THE
ROMANCE
OF
ARTHUR
II

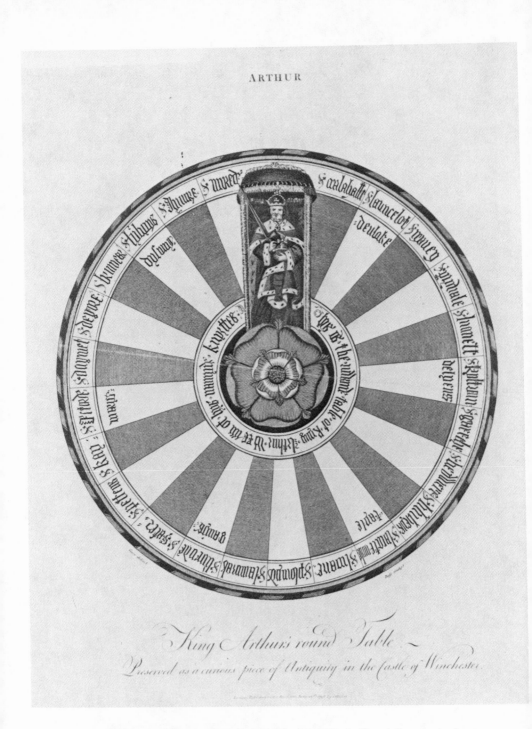

The Round Table in the Great Hall of Winchester Castle. Once believed to be the work of Joseph of Arimathea, it has since been dated to the mid-13th century. In 1486, King Henry VII painted it white and green, and set a Tudor rose in the middle. (Courtesy of the British Tourist Authority)

THE ROMANCE OF ARTHUR

II

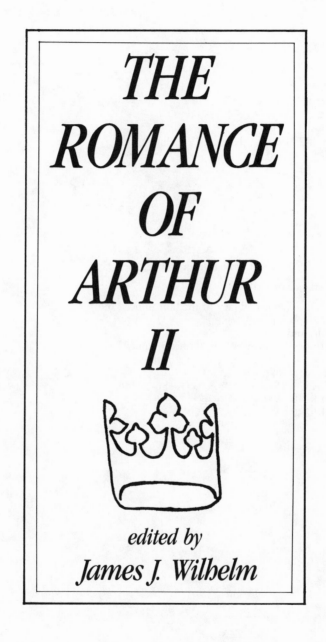

edited by
James J. Wilhelm

GARLAND PUBLISHING, INC. • NEW YORK & LONDON
1986

Library of Congress Cataloging-in-Publication Data

The Romance of Arthur II.

   (Garland reference library of the humanities ; 696)
   Bibliography: p.
   Includes index.
   1. Arthurian romances.   I. Wilhelm, James J.
II. Series: Garland reference library of the
humanities ; v. 696.
PN685.R57   1986   808.8′0351   86-19486
ISBN 0-8240-8936-7 (alk. paper)
ISBN 0-8240-8516-7 (pbk. : alk. paper)

Printed on acid-free, 250-year-life paper
Manufactured in the United States of America

In memory of
LAILA ZAMUELIS GROSS
(1937–1985)

CONTENTS

Preface   ix

I   Wace: Roman de Brut (Merlin Episodes and "The Birth
and Rise of Arthur")
James J. Wilhelm   5

II   Layamon: Brut ("The Death of Arthur")
James J. Wilhelm   19

III   The Story of Peredur Son of Efrog
John K. Bollard   29

IV   The Lay of Graelent
Russell Weingartner   63

V   Chrétien de Troyes: Yvain, *or* The Knight with the Lion
William W. Kibler   81

VI   Béroul: The Romance of Tristan
Norris J. Lacy   151

VII   Marie de France: The Lay of Chievrefueil
(The Honeysuckle)
Russell Weingartner   199

VIII   Thomas of Britain: Tristan ("The Death Scene")
James J. Wilhelm   203

IX   Episodes from the Prose Merlin and the Suite du Merlin
Samuel N. Rosenberg   213

Some General Books for Further Reading   267

Index   269

PREFACE

This sequel to *The Romance of Arthur* fills in some of the gaps necessitated by lack of space in that first volume. To round out the earlier book's coverage of the historical Arthur (as revealed in Latin chronicles, Welsh legendary literature, and Geoffrey of Monmouth), appropriate episodes from Wace and Layamon are included here. Although there was not room enough in Volume I for any Tristan or Grail material, the lack of these was sorely felt by some, and so we present here some smaller versions of the Tristan story, as well as the entire Welsh *Peredur*, an analog of the Perceval-Parsifal versions of the Grail legend.

In using *The Romance of Arthur* in my own classes at Rutgers, I was especially struck by the popularity of the figure of Merlin. Again and again students asked why there was so little of this fascinating person represented. As a result I have added the Merlin episodes in Wace, and Professor Rosenberg has culled appropriate sections from the Prose *Merlin* and the *Suite du Merlin*.

It was obvious that, because of his steadily rising popularity, another masterwork by Chrétien de Troyes should be included. *Yvain*, or *The Knight with the Lion* balances the *Lancelot* that appeared in Volume I. *Graelent* and Marie de France's *Chievrefueil* provide examples of the Breton lay.

The "Further Reading" section of the preceding volume was limited to books in English, but in this volume I have also selected some outstanding works from other literatures.

Chronology was the organizing device for the original *Romance of Arthur*, but that was not feasible here for a variety of reasons. Instead the works are grouped generically, beginning with the pseudo-historical poetic versions of Wace and Layamon, moving through Celtic-inspired samples to a classic French romance, and culminating in works centering on the figures of Tristan and Isolde or Merlin.

I hope that this volume will give the reader as much pleasure as it has given me and my fellow editor-translators. Once again all of the texts have been freshly translated, and with the exception of Chapters I, II, VIII, and IX, everything is entire.

James J. Wilhelm

New York City
May 15, 1986

THE ROMANCE OF ARTHUR
II

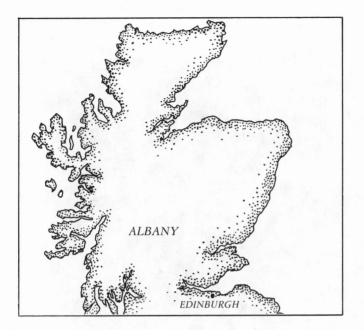

ALBANY

EDINBURGH

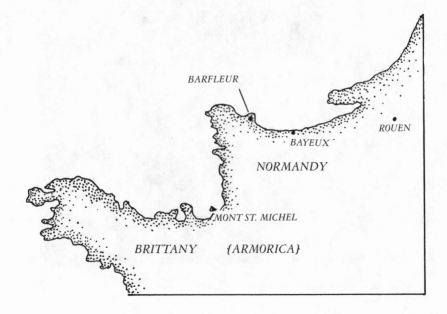

BARFLEUR

ROUEN

BAYEUX

NORMANDY

MONT ST. MICHEL

BRITTANY   {ARMORICA}

Stonehenge. According to legend, Merlin transferred these monolithic stones from Ireland to this location in Wiltshire. (Courtesy of the British Tourist Authority)

chapter I

WACE:
ROMAN DE BRUT
(Merlin Episodes and
"The Birth and Rise of Arthur")

James J. Wilhelm

Wace's *Roman de Brut* is the first full account of the Arthurian story in a vernacular language: Old North French. Other versions may have existed before Wace but none has survived. The little we know about Wace's life comes from his last work, the *Roman de Rou*, a verse history of the dukes of Normandy. He wrote this book for King Henry II of England, beginning it in 1160 but being supplanted in the undertaking by one Master Beneeit, apparently at the king's insistence. Five years before he began his Norman compilation, he undertook the massive task of rendering into French Geoffrey of Monmouth's *History of the Kings of Britain*, which had been written in Latin. This was dedicated to Henry's queen, the famous Eleanor of Aquitaine, and it was presented to the queen in 1155. Before this, Wace also translated some saints' lives from Latin into French.

Wace was born on the Norman-controlled island of Jersey at some point in the early twelfth century, possibly around 1110. He was educated at Caen in Normandy (which he calls the city of Kay) and then near Paris, but he spent most of his later life in his beloved Normandy. Although he was himself of Germanic stock, in his *Roman de Brut* his sympathies are always with the British Celts. Following Geoffrey (the Arthurian part of whose work is available in *Romance of Arthur I*), he tells their early history, beginning with a legendary progenitor named Brutus, who is of Trojan-Roman stock. Brut, as he is called, is a descendant of the great Roman hero Aeneas, celebrated in Vergil's *Aeneid*. He frees some enslaved Trojans in Greece and takes them to the island of Albion, which was then renamed "Britain" in honor of him. Needless to say, none of this is historically proven. Geoffrey (and Wace and Layamon, who followed him) then recounts British history in a highly imaginative and undocumented way, although several of his kings and other characters can be found in Welsh myth and legend (see Chapter II of *Romance of Arthur I*).

Wace is noted for his lively narration and his ability to create scenes and characters with a few strokes of the brush. He excels in dramatic episodes, such as King Uther's wooing of Igerna, and in comic scenes, such as Merlin's being questioned about his father and family history. He is weakest in scenes of violence and valor, just where Layamon is strongest. We have thus selected the Merlin episodes and the early periods of Arthur's life from Wace's work and left the dramatic and violent end of the Arthurian story for Layamon in the chapter that follows. Arthur's battles in the middle portion of his life can be found in Geoffrey of Monmouth's work.

Wace is the first author to mention the Round Table. He also refers directly to Breton storytellers, who served as the link between Celtic Britain and Celtic Brittany, showing that they existed around 1150. These minstrels and narrators would be necessary for the transmission of remote Celtic materials on the British islands to the mainland, where they could then enter the main course of European literature. Wace also mentions the so-called "Breton Hope" that became attached to Arthur's ending. According to this messianic wish, Arthur never fully died, and he will return to free the Celts from their Saxon dominators. This ending to his work is added to the earlier selections here.

Bibliographic note: The 14,800-odd octosyllabic lines in rhymed couplets are not readily translatable into modern English poetry. My prose version is quite free, using compressions and clarifications wherever deemed necessary. I consulted but did not rely on the antiquated translation by S. Evans (Everyman, 1911); the thesis translation by D. A. Light (New York University, 1970) did afford some help with certain problems.

I have used as my base Ivor Arnold's critical edition of *Le Roman de Brut* in two volumes (SATF, 1938–40) and have also consulted the two-volume edition by Le Roux de Lincy (Rouen, 1838), which is antiquated but interesting for its notes. Lincy includes some lines and words rejected by Arnold, and I have adopted a few of these because of the color they add.

The criticism on Wace is extensive. Further reading can be found in the bibliography accompanying extracts from the *Roman* in the edition of Arnold and M. M. Pelan (Klincksieck, 1962): *La Partie arthurienne du "Roman de Brut."* See also the entry "Wace," by William W. Kibler, in *The Arthurian Encyclopedia*, edited by Norris J. Lacy et al. (Garland, 1986).

Roman de Brut

[*After the departure of the Romans from Britain the treacherous Vortigern kills King Constant and forces his two younger brothers, Aurelius Ambrosius and*

Uther, to flee to Brittany. King Vortigern then calls upon the Saxons of Germany under the leadership of Horsa and Hengist to protect him against the Picts. After this victory Vortigern marries Rowena, the daughter of Hengist, who becomes the ruler of Kent; but Hengist soon lusts for the kingship and forces Vortigern to flee to the Gloucester area, where Vortigern wants to enclose himself in a tower. He tries to build one on Mount Snowdon, but every night the day's construction tumbles to the ground. He consults some wise men, who tell him that he has to speak with a man who has no earthly father. Vortigern tries to find such a man, but cannot, until his messengers stumble on two men in Carmarthen, Wales, who are speaking together as follows.]

[*Line 7373*] "Hold your tongue, Merlin!" said Dinabus. "Be still. I am from a much nobler line than you. Don't you know who you are, you evil thing? You shouldn't argue with me or degrade my lineage! I was born of kings and counts; and if *you* tried to account for your parents, you couldn't name your father even, because you don't know who he is, and you never will. You don't know his name because you never had one!"

On hearing this quarrel, the messengers, who were looking for such a man, went over to some neighbors to ask who this creature was who did not have a father. The neighbors replied that, indeed, this fellow had never had a father, and his mother had no idea at all who had engendered the boy. But although Merlin knew nothing about his father, he did have a mother who was known. She was the daughter of the king of Demetia, which is a part of Wales. Now a nun in an abbey in the town, she was a woman of great integrity. The messengers then went to the provost, demanding in the name of the king that this fatherless Merlin and his mother be brought before the king. Unable to refuse, the provost had them summoned before Vortigern.

The king received them kindly and spoke to them warmly. "Lady," he said, "tell me the truth. Without your help I can never learn who fathered your son, Merlin."

The nun stood with head bowed. After she had considered for a moment, she said: "God help me, I never knew or saw the man who fathered this fellow on me. I never heard and I certainly can't tell for sure if it even was a man by whom I had him, but I do know this for certain and I'll swear to its truth: after I had grown up, a certain creature—I don't know if it was a phantom even—used to come to me and kiss me hotly. He used to speak to me like a man and he felt like one, for many times he spoke with me, but he never really revealed himself. He came to me again and again, and he kissed me and slept with me so often that I finally grew pregnant, but I never knew any man but him. This man here—this is the child I had. More than that I do not know, and more I cannot tell."

The king had Magant, a clerk whom he considered very wise, summoned, and he asked if what the lady had said could be true. Magant replied: "We have found it written that between the moon and the earth there is a certain kind of peculiar spirit. If you want to know what they're like—they're partly human and partly celestial. These spirits are known as incubi. Their territory is the air, but their home is the earth. They are not capable of great evil, and they can't hurt us, except to tease and annoy us.

But they can easily assume our human shape and nature. They have deceived many a young girl and tricked her by this disguise. This is the way that Merlin was probably fathered and probably born."

"King!" interrupted Merlin. "You summoned me here. What do you want of me? Why did you bring me here?"

"Merlin," said the king, "that you will learn. Listen well, and you'll hear it. I started to build a tower, and put stone to mortar, but whatever I built during the day tumbled down at night. I don't know if you've heard about this, but the day can do nothing that the night can't undo—and much of my wealth has been squandered. My sages tell me that I'll never get my tower if your blood isn't mixed with the mortar, since you've been born without a father."

"I hope to God," cried Merlin, "that my blood won't make your tower stand! I'll call them liars openly if you summon the men who prescribed my blood, for they are liars indeed!"

The king had the men summoned, and he put them in front of Merlin. When Merlin had looked them over, he said: "My lords who prophesy, tell me why this building won't stand up. If you can't tell me why this tower crumbles to the ground, how can you predict that my blood is needed to make it stand up? Tell us why the foundation gives way so often, and what it lacks and what it needs. If you can't tell us what makes the work fall down, how can you be believed when you say that my blood will make it stand? Tell the king the problem and the solution."

All of the wise men were silent, not knowing how to reply. And when Merlin saw this he immediately said to the king: "Your Majesty, listen! Under the foundation of your tower lies a pool that is broad and deep and that makes your tower crumble. If you want to believe me, then dig down and you'll see!"

The king ordered men to dig, and the pool that Merlin mentioned was found. "Masters," said Merlin, "hear me! You who tried to mix my blood with your mortar, tell me what's in this pool."

They all stood mute and dumbfounded, not wanting to add a word. Turning to the king so that his men could hear, Merlin ordered: "Empty this pool by draining the water off. Down at the bottom are two sleeping dragons lying on two large stones. One of these dragons is white, while the other is as crimson as blood."

When the water was drained into the fields, two dragons rose from the depths and faced each other glaringly. With great ferocity they leaped at each other before the barons. You could truly see them foaming, with flames shooting out of their mouths. The king sat down at the edge of the pool and begged Merlin to tell him the significance of the dragons, which were clashing with such rage. And so Merlin recited his prophecies, which you have heard, I suppose, about the kings to come who would control the earth. I do not want to translate his book since I do not know how to interpret it. I do not want to say anything that is not all true.

The king praised Merlin very highly and considered him a marvelous prophet. He asked when he would die and how, because he was terrified about his end. "Be careful," said Merlin; "be very careful of the sons of Constantine [Aurelius and Uther], because through them you will come to your end. They've already left Brittany and are coming boldly over the sea. I can tell you this for certain: they will arrive at Totnes tomorrow. You did wrong to them, and they'll do wrong to you to avenge your crime. You evilly betrayed their brother [Constant] and made yourself king in an evil manner, and you viciously lured pagans and Saxons into this realm. You face danger on two sides, and I don't know which is worse. On one side the Saxons want to make war on you and destroy you; on the other are the heirs who want to regain their kingdom. They want to wrench Britain away from you and avenge their brother. If you can run, go now, because these two brothers are on the way! Aurelius will be king first, but he will also die first, from poison. Uther Pendragon, his brother, will rule the realm after him, but he will quickly become sick and be poisoned by your heirs. Arthur, his son from Cornwall, who is as fierce as a boar in battle, will devour the traitors against him and will destroy your kinsmen. He will be valiant and fine and will wipe out all of his enemies." Merlin finished this speech, and Vortigern turned away from there.

[*True to Merlin's word, the two brothers reenter Britain and burn Vortigern to death in his tower; the throne falls to Aurelius. The new king wants to build a monument at Ambresbury in honor of his faithful men who had fallen at the hands of the Saxon Hengist.*]

[*Line 8003*] Tremorius, a wise man who was the Archbishop of Caerleon, told Aurelius to send for Merlin and to build according to his advice. No one else could advise him better, since Merlin had no equal when it came to creating and divining. The king wanted to see Merlin and evaluate his wisdom firsthand. At Labenes [Galabes] far away in Wales (a place I do not know, since I have never been there) the king sent for him. Merlin answered the summons and was well received by Aurelius, who welcomed him with great honor, offering him good cheer and companionship and begging him solicitously to teach him about the future, for he eagerly wanted to hear this from him.

"Sir," said Merlin, "I can't do this. I won't open my mouth unless I'm forced to, and this is because of humility. If I spoke braggingly or jestingly or proudly, my guardian spirit, who teaches me all that I know, would leave my lips and take all of my knowledge away. My mouth would not be any more valuable than anyone else's. Let such secrets lie. Think about what you have to do now. If you want to create a lasting work that's beautiful and fitting and will be talked about for all time to come, then bring over here the circle that the giants built in Ireland—a wonderful, huge, round work with stone set on stone—so strong and heavy that no strength of men now alive can ever lift them."

"Merlin," said the king, laughing, "since these stones weigh so much that nobody can budge them, who could possibly bring them over here? Don't we have stones enough in our kingdom already?"

"King," said Merlin, "don't you realize that brains are better than brawn? Strength is fine, but cunning is much better, since it often succeeds where muscles fail. Intelligence and cunning can accomplish much that brute strength would never dare. Cunning can move those rocks and bring them over here to you. After all, they were carried from Africa, where they were first sculpted. Giants transported them from there to Ireland. These stones are beneficial and healthful for the sick. People used to pour water over these rocks and then heat the water as baths for the sick and the infirm. After they bathed, they were cured. They never needed any other kind of medicine for their illness."

When the king and the British heard that those stones had this magic power, they were eager to import the circle that Merlin had described. They chose Uther, who accepted, to lead 15,000 armed men across to Ireland to fight for the stones if they were defended, along with Merlin, who would engineer their transport. When Uther had collected his men, he made the crossing to Ireland, where King Guillomer assembled his own forces to threaten the Britons and drive them out of his land. When the Irish learned that the Britons were searching for these stones, they were full of mockery, saying that it was crazy to come looking for rocks over land and sea. The Britons would not get a single one to carry away. But it is easier to mock someone than to outdo him. The Irish kept ridiculing and threatening and tracking the Britons down until the two forces finally met and were locked in battle. But the Irish were neither so well armed nor so used to fighting, and as a result the once-vilified Britons emerged as the victors. King Guillomer fled madly from town to town.

When the Britons disarmed themselves to rest, Merlin, who was in their company, led them up to a mountain where the eagerly sought circle had been built. The hill was called Killomar, where the circle loomed on top. The Britons gazed at all those rocks, and as they walked around them they told one another that they had never seen such a marvelous feat. "How had all those stones been erected there, and how could they possibly be carried away?"

"My lords," said Merlin, "see if you have the strength to move these rocks and carry them off." The men approached the rocks on every side, front and back. They pushed and they pulled and they heaved and they tugged, but they could not move one of them an inch. "Move away," shouted Merlin, "for your strength won't do a thing. Now see what craft and cunning can accomplish that bodily strength cannot." Then he walked forward and stood gazing around. He moved his lips like a man uttering a prayer; I do not know if he prayed or not. Then he shouted again to the Britons: "Come over here! Come on! Now you can pick up these rocks and carry them down to the ships."

Just as Merlin directed, and exactly the way he prescribed and commanded, the Britons took the stones down to the ships and put them inside. They transported the stones to Britain, putting them on the plain at Ambresbury. The king went there at Pentecost, having ordered his bishops, abbots, and barons to assemble, along with many others; and they held a feast for his coronation. It lasted for three days, and on the fourth he dutifully bestowed croziers on St. Dubris of Caerleon and St. Samson of York, both of whom were great clergymen who led lives of great saintliness. And then Merlin arranged the rocks in order, side by side. The Britons [Welsh] call this the Giants' Carol in their tongue; in English the name of the place is Stonehenge; in French it is "Hanging Rocks."

[*Paschent, a son of Vortigern, flees to Germany and then to Ireland, where he joins forces with the Irish king and attacks Wales. Aurelius rushes to meet him but falls sick and is poisoned by a false doctor in the pay of Paschent.*]

[*Line 8274*] After the king was inflamed and his body was permeated by the poison, O God, what grief! He had to die. When Aurelius was aware of his oncoming death, he made his retainers swear to carry his body to Stonehenge and to inter him there. And then he ended his days, and the traitorous poisoner fled.

Uther had entered Wales and found the Irish in Menevia. Then a star appeared to the view of many, called the Comet according to the clergy. This signified a change of kings. It was marvelously clear as it shot forth its single ray. The fire from this ray assumed the shape of a dragon, and two further beams issued from its jaws. One ray spread over France all the way to Mount St. Bernard [in the Alps]. The other extended toward Ireland and divided into seven other lights. Each of these seven beams shone clearly over the land and the sea. The people were all shaken as they saw this sign. Uther wondered deeply about it and was greatly disturbed. He begged Merlin to tell him what it meant. Merlin also was much troubled, with misgivings in his heart, and he did not answer a word at first. When his spirits returned, he sighed deeply and said sorrowfully: "O God, what great unhappiness, what great loss, what trouble have now descended over our Britain! We have lost our great captain! Our king is dead, that fine champion who delivered our country from grief and evil, wrenching it from the hands of the heathens!"

When Uther heard that the end had come for his brother, that fine lord, he was filled with sadness and dismay. But Merlin comforted him, saying, "Uther, don't be depressed. Nobody escapes from death. Carry out what you started. Fight your enemy. The triumph tomorrow will be yours over Ireland and Paschent. You will win that engagement tomorrow and will become the king of Britain. The sign of the dragon refers to you, who are brave and hardy. The ray to the east is a son you will have who will be very powerful and who will conquer lands beyond France. The other ray to the west with its seven offshoots signifies a daughter who will marry the king of Scotland. Many fine heirs will be born from her who will conquer lands and seas."

When Uther heard what Merlin told him in consolation, he had his men rest that night and arm themselves in the morning. He wanted to attack the city, but when the Irish saw him coming they took up their armor and gear and rushed out to fight. The battle was fierce, and many men were overcome. When the Britons had killed both Paschent and the Irish king, those who left the field alive fled away to their ships. Uther pursued them, harassing them to the bitter end. There were some who escaped by boarding their ships and speeding across the sea so that Uther could not catch them.

On finishing this business, Uther made his way to Winchester with the flower of his knighthood. On the road he met a messenger who told him in all truth that the king had died and how this had happened. The bishops, with great care and ceremony, had arranged his burial inside the Giants'

Carol, as Aurelius had asked his sergeants and barons while he was still alive. When Uther heard this, he rushed to Winchester. The people there ran out crying and shouting in a loud voice: "Uther, my lord! For the sake of God, the man who once looked after us and gave us many favors is now gone! Protect us! Take the crown that is yours by due right and heritage. We all beg you, good sir, since we desire nothing but your profit and honor."

Uther saw that his profit was there, and he could do no better than to seize it. He was happy at what he heard and immediately did as they requested. He took the crown, became king, loved honor, and maintained the people well. In token and memory of the dragon's reference to a bold man who would be king and would have many conquering heirs, upon the advice of his barons he had two golden dragons created. One he always carried into battle; the other he granted to Winchester, to the bishop's church. For this reason he was always thereafter called Uther Pendragon. The British word "Pendragon" means "Dragonhead" [Chief Dragon] in French.

[*Uther is a good king, but he is challenged by the Saxon leader Octa, the son of Hengist, and his cousin Ossa. With the help of Gorlois, the count of Cornwall, Uther captures them in York and takes them back to London to prison.*]

[*Line 8551*] When Uther had finished his affairs in the north, he returned directly to London, and on Easter Day he planned to be crowned. Dukes and counts and knights from far and wide and all his other lieges he summoned by letter and proclamation to come with their wives and retainers to London for the festival, which he wanted to be lavish. They all came as he had requested, bringing wives if they were with them. The festival was celebrated with grandeur, and when the mass had been sung the king sat down for dinner at the head of the table on a dais. The barons sat around him, each according to his rank. Facing Uther was the lord of Cornwall, and beside him was Igerna, his wife, the most beautiful woman in the whole kingdom. She was courteous, elegant, and wise and came from excellent lineage. The king had heard a great deal about her, and it was all praise. Even before he showed it and before he set eyes on her figure, he loved and coveted her because of this extravagant praise.

Uther kept staring at her during dinner, turning his whole attention her way. If he ate or drank or talked or sat silent, he was always thinking about her and glancing her way; and as he looked, he smiled, showing her signs of love. He honored her by having his private pages attend her with little favors. He joked with her, winked at her, and showed her every sign of affection. Igerna controlled herself, neither granting him anything nor denying it.

Her husband noticed these jibes and jests and endearments and compliments and courtesies, and he soon realized that the king was in love with his wife. Never would he show faith to a lord who so blatantly wooed his wife! He leaped up from the table, grabbed his wife by the hand, and darted out of the chamber. Calling his companions, he ran out to mount his horse. The king quickly sent word to Gorlois that it would cast disgrace and shame on him if he left the court without begging His Majesty's leave. Gorlois should act correctly, not discourteously! And if he failed to do this, the king warned him, wherever Gorlois might go he could not trust what would happen. But Gorlois had no desire to return. He left the court without asking the king's permission. The king had threatened him sternly, but the count dismissed this, not guessing the outcome.

Gorlois returned to Cornwall and prepared two of his castles for invasion. He put his wife in Tintagel, which had long been his ancestral holding. Tintagel was easily defensible—hard to take by any craft since it was perched on a steep cliff and largely surrounded by the sea. If one held only the main gate, he had no fear of entry from any other quarter. Gorlois enclosed Igerna there, since no other place could guarantee her from being seized and carried away. Then he took his men-at-arms and the larger part of his knights to another castle that guarded most of his fief.

The king learned that Gorlois had stocked his castles in defense against him. In order to attack the count and draw near his wife, Uther assembled his forces and crossed the River Tamar. He arrived at the castle where the count was enclosed and wanted to storm it, but it held firm. Then he set siege to it, and he stayed there for a week, but he could not capture it. The count would not give up because he was waiting for help to come from the king of Ireland. The British king was angered by this delay, which only caused him anguish, since his love for Igerna, which exceeded everything else, was constantly urging him forward. He called in one of his closest barons and said: "Ulfin, give me your advice. I put all my faith in you. My love for Igerna has overwhelmed me, beaten me down, vanquished me totally. I can't go or come, wake or sleep, rise or lie down, drink or eat without thinking about her. But I don't know how I can win her. I'll die if you can't advise me well."

Ulfin replied: "O what marvels I hear! You've harassed the count with war and cut off his land and enclosed him in his castle. Now do you really think that his wife approves of this? You love his wife and you make war on him—I don't know what counsel you're looking for or what I can give you. But call for Merlin, who's imbued with all the arts and is among our entourage. If he doesn't know how to advise you, nobody can."

Acting on Ulfin's advice, the king sent for Merlin and soon declared all of his needs. He cried and begged him in his mercy to lend some advice, because he would certainly die in a cruel way if he did not win the favors of Igerna: "Please try to do all you can! I'll give you anything you want, since I'm suffering such evil sorrow now."

"Sir," said Merlin, "you shall have her. You won't die for Igerna's sake. I'll give you all you want and you won't have to repay me a thing. But Igerna is closely guarded, locked up in Tintagel, which can't be taken by any force because it's impregnable. Her coming and her going are carefully watched by two loyal guards. But I can get you in there through my powerful enchantments. I know how to change the shape of a man and how to transform one human being into another. I can make one person resemble another, and vice versa. Without any doubt I can give you the body, face, manner, speech, and habits of the count of Cornwall. Why make this talk too long? I'll turn you into the count, and I'll go along with you, taking on the appearance of Bretel, and Ulfin, who'll accompany us, will look like Jordan. The count has these two very dear counselors with him. This way you can enter the castle and get whatever you want. You will never be perceived or mistrusted by anyone there."

The king believed Merlin completely and considered his advice excellent. He privately gave control of his men to one of his barons. Merlin effected his enchantments: he changed their faces and clothing, and so they entered Tintagel that very night. Those who thought they knew the three received and welcomed them and served them with joy. The king lay that night with Igerna, who conceived the good, strong, and certain monarch whom you all know as King Arthur.

The king's men soon realized that the king was not in their midst. There was not a baron whom they respected or for whom they would do a thing. Because of the delay they anticipated, they took up their arms and put them on. Without proper formations or equipment they rushed the castle in disarray, assailing it on every side. The count defended himself bravely, but he was killed and the castle was quickly captured. Some men got away, and they dashed to report at Tintagel how things had gone badly for their lord and how many people they had lost.

On hearing this report about the death of their leader being sorrowfully recounted, the king got up quickly and sprang forward, shouting: "Keep still! It's not at all like that! I'm completely alive and well, thanks to God, as you can plainly see. This news is not true! Don't believe it or disbelieve it. I can tell you why my men so fear for me. I left that other place without saying a word of goodbye to any of them. I never said that I was going and was coming back here to you because I was afraid of treachery. Now they're all afraid that I'm dead because nobody saw me since the king entered the castle. Of course we have to grieve for the men killed and the castle that's fallen, but it still bodes well that I'm alive. I'll still stand up against that king! I'll ask him for peace, promising an accord before he besieges this castle and brings us worse mischief. For if he surprises us here, we'll have to plead more humbly."

Igerna praised this plan, since she was always afraid of the king. And then the king embraced her and kissed her at his departure. And so he left the castle, having enjoyed all his desire.

When the king and Ulfin and Merlin were safely out on the road, everyone changed his shape and once again became the man that he ought to be. Then they arrived quickly back with the main army. The king wanted to know how the castle had fallen so fast, and if the count had been truly slain. He was told the truth on both accounts. Uther said that he was very disturbed by the count's death, since he had not wanted that. He mourned and regretted this deed, acting very angry toward the lieges who had done it. He clearly assumed the appearance of a mourner, but very few of his men believed him.

Then he returned to Tintagel. He called up to the householders, asking them why they defended the place, since the other castle had been taken and their count was dead. They could not expect any aid inside their own country or from abroad. They all realized that the king was telling the truth, and they had no hope whatever of being rescued. And so they opened the gates of the stronghold and handed the fortress over to him. Since the king was so deeply in love with Igerna, he married her without any delay. The night before, she had conceived a son, and after the proper time she gave birth to him. Arthur was his name. Many words have been voiced about his goodness. After him Anna was born, a daughter who was given to the fine and upstanding lord of Lothian, who had the name of Lot.

[*Ossa and Octa, freed from prison, wage war against Uther and Lot; they are slain, but they pass on the torch of rebellion to their cousin Colgrin. When Uther falls sick, he is given a cup from a poisoned well.*]

[*Line 8993*] When the king wanted to drink, and then did drink, he was poisoned and had to die. After downing the water, he swelled up, looking dark and discolored, and soon he passed away. Everyone else who partook of that well also died, so that the treacherous deed was apparent and known to all. The leaders of the city assembled and sealed up the well, filling it with enough earth to create a mound.

After King Uther had met his end, he was carried to Stonehenge and there interred by the side of his brother. The bishops then got together, convening with the barons. They sent for Arthur, Uther's son, and crowned him at Silchester.

Arthur was a young man of fifteen, tall and strong for his years. I shall describe all his qualities, not falsifying anything. He was a very worthy knight, one of great valor and glory. He was arrogant toward the arrogant, and sweet and humble toward the lowly. He was strong and hardy and domineering, but also a gracious and generous giver. If anybody in need asked him for something, he would give it to that person if he could. He loved praise and glory very much, and he wanted all of his good deeds to be remembered. He maintained an elegant court and conducted himself there very nobly. As long as he lived and ruled, he surpassed all other princes in courtesy and nobility and valor and generosity.

[*Arthur attempts to drive the Saxons, especially Colgrin, out of the land, fighting battles from the Caledonian Forest in Scotland to Badon, which Wace interprets as Bath.*]

[*Line 9267*] With all his forces Arthur went to Bath as fast as he could. He wanted to break the Saxon siege and rescue the citizens trapped inside. In a neighboring wood on a great plain Arthur armed his troops. He divided his forces and put them in ranks and then armed himself. He put on his thigh-pieces, which were beautiful and well made, and he donned his fine and handsome hauberk, which was worthy of such a king. He strapped on his sword, Excalibur, which was very long and broad. It had been forged on the island of Avalon, and it always assisted the man who held it. Arthur wore a bright and shiny helmet on his head; its nose-piece was made of gold, and circlets of gold ran around the sides. On its crest a dragon was portrayed. This helmet, which sparkled with many jewels, had belonged to Uther, his father. Arthur rode on a very fine stallion that was strong and fast and lithe; Pridwen, his shield, dangled from his neck. In no way would you take him for a coward or a fool. On his shield was masterfully portrayed an image of Our Lady St. Mary, for her honor and remembrance. He also carried a stiff lance called Ron, which was very sharp at its point and long and sturdy, and was very much feared in time of action.

[*Arthur wins the Battle of Bath with the help of Cador of Cornwall. He then rescues Hoel of Brittany in Scotland.*]

[*Line 9597*] Arthur returned to York and stayed there until Christmas. He celebrated the day of Christ's nativity there. He saw that the city was extremely impoverished, weakened, and degraded. He saw the churches deserted and the houses ruined and fallen. He appointed Pyramus, a wise chaplain, who had always served him well, as the archbishop to maintain the churches and restore the monasteries that had been devastated by the pagans. He then proclaimed peace everywhere and told the farmers to return to the fields. All of the honorable men who had been disinherited he summoned to him and restored their heritages, giving them back their fiefs and increasing their incomes.

There were three brothers of fine, even royal, lineage: Lot, Aguisel, and Urien. Their ancestors had held the land north of the River Humber, as they would during the following peace, most justly and without harming anyone. Arthur gave them back their fiefs and inheritances. To Urien, the eldest of the family, he restored Moray without his having to pay rents or fees, proclaiming him the ruler there; he became the lord of the province of Moray. To Aguisel he gave Scotland, which had been claimed as his fief. To Lot, who had married his sister and had stood by him for a long time, he gave all of Lothian and many other fiefs besides. Gawain, Lot's son, was still just a handsome young courtier at this time.

When Arthur had settled his realm and established justice everywhere and restored the whole kingdom to its ancient dignity, he took for his queen Guinevere, a charming and fresh young maiden. She was lovely, well mannered, and gracious and had noble Roman relatives. Cador had reared her richly in Cornwall for a long time as his near cousin, since his mother was also Roman. Guinevere was a young lady of great charm and noble bearing. She spoke beautifully and acted generously. Arthur adored her and cherished her completely, but the two of them never had an heir; no, she never gave birth to a child.

[*Arthur then subdued the Irish and on returning to Britain established a legendary twelve years of peace; then:*]

[*Line 9751*] Arthur created the Round Table, about which the Britons tell many a tale. There sat his vassals, all in royalty and equality; yes, they sat at his table in equal rank and were served equally; neither one nor another could brag that he sat higher than a peer. They were all gathered closely around the king; nobody was relegated to a corner. No man was considered courtly—not a Scot or Breton or Frank or Norman or Angevin or Fleming or Burgundian or man of Lorraine, wherever he maintained his land from the West to Mount St. Bernard—who did not come and stay for a while with Arthur in equality, and who did not have the clothing, the trappings, and the armor of the sort that those who served at Arthur's court had. People came from many lands seeking praise and honor, some to hear his courteous speech, or to see his elegant court, or to get to know his barons, or to receive rich gifts. He was much adored by the poor and much honored by the rich. Foreign kings envied him because they feared and trembled that he would conquer the whole world and take their possessions away from them.

I do not know if you have heard of the great wonders that occurred during this long period of peace, both out of love of his generosity and out of fear of his prowess, or if you have heard some of the adventures told about Arthur that have turned into fables—some of them lying, some of them true, some of them showing wisdom and some foolishness. The storytellers have narrated and the fable-makers have told tales in order to embellish their plots, and they have made everything seem unreal.

[*From this point Arthur engages in actions on the Continent, eventually warring against the Roman emperor Lucius Hiberius, who is finally slain. This part of the story is continued in Chapter II, as narrated by the Englishman Layamon in his* Brut, *along with the episode of Mordred's betrayal and the king's death. Wace's final words about those cataclysmic events are memorable.*]

[*Line 13,276*] If the chronicle does not lie, Arthur was mortally wounded in his body. He had himself carried to Avalon to heal his wounds. He is still there, and the Britons are still awaiting him. As they always say and firmly believe: he will come back from Avalon; yes, he will live again. Master Wace, who made this book, does not wish to discuss this ending any further than the prophet Merlin did. Merlin said of Arthur (and he spoke rightly) that his death would be a thing of doubt. Yes, the prophet spoke the truth. For all time men have wondered—and indeed they will always wonder—if he is dead or alive. In truth, he was carried to Avalon five hundred and forty-two years after the birth of Christ. It is a pity that he had no heir. He gave his kingdom to his cousin Constantine of Cornwall, son of Cador, telling him to rule until the day when Arthur himself would return.

The Roman amphitheater at Caerleon in Wales, one of the last of the ruins of this once mighty fortress on the River Usk. (Courtesy of the British Tourist Authority)

chapter II

LAYAMON:
BRUT
("The Death of Arthur")

James J. Wilhelm

Layamon's *Brut* is the first full account of the Arthurian story in the English language. It is the second major poetic adaptation of Geoffrey of Monmouth's *History of the Kings of Britain*, taking as its immediate model Wace's *Roman de Brut*. Layamon's poem is extremely long, consisting of over 32,000 half-lines, which cover British history from the time of the mythic Brutus to the retreat of Cadwallader before the Saxons in A.D. 689.

In his prologue Layamon tells us that he was a priest who was living at a noble church at King's Areley in Worcestershire. He says that he used as his primary sources for his poem the *Ecclesiastical History* of the Venerable Bede and, more importantly, Wace, who had presented his work to Queen Eleanor, the wife of King Henry II. Layamon probably composed his own poem after the death of Henry in 1189 and before that of Eleanor in 1204.

Layamon's *Brut* survives in only two manuscripts, both in the British Library: Cotton Caligula A.ix and Cotton Otho C.xiii, both of which were probably copied in the middle of the thirteenth century or not long thereafter. The Caligula manuscript, which is translated here, is both more complete in its composition and more archaic in its language than the often-fragmentary Otho. Layamon (or Lawman, as we believe his name was probably pronounced) clearly tried to be very English in his language, avoiding borrowing any French phrases or locutions from Wace. He was also willfully old-fashioned, writing an alliterative verse that attempted to recall the grandeurs of the Anglo-Saxon epic past. Yet Layamon's alliterations often break down, and sometimes his half-lines are linked by end-rhyme. His poetry is often criticized for being rough and ill hewn; it seems to have descended from popular rather than "classical" Old English verse.

The value of Layamon's work lies precisely in its vigor. Unlike Wace, Layamon is not primarily interested in nuances of character or affairs of love. He is at his best in describing scenes of action and violence. It is for this reason that the "Death of Arthur" segment of his poem has been selected to represent his work. Layamon tells this story dramatically, creating a vivid sense of a massive tragedy stemming from lust, duplicity, and recklessness. His King Arthur acts far more like a primitive British chieftain than a Norman monarch, especially in his brutal handling of the rebels of Winchester. The work's sympathy toward Arthur's crushing of a refractory Britain may reflect Layamon's own sympathy toward the conquering Normans of his own time; but in the work itself, the author is always fiercely on the side of the Celts rather than the Saxons or the French.

Layamon also relates the death and disappearance of Arthur in a way that is mystically suggestive. He has the king go off with Argante (confused in some way with Morgan the Fay) to Avalon, the island of the elves, and elsewhere in the work he mentions these trappings from Celtic mythology. It is obvious that he had access to various kinds of folklore and local legend that a Frenchman like Wace did not have.

The selection chosen here begins at the point where Arthur is finishing his French campaign against the Roman emperor Lucius Hiberius. This occurs at line 13,897 of the Caligula manuscript, and it runs to line 14,297.

Bibliographic note: The text is taken from the 1978 Oxford University Press edition by G. L. Brook and R. F. Leslie, Volume 2. I have also consulted the outmoded translation and edition by Frederic Madden, issued by the Society of Antiquaries in 1847. On Layamon's style see E. G. Stanley, "Layamon's Antiquarian Sentiments," *Medium Aevum*, 38 (1969), 23–37; also the article "Layamon," by E. D. Kennedy, in *The Arthurian Encyclopedia* (Garland, 1986). My thanks to Valerie Krishna for her suggestions for improving the following translation.

Brut

Tidings came to Arthur, who was in his tent,
That the emperor was dead, deprived of his days.
Amid a broad meadow Arthur made a pavilion,
And there he commanded Lucius to be carried,   13,900
And he ordered him covered with golden clothes
And kept under watch for three whole days.
And all this while he had a rich work made:
A chest that was long and overlaid with gold.
Inside this bier he put Lucius's body,
A most lordly man while his lifetime lasted.
Then Arthur did more, that marvelous Briton;
He made a collection of all of the corpses
Of the noblest kings and earls and knights
Who had fallen in battle, had fled from life.   13,910

He had them buried with brilliant pomp.
Three kings he commanded to carry Lucius
In a casket that was grand and exceedingly costly.
And soon afterward he ordered them sent to Rome
And told them to taunt the Roman people
By saying that he sent them the tribute they sought,
And he was prepared to send plenty more
If they still were so callous as to crave Arthur's gold.
Furthermore, he'd be happy to hurry to Rome
To carry the tidings of the British king,   13,920
And to fix up the walls that had long ago fallen:
"Yes, I will rule the unruly men of Rome!"
But these vaunts were in vain; events went elsewhere;
Fate befell otherwise for the folk left behind—
All because of Mordred, that most wicked of men!
    In the oncoming fight Arthur lost many knights:
Five and twenty thousand slain on the sod,
The boldest of the Britons bereft of their lives.
Kay was grievously wounded in the worst of ways;
He was borne to Kinun [Chinon] and there breathed his last.   13,930
He was buried there by the castle's side
Among the many hermits, that most worthy man.
Yes, Kay he was called and his castle Kinun;
Arthur gave him that town where he's now entombed,
And he ordered a new name as a mark of honor:
Kain [Caen] it was called in memory of Kay;
This now and after will live on as the name.
After Bedivere was laid low, giving up his life-days,
Arthur had him borne to the castle of Bayeux,
And there he was buried inside the burg;   13,940
They laid him in a grave by the southern gate.
Howeldin's body was floated north to Flanders
And his noblest knights were also ferried north
Into the counties from which they had come.
In the turf of Terouane they lie totally true;
Lear, the great baron, they bore to Boulogne.
    Arthur then set up his own settlement
In Burgundy, in a place that he thought the best.
He held sway of the land and took over some castles,   13,950
And he said he would handle that land by himself.
Then he threatened that in the summer he'd travel
All the way to Rome to take over that realm
And become the ruler where Lucius had reigned.
Many of the citizens of Rome wished this were so,
For they desperately stood in dread of their deaths.
Many had absconded, abandoning their ownings,
And many sent messages to Arthur the mighty;
Yes, many spoke to him suing for his peace,
While others wanted to fiercely fend off the invader,   13,960
Supporting their city against this new Caesar;

Yet foolishly, for they all were afraid for themselves,
Never claiming any good counsel from Christ.
And so what Merlin had prophesied came to pass:
That the ramparts of Rome would crumble before great Arthur.
This proved true once Emperor Lucius had perished
And fifty thousand Romans fell in the fight—
All those grand Roman legions laid low on the ground!
Then Arthur truly hoped to gain all of Rome
While he lived in Burgundy, the lordliest of lords.   13,970
    But suddenly a single man rode in on saddle,
Carrying new tidings to Arthur the king
From Mordred, his nephew; the man was well met
Since Arthur was guessing that his news was good.
Arthur spent the whole night in talk with the newcomer,
Who was afraid to unfold how affairs had fared,
But when the sun rose and the people were roused,
Arthur bolted up and stretched his arms broadly;
He got up; then he sat as if suddenly sick
Till the newcomer asked: "How fared you last night?"   13,980
Arthur then answered with an uneasy mind:
"Last night in my sleep while I nestled in bed,
I suffered a dream that has filled me with dread:
I dreamed I was raised up high on the roof
Of a hall that I strode as if on saddle,
Where I could survey the land of which I'm lord.
Walwain [Gawain] sat before me, with my sword in my hand,
And Mordred hove up there with numberless hosts.
In his hand he brandished a strong battle-ax,
With which he made swipes very sharp and swift,
Hewing down the posts that propped up the hall.   13,990
I also saw Wenhaver [Guinevere], the dearest of women;
With her fingers she was ripping the roof off the hall.
The building started foundering; I fell to the ground.
My right arm was shattered. Mordred shouted: 'Take that!'
Down fell the whole hall; even Walwain was falling,
Landing on the bottom with both arms broken.
I grabbed my fine sword with my one good hand
And sliced Mordred's head, sending it to the sod.
Then the queen I dismembered with my dearly loved sword,   14,000
Pitching her deep down into a dark pit;
Then all of my fine people began to flee from me.
I can't recall, by Christ! what became of them!
Then all by myself I was alone in a copse;
I started to meander widely on the moors;
Suddenly I spied griffins and grisly birds;
Then a golden lioness glided over the downs,
The crassest of beasts that our Creator makes.
The lioness ran up and lunged for my loins,
Bearing me away to a beach by the sea;   14,010
And I noticed the waves washing over the water,

While the lioness bore me straight into the brine.
As she stepped into the sea, we were sundered by water,
But a fish came by and ferried me back to land.
I felt soaked and weary from sorrow, and sick.
Then I shot up and started to tremble and shake;
I began to quiver as if kindled inside.
For the whole night I was haunted by horrid thoughts,
Since I knew now for certain: my bliss would be gone,
And all my life long I must languish in sorrow.   14,020
Woe is me that I didn't bring my Wenhaver here!"
    The knight replied: "My lord, that's not right!
You should never interpret a dream so dolefully.
You're the richest of men who rule this earth
And the wisest of humans hale under the heavens.
If it so happened—and pray Heaven that it won't—
That your sister's offspring has filched your queen
And grabbed your royal ground as his own right
That you trusted to him as you traveled to Rome,
And if he has done such deeds with deadly fraud,   14,030
Still you could avenge all this with an active hand
And retake your land and rule again your people,
And strike down the wicked who have worked this woe,
Slaying them cleanly, so that none will survive!"
Arthur, the ablest of kings, then answered:
"Never in my entire life did I ever envision
That Mordred, my nephew, the man whom I most love,
Would betray me so totally for the treasure I own,
Or that Wenhaver my queen would waver in her mind;
She shall not accomplish this—not for any man on earth!"   14,040
    Finally the knight spoke these forthright words:
"Since I'm your subject, sir, I shall speak what is so:
Mordred is guilty—he has grabbed your queen,
And your lovely lands now lie in his hands.
He is king, she is queen; they have cast you aside,
Since they're sure that you'll never return from the south.
I'm a tried and true subject; I witnessed this treason,
And I've traveled here to tell you all this myself.
I lay my head in pledge that I haven't lied,
But have spoken the truth of your once-loved spouse,   14,050
And of your sister's son, who has stolen your Britain!"
Then everyone sat very still in King Arthur's hall.
They all felt great sorrow for their fondest king;
All of his British underlings looked most unhappy.
Then, after a little while, some voices were lifted;
Far and wide you could hear all the Britons humming
As they started to tell in their different talks
How they would doom that most damnable pair
And would slay any masses who merged with Mordred.
Then Arthur, the almightiest, gave the final address: 14,060
"Sit down, my fond knights; sit silent in my hall,

For I shall plan out a plot that is stark and strange.
Tomorrow when day dawns, as God shall deem it,
I shall bolt at once toward our birthplace, Britain.
There I'll kill cunning Mordred and torch the queen
And destroy all those who are tied to this treason.
Here I shall leave my most loyal, loving friend,
Howell, most praised of men and prized of our kin.
Half of my army I'll ask to hang back in this land
To cover this kingdom that I now control.   14,070
And when all is restored, I shall rush back to Rome,
Leaving my homeland in the hands of my Walwain;
And I'll answer all my pledges, I quite assure you:
All of my damnable foes shall face down their fates!"
    Then our Walwain arose, the kinsman of Arthur,
And uttered these words in a most unhappy way:
"Almighty God, the dispenser of dooms,
Ruler of all under Heaven, why has it happened
That my brother Mordred did this baleful deed?
Right now I forsake him before all this force;   14,080
I shall destroy him through the destiny of God!
I shall string him up, that most sinful scoundrel,
And I'll pull the queen to pieces with my horses!
For I'll never know bliss as long as they draw breath
Until my beloved uncle's avenged with the best!"
Then the other Britons broke out with bold voices:
"All of our weapons are ready; tomorrow we return!"
    In the morning, as the sun was sent out by the Savior,
Arthur led out the loyalest of his lieges,
Taking about half and leaving half behind him.   14,090
He wended through the land till he came to Whitsand;
Soon he had ships both sundry and well stocked,
But for a full fortnight the army had to stand firm
As they waited for a while for the winds to lift.
There was a vile follower in Arthur's fold
Who, when he heard Mordred's murder widely spoken,
Sent one of his lackeys straight over to Britain
To inform Queen Wenhaver what lay in store:
How Arthur would arrive shortly with his army
And what he planned to breach and how he would behave.   14,100
The queen ran to Mordred, now her dearest consort,
And told him about the coming of Arthur the king,
And how he planned to act and what he was plotting.
Mordred immediately sent someone to Saxony
To confer with Childerich, that most powerful king.
He bade the Saxon come and snatch up some bargains;
Mordred asked Childerich, that mightiest chieftain,
To send out messengers over all of Saxony,
To invite any warriors whom he could win to the cause
To come over with haste to help out the Britons,   14,110
And he would give half of his holdings to Childerich:

Everything north of the Humber was his for his help
If he became Mordred's ally against Arthur.
Childerich charged at once to the British kingdom.
When Mordred had finally gathered his mighty force,
There were sixty thousand soldiers in the sum
Who were hardy, hostile warriors of heathen stock,
All of whom had come over here to harass King Arthur
And to lend aid to Mordred, that most miserable of men!
When his army was pulled together from all the people,   14,120
There were a good hundred thousand in that throng
Of heathens and Christians who claimed Mordred as king.
   Arthur lay two weeks at Whitsand (it was indeed too long!),
While Mordred was fully aware of what Arthur wanted.
Every day a courier came over from Arthur's court.
Then finally it befell—the rains began to fall,
And a wind began to whip up toward the west.
Arthur hurried into his ships with all of his host,
Ordering his mariners to rush him over to Romney,
Where he planned to set foot again on his native sod.   14,130
When he got to the harbor, Mordred was there to greet him.
As the daylight flared, the men fell at once to fighting
For the whole day; and many a man was massacred.
Some struggled on the high ground and some by the shore;
Some shot sharp spears from out of the ships.
Walwain advanced, clearing out the approaches,
And he undid the lives of eleven underlings.
He felled Childerich's son, who had come with his father.
The sun sank westward, with woe to all men!
Walwain was lopped down, loosed from his days,   14,140
By a Saxon baron—cursed be his soul!
Arthur was now wounded deeply within his heart;
This mightiest of Britons sighed these sad words:
"Now I've surrendered the lives of my loyal swains.
I knew from my dream that I was doomed to sorrow!
Dead is King Angel, one of the dearest of men,
And Walwain my nephew—I wish I had never been born!
Come off those ships quickly, my courageous men!"
   With these words some sixty thousand warriors,
Fiercest of men, now rushed into the fray,   14,150
Attacking Mordred's ranks and almost taking him.
Mordred started to run, and his men rushed after him,
Dashing like fiends while all the fields were quaking,
And amid the stones you saw streamings of blood.
The fight would have ended, but nighttime fell;
The enemy would have perished, but it was now pitch-dark.
Darkness split fighters as it spread over dale and dune.
Mordred lunged away madly; he was soon in London.
All the good burghers knew that things had gone badly;
They refused him entry with his entourage;   14,160
So Mordred went with haste westward toward Winchester

And quickly took over the town with his many troops.
Meanwhile Arthur followed with his powerful forces
Till he arrived at Winchester with his awesome army,
Besieging that citadel where Mordred lurked inside.
When Mordred realized that Arthur was around him,
He pondered deeply about what plan to adopt.
That very night he ordered his men to go outside,
To issue forth from the walls, bearing their weapons,
And he told them that there they would have to take a stand.   14,170
He promised the townsfolk their legal privileges
If they would only help him in his hour of need.
When dawn was breaking, the burghers were eager to fight,
And Arthur was outraged when he saw that they were rebels.
He had trumpets blown, warriors readied for battle.
He ordered all of his nobles, his finest knights,
To get ready for the onslaught, to overthrow their foes,
To raise havoc on the town, hang the treacherous townsfolk.
His men moved in masses and hacked with mighty rage.
Mordred was very worried about what he might do.   14,180
And he acted at this time just as he acted elsewhere:
He was utterly wicked, as he was always so.
He betrayed all the burghers there before Winchester.
He cozened up to the closest courtiers he had
And the fondest friends he had among his folk,
And sneaked away from the fray—may the Great Fiend seize him!
He left people who were loyal there to perish.
All the day they labored, thinking their lord among them,
Believing that he stood by them in their hour of need.
But he was galloping on the road that goes to Hampton;   14,190
That perversest of persons was heading for the port.
He annexed all the ships that were active and able,
Told the sailors that he needed to sail them away.
Then he sped off to Cornwall—that crassest of men!
Arthur quickly won over the castle of Winchester,
Slaying all of their citizens, the sorrow was great!
The young and the elderly—he undid them all.
When he killed all the townsfolk, he torched the town,
And he broke the ramparts into little bits.
So it came to pass what Merlin had prophesied: 14,200
"Woe to you, Winchester; the earth shall swallow you up!"
These words Merlin uttered, the wisest of wizards.
    Wenhaver was in York; she was never so worried—
Yes, Wenhaver the queen, most wretched of women.
She had heard all of these most unhappy reports:
How Mordred had fled and how Arthur had followed.
Her life was now loathsome as long as she was living.
In nighttime she slipped out of the shire of York,
Heading for Caerleon as quickly as she could.
There under cover she called for two of her courtiers   14,210

To hallow her head with a holy veil.
She became now a nun—that unhappiest of women.
No man knew then what became of the queen,
And for years thereafter nothing was known,
Whether she was alive or lying in her grave,
Or if she had sunk into some flowing stream.
    Meanwhile in Cornwall Mordred summoned many men.
Swiftly to Ireland he sent over a message
And then to Saxony he also sent some words,
And finally to Scotland he quickly dealt some dispatches.   14,220
He told them all to come if they coveted land
Or silver or gold, some chattel or some goods;
Thus in every which way he watched out for himself,
As does a cunning creature who is cornered by fate.
But Arthur, now angriest of kings, heard this all:
How Mordred in Cornwall cowered with his company
And was waiting for the time that he would approach.
Arthur sent out an order over all his kingdom,
Calling forth all those who were living in his land
Who were ready for war, to come with weapons in hand;   14,230
And if anyone berated what the king now begged,
Arthur would see that he was seared at the stake.
Then countless people came to join in that crowd,
Walking and riding while the rain fell down!
Arthur tramped into Cornwall with a huge train.
Mordred heard this mumbled and hurried out to meet him
With unnumbered warriors—many dooms were weighed.
Near the banks of the Tamar they banded together,
At a place known as Camelford, a name of great fame.
Yes, at Camelford there gathered some sixty thousand,   14,240
With thousands besides who hailed Mordred as their lord.
    Then to that place appeared Arthur the powerful
With legions of forces whose lives were all fated.
On the banks of the Tamar they tangled together;
They lifted their standards and lunged to attack,
Drawing out their long swords, slashing at helmets,
While sparks flinted out and spears flew in two.
Shields started to crumble while shafts were cracking.
Countless men were now clashing together there,
And the River Tamar was now rife with blood.   14,250
Nobody could fathom who fared well in that fighting:
Who did better or worse; the warring was mixed.
They were all slaying outright—whether squire or knight.
Then Mordred was cut down, cut short from his days,
And all of his followers were felled on that field.
Many of the mighty were massacred in that place
Of Arthur's loyal lieges, the high and the low,
And all of the Britons who were attached to his board,
Along with the fosterlings from lands far and wide,

While Arthur was shafted badly by a broad spear;   14,260
In fact he received fifteen fatal gashes.
In the greatest of these you could thrust two gloves!
   Finally not a single person stood on that plain.
Two hundred thousand were hacked down to the ground,
Except for noble Arthur and two of his knights.
Arthur had been sorely wounded in a serious way.
Then up to him crept a youngster of his kin:
He was the son of Cador, the earl of Cornwall.
His name was Constantine; he was cousinly to the king.
Arthur gazed up at him as he groveled on the ground,   14,270
Whispering these words that betokened a woeful heart:
"Dear Constantine, son of Cador, please now hear me.
I bestow upon you now my entire British kingdom.
Please protect my British people for all of your life
And defend the laws that have lasted through my days,
And all of the useful laws that stood under our Uther.
I shall go forth to Avalon to the fairest of maidens,
To Argante [Morgan] the queen, the comeliest of fays,
And she shall heal my wounds and make me healthy
And sound, by preparing for me health-giving potions.   14,280
And then I shall come again into my own kingdom,
And I shall abide with my Britons in joyous bliss."
A light little boat came lilting over the waters
Even as he spoke, gliding in there from the sea,
And two women were in it of wonderful appearance.
They raised Arthur up and rapidly took him away;
They laid him softly down, and outwardly they sailed.
   And so once again there occurred what Merlin had uttered:
Countless cares would be felt when Arthur was faring forth.
The Britons still hold that he is alive in health,   14,290
That he lingers on Avalon with the loveliest of fays,
And they are always awaiting the time when Arthur returns.
There never was a man who was born of a blessed lady
Who can tell you any more about Arthur's true fate.
But once there was a magus whose name was Merlin
And he proclaimed these words; his prophecies were true;
An Arthur will return who will redeem the Britons!

chapter III

THE STORY OF PEREDUR
SON OF EFROG

John K. Bollard

The Story of Peredur Son of Efrog is one of three Welsh tales with close analogs in the romances of Chrétien de Troyes. *Peredur* corresponds to Chrétien's *Perceval*, and the tales of *Owein* (or *The Lady of the Fountain*) and *Gereint* are analogs to Chrétien's *Yvain* and *Erec* respectively. The relationship of these pairs of tales has long been the subject of some debate. Most scholars familiar with the Welsh tales would now agree that neither the French nor the Welsh is a translation of the other. The basic materials of *Peredur*, both of the story and of the Arthurian milieu in which it is set, are Welsh in origin, and there are clear parallels with earlier Irish literature and with common Celtic themes. There is less agreement as to whether the three Welsh tales in their present form are the work of a single author or redactor. Whatever its earlier history, the surviving versions of *Peredur* give evidence of a fairly unified narrative tradition. The particular version translated here is clearly the work of a storyteller with considerable mastery of written Welsh prose.

Much of the study of *Peredur* has been devoted to the question of its relationship to Chrétien's romance, especially because of its importance for an understanding of the development of the theme of the Holy Grail. In this respect *Peredur* perhaps raises more questions than it answers, for there is no Grail *per se* in the story, but rather a bloody, severed head on a platter. Unfortunately this "genetic" approach has obscured the excellence of the tale for many readers, preventing them from understanding and appreciating the Welsh tale's own unity and structure. The author or redactor does not expound the tale's meaning himself; instead he leaves the meaning implicit within the narrative. Yet the almost bewildering array of adventures and events in the tale makes it difficult for us to apprehend the principles of organization and thematic development.

Some of this difficulty is allayed if we recognize that the narrative unit of the tale is the episode. Episodes are not differentiated in the manuscripts, though they are indicated in this translation by a space between paragraphs. Episodes are indicated textually, however, usually by means of the journey motif in such statements as "Peredur went on toward Arthur's court," or simply "And Peredur went on his way." There are three large capitals in the White Book manuscript that do give some indication, at least, of the scribe's understanding of larger divisions in the story. These initials have been indicated in the translation. The narrative, then, is a series of episodes interrelated and interlaced by textual cross-reference, by structural parallelism, and by verbal echoes. Underlying this narrative is the thematic development of the tale, and it is through recognizing the similarities and differences of thematic treatment in various episodes that the meaning of the story becomes apparent.

A number of themes carried throughout the tale are prefigured in the set of instructions Peredur's mother gives him as he sets out for the first time from his secluded forest home. The vocabulary and content of her speech reflect in summary (and from her somewhat biased point of view) the qualities that a knight should possess. He should be accounted among the best of men; he should be generous, brave, noble, and courteous; he should strive for fame; he should help those in trouble, especially women; and his relationships with women should be such as to make him a better man. These ideals appear repeatedly throughout the tale, and such themes often can be seen to account for the inclusion or for the particular emphasis of episodes that otherwise seem unrelated to the surrounding narrative.

The reader, of course, should not be deprived of the joys of discerning at first hand the thematic balance of the tale. Suffice it to say in very general terms that the progress of the untutored boy as he becomes one of the greatest of Arthur's renowned knights provides the primary thematic backdrop. Throughout the story Peredur acts on whatever knowledge he has gained, although that often means that he is acting strangely or imperfectly in the eyes of someone else. While his knowledge and abilities increase steadily, his desire to do right remains constant, even in the face of perplexing and conflicting advice, such as he receives in the closing episodes. It is this quality of steadfast intent, perhaps, that ensures that Peredur remains the true hero of the tale from beginning to end.

It has been suggested above that the tale as we have it is a written one. In the most obvious sense that is, of course, true; the story has been preserved in written form by fourteenth-century scribes, who themselves copied it from earlier manuscripts. There are also, perhaps, evidences of an oral tradition to be discerned in the sentence structure and the repetitive phraseology. This may indicate merely that the developing written style of Middle Welsh narrative had not diverged markedly from an earlier oral tradition. There is no need to assume that *Peredur*, as we now have it, was originally transmitted orally, although that may have been the case. Perhaps the most jarring element to the English reader is the frequent use of "and" as a sentence connector, or even as the opening word of a sentence or paragraph. In part this effect is less obtrusive in Welsh; in part it is a stylistic device (oral in origin) that presents the reader with a series of coordinate clauses and statements, rather than an array of complex subordinate constructions. As a result the story keeps moving fairly rapidly. Although at times it may seem awkward, I have chosen to retain this feature in order to maintain an effect similar to the original. The present translation attempts to stay as close to the original form of the Middle Welsh text as is consistent with modern English usage. Such weaknesses as this translation may have are my own; its strengths are reflections of the Welsh text, the work of one of the finest prose writers in the course of Welsh literature.

Bibliographic note: Peredur is known to us from four medieval manuscripts. The present translation, based on a fresh review of these manuscripts, takes as its primary text the earliest complete version in the White Book of Rhydderch (ca. 1350), now in the National Library of Wales, with help from the version in the Red Book of Hergest (ca. 1382–1410), now held by Jesus College, Oxford. There is some evidence that the latter part of *Peredur* may have been copied by the Red Book scribe, Hywel Vychan, directly from the White Book itself. The two earliest manuscripts (National Library of Wales Manuscripts Peniarth 7 and 14, both ca. 1300), are fragmentary but provide us with important evidence as to variations in the early transmission of the written form of this tale. The title of this translation, for instance, is based on the rubric at the beginning of Peniarth 14: *Ystoria Beredur.*

Since 1849, when Lady Charlotte Guest published her famous translations of *The Mabinogion, Peredur* has been translated into English in 1849, 1929, 1948, and 1976. The most influential English translation is the version by Gwyn Jones and Thomas Jones in *The Mabinogion* (Dent, Everyman's, 1949; revised 1974), although the vocabulary and syntax of their translation are often archaic.

Scholarly interest in *Peredur* has grown in recent years, and the focus of debate has shifted from its relationship to continental romances to the virtues, structure, and meaning of the Welsh tale itself. A brief but perceptive introduction to this and other Welsh tales is Brynley F. Roberts's chapter "Tales and Romances" in *A Guide to Welsh Literature*, Vol. 1, edited by A. O. H. Jarman and G. R. Hughes (Christopher Davies, 1976), pp. 189–243. *Peredur: A Study of Welsh Tradition in the Grail Legends*, by Glenys Goetinck (University of Wales, 1975), is an exposition of her theory of the development of the mythological background and especially the sovereignty and vengeance themes. An important article on the structure and narrative method of the story is Ceridwen Lloyd-Morgan's "Narrative Structure in *Peredur*," *Zeitschrift für Celtische Philologie*, 38 (1981), 187–231.

Note on the pronunciation of Welsh names and words, in order of appearance: Peredur (pe-RED-ear; *r*'s trilled), *Efrog* (EV-rog), *Gwalchmai* (GWAHLCH-mye; *ch* as in Scottish *loch*), *Gwyar* (GOOEY-are), *Gwair* (GWIRE), *Gwestl* (GWES-tl), *Owain* (O-wine), *Urien* (EAR-yen), *Arthur* (ARTH-ear), *Gwenhwyfar* (gwen-HOOEY-vahr), *Cai* (KY), *Caer Loyw* (kire-LOY-oo), *Angharad* (ahng-HAHR-ahd), *Caer Llion* (kire-LLEE-on; pronounce *ll* with the tongue in the same position as for *l* by gently blowing air, without voice, past the side of the tongue—the *l* of English *clean* is similar), *gwyddbwyll* (GWITH-booill; *th* as in *this*), *addanc* (AH-thahnk, *th* as in *this*), *Edlym* (ED-limb), *Hywel* (HU-wel; *u* as in *up*), *Emyr Llydaw* (EM-er LLU-dow; *u* as in *up*, *ow* as in *now*), *Ysbidinongl* (us-bid-IN-ong-gul).

The Story of Peredur Son of Efrog

Earl Efrog held an earldom in the North and he had seven sons. And not chiefly by his realm did Efrog sustain himself but by tournaments and battles and wars. And as is frequent with one who follows war, he was slain, both he and his six sons. And his seventh son was called Peredur, and he was youngest of his seven sons. He was not of age to go to war or battle. Were he of age, he would have been slain as his father and brothers were slain.

A clever, wise woman did he have for a mother. She thought about her son and his realm. She decided to flee with the boy to the desert and wilderness, and to leave the settled parts. She took none in her company except women and boys and humble, contented men who were incapable of battles and wars and to whom they were not seemly. No one would dare to mention, where her son might hear, either horses or arms lest he set his heart on them.

And to the deep forest every day the boy would go to play and to throw holly darts. And one day he could see a flock of goats that was his mother's, and two hinds near the goats. The boy stood and marveled at seeing those two without horns but horns on each one of the others, and he supposed they had been long lost and because of that they had lost their horns. And by might and fleetfootedness he drove the hinds along with the goats into a house that was at the end of the forest.

He came back home. "Mother," he said, "a strange thing have I seen nearby—two of your goats have gone wild and have lost their horns, so long have they been lost in the wood. And no one ever had more trouble than I have had chasing them in."

Upon that everyone arose and came to look. And when they saw the hinds, they marveled greatly that anyone had the strength and fleetfootedness that he could overtake them.

And one day they could see three knights coming along a bridle path beside the forest. These were Gwalchmai [Gawain] son of Gwyar, Gwair son of Gwestl, and Owain [Yvain] son of Urien, with Owain keeping the rear, following the knight who had distributed the apples in Arthur's court.

"Mother," he said, "what are those yonder?"

"Angels, my son," she said.

"I will go as an angel with them," said Peredur. And he came to the path to meet the knights.

"Tell me, friend," said Owain, "have you seen a knight going past either today or yesterday?"

"I do not know," he said, "what a knight is."

"The kind of thing I am," said Owain.

"If you will tell me that which I ask of you, I will tell you that which you ask."

"I will gladly."

"What is this?" he said of the saddle.

"A saddle," said Owain.

Peredur asked what everything was and what was intended and what could be done with it. Owain told him fully what everything was and what could be done with it.

"Go on ahead," said Peredur. "I have seen the sort of man you are asking about. And I will go after you as a knight now."

Then Peredur returned to where his mother and the company were. "Mother," he said, "those are not angels there, but knights."

Then she fell into a dead faint. And Peredur went on to where the horses were that carried firewood for them and that brought food and drink from the inhabited parts to the desert, and he took a bony, dapple-grey horse (the strongest, he supposed), and he pressed a pannier on it as a saddle. And back he came to where his mother was.

And upon that, lo, the countess revived. "Well," she said, "do you wish to set out?"

"Yes," he said.

"Wait. I have advice before you leave."

"Speak," he said, "quickly; I will wait for it."

"Go on," she said, "to Arthur's court, where there are the best men and the most generous and the bravest. Where you see a church, recite your paternoster to it. If you see food and drink, if you have need of it and there is no one to give it to you out of courtesy and goodness, take it yourself. If you hear a cry, go to it, and the cry of a woman before any cry in the world. If you see a fair jewel, take it and give it to another, and from that you will get fame. If you see a fair woman, court her. Though she may not desire you, a better and more fervent man it will make you than before."

And with withes he imitated in every respect the trappings that he had seen, and he set forth with a fistful of sharp-pointed darts in his hand. And for two nights and two days he was traveling through desert and wilderness without food, without drink. And then he came to a great, desolate wood. And in the midst of the wood he could see a clearing as of a field, and in the clearing he could see a pavilion. And as if it were a church, he recited his paternoster to the pavilion. And toward the pavilion he came. And the door of the pavilion was open, with a chair of gold near the door and a fair auburn-haired maiden sitting in the chair with a golden frontlet about her brow and a sparkling stone in the frontlet and a thick gold ring on her hand.

And Peredur dismounted and came in. The maiden was pleasant to him and she greeted him. And at the end of the pavilion he could see a table with two flagons full of wine and two loaves of white bread and cutlets of porkling. "My mother," said Peredur, "bade me wherever I might see food and drink to take it."

"Go, then, sir," she said, "to the table, and God's welcome to you."

Peredur went to the table, and one half of the food and the drink Peredur took for himself, and the other he left for the maiden. And after he finished eating, he arose and came where the maiden was. "My mother," he said, "bade me to take a fair jewel wherever I saw one."

"Take it, friend," she said. "It is not I who will begrudge it to you."

Peredur took the ring and bent down on his knee and gave a kiss to the maiden and took his horse and set out.

After that, lo, the knight who owned the pavilion came. He was the

Proud One of the Clearing. And he could see the tracks of the horse. "Tell me," he said to the maiden, "who has been here after me?"

"A man of strange appearance, lord," she said, and she related Peredur's appearance and his manner.

"Tell me," he said, "has he been with you?"

"He has not, by my faith," she said.

"By my faith, I do not believe you. And until I myself meet with him to take vengeance for my anger and my shame, you shall not be two nights in one place or another."

And the knight arose and set out to seek for Peredur.

Peredur went on toward Arthur's court. But before he came to Arthur's court another knight came to the court and gave a thick gold ring to a man at the gate for holding his horse. And he himself came into the hall where Arthur was with his warband and Gwenhwyfar with her maidens, and a chamberlain was serving Gwenhwyfar with a goblet. And the knight took the goblet from Gwenhwyfar's hand and poured the drink that was in it over her face and her breast and gave Gwenhwyfar a great box on the ear.

"If there is," he said, "anyone who wishes to fight with me for this goblet and to avenge this insult to Gwenhwyfar, let him come after me to the meadow, and I will wait for him there."

And the knight took his horse and made for the meadow. Then everyone lowered his head lest he be asked to go to avenge the insult to Gwenhwyfar, and it seemed likely to them that no one would do such an outrage as that unless he had such might and strength or magic and enchantment that no one could take revenge upon him.

Upon that, lo, Peredur came into the hall on a bony dapple-grey horse with crude, clumsy trappings upon it. And Cai [Kay] was standing in the middle of the floor of the hall.

"Tell me," said Peredur, "tall man yonder, where is Arthur?"

"What do you want," said Cai, "with Arthur?"

"My mother bade me come to Arthur to be ordained as an ordained knight."

"By my faith," said Cai, "too crudely have you come with regard to horse and arms."

And upon that the warband saw him and began to ridicule him and throw sticks at him, and they were pleased that one such as that came to drive the other matter from memory.

And upon that, lo, the dwarf came in who had come the space of a year before that to Arthur's court, he and his she-dwarf, to ask hospitality of Arthur. And they got that from Arthur, except that in the space of the year they did not speak a single word to anyone. When the dwarf saw Peredur, "Aha," he said, "God's welcome to you, fair Peredur son of Efrog, chief of warriors and flower of knights."

"Truly, boy," said Cai, "that is an evil stroke: being for a year mute in Arthur's court, having your choice of fellow-talker and your choice of companion, and calling this sort of person, in the presence of Arthur and his warband, chief of warriors and flower of knights." And he gave him a box on the ear so that he went head over heels to the floor in a dead faint.

Upon that, lo, the she-dwarf came in. "Aha," she said, "God's welcome to you, fair Peredur son of Efrog, flower of warriors and candle of knights."

"Well, girl," said Cai, "that is an evil stroke: being for a year mute in Arthur's court, without saying a single word to anyone, and calling this sort of person today, in the presence of Arthur and his warriors, flower of warriors and candle of knights," and kicked her so that she fell in a dead faint.

"Tall man," said Peredur then, "tell me, where is Arthur?"

"Be silent," said Cai. "Go to the meadow after the knight who came here, and take the goblet from him and overthrow him and take his horse and his arms. And after that you may be ordained as an ordained knight."

"Tall man," he said, "I will do that." And he turned his horse's head and went out to the meadow.

And when he arrived, the knight was riding his horse in the meadow with great arrogance in his ability and his bravery. "Tell me," said the knight, "did you see anyone from the court coming after me?"

"The tall man who was there," he said, "asked me to overthrow you and take the goblet and the horse and the arms for myself."

"Silence," said the knight. "Go back to the court for me and ask for Arthur to come, either he or another, to joust with me. But if he does not come quickly, I will not wait for him."

"By my faith," said Peredur, "you choose; either by your will or against your will, I wish for the horse and the arms and the goblet."

And then the knight attacked him angrily and with the butt of his spear struck him a great, painful blow between shoulder and neck.

"Ah, fellow," said Peredur, "my mother's servants would not play with me thus. I will play with you like this." And he took aim with a sharp-pointed dart and hit him in his eye so that it went out through the nape of the neck, and he fell stone-dead to the ground.

"Truly," said Owain son of Urien to Cai, "wrongly have you struck with regard to the foolish man whom you sent after the knight. And one of two things has happened: either he has been overthrown or he has been killed. If he has been overthrown, he will be reckoned a gentleman by the knight, and there will be eternal disgrace upon Arthur and his warriors. If he has been killed, the disgrace as before will come about, and the sin of it upon you in addition. [Peniarth MS 14 reads: "and the sin of it upon us all."] And may I lose face unless I go to find out what adventure has happened to him."

And then Owain went toward the meadow. And when he arrived, Peredur was dragging the man behind him across the meadow.

"Ah, sir," said Owain, "wait. I will remove the armor."

"Never," said Peredur, "will this iron tunic come off him. It is part of his own self."

Then Owain removed the armor and the garments.

"Behold now for you, friend," he said, "a horse and arms better than the others. And take them gladly, and come with me to Arthur, and you shall be ordained as an ordained knight."

"May I lose face," said Peredur, "if I go. But take the goblet from me to Gwenhwyfar, and say to Arthur that, wherever I may be, I will be his man, and if I can do good and service to him, I will do it. And say to him that I will never go to his court until I meet with the tall man who is there to take vengeance for the insult to the dwarf and the she-dwarf."

Then Owain went on to the court, and he told the adventure to Arthur and Gwenhwyfar and to all of the warband, and the threat to Cai.

And Peredur went on his way. And as he was going, lo, a knight met with him. "Where do you come from?" asked the knight.

"I come from Arthur's court," he said.

"Are you a man of Arthur's?"

"Yes, by my faith," he said.

"A fine place to acknowledge Arthur!"

"Why?" asked Peredur.

"I will tell you," he said. "I have always been a pillager and a despoiler of Arthur, and whatever man of his met with me, I would kill him."

Without delay they jousted, and they were not long at it. Peredur overthrew him so that he went over the hindquarters of his horse to the ground. The knight asked for mercy.

"You will get mercy," said Peredur, "upon your oath to go to Arthur's court and tell to Arthur that I overthrew you for honor and service to him. And tell him I will never set foot in his court until I meet with the tall man who is there to take vengeance for the insult to the dwarf and the she-dwarf."

And with his promise of that the knight set out for Arthur's court, and he told the adventure in full, and the threat to Cai.

And Peredur went on his way. And in the same week sixteen knights met with him and he overthrew every one. And they came to Arthur's court with the same tale as from the first one whom he overthrew, and the same threat to Cai. And Cai was blamed by Arthur and the warband, and he was worried about that.

Peredur set out on his way, and in the end he came to a great, desolate wood. And beside the wood was a lake, and on the other side of the lake was a great court with a fine fortress around it. And on the shore of the lake was a grey-haired man sitting on a cushion of brocade with a garment of brocade about him, and youths were fishing in a boat on the lake. As the grey-haired man saw Peredur coming, he rose up and went toward the court. And the man was lame.

Peredur came toward the court, and the gate was open and he came to the hall. And when he arrived, the grey-haired man was sitting on a cushion of brocaded silk, and a great fire was beginning to burn. And both warband and retinue rose up to meet Peredur, and they helped him dismount and took off his armor. And the man struck his hand on the end of the cushion and asked the youth to sit on the cushion. And they sat together and conversed.

And when it was time to set up the tables and go to eat, Peredur was placed next to the man to sit and to eat. After they finished eating, the man asked Peredur if he knew well how to strike with a sword.

"I do not know," said Peredur, "that if I were to get instruction I would not know it." [Peniarth MSS 7 and 14 say more simply: "If I were to get instruction, (I suppose) I would know it."]

"Whoever knew," he said, "how to play with a stick and with a shield, he would know how to strike with a sword." The grey-haired man had two sons, a yellow-haired youth and an auburn-haired youth. "Rise up, lads," he said, "to play with the sticks and with the shields." The youths went to play.

"Tell me, friend," the man said, "which of the lads plays best."

"It is my opinion," Peredur said, "that the yellow-haired youth for some time could have drawn blood from the auburn-haired youth, if he had wished it."

"Friend, you take the stick and the shield from the hand of the auburn-haired youth, and draw blood from the yellow-haired youth if you can."

Peredur rose up and took the stick and the shield, and he struck a blow on the yellow-haired youth so that his eyebrow was down over the eye and the blood was running freely in streams.

"Well, friend," said the man, "come and sit now. And you will be the best man who strikes with a sword in this island. And I am your uncle, your mother's brother. And you will be with me for a while learning manners and courtesy. Leave now your mother's advice, and I will be your teacher and will ordain you as an ordained knight. From now on here is what you should do: though you see something that may be strange to you, do not ask about it if it is not told to you out of politeness. The blame will not be on you but on me, since I am your teacher."

And they received various kinds of honor and service; and when it was time, they went to sleep.

When daybreak came, Peredur rose up and took his horse and, with his uncle's permission, set out. And he came to a great wood, and at the end of the wood he came to a flat meadow, and on the other side of the meadow he could see a great fortress and a fine court. And Peredur made for the court, and he found the gate open and he made for the hall. And when he arrived, a handsome, grey-haired man was sitting at the side of the hall with a great number of youths around him. And everyone rose up to meet the youth, and their politeness and their service to him were good. He was placed to sit next to the nobleman who owned the court, and they conversed.

And when time came to go to eat, he was placed next to the nobleman to sit and to eat. After they had finished eating and drinking as long as it was pleasant to them, the nobleman asked him if he knew how to strike with a sword.

"If I were to get instruction," said Peredur, "I suppose I would know."

There was a great iron column in the floor of the hall, a warrior's grasp in girth. "Take," the man said to Peredur, "the sword yonder and strike the iron column."

Peredur rose up and he struck the column so that it was in two pieces and the sword in two pieces.

"Put the pieces together and join them."

Peredur put the pieces together, and they joined as before. And a second time he struck so that the column broke into two pieces and the sword into two pieces; and as before they joined. And a third time he struck so that the column broke into two pieces and the sword into two pieces.

"Put them together again and join them."

Peredur put them together the third time, but neither the column nor the sword would join.

"Well, lad," he said, "come and sit, and God's blessing be with you. You are the best man who strikes with a sword in the kingdom. Two thirds of your bravery you have achieved, and the last third is yet to be gained. And after you gain the whole, none will be able to withstand you. And I am your uncle, your mother's brother, brother of the man whose court you were in last night." At the one hand of his uncle Peredur sat, and they conversed.

Upon that he could see two youths coming into the hall, and from the hall going into a chamber, and they had a spear of immeasurable size, with three streams of blood along it running from the socket to the floor. And when they saw the youths coming in that manner, everyone took to crying and lamenting until it was not easy for anyone to endure it. The man did not break off his conversation with Peredur because of that. The man said nothing to Peredur about what that was. Nor did Peredur ask him. After it was quiet for a short while, lo, two maidens came in with a large dish between them and a man's head on the dish, with a lot of blood around the head. And then everyone lamented and cried so that it was difficult for anyone to be in the same building as they. In the end they stopped that and sat as long as they wished and drank. After that a chamber was prepared for Peredur, and they went to sleep.

The next morning Peredur rose up and with his uncle's permission set out on his way. From there he came to a wood, and deep in the wood he could hear a cry. He went toward the place where the cry was, and when he arrived he could see a handsome, auburn-haired woman and a horse with a saddle on it standing beside her, and a man's body in the woman's arms. And as she tried to put the body into the saddle, the body would fall to the ground, and then she would give a great cry.

"Tell me, my sister," he asked, "what are you crying out about?"

"Oh, accursed Peredur," she said, "little relief from my trouble did I ever get from you!"

"Why," he said, "would I be accursed?"

"Because of your being the cause of your mother's death, for when you set out against her will, a pain leaped within her and from that she died. And because of your being the cause of her death, you are accursed. And the dwarf and the she-dwarf whom you saw in Arthur's court, that was the dwarf of your father and your mother. And I am your foster-sister and this is my husband, whom the knight who is in the wood killed. And do not go near him, lest you be killed."

"Wrongly, my sister," he said, "do you rebuke me. Because I have been with you as long as I have, I will barely overcome him. And if I were any longer, I would never overcome him. And you, cease any further your lamentation, since relief is nearer to you than before. And I will bury the man and I will go with you to where the knight is, and if I can take vengeance, I will do it."

After burying the man, they came to where the knight was in the clearing riding his horse. Without delay the knight asked Peredur where he came from.

"I come from Arthur's court."

"Are you Arthur's man?"

"Yes, by my faith."

"A fine place to claim an alliance to Arthur!"

It was no longer than that till they attacked each other, and on the spot Peredur overthrew the knight. The knight asked for mercy.

"You will get mercy by taking this woman as a wife and, whatever good you may do for a woman, doing it for her, because you killed her husband without cause; and by going on to Arthur's court and telling him that I overthrew you in honor and service to Arthur, and telling him that I will not go to his court until I meet with the tall man who is there to take vengeance for the insult to the dwarf and the maiden."

And Peredur took surety on that from him. And he set the woman on a well-arrayed horse along with him, and he went on to Arthur's court and told to Arthur the adventure and the threat to Cai. And Cai was blamed by Arthur and the warband for driving a youth as good as Peredur from Arthur's court.

"That youth will never come to the court," said Owain. "Cai, for his part, will not go out of the court."

"By my faith," said Arthur, "I will search the wilderness of the Isle of Britain for him until I find him. And then let each one of them do the worst he can to the other."

And Peredur went on his way, and he came to a great, desolate wood. He could not see the tracks of men or cattle in the wood, but thickets and plants. And when he came to the end of the wood, he could see a large, ivy-covered fortress with many strong towers on it. And near to the gate the plants were taller than elsewhere.

With the butt of his spear he knocked on the gate. Upon that, lo, a thin, ginger-haired youth was in the battlement above his head. "Choose, sir," he said; "either I will open the gate for you or tell the one who is chief that you are at the gate."

"Say that I am here, and if it is wished that I come in, I will come."

The youth came quickly back and opened the gate for Peredur and went ahead of him to the hall. And when he came to the hall, he could see eighteen slender, red-haired youths of the same height, the same features, the same age, and the same clothing as the lad who had opened the gate for him. And their courtesy and their service were excellent. They helped him dismount and took off his armor, and they sat and conversed.

Upon that, lo, five maidens came from a chamber to the hall. And the chief maiden of them—he was certain that he had never seen in another a vision as beautiful as she. Around her was an old, torn garment of brocade that had been good. Where her skin could be seen through it, it was whiter than powder of the whitest crystal. Her hair and her eyebrows—they were blacker than jet. Two small red spots in her cheeks—they were redder than the reddest anything.

The maiden greeted Peredur, embraced him, and sat next to him. Not long after that he could see two nuns coming in, and one with a flagon full of wine and the other with six loaves of white bread. "Lady," said they, "God knows there was not but as much again of food and drink for the convent yonder tonight."

Then they went to eat. And Peredur observed that the maiden wished to give him more of the food and drink than to another.

"You, my sister," he said, "I will share out the food and the drink."

"No, sir," she said.

"Shame on my beard," he said, "if I do not."

Peredur took the bread and he gave to each as much as to the other, and thus also of the drink, to the measure of a cup. After they finished eating, "I would be pleased," said Peredur, "if I could get a comfortable place to sleep." A chamber was prepared for him, and Peredur went to sleep.

"Here, sister," said the youths to the maiden, "is what we counsel you."

"What is that?" she said.

"Go to the youth in the chamber above to offer yourself to him in the manner that may be pleasing to him, either as a wife or as a lover."

"That," she said, "is a thing that is not fitting. I have never had relations with a man, and to offer myself to him before he courts me, I cannot do for anything."

"By our confession to God," they said, "if you do not do that, we will leave you here to your enemies."

Upon that the maiden rose up, letting go her tears, and went to the chamber. And with the noise of the door opening, Peredur awoke, and there was the maiden with her tears running down her cheeks. "Tell me, my sister," said Peredur, "why are you weeping?"

"I will tell you, lord," she said. "My father held this court and the best earldom in the world under him. There was a son of another earl asking my father for me. I would not go to him by my own will; my father would not give me against my will, either to him or to anyone. And my father had no children except myself, and after my father's death the realm fell into my hand. More reluctantly did I desire him then than before. What he did was to make war upon me and to overrun my realm, except for this one house. And so good are the men whom you have seen, my foster-brothers, and so strong the house, it could never be taken from us while food and drink lasted. But those have ended, except that the nuns whom you have seen were supporting us because the country and the realm are free to them. But now they too have neither food nor drink. And there is no time beyond tomorrow before the earl will come with all his might upon this place. And if he takes me, my fate will be no better than giving me to the grooms of his horses. And I came to offer myself to you, lord, in the manner that may be pleasant to you in exchange for being a help to us—to take us from here or to defend us here."

"Go to sleep, my sister," he said. "And I will not leave you without doing one of those things."

The maiden went back and went to sleep.

The next morning the maiden arose and came to where Peredur was and greeted him. He said: "God reward you, friend. And do you have news?"

"There is nothing but good, lord, as long as you are well—and that the earl and all his might have descended upon the house. And no one has seen a place more full of pavilions and knights calling upon each other to joust."

"Well," said Peredur, "let my horse be prepared for me and I will get up."

His horse was prepared, and he arose and went toward the meadow. And when he arrived, there was a knight riding his horse who had raised a signal to joust. Peredur threw him over the hindquarters of his horse to the ground. And he overthrew many that day. And in the afternoon toward the end of the day a particular knight came to joust with him, and he overthrew that one. He asked for mercy.

"Who are you?" said Peredur.

"Truly," he said, "captain of the earl's warband."

"What is there of the lady's realm in your power?"

"Truly," he said, "a third."

"Well," he said, "restore to her the third of her realm in full, and whatever you have gained as benefit from it in full, and food for a hundred men, their drink, their horses, and their arms tonight in the court for her, and you, too, as her prisoner, except that you will not be under sentence of death."

That was obtained without delay. The maiden was joyfully happy that night; the third of her realm was hers, with an abundance of horses, arms, food, and drink in the court. They took their ease while it was pleasing to them, and they went to sleep.

The next morning Peredur made for the meadow, and that day he overthrew multitudes. And at the end of the day a certain arrogant knight came, and he overthrew that one. And he asked for mercy.

"Which one are you?" said Peredur.

"Steward," he said.

"What is there in your hand of the maiden's realm?"

"A third," he said.

"The third of her kingdom to the maiden, and what you have gained as benefit from it in full, and food for two hundred men, their drink, their horses, and their arms, and you as a prisoner of hers."

That was obtained without delay.

And a third day Peredur came to the meadow, and he overthrew more that day than any other day. And in the end the earl came to joust with him, and he threw him to the ground. And the earl asked for mercy.

"Who are you?" said Peredur.

"I will not hide it," he said; "I am the earl."

"Well," he said, "all of her earldom to the maiden, and your earldom also in addition, and food for three hundred men, their drink, their horses, and their arms, and you in her power."

And thus Peredur was taking tribute and homage for the maiden for three weeks. And after establishing her and securing her in her realm: "With your permission," said Peredur, "I will set out."

"Is that, my brother, what you wish?"

"Yes, by my faith. And if it had not been for love of you, I would not have been here for a good while."

"Friend," she said, "who are you?"

"Peredur son of Efrog from the North. And if trouble or peril comes to you, tell me, and I will defend you if I can."

Then Peredur set out, and far from there a lady with a thin, sweated horse under her met with him. And she greeted the knight.

"Where do you come from, my sister?" said Peredur.

She told him the situation she was in, and her journey. She was the wife of the Proud One of the Clearing.

"Well," said Peredur, "I am the knight because of whom you have gotten into that trouble. And the one who did it to you will be sorry."

And upon that, lo, a knight came and asked Peredur if he had seen the kind of knight he was after.

"Be silent," said Peredur. "You are seeking me. And by my faith the maiden is innocent with regard to me."

They jousted nevertheless, and Peredur overthrew the knight. He asked for mercy.

"Mercy you shall get by going back the way you have been, to report that the maiden has been found innocent. And as compensation to her I overthrew you."

The knight gave his promise of that.

And Peredur went on. And on a mountain before him he could see a castle. And he went toward the castle, and he struck the gate with his spear. Upon that, lo, a handsome, auburn-haired youth opened the gate, with the size and stoutness of a warrior, but the age of a boy upon him. When Peredur came to the hall, there was a large, handsome woman sitting in a chair with plenty of handmaidens around her. And the noblewoman made him welcome. And when it was time to go to eat, they went. And after eating: "You would do well, sir," said the woman, "to go to another place to sleep."

"May I not sleep here?"

"Nine witches, sir," she said, "are here, and their father and mother with them. They are the witches of Caer Loyw ["the Bright Fortress," perhaps the English city of Gloucester], and by daybreak we will no sooner escape than be killed. And they have overrun and laid waste to the realm except for this one house."

"Well," said Peredur, "I will be here tonight. And if trouble comes, if I can do good, I will do it. Harm I will not do."

They went to sleep.

And at daybreak Peredur could hear a cry. And Peredur rose up quickly in his shirt and trousers with his sword around his neck and came out. And when he arrived, there was a witch overtaking the watchman, and he was crying out. Peredur made for the witch, and he struck her with his sword on the head so that he flattened her helmet and her mail-cap like a dish on her head.

"Your mercy, fair Peredur son of Efrog, and God's mercy!"

"How do you know, hag, that I am Peredur?"

"It is fated and foreseen that I will suffer trouble from you and that you will take horse and arms from me. And you will be with me a while learning to ride your horse and to handle your arms."

"This is how," he said, "you shall get mercy: on your oath that you will never do wrong to the realm of this countess."

Peredur took surety on that, and with the permission of the lady set out with the witch to the court of the witches. And he was there for three weeks on end.

And then Peredur took his choice of horse and arms and set out on his way. And at the end of the day he came to a valley and at the end of the valley he came to a hermit's cell. And the hermit made him welcome and he was there that night.

The next morning he rose up. And when he came out there was a shower of snow that had fallen the night before, and a wild hawk had killed a duck in front of the cell. And with the noise of the horse the hawk arose and a raven descended on the flesh of the bird. Peredur stood and compared the blackness of the raven and the whiteness of the snow and the redness of the blood to the hair of the woman he loved most, which was as black as jet, and her skin to the whiteness of the snow, and the redness of the blood in the white snow to the two red spots in the cheeks of the woman he loved most.

Upon that, there were Arthur and his warband seeking Peredur.

"Do you know," said Arthur, "who is the long-speared knight who is standing in the vale above?"

"Lord," said one, "I will go to find out who it is."

Then the youth came to where Peredur was and asked him what he was doing there and who he was. But so firmly was Peredur's thought on the woman he loved most, he gave him no answer. He struck Peredur with a spear, and Peredur turned on the youth and thrust him over the hindquarters of his horse to the ground. And one after another there came twenty-four knights, and he would not answer one more than another, except with the same game to each one, thrusting him with one blow over his horse to the ground.

Cai came to him and spoke harshly and unpleasantly to Peredur. And Peredur took him with a spear under his jaws and threw him a great space away from him, so that he broke his arm and his shoulder blade. And while he was in a dead faint from the greatness of the hurt he had received, his horse returned with a capering trot. And when every one of the warband saw the horse coming without a man upon it, they came quickly toward the place where the encounter had been. And when they came there, they supposed that Cai had been killed. They saw, however, that if he were to get a physician to set his bone and to bind his joints, he would be none the worse. Peredur did not move from his thought any more than before at seeing the commotion over Cai. And Cai was brought to Arthur's pavilion, and Arthur sent skillful physicians to him. Arthur was sorry that Cai had met with that trouble, since he loved him greatly.

And then Gwalchmai said: "No one ought to awaken an ordained knight discourteously from the thought that is upon him, since it may be either that loss has come upon him or that he is thinking about the woman he loves most. And that discourtesy, perhaps, befell the man who met him last. And if it please you, lord, I will go to see whether the knight has moved from that thought. And if it is thus, I will ask him pleasantly to come to meet you."

And then Cai sulked and spoke angry, envious words. "Gwalchmai," he said, "it is obvious to me that you will bring him back by the reins. Little fame, however, and praise is it for you to overcome a weary knight, tired from fighting. Thus, however, you have overcome many of them. And while your tongue and your fair words last, a tunic of thin, fine linen about you will be sufficient arms for you. And there will be no need for you to break either spear or sword fighting with the knight that you can get in that manner."

And then Gwalchmai said to Cai: "You could have said something that was more pleasant if you wished. But not against me should you avenge your wrath and your anger! It seems likely to me, however, that I will bring the knight with me without breaking either an arm or shoulder of mine."

Then Arthur said to Gwalchmai: "You speak like a wise and prudent man. And you go on, and take enough armor upon you and choose your horse."

Gwalchmai armed himself and went on slowly at his horse's pace toward the place where Peredur was. And he was leaning on the shaft of his spear and thinking the same thought. And Gwalchmai came toward him with no sign of hostility about him and said to him: "If I knew it would please you as it pleases me, I would converse with you. Nevertheless I am a messenger from Arthur to you to ask you to come to meet him. And two men came before me on that same errand."

"That is true," said Peredur, "but they came unpleasantly. They fought with me, and I was not pleased at that, insofar as I was not pleased to be taken from the thought that I was in. I was thinking about the woman I loved most. This is the reason the memory of that came to me: I was looking at the snow and at the raven and at the drops of the blood of the duck that the hawk had killed in the snow. And I was thinking that the whiteness of her skin was similar to the snow, and the blackness of her hair and her eyebrows to the raven, and the two red spots there were in her cheeks to the two drops of blood."

Gwalchmai said: "That thought was not ignoble, and it was not surprising that you were not pleased to be taken from it."

Peredur said: "Will you tell me: is Cai in Arthur's court?"

"He is," he said. "He was the last knight who jousted with you. But no good came to him from that joust; he broke his right arm and his shoulder blade with the fall that he got from the thrust of your spear."

"Well," said Peredur, "I do not mind beginning to avenge the insult to the dwarf and the she-dwarf thus."

Gwalchmai marveled to hear talk about the dwarf and the she-dwarf, and he drew near to him and embraced him and asked what his name was.

"I am called Peredur son of Efrog," he said. "And you—who are you?"

"I am called Gwalchmai," he said.

"I am pleased to see you," said Peredur. "I have heard of your fame for might and fidelity in every land that I have been in; and I wish for your friendship."

"You shall have it, by my faith; and you give me yours."

"You shall have it gladly," said Peredur.

They set out together pleasantly in accord toward the place where Arthur was. And when Cai heard they were coming, he said: "I knew there would be no need for Gwalchmai to fight with the knight. And it is not surprising that he has achieved fame. He does more with his fair words than we by the strength of our arms."

And Peredur and Gwalchmai went to Gwalchmai's tent to remove their arms. And Peredur took the same sort of garment as Gwalchmai had. And they went hand in hand to where Arthur was and greeted him. "Here, lord," said Gwalchmai, "is the man you have been seeking for some time."

"Welcome to you, sir," said Arthur, "and you shall remain with me. And if I had known that your development would be as it has been, you would not have gone from me when you went. That, however, the dwarf and the she-dwarf to whom Cai was mean prophesied of you. And you have avenged them."

And upon that the queen and her handmaidens came up. And Peredur greeted them, and they were pleasant to him and welcomed him. Arthur showed great respect and honor to Peredur, and they returned toward Caer Llion.

And the first night Peredur came to Caer Llion to Arthur's court, it happened that he was walking in the fortress after eating. Lo, Angharad Golden-Hand met with him.

"By my faith, my sister," said Peredur, "you are a pleasant, lovely maiden, and I could love you the most of women, if it would please you."

"I give my promise," she said, "thus: I do not love you and I will not desire you for eternity."

"I give my promise," said Peredur, "that I will not ever speak a word to a Christian until you admit that you love me most of men."

The next day Peredur went on his way, and he followed the highway along the ridge of a great mountain. And at the end of the mountain he could see a round valley, and the borders of the valley were wooded and stony. And the floor of the valley was meadows, with plowed lands between the meadows and the wood. And in the heart of the wood he could see large, black houses of rough workmanship. And he dismounted and led his horse toward the wood. And a little way into the wood he could see the side of a sharp stone, and the road going beside the stone, and a lion bound by a chain and sleeping at the side of the stone. And a deep pit of huge size he could see below the lion, with its fill of the bones of men and animals in it. And Peredur drew his sword and struck the lion so that he fell hanging by the chain above the pit. With a second blow he struck the chain so that it broke, and so the lion fell into the pit.

And past the side of the stone Peredur led his horse until he came to the valley. And about the center of the valley he could see a fair castle, and he went toward the castle. And on the meadow by the castle he could see a large, grey-haired man sitting, who was larger than any man he had ever seen, and two young boys shooting at the walrus-tusk hilts of their knives, the one of them an auburn-haired youth and the other a yellow-haired youth. And he went on to where the grey-haired man was, and Peredur

greeted him. And the grey-haired man said: "Shame on my porter's beard!"
And then Peredur understood that the lion was the porter.

And then the grey-haired men and the youths with him went to the
castle, and Peredur went with them. And he could see a fair, majestic place
there. And they made for the hall. And the tables had been set up, with
abundant food and drink upon them. And upon that he could see an aged
woman and a young woman coming from the chamber, and they were the
largest women he had ever seen. And they washed and went to eat. And the
grey-haired man went to the head of the table in the highest place, with
the aged woman next to him. And Peredur and the maiden were placed
together, with the two young boys waiting on them.

And the maiden looked at Peredur and grew sad. And Peredur asked the
maiden why she was sad.

"You, friend; since I first saw you I have loved you most of men. And it
is hard for me to see for a youth as noble as you the death that will come to
you tomorrow. Did you see the many black houses in the midst of the
wood? Those are all men of my father, the grey-haired man yonder, and
they are all giants. And tomorrow they will gather against you and kill you.
And this valley is called the Round Valley."

"Alas, fair maiden, will you have my horse and my arms put in the same
lodging as I tonight?"

"I will, between me and God, if I can, gladly."

When it was more the time for them to take sleep than carousal, they
went to sleep. And the maiden had Peredur's horse and his arms put in the
same lodging as he. And the next day Peredur could hear a tumult of men
and horses around the castle. And Peredur arose and put his arms upon him
and upon his horse, and he came to the meadow.

And the aged woman and the maiden came to the grey-haired man.
"Lord," they said, "take the promise of the youth that he will not tell
anything he has seen here, and we will vouch for him to keep it."

"I will not, by my faith," said the grey-haired man.

And Peredur fought with the host. And by evening he had killed a third
of the host without anyone harming him. And then the aged woman said:
"The youth has killed many of your host. Will you show mercy to him?"

"I will not, by my faith," he said.

And the aged woman and the fair maiden were watching on the battlement of the fortress. And upon that Peredur met with the yellow-haired
youth and killed him.

"Lord," said the maiden, "show mercy to the youth."

"I will not, between me and God."

And upon that Peredur met with the auburn-haired youth and killed
him.

"It would have been better for you if you had shown mercy to the youth
before he killed your two sons. And with difficulty will you yourself escape, if you escape."

"You go, maiden, and beg the youth to show mercy to us, since we have
not shown it to him."

And the maiden came to where Peredur was and asked for mercy for her
father and for those of his men who had escaped alive.

"You shall get it under the condition that your father and all of those who are under him go to swear homage to the emperor Arthur, and tell him that it is Peredur, a man of his, who did this service."

"We will do it, between me and God, gladly."

"And that you receive baptism. And I will send to Arthur to ask him to give this valley to you and to your heirs after you forever."

And then they came in, and the grey-haired man and the large woman greeted Peredur. And then the grey-haired man said: "Since I have ruled this valley, I have not seen a Christian who left it with his life except you. And we will go to swear homage to Arthur and to receive the faith and baptism."

And then Peredur said: "I give thanks to God that I have not broken my oath to the woman I love most that I would not say one word to a Christian."

They remained there that night.

The next day the grey-haired man and his retinue with him went to Arthur's court. And they swore homage to Arthur, and Arthur had them baptized. And the grey-haired man told Arthur that it was Peredur who had overcome him. And Arthur gave the valley to the grey-haired man and his retinue to hold it under him, as Peredur had asked. And with Arthur's permission the grey-haired man left for the Round Valley.

Peredur set out the next morning through a great stretch of wasteland without reaching a dwelling. But in the end he came to a poor, small dwelling. And there he heard that there was a serpent lying on a gold ring without leaving a dwelling seven miles on any side of it. And Peredur went to where he heard the serpent was, and he fought with the serpent angrily, fiercely, and fervently brave. And in the end he killed it and took the ring for himself. And thus he was for a long time wandering, without saying one word to any Christian, so that he lost his color and his appearance from great longing for Arthur's court and the woman he loved most and his companions.

Then Peredur went on to Arthur's court. And on the way Arthur's warband, with Cai in the front going on an errand for them, met with him. Peredur recognized each one of them, but none of the warband recognized him. "Where do you come from, sir?" asked Cai, and two times, and three. But he did not answer.

Cai stabbed him with a spear through his thigh. But lest he be compelled to speak and to break his oath, he went past without avenging himself upon him.

And then Gwalchmai said: "Between me and God, Cai, wrongly have you struck to injure a youth like this, because he could not speak." And he turned back to Arthur's court. "Lady," he said to Gwenhwyfar, "do you see how bad an injury Cai did to that youth because he could not speak? And for God's sake and for mine have him cured by my return and I will repay the price to you."

And before the men came from their errand, a knight came to the meadow beside Arthur's court to ask for a man to joust with. And he got that and he overthrew him. And for a week he overthrew a knight daily.

And one day Arthur and his warband were coming to the church. They could see the knight with a raised signal to joust. "Ha, men," said Arthur, "by the valor of men, I shall not go from here until I get my horse and my arms in order to overthrow the knave yonder!"

Then servants went after his horse and arms for Arthur. And Peredur met the servants going past, and he took the horse and the arms, and he made for the meadow. At seeing him arise and go to joust with the knight, everyone went to the housetops and the hills and high places to watch the joust.

Peredur beckoned with his hand to the knight to ask him to start against him. And the knight set upon him, but he did not stir from the place despite that. And Peredur urged on his horse and attacked him angrily, fiercely, terribly bitter, eagerly brave, and struck him a venomously sharp, fiercely harsh, powerfully mighty blow under his jaws and lifted him from his saddle and cast him a great throw from him. And he turned back and left the horse and the arms with the servants as before, and on foot he made for the court. And Peredur was called the Mute Squire then.

Lo, Angharad Golden-Hand met with him. "Between me and God, sir, it was grievous that you could not speak. And if you could speak, I would love you most of men. And by my faith, though you cannot speak, I will love you most."

"God repay you, my sister. By my faith, I will love you."

And then it was known that he was Peredur. And he held companionship with Gwalchmai and with Owain son of Urien and with all of the warband. And he remained in Arthur's court.

Arthur was at Caer Llion on [the River] Usk, and he went to hunt, and Peredur with him. And Peredur loosed his dog on a stag, and the dog killed the stag in a wilderness. And some distance away from him he could see a sign of habitation, and he went toward the habitation. And he could see a hall, and at the door of the hall he could see three bare-faced, ruddy youths playing gwyddbwyll [a medieval Welsh board game]. And when he came in, he could see three maidens sitting on a couch with golden garments about them such as ought to be about nobles. And he went to sit with them on the couch. And one of the maidens looked at Peredur keenly, and she wept. And Peredur asked her why she was weeping.

"Because of how sorry I am to see a youth as fair as you killed."

"Who would kill me?"

"If it were not dangerous for you to remain in this place, I would tell you."

"However great the peril of remaining may be to me, I will hear it."

"The man who is our father owns this court. And he kills everyone who comes to this court without his permission."

"What kind of man is your father that he is able to kill everyone thus?"

"A man who does violence and displeasure to his neighbors and who does not make amends to anyone for it."

And then he could see the youths rising and clearing the board of the pieces. And he could hear a great commotion, and after the commotion he could see a large, black, one-eyed man coming in. And the maidens arose to meet him, and they removed his garments from him, and he went to sit.

And after gathering his thoughts and relaxing, he looked at Peredur and asked who the knight was.

"Lord," she said, "the fairest and the noblest youth you have ever seen. And for God's sake and for your pride, be considerate toward him."

"For your sake I will be considerate and I will leave him his life tonight."

And then Peredur came to them by the fire and took food and drink and conversed with the young ladies. And then Peredur said, after becoming intoxicated: "It is strange to me how strong you say that you are. Who put out your eye?"

"One of my practices has been that whoever would ask me what you are asking, he would not have his life from me either freely or for a price."

"Lord," said the maiden, "though he speaks foolishness and intoxication and drunkenness to you, make good the word that you spoke a short while ago and that you promised me."

"And I will do that gladly for you. I will leave him his life gladly tonight."

And they left it at that that night.

And the next day the black man arose and put his arms upon him and ordered Peredur: "Rise up, man, to suffer death," said the black man.

Peredur said to the black man: "Do one of two things, black man, if you wish to fight with me: either remove your arms from upon you, or you give me other arms in order to fight with you."

"Ha, man," he said, "could you fight if you had arms? Take the arms that you wish."

And upon that the maiden came with arms for Peredur that were pleasing to him. And he fought with the black man until it was necessary for the black man to ask for mercy from Peredur.

"Black man, you shall have mercy while you are telling me who you are and who plucked out your eye."

"Lord, I will tell it: fighting with the Black Beast of the Cairn. There is a mound that is called the Sorrowful Mound, and in the mound there is a cairn, and in the cairn there is a beast, and in the tail of the beast there is a stone. And the virtues of the stone are that whoever would have it in his one hand, whatever he would wish of gold, he would get with his other hand. And fighting with that beast I lost my eye. And my name is the Tyrannical Black. This is the reason I was called the Tyrannical Black: I would not leave a single man around me to whom I would not do violence, and I would not make amends with anyone."

"Well," said Peredur, "how far from here is the mound that you speak of?"

"I will recount for you the journey there, and I will tell you how far it is. The day you set out from here, you will come to the court of the sons of the King of Suffering."

"Why are they called thus?"

"An addanc [water-monster] of the lake kills them once each day. When you go from there, you will come to the court of the Countess of the Feats."

"What feats are hers?"

"She has a three-hundred-man warband. Every stranger who comes to the court is told the feats of her warband. This is because the three-hundred-man warband sits next to the lady, and not out of disrespect to the guests but to tell the feats of her warband. The night you set out from there you will come to the Sorrowful Mound. And there are there the owners of three hundred pavilions around the mound guarding the beast."

"Since you have been a plague for so long, I will make it so that you will never be one again!" And Peredur killed him.

And then the maiden who had begun conversing with him said: "If you were poor coming here, you will be wealthy henceforth from the treasure of the black man you have killed. And do you see the many pleasant maidens who are in this court? You could get as a lover any one you wished."

"I did not come here from my country to get a wife. But I see pleasant youths here; let each of you match with another as she desires. And I do not desire any of your goods and I have no need of it."

Then Peredur set out and he came to the court of the sons of the King of Suffering. And when he came to the court, he saw only women. And the women rose up before him and they welcomed him. And at the beginning of their conversation he could see a horse coming with a saddle on it and a corpse in the saddle. And one of the women rose up and took the corpse from the saddle and bathed it in a tub that was below the door with warm water in it, and she put precious ointment on it. And the man arose alive and came where Peredur was and welcomed him and was pleasant to him. And two other men came in over their saddles. And the maiden gave the same remedy to those two as to the one before. Then Peredur asked the chieftain why they were thus. And they said there was an addanc in a cave, and it would kill them each day. And they left it at that that night.

And the next day the youths rose up, and Peredur asked for the sake of their lovers to let him go with them. They refused it: "If you were killed there, you would have no one by whom you could be made alive again." And then they went on and Peredur went after them, but afterward they disappeared so that he could not see them.

And then the fairest woman he had ever seen met him sitting on top of a mound. "I know your venture. You are going to fight the addanc, and he will kill you—and not by his bravery but by cunning. He has a cave, and there is a stone pillar at the entrance of the cave, and he sees everyone who comes in, but no one sees him. And with a poison stone spear he kills everyone from the shadow of the pillar. But if you would give me your oath to love me most of women, I would give you a stone so that you could see him when you went in, but he would not see you."

"I will, by my faith," said Peredur. "Since I first saw you, I have loved you. But where should I look for you?"

"When you look for me, look toward India." And then the maiden disappeared after putting the stone in Peredur's hand.

And he went on toward a river valley. And the boundaries of the valley were wooded and on each side of the river were level meadows. And on one side of the river he could see a herd of white sheep, and on the other side he could see a herd of black sheep. And as one of the white sheep would bleat, one of the black sheep would come across and would be white. And as one of the black sheep would bleat, one of the white sheep would come across and would be black. And he could see a tall tree on the bank of the river, and one half of it was burning from the roots to the top, and the other half with green leaves on it.

And beyond that he could see a youth sitting on top of a mound, with two white-breasted, spotted greyhounds on a leash resting beside him. And he was certain he had never seen a youth as princely as he. And in the wood opposite him he could hear staghounds raising a herd of stags. And he greeted the youth, and the youth greeted Peredur. And Peredur could see three roads going past the mound, two roads large and the third smaller. And Peredur asked where the three roads went.

"One of these roads goes to my court. And I will counsel you to do one of two things: either go to the court ahead to my wife who is there, or wait here, and you will see the staghounds driving the tired stags from the wood to the field. And you will see the best greyhounds you have ever seen, and the boldest for stags, killing them at the water near at hand. And when it is time for us to go for our food, my servant will come with my horse to meet me, and you shall have joy there tonight."

"God repay you. I will not stay, but I will go on."

"The second road goes to the town that is there nearby, and there food and drink can be had for sale. And the road that is smaller than the others goes toward the cave of the addanc."

"With your permission, lad, I will go toward there."

And Peredur came toward the cave and took the stone in his left hand and his spear in his right hand. And as he entered, he caught sight of the addanc and ran him through with a spear and struck off the head. And when he came out of the cave, lo, in the entrance of the cave were his three companions. And they greeted Peredur and said that it was about him that there was a prophecy of someone killing that plague. And Peredur gave the head to the youths. And they offered to him whichever one he would choose of their three sisters and half of their kingdom with her.

"I did not come here to get a wife, but if I did desire any woman, perhaps it is your sister whom I would desire first."

And Peredur went on his way. And he could hear a noise behind him. And he looked behind him and he could see a man on a red horse, and red armor on him. And the man came level with him and he greeted Peredur in the name of God and of man. And Peredur greeted the youth kindly.

"Lord, I am come to make a request of you."

"What do you request of me?" said Peredur.

"To take me as a man of yours."

"Whom would I take as a man if I took him?"

"I will not hide my identity from you. I am called Edlym Red-Sword, an earl from the east."

"It is strange to me that you offer yourself as man to a man whose realm is not greater than yours. I have nothing but an earldom as well. But since it is suitable to you to become my man, I will take you gladly."

And they came toward the court of the countess. And they were made welcome in the court. And it was told to them that not out of disrespect were they placed below the warband, but the custom of the court was thus, since the one who overthrew her three-hundred-man warband would get to eat next to her, and she would love him most of men.

And after Peredur threw her three-hundred-man warband to the ground and sat at her hand, she said: "I thank God I have gotten a lad as fair and as brave as you since I have not gotten the man I love most."

"Who was the man you loved most?"

"By my faith, Edlym Red-Sword was the man I loved most, but I have never seen him."

"Truly," he said, "Edlym is my companion, and here he is. And for his sake I came here to trifle with your warband, and he could have done it better than I if he had wished. And I will give you to him."

"God thank you, fair youth. And I will take the man I love most."

And that night Edlym and the countess slept together [in medieval Welsh narrative, the usual idiom for "they got married"].

And the next day Peredur set out toward the Sorrowful Mound.

"By your hand, lord, I will go with you," said Edlym.

They went on to where they could see the mound and the pavilions.

"Go," said Peredur to Edlym, "to the men yonder and ask them to come to do homage to me."

Edlym went to them and spoke thus: "Come to do homage to my lord."

"Who is your lord?" they asked.

"My lord is Peredur Long-Spear," said Edlym.

"Were it proper to slay a messenger you would not return alive to your lord for making a request so arrogant to kings, earls, and barons as to come to do homage to your lord."

Edlym came back to Peredur. Peredur asked him to go back to them to give them a choice, either to do homage to him or to joust with him. They chose to joust with him, and Peredur threw the owners of a hundred pavilions that day to the ground. And the next day he threw the owners of another hundred to the ground. And the third day they decided in their council to do homage to Peredur. And Peredur asked them what they were doing there. And they said that they were guarding the beast until it died: "And then we would fight for the stone, and whoever would be strongest of us would get the stone."

"Wait for me here. I will go to meet the beast."

"No, lord," they said. "We will go together to fight the beast."

"Well," said Peredur, "I do not desire that. If the beast were slain, I would not get more fame than one of you."

And he went to where the beast was and killed it, and returned to them. "Reckon your expense since you came here and I will repay you with gold," said Peredur. He paid them as much as each one said was owed to him, and he did not ask anything of them except to acknowledge that they were men of his. And he said to Edlym: "You go to the woman you love most, and I will go on. And I will repay you for becoming my man." And then he gave the stone to Edlym.

"May God repay you and God make your way easy."

And Peredur went away. And he came to a river valley, the fairest he had ever seen, and many multicolored pavilions he could see there. But stranger to him than that was to see as many watermills and windmills as he could see. A large auburn-haired man, with the look of a builder about him, met him, and Peredur asked him who he was.

"I am head miller over all the mills yonder."

"Will I get lodging with you?" asked Peredur.

"Yes," he said, "gladly."

He came to the house of the miller, and he saw the miller's fair, pleasant lodging. And Peredur asked for money as a loan from the miller in order to buy food and drink for him and for the family of the house, and he would pay him before going from there. He asked the miller what was the reason for that gathering.

The miller said to Peredur: "It is one of two things: either you are a man from afar, or you are a fool. There is the empress of Constantinople the Great, and she desires none but the bravest of men, since she has no need of goods. And food could not be brought for the many thousands who are here and because of that there are so many mills."

And that night they took their ease.

And the next day Peredur rose up and armed himself and his horse in order to go to the tournament. And he could see a pavilion in the midst of the other pavilions that was the fairest he had ever seen. And he could see a fair maiden sticking her head through a window of the pavilion, and he had never seen a fairer maiden, with a golden garment of brocade around her. And he looked at the maiden intently and a great love for her went through him. And he was thus looking at the maiden from the morning until midday and from midday until it was afternoon; and then the tournament had finished. And he came to his lodging and drew his arms from upon him and asked for money from the miller as a loan. And the miller's wife was angry at Peredur, but nevertheless the miller gave him money as a loan. And the next day he did the same as he had done the day before. And that night he came to his lodging and took money as a loan from the miller. And the third day, when he was in the same place looking at the maiden, he felt a great blow between the shoulder and neck with an ax-handle. And when he looked behind him at the miller, the miller said to him: "Do one of two things," said the miller: "either draw your head away or go to the tournament."

And Peredur smiled at the miller and went to the tournament. And whoever met with him that day, he threw them all to the ground, and as many as he overthrew he sent the men as a gift to the empress, and the horses and the arms as a gift to the miller's wife for waiting for her borrowed money. Peredur pursued the tournament until he threw everyone to the ground, and whomever he threw to the ground he sent the men to the empress's prison, and the arms to the miller's wife for waiting for the borrowed money.

The empress sent after the Knight of the Mill to ask him to come to see her. But the first messenger failed, and the second who went after him. And the third time she sent a hundred knights to ask him to come to see her, and if he would not come of his own will, she asked them to bring him against his will. And they came to him and spoke their message from the empress. He played with them nicely. He had them bound with roebuck fetters and thrown into the mill ditch. And the empress asked for advice from a wise man who was in her council, and he said to her: "I will go to him on your errand."

And he came to Peredur and greeted him and asked him for his lover's sake to come to see the empress.

And he came, he and the miller; and he sat in the first place he came to in the pavilion. And she came to his hand, and there was a short conversation between them. And Peredur took leave and went to his lodging. The next day he came to see her, and when he came to the pavilion there was no place in the pavilion that was in a poorer condition than any other, since they did not know where he would sit. Peredur sat at the hand of the empress, and he conversed graciously.

While they were thus, they could see a black-haired man coming in with a golden goblet in his hand, full of wine. He fell to his knee before the empress and asked her to give it only to one who would come to joust with him for it. And she looked at Peredur.

"Lady," he said, "give me the goblet." And he drank the wine and gave the goblet to the miller's wife. And while they were thus, lo, a black-haired man came who was larger than the other, with the claw of a beast in his hand in the shape of a goblet with its fill of wine, and he gave it to the empress and asked her to give it only to one who would joust with him.

"Lady," said Peredur, "give it to me." And she gave it to Peredur, and Peredur drank the wine and gave the goblet to the miller's wife. And while they were thus, lo, a curly red-haired man came who was larger than either of the other men, with a goblet of stone crystal in his hand with its fill of wine in it. And he bent down on his knee and put it into the empress's hand and asked her to give it only to one who would joust with him for it. And she gave it to Peredur and he sent it to the miller's wife.

That night Peredur went to his lodging, and the next day he armed himself and his horse and came to the meadow and killed the three men. And then he came to the pavilion. And she said to him: "Fair Peredur, remember the promise you gave to me when I gave you the stone when you killed the addanc."

"Lady," he said, "you speak truly, and I do remember it."

And Peredur ruled with the empress for fourteen years as the story tells. [Instead of "as the story tells," Peniarth MS 7 concludes here with the colophon: "And thus ends the progress of Peredur son of Efrog."]

Arthur was at Caer Llion on Usk, a chief court of his, and in the middle of the floor of the hall there were four men sitting on a mantle of brocade: Owain son of Urien, Gwalchmai son of Gwyar, Hywel son of Emyr Llydaw, and Peredur Long-Spear. And upon that they could see coming in a curly, black-haired maiden on the back of a yellow mule, with rough thongs in her hand, driving the mule, and a rough, unlovely look about her. Blacker were her face and her hands than the blackest iron that had been covered with pitch. And it was not her color that was ugliest, but her form—high cheeks with a baggy-fleshed face below and a short wide-nostriled nose, and one eye blue-speckled, very piercing, and the other as black as jet in the hollow of her head, long yellow teeth, yellower than the flowers of the broom, and her belly rising from her breastbone higher than her chin. Her backbone was in the shape of a crutch; her hips were broad-boned, but everything thin from there down, except that her feet and knees were thick. ,

She greeted Arthur and his whole warband except for Peredur, and to Peredur she spoke angry, unpleasant words: "Peredur, I do not greet you, since you do not deserve it. Fate was blind when she gave you favor and fame. When you came to the court of the lame king and when you saw there the youth carrying the sharpened spear, and from the tip of the spear a drop of blood, and that running in a torrent to the fist of the youth, and other marvels you saw there also, but you did not ask their meaning or their cause. And if you had asked, the king would have obtained his health and his kingdom in peace, but henceforth battles and strife and loss of knights and women left widowed and maidens without sustenance, and all of that because of you."

And then she said to Arthur: "With your permission, lord, my lodging is far from here, none other than in the Proud Castle. I do not know if you have heard of it. And in it there are five hundred and sixty-six ordained knights, and the woman each one loves most together with him. And whoever wishes to win fame in arms and in jousting and in fighting, he will get it there if he deserves it. Whoever wishes, however, for pre-eminence in fame and praise, I know where he may get it. There is a castle on a conspicuous mountain, and in it there is a maiden, and it is being besieged. And whoever is able to free her, he will get the highest fame in the world."

And upon that she went on her way. Gwalchmai said: "By my faith, I will not sleep a peaceful sleep until I know if I can release the maiden." And many of Arthur's warband were in agreement with him.

Peredur, however, spoke otherwise: "By my faith, I will not sleep a peaceful sleep until I know the story and the meaning of the spear that the black maiden spoke about."

And when everyone was getting ready, lo, a knight came to the gate with the size and strength of a warrior in him, arrayed with horse and arms. And he came forward and greeted Arthur and all of his warband except for Gwalchmai. And on the knight's shoulder was a gold-embossed shield with a bar of blue azure on it, and all of his arms were the same color as that. And he said to Gwalchmai: "You killed my lord through your deceit and treachery, and I will prove that upon you."

Gwalchmai rose up. "Here," he said, "is my pledge against you, either here or in the place you wish, that I am neither a deceiver nor a traitor."

"Before the king who is over me do I wish the encounter between you and me to be."

"Gladly," said Gwalchmai. "You go on; I will follow you."

The knight went on and Gwalchmai prepared himself. And many arms were offered to him, but he did not desire any but his own. Gwalchmai and Peredur armed themselves and they set out after him because of their friendship and how much they loved each other. But they did not stay together; rather each one went his own way.

Gwalchmai, in the young of the day, came to a valley, and in the valley he could see a fortress and a great court in the fortress and proud high towers around it. And he could see a knight coming out of the gate to hunt on a shining black, wide-nostriled, well-paced palfrey with a steady-proud, keenly quick, unfaltering step. That was the man who owned the court. Gwalchmai greeted him.

"God reward you, sir; and where do you come from?"

"I come," he said, "from Arthur's court."

"Are you a man of Arthur's?"

"Yes, by my faith," said Gwalchmai.

"I know of good counsel for you," said the knight. "I see that you are tired and weary. Go to the court and you can stay there tonight, if it pleases you."

"It does, lord, and God repay you."

"Take a ring as a sign to the porter and go on to the tower yonder. And there is a sister of mine there."

And Gwalchmai came to the gate and he showed the ring and made for the tower. And when he arrived, there was a great blazing fire burning, with a high, bright, smokeless flame from it and a fair, majestic maiden sitting in a chair by the fire. And the maiden was pleasant to him and welcomed him and went to meet him. And he went to sit at the maiden's hand.

They took their dinner, and after their dinner they held a pleasant conversation. And when they were thus, lo, a fair grey-haired man came in to them. "Oh, beggar whore," he said, "if you knew how right it is for you to play and to sit with that man, you would not sit and you would not play." And he withdrew his head and went away.

"Ah, sir," said the maiden, "if you would take my advice for fear of danger to you from the man, you would fasten the door," she said.

Gwalchmai rose up and when he came toward the door, the man, one of three score, fully armed, was making his way up the tower. With a gwydd-bwyll board Gwalchmai defended against anyone coming up until the man came from hunting.

Upon that, lo, the earl arrived. "What is this?" he said.

"An ugly thing," said the grey-haired man; "that beggar-woman yonder is sitting and drinking till evening with the man who killed your father. And he is Gwalchmai son of Gwyar."

"Stop now," said the earl. "I will go in." The earl was pleasant to Gwalchmai. "Ah, sir," he said, "wrong was it for you to come to our court if you knew you killed our father. Since we cannot avenge it, God will avenge it upon you."

"Friend," said Gwalchmai, "here is how it is about that: I came neither to confess to killing your father nor to deny it. I am going on an errand for Arthur and for myself. I will ask for the space of a year, however, until I shall come from my errand, and then on my oath I will come to this court to do one of the two—either to confess it or to deny it."

He got the time gladly, and he was there that night. The next day he set out, but the story does not say anything more than that about Gwalchmai in that area.

And Peredur went on his way. Peredur wandered the island seeking tidings of the black maiden, but he got none. And he came to a land he did not know in a river valley. And as he was traveling through the valley, he could see a rider coming to meet him, with the sign of a priest upon him, and he asked for his blessing.

"Ach, wretch," he said, "you do not deserve to receive a blessing, and it would not benefit you, for wearing arms on a day as exalted as today."

"And what day is today?" asked Peredur.

"Today is Good Friday."

"Do not blame me; I did not know that. A year from today I set out from my country." And then he dismounted and led his horse in his hand.

And he traveled a stretch of the highway until a by-road met with him, and he went along the by-road through the wood. And on the other side of the wood he could see a bare fortress and he could see a sign of habitation about the fortress. And he came toward the fortress, and at the gate of the fortress there met with him the priest who had met with him before that, and he asked for a blessing.

"God's blessing to you," he said, "and it is more proper to travel thus. And you will be with me tonight." And Peredur stayed that night.

The next day Peredur sought leave to depart.

"Today is not a day for anyone to travel. You will be with me today and tomorrow and the next day, and I will give you the best guidance I can about that which you are seeking."

And the fourth day Peredur sought leave to depart and requested the priest to give him guidance concerning the Fortress of the Wonders.

"As much as I know, I will tell you. Go over the mountain yonder, and on the far side of the mountain there is a river, and in the river valley there is a king's court, and the king was there at Easter. And if you can get news anywhere about the Fortress of the Wonders, you will get it there."

And then he set out and he came to the river valley, and he met with a company of men going to hunt, and he could see in the midst of the company a high-ranking man. And Peredur greeted him.

"You choose, sir, whether you will go to the court or you will come with me to hunt, and I will send one of the warband to commend you to a daughter of mine there, to take food and drink until I come from hunting. And if your errands are such that I can obtain them, you shall obtain them gladly." And the king sent a short yellow-haired youth with him.

And when they came to the court, the lady had arisen and was going to wash. And Peredur came forward, and she welcomed Peredur pleasantly and made room for him at her hand, and they took their dinner. And whatever Peredur would say to her, she would laugh loudly, so that everyone of the court could hear. And then the short yellow-haired youth said to the lady: "By my faith," he said, "if you have ever had a man, it was this youth. And if you have not had a man, your mind and your thought are upon him."

And the short yellow-haired youth went toward the king, and he said that it was most likely to him that the youth who had met with him was his daughter's man, "and if not her man, I think he will be her man on the spot if you are not wary of him."

"What is your counsel, lad?"

"My counsel is to set brave men upon him and to seize him until you know for certain about that."

And he set men upon Peredur and seized him and put him in prison.

And the maiden came before her father and asked him why he had caused the youth from Arthur's court to be imprisoned.

"Truly," he said, "he will not be free tonight nor tomorrow nor the next day, and he shall not come from where he is."

She did not oppose the king for what he said, but she came to the youth. "Is it unpleasant for you to be here?"

"I would not mind it even though I were not."

"No worse shall your bed and your fare be than those of the king, and you shall have the best songs in the court at your discretion. And if it were more pleasing to you than before that my bed be here for conversing with you, you should have it gladly."

"I will not oppose that." He was in prison that night, and the maiden fulfilled what she had promised to him.

And the next day Peredur could hear a commotion in the town. "Oh, fair maiden, what tumult is this?"

"The king's host and his might are coming to the town today."

"What do they desire thus?"

"There is an earl near here with two earldoms, and he is as strong as a king. And there will be an encounter between them today."

"I have a request," said Peredur: "for you to get for me a horse and arms to go to observe the encounter, on my word of honor to come back to my prison."

"Gladly," she said. "I will get a horse and arms for you." And she gave him a horse and arms and a pure red surcoat over his arms and a yellow shield on his shoulder.

And he came to the encounter. And whoever of the earl's men met with him that day, he threw them all to the ground. And he came back to his prison. She asked Peredur for news, but he did not say one word to her. And she went to ask news of her father, and she asked who had been the best of his warband. He said that he did not know him. "He was a man with a red surcoat over his arms and a yellow shield on his shoulder."

And she smiled and came to where Peredur was. And good was his respect that night.

And for three days on end Peredur killed the men of the earl, and before anyone got to know who he might be, he would come back to his prison. And the fourth day Peredur killed the earl himself. And the maiden came before her father and asked him for news.

"Good news," said the king. "The earl is slain," he said, "and the two earldoms are mine."

"Do you know, lord, who killed him?"

"Yes," said the king, "the knight of the red surcoat and the yellow shield killed him."

"Lord," she said, "I know who that is.":

"For God's sake," he said, "who is he?"

"Lord, that is the knight whom you have in prison."

He came to where Peredur was and he greeted him and told him that for the service he had done, we would pay him however he himself might wish.

And when they went to eat, Peredur was placed at the hand of the king and the maiden on the other side of Peredur. And after the meal the king said to Peredur: "I will give you my daughter as a wife and half of my kingdom with her, and the two earldoms I will give you as your reward."

"Lord, may God repay you; I did not come here to get a wife."

"What are you seeking, sir?"

"I am seeking news about the Fortress of the Wonders."

"Greater is the chieftain's thought than we expect to find," said the maiden. "You shall have news of the fortress, and a guide for you through my father's realm, and sufficient provisions. And you, sir, are the man I love most."

And then she said to him: "Go over the mountain yonder and you will see a lake and a fortress in the lake. And that is called the Fortress of the Wonders. But we do not know anything about its wonders, except that it is called thus."

And Peredur came toward the fortress, and the gate of the fortress was open. And when he came to the hall, the door was open. And as he came in, he could see a gwyddbwyll in the hall, with each one of the two sides playing against the other. And the one that he would support would lose the game, and the other would give a shout, just as if they were men. He grew angry and took the pieces in his lap and threw the board into the lake.

And while he was thus, lo, the black maiden came in. "God's welcome be not to you. More often do you do harm than good."

"Of what are you accusing me, black maiden?"

"You have deprived the empress of her board, and she would not desire that for her empire."

"Would there be a way the board can be gotten?"

"Yes, if you go to the Fortress of Ysbidinongl. There is a black man there laying waste to much of the realm of the empress. Kill him and you shall get the board. But if you go there, you will not come back alive."

"Will you be a guide for me there?"

"I will tell you the way there."

He came to the Fortress of Ysbidinongl and fought with the black man, and the black man asked Peredur for mercy.

"I will give you mercy. Cause the board to be where it was when I came to the hall."

And then the black maiden came. "God's curse on you for your labor, for leaving the plague alive who is laying waste to the realm of the empress."

"I left him his life for getting the board."

"The board is not in the first place that you found it. Go back and kill him."

Peredur went and killed the man. And when he came to the court, the black maiden was in the court.

"Ah, maiden," said Peredur, "where is the empress?"

"Between me and God, you will not see her now unless you kill a plague that is in the forest yonder."

"What kind of plague is it?"

"There is a stag there, and it is as swift as the swiftest bird. And there is one horn in its brow as long as a spear shaft and as sharp as anything sharpest. And it grazes on the tops of the trees and whatever there may be of grass in the forest. And it kills every animal that it finds in it, and what it does not find will die from hunger. And what is worse than that, it comes every night and drinks the fish pond for its drink and leaves the fish exposed, and they die, for the most part, before the water comes back to it."

"Ah, maiden," said Peredur, "will you come to show me that animal?"

"No. No one has dared to go to the forest for a year. There is the lady's spaniel, and that will raise the stag and will bring it to you. And the stag will rush at you."

The spaniel went as a guide to Peredur and raised the stag and brought it toward the place where Peredur was. And the stag rushed at Peredur, and he let its attack go by, and he struck the head from it with a sword. And while he was looking at the head of the stag, he could see a rider coming toward him and taking the spaniel in the sleeve of her cloak and the head between her and the pommel, and the red-gold collar that was around the stag's neck. "Ah, sir," she said, "discourteously have you acted, killing the fairest jewel that was in my realm."

"That was requested of me. And would there be a way I could gain your friendship?"

"Yes. Go to the breast of the mountain and there you will see a bush, and at the base of the bush there is a stone slab. Ask three times for a man to joust and you shall gain my friendship."

Peredur went on and he came beside the bush and he asked for a man to joust. And a black man rose up from under the stone slab, with a bony horse under him and great rusty armor upon him and on his horse. And they jousted. And as Peredur would throw the black man to the ground, he would leap back into the saddle. And Peredur dismounted and drew his sword. And upon that the black man disappeared, and Peredur's horse and his own horse with him, so that he did not get a second look at them.

And Peredur walked along the mountain. And on the other side of the mountain he could see a fortress in a river valley, and he came toward the fortress. And as he came to the fortress, he could see a hall, and the door of the hall was open. And he came in, and he could see a lame, grey-haired man sitting at the end of the hall, and Gwalchmai sitting at his hand. And Peredur's horse he could see at the same manger as Gwalchmai's horse. And they welcomed Peredur. And he went to sit on the other side of the grey-haired man. And a yellow-haired youth went to his knee before Peredur and asked for Peredur's friendship.

"Lord," said the youth, "I came in the form of the black maiden to Arthur's court, and when you threw the board, and when you killed the black man of Ysbidinongl, and when you killed the stag, and when you were fighting with the black man of the stone slab. And I came with the bloody head on the dish and with the spear that had the stream of blood from the head to the hilt along the spear. And the head was your cousin's, and the witches of Caer Loyw had killed him, and they had lamed your uncle. And I am your cousin, and it is prophesied that you will avenge that."

And Peredur and Gwalchmai decided to send to Arthur and his warband to ask him to come against the witches. And they began to fight with the witches. And one of the witches killed a man of Arthur's in front of Peredur, and Peredur forbade her. And a second time the witch killed a man in front of Peredur, and a second time Peredur forbade her. And a third time the witch killed a man in front of Peredur, and Peredur drew his sword and struck the witch on top of the helmet so that the helmet and all the arms and the head were in two halves. And she gave a cry and bade the other witches to flee and said that it was Peredur, the man who had been with them learning horsemanship, who was destined to kill them. And then Arthur and his warband attacked the witches, and all the witches of Caer Loyw were killed. And thus it is told of the Fortress of the Wonders.

Beaumaris Castle of Anglesey in North Wales, in country associated with Peredur and the wanderings of Gawain in Sir Gawain and the Green Knight. (Courtesy of the British Tourist Authority)

chapter IV

THE LAY OF GRAELENT

Russell Weingartner

The *Lay of Graelent* is a sample of the genre known as the Breton lay, a short story in verse that is based on Celtic legend. Like most other Old French courtly writings of the period, it is written in eight-syllable verse with rhyming couplets. Neither of the two extant manuscripts has any indication of the author's identity. Scholars have therefore been forced to turn to internal evidence to establish a probable date and provenance. A study of vocabulary, rhymes, and other language features suggests that the author was a Norman writing in his dialect in the latter half of the twelfth century.

The last half of the 1100s saw the enthusiastic reception in both England and France of a large group of Celtic tales that provided fascinating new source material to writers who had exhausted their Latin sources. Transmitted by word of mouth in both narrative and song from Ireland, Wales, and Brittany, the Celtic legends were woven into the Arthurian romances of Chrétien de Troyes; the Tristan story of Béroul, Thomas, and others; and the lays of Marie de France and those of the anonymous poets. In a creative burst of energy poets wrote the tales down, adapting them to please their audiences with an overlay of current social customs. Celtic exploits, heroes, and supernatural events, by now stripped of their ancient pagan significance, were artfully combined with elements of Christianity and courtliness in twelfth-century France. The result was a literature that is hard to resist, and one that was to influence the course of European literature for centuries to come.

The author of *The Lay of Graelent* has given us a romantic tale of a likable young knight who, after proclaiming himself unready for the responsibilities of love, succumbs to a magical and obsessive love that propels him to near-disaster. After being chosen by his otherworldly mistress, Graelent is as unable to control his fate as is Tristan after drinking the magic potion;

nor can such singleminded love exist in the real world without unhappiness and suffering. Only in the otherworld can it thrive. It is no wonder that the legend of *Graelent*, with its elements of charmed love, supernatural mystery, and destruction only barely missed, was so popular.

Our unknown author presumably had access to some legendary account of Graelent, which he says he will narrate to us "as I understand it," having heard it related and sung. With little embellishment and great economy he takes us through a fast-moving series of events in which our imagination fills in descriptions and the hero's thoughts, giving us the same type of satisfaction as that received from fairy tales. It is a story earnestly told, with a charming naiveté and a two-dimensional quality reminiscent of medieval tapestries. The author took his Celtic legend more seriously than did Marie de France in her treatment of similar material in *Lanval*, with which *Graelent* is often compared. The fairy mistress waiting in the pool of water for Graelent, whom she knew would come, is very close to an ancient Irish water sprite, whose habitat was a spring and who was worshiped for the rewards she dispensed to those she favored. Failure to obey her commands, however, led to an equally extreme punishment, so that, when Graelent broke his promise never to speak of his mistress, he was subjected not only to the disappearance of his beloved and her gifts but almost to the loss of his life.

By contrast Marie makes only slight reference to the water-deity motif when she has Lanval dismount "near a running stream." Thereafter she turns her attention to a lavish description of a nearby tent to which Lanval is led by beautiful maidens carrying gold basins, a tent that no king could afford. Inside, their mistress, who has sent for Lanval, lies on a beautiful bed with an ermine cloak over her. As in *Graelent*, she and her gifts will also disappear after Lanval breaks his pledge of silence, but the Celtic harshness is softened in Marie's lay, and a single punishment for Lanval is deemed sufficient. In the final scene, at the trial, fully twenty-five lines are devoted to cuts of dresses and their fabrics, as the pairs of beautiful maidens and finally their mistress arrive, after which the rest of the Celtic tale is dispatched in only nine more hasty lines. Nor did Marie hesitate to please her audience by using the instantly recognized names from Chrétien's popular romances of the day. Thus the king in *Lanval* is Arthur, and no gathering of knights is complete without the presence of Gawain, who is once linked with "his cousin Yvain," neither of whom has any function in the story. Lanval's mistress takes him off to Avalon.

The author of *Graelent*, on the other hand, mentions no name other than that of his hero, making it more likely that his is the earlier lay, or that it is at least closer to the original Celtic myth. Indeed the artlessness of the poet in faithfully recording his legend, without tongue-in-cheek ornamentation, permits us to respond more fully to the affecting elements of the Celtic legend. After only a brief description of Graelent's mistress two simple lines make us feel the excitement and anticipation of the spectators at the trial: "And when the mistress came / The entire court fixed its eyes upon her." When the trial is over, she shows her unforgiving Celtic sternness once again by ignoring the pleas of a disconsolate Graelent. We share in the shock shown by her hysterical maidens as they watch her allow Graelent to drown. Despite the superficial similarities of *Graelent* and *Lanval*, which have at times led critics fond of Marie's more sophisticated style to view

Graelent as a sort of *Lanval* manqué, it should come as a pleasant surprise to discover that both the events and their thrust are completely different in the two works, and that a good case can be made for *Graelent* as the more compelling and honestly told Celtic lay. Because the story has been available to readers of English only in the strangely archaic and frequently inaccurate rendering by Eugene Mason (1911), it is hoped that the present line-by-line translation will permit readers to enjoy both the naiveté and the charm of the well-known legend.

Bibliographic note: For the Old French text of *Graelent*, based on the manuscript Bibliothèque Nationale 1104 nouv. acq. fr., see my edition *Graelent and Guingamor: Two Breton Lays* (Garland, 1985). The same edition contains a lengthy bibliography of works published prior to 1985.

The Lay of Graelent

The adventure of Graelent
I will tell you as I understand it;
The lay is good to hear,
And the melody good to remember.
Graelent was born of Bretons,
Noble and of good family;
He was handsome of body and noble of heart;
They called him Graelent Muer [the Great].
He did not have very great inheritances,
But he was courteous and wise,   10
A good knight and of great renown;
There was no lady of the country so highly placed
Who, had he requested her love,
Would not have listened to him more attentively.
    The king who held Brittany
Waged a great war with his neighbors;
He sent for and retained knights;
It was true that Graelent came there.
The king retained him willingly
Because he was a good knight;   20
Much did the king cherish and honor him,
And Graelent strove mightily
To fight and joust,
To do harm to the enemies of the king;
Good hospitality he offered and often,
And he gave very generously.
    The queen heard him praised,
And much good spoken about him:
His great valor and knightly prowess,

And his beauty and generosity.   30
In her heart she fell in love with him.
She called one of her chamberlains.
"Tell me," she said, "and don't hide anything from me,
Have you heard people speak much
Of the good knight Graelent?
Is he praised by many people?"
"Madam," he replied, "he is very valiant,
And he earns the great love of everyone."
    The queen replied to him:
"I wish to make him my lover;   40
Because of him I am in turmoil;
Go, tell him to come to me;
I will put my love at his disposal."
"You will give him an exceedingly great gift;
It would be amazing if it did not give him great joy;
There isn't any good monk from here to Troyes
Who, if he looked at your face,
Would not change his sentiments completely."
When he had said that, he left his lady;
To the dwelling of Graelent he went off;   50
He greeted him properly
And gave him his message:
That he should go to the queen and speak with her,
And take care not to delay.
The knight replied:
"Go ahead of me, my dear friend."
The chamberlain departed,
And Graelent made his preparations.
He mounted an iron-grey horse
And took one knight with him.   60
Both came to the castle;
Before the great hall they dismounted;
Passing in front of the king,
To the queen's chamber they went.
When she saw them, she called them to her;
Much did she cherish and honor them.
She took Graelent into her arms
And embraced him warmly;
She had him sit next to her
On a carpet beside her bed;   70
Very affectionately did she glance
At his body, at his face, and at his beauty;
She spoke to him without ceremony,
And he replied courteously;
He said nothing that was not completely proper.
The queen thought for a long time;
She was surprised that he did not beg her
To love him as his mistress.
Since he did not make this request,

She asked him if he had a mistress   80
And if his heart was already taken,
For he should certainly be well loved.
"Madam," said he, "that is something I do not wish;
To be in love is not a joke;
The man should be of very great worth
Who undertakes to be a lover;
Some five hundred talk of love
Who know not the least thing about it,
Nor what loyal love service is;
Such is their madness and their folly.   90
Indolence, lies, and deception
Ruin love in many ways.
Love requires chastity
In deed, in word, and in thought;
If one of the lovers is loyal,
And the other wanton and unfaithful,
Then the love will be made quite false;
It cannot endure for long.
Love is not worthy without a companion.
It is not good unless there are two,   100
From body to body, from heart to heart;
Otherwise it is not noble in any way.
Tullius, who spoke of friendship,
Said it very well in his work:
What the lover desires, so should the mistress;
Then the companionship will be close.
If she stops loving, let him stop as well;
Otherwise the love affair will not be equitable.
Since each one has gone back on his word,
There remains only a trace of love.   110
One can find love easily enough,
But one must hold to the good,
To gentleness, nobility, and moderation
(Love cares not for serious wrongdoing)
And must promise and maintain loyalty;
Because of that I don't dare engage in it."
     The queen listened to Graelent,
Who was speaking so courteously;
Had she not had the desire to love,
He would have made her think of it;   120
She knew and saw, and had no doubt,
That he possessed wisdom and courtesy.
She spoke to him more openly;
Completely did she reveal her heart to him:
"Dear Graelent," she said,
"I love you passionately;
Never have I loved anyone except my husband,
But I love you with such a love
That I grant you the right to be my lover;

Be my lover, for I will be yours."   130
"My lady," said he, "by your leave,
It certainly cannot be thus,
For I am in the pay of the king;
I promised him loyalty and faithfulness
Toward both his life and his honor
When I became his liege the other day;
Indeed he will never have shame because of me."
Then he took leave of her and departed.
    The queen saw him go away.
She began to sigh;   140
She was extremely sad, and did not know what to do;
She did not, however, want to abandon her pursuit.
Many times did she beg him to come;
She dispatched her messengers to him
And sent him expensive presents,
But he refused them outright.
When she saw that she had failed
With him completely, she hated him intensely;
She turned her lord against him
And eagerly slandered him.   150
As long as the king waged war,
Graelent remained in his domain.
So much did he spend that he was forced to borrow,
For the king made him wait,
Since he was holding back his wages;
He had given him none;
The queen had persuaded him to do that;
She had given her advice to the king
To give Graelent nothing at all
Beyond subsistence, to keep him from leaving;   )   160
By that means she kept him near the king,
So that he could not serve another.
    What will Graelent do now?
It is not surprising that he is sad;
There remained nothing on which he could borrow,
Except one old horse worth very little,
And one young servant whom he had reared
(His men had all left him).
He could not leave the city,
For he had nothing on which to ride,   170
Nor did he expect the slightest help.
It was in May, on one of those long days,
That his landlord arose early;
With his wife he went to the town
To dine at the home of one of his neighbors.
He left the knight quite alone.
There was no one with him in the house,
Squire, servant, or boy,
Except the daughter of his hostess,
Who was very well bred and courteous.   180

When it was time to have dinner
She went to speak to the knight;
Strongly did she urge him to be more cheerful
And to have dinner with her.
He had no desire at all to grant her request,
But he called his squire
And told him to bring his hunting horse
And to put the saddle and bridle on it:
"I shall go outdoors for amusement,
Because I do not care to eat."   190
His squire replied that he did not have a saddle.
"Friend," said the young woman,
"I will lend you one,
And I will furnish you with a good bridle."
The squire brought the horse;
Inside the house he saddled it.
Graelent mounted
And passed through the town.
He had donned an old suit of leather
That he had worn much too long.   200
Those who looked at him
Mocked and teased him;
He paid no attention to that.
Outside the city there was a clearing
In a large and abundant forest;
Through it ran a stream;
Graelent made his way in that direction,
Lost in thought, sad and miserable.
    He had scarcely entered the woods
When, in a dense thicket,   210
He saw a pure white doe;
Whiter it was than snow that lies on a branch.
The doe leaped forward ahead of him;
He hallooed and spurred his mount toward it,
But he would never overtake it on that day;
Nevertheless he followed it closely
Until it led him onto a heath,
Toward the spring that formed a pool,
The water of which was clear and beautiful.
In it a maiden was bathing,   220
Served by two handmaidens
Who were on the edge of the pool.
The clothing that she had removed
Was in a leafy bower.
Graelent saw the maiden
Who was naked in the pool.
He went there at great speed,
Thinking no more about the doe.
    He saw that she was beautiful and shapely,
White, rosy, and with a fresh complexion,   230
With laughing eyes and beautiful forehead;

There was not a woman of such beauty in the world;
Nothing under heaven pleased him so much;
He quite forgot his unhappiness.
Not wishing to disturb her in the water,
He allowed her to bathe at her leisure.
He went to seize her clothing;
With that he hoped to prevent her flight;
The handmaidens noticed him
And were frightened to see the knight.   240
Their mistress spoke to him;
Angrily she called to him:
"Graelent, leave my clothes alone!
You could hardly improve your good reputation
If you carried them off
And left me naked like this;
That would be an exceedingly poor sort of greed.
Give me back at least my chemise;
The coat can be yours;
Get a good sum for it, because it's a good one."   250
Graelent replied laughingly:
"I'm not a merchant's son,
Nor a bourgeois, who sells cloaks;
If it were, right now, worth three castles
I wouldn't take it.
Come out of the water, my dear;
Take your clothing and get dressed;
I beg you to talk with me."
"I don't wish to come out," she said,
"So that you can lay hold of me;   260
I have no respect for your word;
I am not your kind."
He replied to her: "I will wait;
I will keep your clothing
Until you come out from there;
My beautiful one, you have a lovely body."
    When she saw that he intended to wait,
And that he would not give back her clothing,
She asked him for assurance
That he would do her no harm.   270
Graelent gave her his promise
And handed over her chemise.
She dressed immediately.
He held the coat in front of her,
Then put it on her, giving it to her;
He took her by the left hand
And then brought her close to him;
He asked for her love and beseeched her
To make him her lover.
The maiden replied: 280
"Graelent, you desire the unthinkable;

I don't consider you at all proper;
Greatly must I marvel
When you dare to speak to me of that.
Don't be so bold;
You would soon be ruined by it;
It is not suitable for one of your birth
To love a woman of my rank."
Graelent found her very haughty;
He understood well that by pleading   290
He would not be granted his pleasure,
But he did not wish to be separated from her.
So much did he implore and flatter her
Until he had pleased her,
That, in the dense part of the forest,
He did with her what he wished.
When he had had his way,
He pleaded with her very gently
Not to be too angry with him,
But instead to be noble and well-bred   300
And to permit him to be her lover,
And he would take her for his mistress;
He would love her very loyally
And never depart from her.
The maiden heard and understood
Graelent's plea,
And she saw that he was courteous and wise,
A handsome knight both brave and generous,
And if he departed from her,
Never would she have such a good lover.   310
Her love she promptly granted him,
And he gently kissed her.
The woman spoke in this way:
"Graelent, you took me by surprise.
I love you with all my heart,
But one thing I forbid you:
That you say a single word openly
By which our love could be discovered.
I will give you in abundance
Money and clothing, gold and silver.   320
The love between us is very good;
Night and day I shall be near you;
With me you can laugh and play;
You will see me accompany you;
No companion of yours will see me
Nor indeed know who I am.
Graelent, you are loyal,
Brave, and courteous, and very handsome;
For you I came here to the pool.
I will suffer greatly because of you;   330
I knew well this adventure would happen.

Now be greatly restrained;
Make certain that you do not boast;
Say nothing by which you could lose me.
For one year, my love, you must
Remain nearby in this country,
And then, often, beloved,
Let it be the place you come back to,
For I love this country.
Leave now; it is past three o'clock;   340
My messenger I will send to you;
My commands will be conveyed to you."
    Graelent took leave of her;
She embraced him and kissed him.
He went to his lodgings
And dismounted from his horse.
He entered a chamber,
And leaned his elbows on the windowsill;
He was greatly preoccupied with what had happened.
Toward the town he turned his glance;   350
He saw a young manservant coming quickly,
Mounted on an iron-grey hunter;
With his hand the servant was leading
A pure white steed by the bridle;
On its back was tied a large trunk.
He crossed the main street
And came to Graelent's dwelling;
He dismounted from the horse
And greeted the knight
Who had come out to meet him;   360
The knight asked him where he came from,
What his name was, who he was.
"Sir," said he, "have no fear;
I am the messenger of your mistress;
This steed, by me, she sends to you;
She wishes me to remain with you.
I will pay your debts;
I will take charge of your lodging."
    When Graelent heard the news,
Which was to him both good and beautiful,   370
He kissed the servant warmly;
Then he received the present, the steed;
Under heaven was there none more beautiful,
Nor healthier, nor more swift;
He put it in the stable himself,
As well as the servant's hunting horse.
The servant took down his trunk;
He removed from it a large coverlet
That was made of a rich brocade;
On the other side was a costly silk material;   380
He put it on Graelent's bed.

Afterward he brought forth gold and silver,
And fine garments to clothe his lord.
He had the landlord come to him.
He gave him money in great abundance;
Then he said to him and ordered
That his lord be free of debt,
And his lodgings be well furnished;
That he make sure that his lord be well fed,
And if, in the city, there were a knight   390
Who desired lodging and food,
He should bring him back home with him.
    The landlord was good and courteous,
And an excellent, noble bourgeois;
He had a festive meal prepared;
Throughout the city he went, seeking
Knights in difficulty,
Both prisoners and crusaders;
To the dwelling of Graelent he brought them;
He took great pains to honor them.   400
At night there was abundant joy,
Both in music and in entertainment;
That night Graelent was happy
And richly dressed;
He gave great gifts to the harpers,
To the prisoners, and to the singers;
There was not a single bourgeois in the city
Who had made loans to him
To whom he did not give presents and do honor,
So much so that they considered him their lord.   410
From that time on Graelent was happy;
He saw nothing any more that displeased him;
His mistress he saw at his side;
He could laugh and play a great deal;
At night he felt her close to him;
How could he have been unhappy?
Graelent traveled very often;
There was no tournament in the land
In which he was not the very first;
He was greatly loved by knights.   420
Now Graelent had a good life;
He knew great joy with his beloved;
Had that lasted a long time,
He could not have asked for anything more.
Thus it was for a full year,
Until the king was to give a feast.
At Pentecost each year
He summoned his barons by proclamation,
And all those who were his vassals
Were together with him on that day;   430
They were served with great honor.

When, on that day, they had eaten,
He had the queen mount
Onto a high bench and remove her cloak;
Then he asked all those assembled:
"Lord barons, what is your opinion?
Is there, under heaven, a more beautiful queen,
Maiden, woman, or young girl?"
    It was proper for everyone to praise her
And to say and affirm to the king   440
That they knew of no one so beautiful,
Young girl, woman, or maiden.
    That year there was a great assembly;
The court was convened for a week;
There was an unusually large number of people;
The king sent for Graelent.
After dinner the king had his wife
Climb up onto a great raised table;
He urged and commanded his barons
And, by the friendship they owed him, asked   450
That they inform him of the truth,
If they knew of another woman so beautiful.
There was no one who did not praise her
Or fail to speak most highly of her beauty,
Except Graelent; he was silent;
He laughed to himself over this;
In his heart he thought of his mistress.
He considered the others mad
For shouting on all sides
And praising the queen in this way.   460
    He covered his head, he lowered his face,
And the queen looked at him;
She pointed him out to her husband, the king:
"Sir, see what a dishonor this is!
There's not a baron here who has not praised me,
Except Graelent, who has been making sport of me;
I know well that he has hated me for some time;
I think that he is envious of me."
    The king called Graelent
And asked him, before his subjects,   470
By the loyalty that Graelent owed him
As his rightful liege,
Not to conceal from him but to tell him
Why he had lowered his head and laughed.
Graelent replied to the king:
"Sir," he said, "listen to me:
Never did a man of your rank
Do such a thing or act so rashly;
You're making a spectacle of your wife.
You have not a single baron   480
Whom you have not forced to praise her;

They say that they know no one who is her peer;
Truly I will tell you some news:
One can easily find someone more beautiful."
The king heard him, though it pained him greatly;
He pressed him to tell on oath
If he knew of anyone more attractive.
"Yes," he said, "one worth thirty of this one."
The queen was greatly chagrined;
To her lord she cried for mercy,   490
Asking that he have the knight bring forward
The lady whom the king had heard mentioned thus,
Whom Graelent was praising so much;
Let both of them be put on display;
If the other is more beautiful, let him be freed,
Or, if otherwise, let him suffer the punishment
For slander and insult.
The king ordered that he be arrested;
He would have from him neither love nor peace,
Nor would he ever again leave prison   500
If he did not first bring forward this woman
Whose beauty had been praised so much.
Graelent was taken and held;
It would have been better had he remained silent.
He asked the king for a delay;
Clearly he saw that he had spoken badly.
He believed that he had lost his mistress;
From anger and chagrin he was perspiring.
He deserved to have things turn out badly.
Several members of the court had pity for him;   510
That day there was a large crowd around him.
The king postponed the matter until the next year
When he would hold his feast again;
All his friends would be called together again,
His barons and all his intimates.
Let Graelent be brought there;
Let him bring with him the woman
Whom he has praised so much before the king;
If she is as beautiful and as marvelous
As he has said, let that be the proof;   520
Let him be freed; he will lose nothing.
If she does not come, he will be judged;
He will be at the mercy of the king.
Everyone knew that this was proper.
    Graelent departed from the court,
Angry, sad, and unhappy;
He was mounted on his good steed;
To his dwelling he went to take lodging.
He called for his chamberlain,
The one his mistress had sent to him,   530
But found no trace of him.

Now Graelent was greatly upset;
He would rather be dead than alive.
He went to a room alone
And begged that his mistress have mercy,
That she consent to speak to him;
This did no good; she would not speak to him;
He would not see her for a year.
Graelent was overcome with grief;
He could rest neither night nor day;   540
Since he could not have his mistress,
He cared nothing for his life.
   Before the year had passed
Graelent knew such anguish
That he had neither strength nor vigor;
Those who saw him said that
It was surprising that he had lasted so long.
On the day that the king had named,
When his feast was to be held,
He assembled a great many people.   550
The guarantors brought Graelent
Before the king, into his presence;
The king asked him where his lady was.
"Sir," said he, "she is not here;
I cannot get in touch with her at all;
Do with me as you wish."
The king spoke first to Graelent:
"You spoke extremely discourteously;
You wronged the queen
And contradicted all my barons;   560
Never will you slander another
When you depart from me."
The king raised his voice:
"Lords," he declared, "concerning the sentence,
I beg you not to be too lenient,
In accordance with the statement that you heard
Graelent make in your presence;
In my court he brought shame upon me.
The man does not love me very well
Who does dishonor to my wife;   570
If someone enjoys beating your dog,
Don't imagine that he loves you well."
   Those who were to judge went outside;
They assembled for the sentence;
For a long time they all were quiet;
There was neither argument nor discord;
They felt great sadness for the knight
Whom they would have to judge among themselves.
Before any of them had uttered a word,
Or anyone had testified,   580
There came a servant who said to them

That they should wait a little while:
Two maidens were coming to the court.
In the kingdom there were none so beautiful;
They would greatly help the knight
And would, God willing, set him free.
    They gladly agreed to wait
Instead of moving away from there;
The young ladies arrived;
They were of great beauty and nicely dressed   590
In two tightly laced embroidered dresses;
They were very attractive and fine-featured.
They dismounted from their palfreys
And had two servants hold them;
Into the hall they came, up to the king.
"Sir," said one, "listen to me;
My mistress commands you
And, through the two of us, begs and asks
That you delay the trial for a little while,
That there be no sentence passed;   600
She is coming here to speak with you
In order to free the knight."
As she was telling her tale
The queen felt very great shame.
    She left quickly after that.
Before the king, in his palace
There came two others, much more beautiful,
With white and rosy complexions;
They asked the king to wait
Until their mistress arrived.   610
They were greatly admired
And their beauty praised by many;
There were indeed women more beautiful
Than was the queen.
And when the mistress came,
The entire court fixed its eyes upon her;
She was extraordinarily beautiful,
With a gentle appearance, a soft countenance,
Beautiful eyes, lovely face, gracious manner;
In her there was no flaw.   620
Everyone stared at her with amazement;
She wore a red silk dress,
Richly embroidered with gold,
That was tight-fitting;
Her cloak was worth a castle.
She had a fine handsome palfrey;
Its bridle, its saddle, and its harness
Were worth a thousand pounds in Chartres coin.
Everyone came outdoors in order to see her;
They praised her face and body   630
And her countenance and figure.

She came galloping up;
She came before the king on horseback;
No one found fault with her for doing so;
She dismounted, away from the crowd,
And allowed her palfrey to wander off.
She spoke to the king courteously:
"Sir," she said, "hear me,
And all of you, my lord barons,
Listen now to my words.   640
You know all about Graelent,
That he said to the king before his people,
At the time of the great assembly
When the queen was on display,
That he had seen a more beautiful woman;
That speech is well known.
In truth he spoke improperly,
Since the king was angered by it;
But, in saying that, he told the truth;
No one is of such great beauty   650
That another, just as beautiful, does not exist.
Now look, and tell the truth;
If, by my appearance, I can have him acquitted,
The king should declare him exonerated."
There was not a soul, of low or high rank,
Who did not say publicly
That even a servant accompanying her
Was equal to the queen in beauty.
The king himself made the judgment
Before his subjects, and stated   660
That Graelent was acquitted;
Clearly he had to be declared innocent.
As long as the trial had lasted,
Graelent had not failed in his duty;
Now he sent for his good steed;
With his mistress he wished to depart.
    When she had done what she wanted to do,
And had heard what the court said,
She received permission from the king to depart;
Then she mounted her palfrey;   670
Out of the hall she went
Together with her maidens.
Graelent mounted up and followed her
Through the city at great speed,
Never stopping, crying out for mercy,
But she replied to him not at all.
They kept to the straight road
Until they came to the forest;
They maintained their route through the woods
Until they came to the river   680
Which had its source in the middle of the heath

And ran through the forest.
The water in it was clear and beautiful.
The young woman rode into it;
Graelent tried to enter after her,
But she began to cry out to him:
"Flee, Graelent! Don't come in!
If you enter, you will drown!"
He paid no attention to that;
He plunged in; he could not wait;   690
The water closed over his forehead;
With great effort he came to the surface;
But she took hold of his rein
And led him back to dry land.
Then she said to him: "You cannot cross,
No matter how much you struggle."
She commanded him to go back;
Then she entered the river once again;
But he could not bear
To see her depart from him;   700
Into the water he went, still on horseback;
The current carried him downstream;
It separated him from his steed;
He was close to drowning
When the maidens cried out,
The ones who were with the young woman:
"My lady, in God's name, have mercy!
Take pity on your lover!
Look, he is dying with great suffering.
God, what an ill-fated day it was for him   710
When you first spoke to him
And granted him your love!
Look, my lady, the current is carrying him away;
For the sake of God, save him from danger;
The grief will be unbearable if he perishes.
How can your heart endure it?
My lady, your lover is drowning;
Let him have help from you;
You are far too cruel and hard!
If you don't give thought to helping him,   720
You will sin greatly against him."
The young woman took pity on him
Because she heard them lamenting so much;
No longer could she hold back or hesitate.
Hastily she returned;
She went downstream
And seized her lover by the waist
And led him off with her.
   When they arrived on the other side,
She removed his wet clothing;   730
She wrapped him in her cloak

And led him off with her to her land.
Still today the people of this region say
That Graelent is there and quite alive.
His horse, which had been separated from him,
Went back into the forest;
It was very sad over the loss of its master;
It was at peace neither night nor day.
Then, for a long time, it neighed in the region;
Throughout the countryside it was heard.   740
Many wanted to capture and hold the steed,
But no one could ever catch it;
Never again would it let any man approach,
Nor could it be either ensnared or captured.
A very long time afterward, people heard
For many years, in the season
In which its master had left it,
The noise, the neighing, and the cries
Made by this good steed
For the master whom it had lost.   750
The marvel of the good steed,
The knight's adventure,
How he went off with his mistress,
Were heard throughout all of Brittany.
The Bretons made a lay about it;
They called it *Graelent Muer*.

chapter V

CHRÉTIEN DE TROYES: YVAIN, *or* THE KNIGHT WITH THE LION

William W. Kibler

Chrétien de Troyes is regarded by many as one of France's most creative and influential medieval authors. He lived and wrote in the second half of the twelfth century, a time when both ideas and the arts were flourishing in central France. The Gothic arches of St. Denis had already been built, Abelard had launched the scholastic method in philosophy, Leonin was composing the new liturgical polyphony for services in the rising cathedral of Notre Dame de Paris, the Parisian schools were attracting scholars from all over Europe, and many new forms of literature were being tried and developed. In this artistic and intellectual explosion Chrétien was one of the greatest innovators, bringing together legendary Celtic motifs, a nascent interest in love intrigues, and the newly perfected octosyllabic rhymed couplet to create an original genre that was destined for unprecedented success: the Arthurian romance.

Many scholars agree that *Yvain*, or *The Knight with the Lion*, which was the third or fourth of his major poems, is Chrétien's most perfectly developed romance. It was preceded by *Erec and Enide, Cligés,* and possibly *Lancelot,* or *The Knight of the Cart*, and was followed by *Perceval*, or *The Story of the Grail.* By the time he composed *The Knight with the Lion*, Chrétien had mastered not only his source but his poetic medium as well. *The Knight with the Lion* flows fluidly on its octosyllables, combining swift-moving narrative, lively and immediate dialogue, and passages of great lyric beauty. Chrétien's use of humor and irony has been frequently commented upon, as has his ability to incorporate keenly observed realistic details into the most fantastic adventures. His lengthy portrait of the ugly peasant (lines 288–326) is a justly famous tour de force.

Chrétien was an unusually self-conscious artist for his period. He alludes in several of his prologues to the processes of composition, and he proudly signed all his works in an era when many literary productions remained anonymous. Yet in spite of this we know next to nothing about his life. His name does not appear on any official records, so what little we can glean about his biography must come from infrequent references within his own works. In the prologue to *Erec and Enide* our author refers to himself as *Crestiens de Troies* (line 9), from which we can assume that he was born or at least spent the better part of his formative years in Troyes, one of the leading cities in the region of Champagne. Dialectal features of his language also support this contention. At Troyes he was most assuredly associated with the court of the Countess Marie de Champagne, to whom he dedicated his romance *Lancelot*, or *The Knight of the Cart*. This Marie, a daughter of Eleanor of Aquitaine by her first marriage, to King Louis VII of France, was married in 1159 to Henry the Liberal, Count of Champagne. Sometime after Henry's death in 1181 Chrétien shifted patrons and began his unfinished romance *Perceval*, or *The Story of the Grail*, for Philip of Flanders.

The dates of Chrétien's romances have not been firmly established. Although some critics suggest that his primary literary activity took place in the 1180s, the information presented above argues for an active period from the mid-1150s to around 1190. In the prologue to *Cligés* he tells us that he had previously composed some adaptations of Ovidian materials as well as a poem treating the Tristan legend, which he enigmatically refers to as being "about King Mark and Isolde the Blonde." All of this early material, with the possible exception of an adaptation of the Philomela story (Ovid's *Metamorphoses*, Book 6), has been lost. After honing his technique on these adaptations, Chrétien created his first masterpiece when he turned from Rome to the Celtic world for his inspiration and composed *Erec and Enide*. This fine psychological study of a knight and his new bride is the first extant literary work to incorporate Arthurian material. Its success was followed by *Cligés*, which, though set in part at Arthur's court, is principally an adventure romance based on Greco-Byzantine materials.

There is some indication that Chrétien composed *Yvain* simultaneously with *Lancelot*, but in inspiration it instead harkens back to *Erec and Enide*. While *Lancelot* appears to champion adulterous love, *Yvain* and *Erec* explore the mutual interdependencies of love, marriage, and knightly prowess. *Yvain* is in many respects a "mirror-image" of *Erec*: where the latter shows what can occur when the pursuit of knightly acclaim takes a secondary role to the pleasures of conjugal love, *Yvain* teaches the dangers of placing worldly glories above the demands of love. In these, as in his other romances, Chrétien opts for the typically medieval virtue of *mesure*, a delicate middle-line position in which no one virtue (or vice) is allowed to predominate.

Although Chrétien drew upon disparate sources, both classical and Celtic, in composing *The Knight with the Lion*, he consciously combined these elements to form a harmonious whole, *une molt bele conjointure* ("a very beautiful arrangement"), as he termed it in *Erec*. The intrigue of *Yvain*, like that of most of his romances, is organized around the motif of the quest. He used this motif to explore the technical possibilities for organizing a romance. Whereas in *Erec and Enide* he carefully arranged a linear series of adventures to culminate in the "Joy of the Court" episode, and in *Lancelot* he organized his adventures according to the principle of *contrapasso*, by which the nature of the adventure corresponded to the nature of the offense, in *The Knight with the Lion* Chrétien introduced a new technique that, in its later and more complex manifestations, would have widespread repercussions: the technique of *entrelacement* (interlacing). The interlacing in *Yvain* is of the simplest sort, but occurs twice, as if to call attention to itself. In each instance Yvain begins an adventure, only to be forced to interrupt it to complete another before he can return to his original pursuit. In this way the second adventure is, as it were, embraced by or "interlaced" with the first. A second technical innovation in *Yvain* involves the series of intertextual cross-references to *Lancelot*. We learn that Sir Gawain cannot help his sister, whose husband is besieged by Harpin of the Mountain, because Sir Gawain is off rescuing Queen Guinevere in the other romance.

One cannot hope to capture Chrétien's technical virtuosity in a translation, and much of what was original with Chrétien may appear to us eight centuries later as unexceptional, or even naive. But in the history of French letters Chrétien remains one of the great innovators as well as one of the finest poets. Perhaps this translation will help us realize that he also could tell a very good story.

Bibliographic note: A detailed bibliography up to the mid-1970s is provided by F. Douglas Kelly, *Chrétien de Troyes: An Analytic Bibliography* (Grant & Cutler, 1976). Good general introductions to Chrétien in English can be found in Jean Frappier, *Chrétien de Troyes, the Man and His Work*, English translation by Raymond J. Cormier (Ohio University, 1982), and U. T. Holmes, *Chrétien de Troyes* (Twayne, 1970). Important recent studies in English include Peter Haidu, *Aesthetic Distance in Chrétien de Troyes* (Droz, 1968); Norris J. Lacy, *The Craft of Chrétien de Troyes: An Essay on Narrative Art* (Brill, 1980); L. T. Topsfield, *Chrétien de Troyes: A Study of the Arthurian Romances* (Cambridge University, 1981); and Peter S. Noble, *Love and Marriage in Chrétien de Troyes* (University of Wales, 1982).

Yvain, or *The Knight with the Lion*

Arthur, the good king of Britain, whose valor teaches us to be brave and courteous, held a court of truly royal splendor at Carduel in Wales at that precious feast that is known as Pentecost. After dining, the knights gathered in the halls at the invitation of ladies, damsels, or maidens. Some told of past adventures, others spoke of Love: of the anguish and sorrows, but also of the great blessings often enjoyed by the disciples of His order, which in those days was sweet and flourishing. But today very few serve Love, for nearly all have abandoned Him; and Love is greatly abased, because those who loved in bygone days were known to be courtly and valiant and generous and honorable. Now Love is a matter for pleasantries, since those who know nothing about it say that they love, but they lie, and those who boast of loving and have no right to do so make a lie and a mockery of Love.

But let us speak now of those who were, leaving those who are still among us, for to my mind a courteous man, though dead, is more worthy than a living boor. Therefore it is my pleasure to tell something worthy to be heard about the king whose fame was such that men still speak of him both near and far; and I agree wholly with the Bretons that his fame will last forever, and through him we can recall those good chosen knights who strove for honor.

On that Pentecost of which I speak the knights were very surprised to see the king arise early from table, and some among them were greatly disturbed and discussed it at length, because never before at such a great feast had they seen him enter his room to sleep or rest. But that day it happened that the queen detained him, and he tarried so long at her side that he forgot himself and fell asleep. At the entrance to his chamber were Dodinel and Sagremor and Kay and my lord Gawain; and my lord Yvain was there too, and with them was Calogrenant, a very handsome knight, who began telling them a tale, not of his honor, but of his disgrace.

As he was telling his tale, the queen began to listen to him. She arose from beside the king and came to them so quietly that before anyone could notice her, she had settled in among them. Calogrenant alone leapt to his feet to show her honor. And Kay, who was spiteful, wicked, sharp-tongued, and abusive, said to him: "By God, Calogrenant, I see how gallant and sharp you are, and indeed I'm delighted that you're the most courteous among us. And I'm sure you think so, since you're so lacking in good sense! It's natural that my lady should believe you are more gallant and courteous than all the rest of us: perhaps it appears that it was out of laziness we neglected to rise, or because we didn't deign to do so? But by God, sir, that wasn't it; rather it was because we didn't see my lady until after you'd risen."

"Indeed, Kay," said the queen, "I think you'd soon burst if you couldn't pour out the venom that fills you. You are tiresome and base to reproach your companions so."

"My lady, if we are not better for your company," said Kay, "make sure that we don't lose by it. I don't believe I've said anything that should be noted to my discredit, so, if you please, let's talk no more of it. It is not courteous or wise to speak of idle things; such talk should go no farther, nor should anyone make any more of it. Instead have him tell us more of the tale he started, for there should be no quarreling here."

At these words Calogrenant joined in and answered: "My lady, I'm not greatly upset by the quarrel; it's nothing to me, and I don't care. Though Kay has wronged me, it will do me no harm: to braver and wiser men than I, my lord Kay, have you spoken your slander and spite, for you do it habitually. The dungheap will always smell, wasps will always sting and hornets buzz, and a cad will always slander and vex others. Yet I'll not continue my story today, if my lady will excuse me, and, by her grace, not command that which displeases me."

"My lady, all those who are here," said Kay, "will be grateful to you and will willingly hear him out; don't do anything on my account, but, by the loyalty you owe the king, your lord and mine, order him to continue—you will do well in doing so."   [130]

"Calogrenant," said the queen, "don't pay any heed to this attack by my lord Kay the seneschal; he so frequently speaks ill of people that we cannot punish him for it. I urge and pray you not to be angry in your heart, nor fail on his account to tell of things it would please us to hear. If you wish to enjoy my love, pray begin again at once."

"Indeed, my lady, what you order me to do is very difficult. I'd rather let one of my eyes be put out, if I did not fear to anger you, than to tell them anything more this day; but though it pains me, I'll do what pleases you.

"Since it suits you, listen to me now! Lend me your hearts and ears, for words that are not understood by the heart are lost completely. There are those who hear something without understanding it, and praise it; they have only the faculty of hearing, since the heart does not comprehend it. The word comes to the ears like whistling wind, but doesn't stop or tarry there; instead it quickly leaves if the heart is not alert enough to be ready to seize it. However, if the heart can take and enclose and retain the word when it hears it, then the ears are the path and channel through which the voice reaches the heart; and the voice, which enters through the ears, is received within the breast by the heart. So he who would hear me now must surrender heart and ears to me, for I do not wish to speak of a dream, nor a fable, nor a lie, which many others have served you; instead I'll tell what I saw.   [174]

"It happened more than seven years ago that I, alone like a farmer, was riding along in search of adventures, fully armed as a knight should be; I discovered a path to the right leading through a thick forest. The way was very treacherous, full of thorns and briars; with considerable effort and difficulty I kept to this way and this path. Nearly the whole day I rode along in this manner, until I came out of the forest, which was named Broceliande.

"From the forest I entered into open country, where I saw a wooden tower half a Welsh league away; if it was that far, it was no farther. I rode that way faster than a pace, saw the fortification and the moat deep and wide all around; and on the drawbridge was he to whom the castle belonged, with a molted goshawk upon his wrist. I had no sooner greeted him than he came to hold my stirrup and invited me to dismount. I had no inclination but to do so, for I needed lodging; and he told me at once more than seven straight times that blessed was the way by which I had come therein. Thereupon we crossed the bridge and passed through the gate into the courtyard.

"In the middle of the vavasor's courtyard—may God grant him as much joy and honor as he showed to me that night—there hung a gong; I don't believe it was made with any iron or wood, or of anything but pure copper. Upon this gong, with a hammer that was hanging from a little post, the vavasor struck three blows. Those who were within, hearing the voices and this sound, came out of the house and down into the courtyard. Some ran to my horse, which the good vavasor was holding. And I saw that a fair and noble maiden was coming toward me. I looked at her intently, for she was beautiful, tall, and proper; she was skillful in helping me disarm, which she did quickly and well. Then she dressed me in a short, bright-colored mantle of peacock-blue. And I was pleased to notice that no one remained there with us, for I had eyes for no one else. And she led me to sit down in the most beautiful meadow in the world, enclosed roundabout with a small wall. There I found her to be so talented, so charming in speech, so gifted, so comforting, and of such a nature, that I was very delighted to be there, and no duty could ever cause me to leave.

"But that night the vavasor made war upon me by coming to fetch me when it was the time and hour to sup; since I could tarry no longer, I did his bidding at once. Of the supper I'll tell you in short that it was entirely to my liking, since the maiden, who was in attendance, was seated opposite me. After dinner the vavasor told me that he couldn't recall how long it had been since he had given lodging to a knight-errant riding in search of adventure; he had not lodged any in a long while. Then he beseeched me to accord him the service and recompense of returning by way of his lodging, and I told him: 'Willingly, sir.' For it would have been a shame to refuse him; I would have seemed ungrateful had I refused my host this boon.   [268]

"That night I was well lodged, and my horse was saddled as soon as one could see the dawn; I had ardently requested it the evening before, and my request had been honored. I commended my good host and his dear daughter to the Holy Spirit; I begged leave of all and set off as soon as I could. I had scarcely left the castle when I discovered, in a clearing, wild bulls at large, who were fighting among themselves and making such an uproar and commotion and disturbance, if the truth be told you, that I backed off a little way, for no beast is as fierce as or more bellicose than a bull.

"A peasant who resembled a Moor, ugly and hideous in the extreme—such an ugly creature that he cannot be described in words—was seated on a stump, with a great club in his hand. I approached the peasant and saw that his head was larger than a nag's or other beast's. His hair was in tufts and his bare forehead was more than two spans wide; his ears were as hairy and as huge as an elephant's; his eyebrows heavy and his face flat; he had the eyes of an owl and the nose of a cat, jowls split like a wolf's, with the sharp, reddish teeth of a boar; he had a russet beard, unkempt moustache, a chin down to his breast, a long twisted, humpbacked spine. He was leaning on his club, wearing a most unusual cloak. It was made neither of wool nor linen; instead at his neck he had attached two pelts freshly skinned from two bulls or two oxen.

"The peasant leaped to his feet as soon as he saw me approaching him; I didn't know if he wanted to strike me, or what he intended to do, but I made ready to defend myself, until I saw that he stood there perfectly still, without moving. He had climbed up on a tree trunk, where he towered a good seventeen feet high. He looked down at me, without saying a word, no more than a beast would have; and I thought he didn't know how to talk and was mute. Nonetheless I got up enough nerve to say to him: 'Come now, tell me if you are a good creature or not?' And he answered: 'I am a man.'   [329]

"'What sort of man are you?' I asked.

"'Just as you see; and I'm never anything else.'

"'What are you doing here?'

"'I stand here and watch over the beasts of this wood.'

"'Watch them? By St. Peter in Rome, they've never been tamed! I don't believe anyone can watch over wild beasts on the plain or in the woods, nor anywhere else, in any way, unless they are tied up and fenced in.'

"'I watch over these and herd them so that they'll never leave this clearing.'

"'How do you do it? Tell me truly.'

"'There's not a one of them that dares move when it sees me coming, for whenever I catch hold of one I grab it so by its two horns with my tough and strong hands that the others tremble in fear and gather around me as if to cry out for mercy. No one except me could trust himself among them, for he would be killed at once. Thus I am lord over my beasts. Now it's your turn to tell me what sort of man you are and what you're seeking.'

"'I, as you see, am a knight seeking what I cannot find; I've sought long and yet find nothing.'

"'And what do you wish to find?'

"'Adventure, to test my courage and my strength. Now I pray and beseech you to advise me, if you know, of any adventure or marvelous thing.'

"'In this,' he replied, 'you will surely fail: I know nothing of adventure, nor have I ever heard any talk of it. But should you wish to go to a spring near here, you will not return without difficulty unless you abide by the custom of the place. Nearby you will soon find a path that will lead you there. Follow the path straight ahead if you don't wish to waste your steps, for you could easily stray: there are many other paths. You will see the spring that boils and yet is colder than marble. It is shaded by the most beautiful tree that Nature ever formed. Its leaves stay on in all seasons; it doesn't lose them in even the harshest winter. Also hanging there is an iron basin on a chain that's long enough to reach the spring. Beside the spring you'll see a stone; I can't tell you what kind it is, as I've never seen any like it. And on the other side is a chapel, small but very beautiful. If you will take water in the basin and cast it upon the stone, then you'll see such a storm come up that no beast will remain in this wood: stags, does, deer, boars, and even birds will fly before it. There'll be so much lightning, such wind and splitting of trees, so much rain, thunder, and lightning, that if you escape without great trouble and distress, you will be more fortunate than any knight who ever went there.'   [407]

"I left the peasant as soon as he had shown me the way. It was probably after tierce and might even have been near midday when I saw the tree and the spring. I know for a fact that the tree was the most beautiful pine that ever grew upon the earth. I don't believe it could ever rain so hard that a single drop could penetrate it; rather it would all drip off. From the tree I saw the basin hanging, made of the purest gold that was ever sold at any fair. As for the spring, you can be assured that it was boiling like hot water. The stone was of emerald pierced through like a cask, and it sat upon four rubies, brighter and redder than the morning sun when it first appears in the east—everything I say is the truth, so far as I know it. I was eager to see the miracle of the storm and tempest, but this was unwise on my part, and had I been able I would immediately have retracted my action, after sprinkling the perforated stone with the water from the basin. But I poured too much, I fear, because I then saw the heavens so rent apart that lightning blinded my eyes from more than fourteen directions; and the clouds all pell-mell dropped rain, snow, and hail. The storm was so terrible and severe that a hundred times I feared I'd be killed by the lightning that struck about me or by the trees that were split asunder. You can be sure that I was very frightened until the storm died down.

"But God brought me swift comfort, for the storm did not last long and all the winds diminished; they dared not blow against God's will. And when I saw clear, pure air, I was filled again with joy; for joy, as I've come to learn, causes great cares to be soon forgotten. As soon as the storm abated, I saw gathered upon the pine tree so many birds—believe it if you will—that not a leaf or branch could be found that was not completely covered with birds. The tree was more beautiful because of them, and they were singing softly, in perfect harmony; yet each sang a different song, so that I never heard one sing what the other was singing. I rejoiced in their joyousness, and I listened until they had completely finished their service, for I had never heard such perfect joy, nor do I believe anyone would hear its equal unless he too goes there to hear what so pleased and delighted me that I was totally enraptured.

"I stayed there so long that I heard what sounded like a knight coming; indeed I thought there might be ten of them, such a racket and clatter did a single knight who was approaching make. When I saw him coming all alone, I caught my horse at once and did not delay in mounting; and he, as if with evil intent, flew at me swifter than an eagle, looking as fierce as a lion.

"In his loudest voice he began to challenge me, saying: 'Vassal, greatly have you shamed and injured me, without proper challenge. If you had just cause, you ought first to have challenged me, or at least claimed your rights, before bringing war against me. So now if I can, sir vassal, I'll make you suffer punishment for the manifest damage you've done. The evidence is all around me, in my woods that have been felled. He who is injured has the right to lodge a complaint; and I do claim, and rightly so, that you have driven me from my house with lightning and rain; you have wronged me (and cursed be he who finds it good), for against my woods and my castle you have leveled such an attack that great towers and high walls would have been of no avail to me. No man would have been safe in any fortress whatsoever, whether of timber or solid stone. But know well that from now on you will have no truce or peace from me.'   [516]

"At these words we came together; we held our shields on our arms, each covering himself with his own. The knight had a good horse and a stiff lance, and was certainly a full head taller than I. I was thus in a very bad way, because I was smaller than he and his horse was better than mine. (I am telling you the truth, you must understand, so as to explain the cause of my shame.) I dealt him the mightiest blow that I could, sparing him nothing, and struck the end of his shield. All my strength was behind my blow, and my lance shattered to pieces. But his remained whole, since it was not light at all but weighed more, I think, than the lance of any other knight, for I'd never seen such a huge one. And the knight struck me such a blow that it knocked me over my horse's crupper and flat upon the ground; he left me ashamed and defeated there, without glancing even once at me. He took my horse, leaving me alone, and started back along the path. And I, who didn't know what to do, remained there bewildered and depressed.

"I sat for a while beside the spring and waited; I didn't dare follow the knight for fear of doing something rash. And even had I dared to follow him, I didn't know what had become of him. Finally I decided that I would keep my word to my host and return to him. This decision pleased me, and so I set off; but first I took off all my armor in order to proceed more easily, and I returned in shame.

"When I reached his lodgings that night, I found my host quite unchanged, just as happy and as courteous as I had found him earlier. I did not in the least sense that either his daughter or he was any less happy to see me or paid me any less honor than they had the night before. In their goodness everyone in that house bore me great honor; and they said that never before had anyone escaped from where I had come, as far as they knew or had heard tell, but all had been killed or captured. Thus I went, and thus I returned; upon returning I considered myself a fool. Now like a fool I've told you what I never before wanted to tell."

"By my head," said my lord Yvain, "you are my first cousin and we should love one another dearly; yet I must agree you were a fool for having hidden this from me so long. If I have called you a fool, I beg you not to be offended by this, for I'll go forth to avenge your shame if I can."

"It's clear that it's after dinner," said Kay, who could not restrain his tongue. "There are more words in a pitcher full of wine than in a hogshead of beer. They say the drunken cat makes merry: after dinner, without ever stirring from his place, everyone goes forth to kill the Sultan Noradin. And you're off to avenge Forré! Are your saddle-cloths stuffed, your iron greaves polished, and your banners unfurled? Swiftly now, by God, my lord Yvain, will you set out tonight or tomorrow? Let us know, fair sir, when you'll start on this dangerous adventure, because we'd like to accompany you; there's not a provost or constable who wouldn't gladly escort you. And I beg you, whatever happens, don't go off without our leave. But should you have a bad dream this night, then stay here!"   [611]

"What? Are you out of your mind, my lord Kay?" said the queen. "That tongue of yours never stops! Cursed be your tongue that's so full of bitterness! Indeed your tongue must hate you, because it says the worst it knows to every man, no matter who he is. May the tongue that never tires of speaking slander be damned! The way your tongue behaves, it makes you hated everywhere: it couldn't betray you any more completely. I assure you I'd accuse it of treason if it were mine. Anyone who cannot learn by chastisement should be bound before the choir-grill in church like a lunatic."

"Indeed, my lady," said my lord Yvain, "I don't pay any heed to his insults. My lord Kay is so clever and able and worthy in all courts that he'll never be deaf or dumb. He knows how to answer insults with wisdom and courtesy, and has never done otherwise. (Now you know perfectly well whether I am lying!) But I have no wish to quarrel or start something foolish, because it isn't the man who strikes the first blow who starts the fight, but he who strikes back. He would gladly quarrel with a stranger who insults his companion. I don't want to behave like the mastiff who bristles and snarls when other dogs show their teeth."   [648]

As they were speaking thus, the king came out of his chamber, where he had been a long while, having slept until this moment. And the barons, when they saw him, all leaped to their feet before him, and he had them all be seated again. He took his place beside the queen, who immediately told him Calogrenant's adventures, word for word, for she knew well how to tell a tale. The king listened eagerly to it, then swore three solemn oaths—on the soul of his father Uther Pendragon, on that of his son, and on that of his mother—that before two weeks had passed he would go to see the spring, the storm, and the marvel, and would arrive on the eve of the feast of St. John the Baptist and take his lodging there. And he added that all those who wished to might accompany him there. Everyone at court approved of the king's decision, for the barons and young knights were all very eager to go there.

But though others might be happy and joyful, my lord Yvain was sorrowful, for he had intended to go there all alone; so he was distressed and upset that the king had decided to go. This is what upset him: he knew that my lord Kay would undoubtedly be granted the battle rather than himself; if Kay were to request it, it would never be refused him; or perhaps my lord Gawain himself would ask for it first. If either of these two requested it, it would never be denied them. So Yvain, who had no desire for their company, did not wait for them; he resolved instead to set off alone, whether it might bring him joy or grief. With no thought as to who might be left behind, he determined to be in Broceliande within three days and would seek, as he could, until he found the narrow wooded path, which he was most eager to find, and the heath and the castle and the comfort and pleasure of the courteous damsel who was so comely and so fair, and the nobleman who, along with his daughter, strove to act honorably, for he was so generous and nobly born. Then he would see the clearing and the bulls, and the huge peasant who watched over them. He was eager and impatient to see this peasant, who was so stout, tall, hideous, and deformed, and as black as a smithy. Then he would see, if he could, the stone and the spring and the basin, and the birds of the pine tree; and he would make it rain and blow. But he did not want to boast of it yet, and did not intend anyone to learn of it until he had won either great shame or great honor; then only should it be made known.

My lord Yvain stole away from the court without encountering anyone and returned alone to his lodgings. He found all his household assembled there, asked that his horse be saddled, and summoned one of his squires from whom he hid nothing. "Say there," he said, "follow me outside the city and bring me my armor. I'll leave by this gate upon my palfrey at a slow walk. Be careful not to delay, for I have a long way to travel. And have my horse well shod and lead him after me; then you will bring my palfrey back. But take care, I command you, that if anyone should ask after me, you tell him nothing. Otherwise, though you trust in me now, you will never again be able to count on me."

"My lord," he answered, "have no fear, for no one will ever learn anything from me. You go first and I'll follow after you."   [746]

My lord Yvain mounted at once, for he intended to avenge his cousin's shame before his return. The squire ran for the arms and the horse, and mounted it; there was no need to delay further, since the horse lacked neither shoes nor nails. He galloped swiftly after his master until he saw him dismounted, for he had been awaiting him for a while some distance from the road, in a secluded place. The squire brought him all his harness and trappings, and helped him with the armor.

Once he was armed, my lord Yvain didn't delay in the slightest but rode on each day, over mountains and across valleys, through forests deep and wide, through strange and wild places, crossing many treacherous passes, many dangers, and many straits, until he reached the narrow path, full of thorn bushes and dark shadows. Only then was he certain that he would not lose his way again. No matter what the price, he would not stop until he saw the pine tree that shaded the spring, and the stone, and the storm that hailed, rained, thundered, and blew.

That night, you can be sure, he found such a host as he sought, for he received more favor and respect from the vavasor than I've recounted to you; and in the maiden he perceived a hundred times more sense and beauty than Calogrenant had spoken of, for one cannot tell the sum of the virtue of a noble lady and a good man. Once one devotes oneself to true goodness, his full worth can never be told, for no tongue can rehearse all the goodness a noble man can do. My lord Yvain was well lodged that night, and it pleased him greatly.

The next day he went to the clearing and saw the bulls and the peasant who showed him the way to proceed; but he crossed himself more than a hundred times in wonder at how Nature could have created such an ugly and baseborn creature. Then he rode up to the spring and beheld all that he had come to see. Without stopping to rest, he poured the full basin of water all over the stone. At once it began to blow and rain and storm just as it was supposed to. And when God restored the good weather, the birds alighted upon the pine tree and made a wondrously joyful sound above the perilous spring. Before the joyful sound abated, there came a knight, more burning with anger than a glowing coal, making as much racket as if he were pursuing a rutting stag.

As soon as they caught sight of one another, they attacked as if they bore each other a mortal hatred. Each had a sturdy and strong lance with which they struck one another such mighty blows that they pierced through the shields at their sides and smashed their hauberks; the lances shattered and splintered, and the pieces flew into the air. They then drew their swords and struck each other with blows that sliced through the shield straps and completely split their bucklers, both top and bottom, leaving the pieces hanging so that they were useless to cover or defend them. Their shields had so many holes that the shining swords struck directly on their sides, their breasts, and their flanks. They tested one another cruelly, yet they stood their ground like two blocks of stone; never were two knights more eager to hasten one another's deaths. They had no wish to waste their blows and delivered them as best they could. Helmets were dented and bent, and links of mail flew from their hauberks, amid much loss of blood. The hauberks grew so hot from their exertion that they were of scarcely more avail than a frock. They struck one another's faces with their blades: it's a wonder how such a fierce and bitter battle could last so long. But each was so proud of heart that neither would yield a foot of ground to the other on any account, unless he were wounded to the death.

They fought most honorably all the while, for they never struck or wounded their horses at all, nor did they deign or desire to. They remained on horseback and never fought on foot, and the battle was more splendid for it. Finally my lord Yvain smashed the knight's helmet. The knight was stunned and weakened by the blow; he was confounded, for never before had he felt such a blow, which had split his head to the brain beneath his hood, until the chainmail of his shining hauberk was stained with brains and blood, which caused him such great pain that his heart nearly failed him.   [872]

If he fled, he was not to be blamed, since he felt himself mortally wounded; no defense could help him now. As soon as he could gather his wits, he fled in all haste toward his town; the drawbridge was lowered for him and the gate opened wide. My lord Yvain spurred hotly after him, as fast as he could. As the gyrfalcon pursues the crane, soaring in from the distance until it thinks to strike, but then misses, thus the knight fled and Yvain pursued so closely that he could nearly touch him; yet he couldn't quite reach him, though he was so close that he could hear him groan from the distress he felt; all this time he was intent upon escaping and Yvain likewise upon his pursuit. My lord Yvain feared his efforts would be wasted if he were unable to take the knight dead or alive, for he recalled the insults that my lord Kay had flung his way. He had not yet acquitted himself of the promise he had made his cousin, and no one would believe him at all if he did not bring back real proof. Spurring ahead, the knight led him to the gate of his town, through which both entered; they encountered neither man nor woman on the streets along which they passed as both went racing toward the palace gate.

This gate was very high and wide but had such a narrow entryway that two men or two horses could not pass through together or meet one another in the gate without crowding or great difficulty; for it was built just like a trap that awaits the rat when it comes sneaking in: it had a blade poised above, ready to fall, strike, and pin, which is released and falls whenever anything touches the trigger, no matter how slightly. In like manner there were two fulcrums beneath the gate connected to a portcullis above of sharpened, cutting iron; if anything stepped upon these devices the portcullis overhead dropped and whoever was struck by the gate was completely cut to pieces. And precisely in the middle the passageway was as narrow as a forest trail.

The knight skillfully maneuvered his way along this narrow path, and my lord Yvain hurtled on madly at full speed after him. He was so near catching him that he had seized hold of his saddlebow; and it was fortunate for him that he had stretched forward, for had he not been so lucky he would have been split asunder, because his horse tripped the beam that supported the iron portcullis. Just like the Devil of Hell, the door came crashing down, striking the saddle and horse behind, and slicing them both in half. But thank God it didn't touch my lord Yvain, except that as it came slicing down along his back, it cut off both his spurs right at his heels, and he fell down stunned. The other knight, wounded to the death, escaped him in this way.

There was another gate at the back like the one in front; as the fleeing knight fled through this gate, a second portcullis fell closed behind him. Thus was my lord Yvain trapped. Very surprised and discomfited, he remained locked within the great hall, whose ceiling was studded with gilded bosses and whose walls were painted masterfully in the richest colors. But nothing troubled him more than not knowing where the knight had gone.   [969]

While he was in his misery, he heard the narrow door of a tiny room beside him open, and he saw a damsel approaching, fair of body and handsome of face, who closed the door after her. When she discovered my lord Yvain, she was dismayed at first. "Indeed," said she, "sir knight, I fear you are unwelcome. If you are found in here, you will be promptly torn to pieces, for my lord is wounded to the death and I am certain that you have slain him. My lady is grieving so deeply and her people are weeping around her so much that they nearly kill themselves for grief. They know that you are here within, but the grief they share is so great that presently they can think of nothing else. Yet when they are ready to kill or hang you, they'll not fail to do so as soon as they choose to attack you."

And my lord Yvain answered her: "If it please God, they never will kill me, nor will I ever be captured by them."

"No," she said, "for I will do everything in my power to assist you. He's not brave who fears too much; but since you have not been too frightened, I believe you are a man of courage. Rest assured that, if I am able, I will render you service and honor, for you have already done so for me. Once my lady sent me with a message to the court of the king; perhaps I was not as prudent or courteous or proper as a maiden should be, but there was not a knight there who deigned to speak a single word to me, except you alone, who stand here now. But you, to your great credit, honored and served me there; for the honor that you paid me then I'll now give you the recompense. I know your name well and recognized you at once: you are the son of King Urien and are named my lord Yvain. Be reassured and certain now that if you trust in me you will never be captured or harmed. Now take this little ring of mine and, if you please, return it to me after I have freed you."

Then she gave him the little ring and told him that its effect was like that of bark over wood, which covers it so it cannot be seen. The ring was to be worn with the stone enclosed within the fist; then whoever was wearing the ring on his finger need have no fear of anything, for no one could ever see him, no matter how wide open his eyes, any more than he could see the wood with the bark growing over it. This pleased my lord Yvain. And after she had told him this, she led him to sit upon a bed covered with such a costly quilt that even the Duke of Austria didn't have its equal. She told him that if he liked she would bring him something to eat, and he said that this would please him. The damsel ran swiftly to her room and returned at once bearing a roast capon and a full jug of good vintage wine, covered with a white linen. Thus she who served him gladly provided him with something to eat; and he, who was greatly in need, ate and drank very gladly.   [1054]

By the time he had eaten and drunk, the knights were milling about outside and searching for him, for they wished to avenge their lord, who by now had been placed in his bier. The damsel said to him: "Friend, do you hear them all looking for you? There's a lot of noise and commotion but, no matter who comes or goes, don't move on account of their noise, for you'll never be found if you don't stir from this bed. Soon you'll see this room full of hostile and troublesome people who expect to find you here. And I believe they'll carry the body through here for burial; they'll start to look for you under the benches and beds. To a man who is unafraid it will be an amusing sport to see people so blinded; for they'll all be so blinded, so confused, and so deceived that they'll be beside themselves with rage. I have nothing more to tell you, nor do I dare stay here any longer. But let me praise God for having given me the time and occasion to do something to please you, for I was most eager to do so."

Then she set off on her way and, as soon as she had departed, the people began to gather at the gates on both sides, with clubs and swords in hand; there was a dense crowd and great press of cruel and hostile people. They saw the half of the horse that had been sliced in two lying before the portcullis; this convinced them that when the doors were opened, they would find there within the one they were seeking to kill. Then they had the portcullis, which had been the death of many people, hauled up; but they did not reset the snares or traps, and everyone entered abreast. At the threshold they found the other half of the horse that had been slain, but not a one of them had an eye sharp enough to see my lord Yvain, whom they would gladly have killed. And he saw them going mad with rage and anger, saying: "How can this be? There's no door or window in here through which anything could escape, unless it were a bird that flew, or a squirrel or marmot or other beast that small or smaller, because the windows are barred and both portcullises were closed after my lord escaped through them. The body has to be dead or alive inside, since it isn't outside! More than half the saddle is inside here, as we clearly see, yet we find no trace of him except the severed spurs that fell from his feet. Now let's search every corner and leave off this idle talk, for he must still be in here, I think, or else we are all bewitched, or the devils have stolen him from us."   [1131]

Thus enflamed with anger, they all sought for him within the room, striking through the walls and the beds and the benches; but the bed where Yvain was lying was passed over and spared, and he was not hurt or touched. They struck all around it, and made a tremendous uproar with their clubs everywhere in the room, like a blind man who taps along as he looks for something.

While they were ransacking under the beds and stools, there entered one of the most beautiful women that ever earthly creature had beheld—such an exceptionally beautiful lady has never before been reported or told of. But she was so crazed with grief that she was on the verge of killing herself. All at once she cried out as loudly as she could and fell down in a faint. When she was lifted back to her feet, she began clawing at herself and tearing out her hair like a madwoman; her hands grabbed and ripped her clothing and she fainted with every step. Nothing could comfort her, for she beheld her lord being carried before her dead upon the bier; she felt she could never be comforted again, and so she cried out at the top of her voice. Holy water, crosses, and candles were carried in by nuns from a convent, along with missals and censers; then came priests who were charged with seeking solemn absolution for the object of that poor soul's thoughts.

My lord Yvain heard the indescribable cries and moanings, which surpassed all words and could never be recorded in a book. The procession passed on, but in the middle of the room there was a great commotion about the bier, for warm blood, clear and red, was flowing again from the dead man's wound. This was taken as proof positive that he who had done battle with him, and who had defeated and killed him, was undoubtedly still there within. Then they searched and looked everywhere, overturning and moving everything, until they were all in a sweat from the great anguish and turmoil they felt upon seeing the red blood flowing forth before them. My lord Yvain was constantly struck and jostled there where he lay, but he never moved for all that. And the more the wounds bled, the more distraught the people became; and they wondered why they bled when they could not find the cause. And each and every one of them said: "Among us is the one who killed him, yet we can't see him at all; this is a wondrous and devilish thing!" [1202]

Because of this the lady was so grief-stricken that she quite lost her mind and cried out as if she were mad: "Ah! my God! will they never find him, the murderer, the traitor, who has killed my good husband? Good? Indeed the best of the good! True God, you will be to blame if you let him escape from here; I should blame no one but you, for you have stolen him from my sight. Such violence has never been seen, nor such despicable wrong as you do me, in refusing even to let me see the man who is here so near to me. Indeed, since I cannot see him, I can affirm that either a phantom or a devil has come between us here, and I'm completely bewitched. Or else he's a coward and afraid of me. I'm sure he must be a great coward when he doesn't even dare to show himself before me. Ah! Phantom, cowardly creature, why are you afraid of me when you were so bold before my husband? Empty and elusive creature, if only I had you in my power! Why can't I get you in my grasp? Yet how did you manage to kill my husband, if it wasn't through deceit? Truly my husband would never have been defeated by you had he been able to see you, for there was no one in the world his equal; neither God nor man knew his equal, and never was there another his match. Indeed, had you been a mortal man, you would never have dared attack my husband, for no one could capture him."

Thus the lady argued within herself; thus she struggled alone; thus she confounded herself. And her people likewise were so sad that it was impossible to grieve more. They carried the body away to bury it. After having spent so much effort looking for Yvain, they grew weary from the search and finally gave up from fatigue when they couldn't find anyone in the least suspicious.

Meanwhile the nuns and priests had finished the entire service; the people left the church and came to the place of burial.

But the maiden from the chamber had no desire to accompany them; she remembered my lord Yvain, returned quickly to him, and said: "Fair sir, there was a great crowd of these people in here. They stormed around here a lot and poked about every hiding place more closely than a hound pursuing partridge or quail. You were undoubtedly afraid."

"In faith," he answered, "you speak the truth; I never thought I'd be so afraid. Yet now, if it's possible, I'd like to look through some window or tiny opening and watch the procession and the corpse."

But it was not the corpse or the funeral procession that he was interested in, and he would gladly have consigned them to the fire, even had it cost him a hundred marks. A hundred marks? Indeed more than a hundred thousand. No, he had only said this because he wished to see the lady of the town. The damsel placed him before a little window, thus repaying him as best she could for the honor he had once done her. Through this window my lord Yvain observed the beautiful lady, who was saying: "Fair sir, may

God have mercy on your soul, for I firmly believe that no knight who ever mounted a horse could compare with you in any way. Fair dear sir, no knight ever equaled you in honor or in companionship; generosity was your friend and boldness your companion. May your soul join the company of the saints, fair sweet sir!"

Then she ripped at her clothing, tearing whatever came into her hands. Only with great difficulty did my lord Yvain restrain himself from running to seize her hands. But the damsel beseeched and begged and ordered and warned him, though with courtesy and graciousness, not to do anything foolish, saying: "You are well off here. Be careful not to move on any account until this grief is abated; let these people leave first, for they will soon depart. If you heed my advice as I urge you to heed it, great good may come to you from it. You can stay here and watch the people coming and going, as they pass through this way; no one can possibly see you and you will be at a great advantage. So refrain from speaking rashly, for someone who rants and raves, and exerts himself to rash acts whenever he has the time and place, I consider more foolish than brave. Though you may be thinking folly, be careful to refrain from doing it. The wise man conceals his foolish thoughts and, if he can, puts wisdom to work. Act sensibly now and be careful not to leave your head as hostage, for they'll accept no ransom. Watch out for yourself and remember my advice: stay still until I return. I dare not remain here any longer, because if I stayed too long they'd begin to suspect me when they didn't see me in the crowd with the others, and I'd pay dearly for it."

Thereupon she departed and Yvain remained, not knowing what to do. He was upset to see them burying the body, since he didn't have anything to prove that he had killed the knight; if he didn't have some proof to show in the assembly, he'd be thoroughly embarrassed, because Kay was so wicked and perverse, so full of insults and mockery, that he'd never convince him. Instead Kay would keep on hurling insults and taunts at him, just as he had done the other day.

The wicked taunts are still rankling and fresh within him. But new love has sweetened him with its sugar and honeycomb and has made a foray into his lands, where it's captured its prey: his enemy has led away his heart, and he loves the creature who most hates him. The lady, although she doesn't know it, has fully avenged the death of her husband; she has taken greater vengeance than she could have imagined, had Love herself not avenged her, by striking Yvain such a gentle blow through the eyes into the heart. This blow is more enduring than any from lance or sword: a sword blow is healed and cured as soon as a doctor sees to it; but the wound of Love grows worse when it is nearest to its doctor.   [1378]

My lord Yvain has suffered this wound from which he'll never be healed, for Love has completely overwhelmed him. Lady Love has sought out all those places in which she was spread thin and left them; she wants no host or lodging except him, and indeed she behaves nobly by withdrawing from base places in order to give herself entirely to him. I don't believe a bit of love remained elsewhere: she had ransacked all those lowly lodgings. It's truly a shame Love behaved like that and showed herself so base as to accept lodging in the lowliest place she could find just as willingly as she would in the best. Now, however, she is well housed; here she will be held in honor, and here it is good for her to stay. This is the way Love should behave, being such a noble thing; it's a wonder she dared shame herself by descending to such base places. She behaves like someone who pours out his balm on the ashes and dust, who hates honor and loves baseness, who mingles soot with honey, and mixes sugar with soot. But this time she has not done so: she has taken lodging in freeheld land, for which no one can reproach her.

After they had buried the knight, all the people departed; neither priest, knight, retainer, nor lady remained behind, except the one who could not hide her grief. She remained all alone, frequently grasping her throat, wringing her hands, and striking her palms, as she read her psalms from a psalter illuminated with gilded letters. And my lord Yvain was still at the window observing her; and the more he paid heed to her, the more he loved her and the more she pleased him. He wished that she would cease her weeping and her reading and that it were possible for him to speak to her. Love, who had caught him at the window, filled him with this wish; but he despaired of his desire, for he could not believe or hope that his wish could come true. "I consider myself a fool," he said, "to desire what I cannot have; I wounded her husband to the death, yet I want to have peace with her! By my faith, such thoughts are senseless, for right now she hates me more than anything, and rightfully so. I was correct to speak of 'right now,' for a woman has more than a hundred moods. This mood she is now in will yet change, perhaps; in fact there is no 'perhaps': she *will* change it. I'm a fool to despair of it, and may God grant that she change, for I am destined to be in her power from this time on, since Love wishes it. He who refuses to welcome Love eagerly as soon as she draws near to him commits a felony and treason; and I say—heed it who will—that such a one doesn't deserve any happiness. But I shall not lose on this account; I shall love my enemy forever, for I must not bear her any hatred if I do not want to betray Love. I must love whomever Love chooses.

"And should she consider me her friend? Yes indeed, because I love her. Yet I must call her my enemy because she hates me, and rightfully so, since I have killed the one she loved. Am I therefore her enemy? Indeed I am not, but her friend instead, for I've never before loved anyone so much. I grieve for her beautiful hair, which surpasses pure gold as it glistens; it kindles and enflames me with passion when I see her tearing and pulling it out; nor can it ever again dry the tears that flow from her eyes: all these things displease me. Although they are filled with tears unceasing, there never were more beautiful eyes. It grieves me that she is weeping, but nothing causes me more distress than to see her doing injury to her face, which has not deserved it: I've never seen a more perfectly shaped face, nor one fresher or more full of color; but it pierces my heart through that she is an enemy to it. And truly she is not holding back but is doing the worst she can to it, yet no crystal or mirror is so bright or smooth.

"God! Why is she acting so madly? Why does she hurt herself so? Why does she wring her beautiful hands and strike and scratch at her breast? Would she not be a true wonder to look upon if she were happy, when even now she is so beautiful in anguish? Indeed yes, I swear it's true; never again will Nature be able to create such immeasurable beauty, for in making her Nature has surpassed every limit. Or else, perhaps, Nature had no hand in creating her? Then how could she have come to be? Where did such great beauty come from? God with His bare hands must have made her to make Nature marvel at her. Nature's time would all be wasted if it tried to make another like her, for even God could not succeed again. And I believe that even if He decided to make the effort, He'd never be able to make another like her, no matter how hard He tried."   [1510]

Thus my lord Yvain observed her who was wracked with grief, and I don't believe it ever happened that any man in prison, as my lord Yvain was imprisoned and in fear of losing his head, was ever so madly in love that he could not express his feelings to her nor, perhaps, find anyone to do so for him. He remained at the window until he saw the lady leave and both portcullises had been lowered again. Someone else, who preferred his freedom to remaining here, might have been upset; but for him it was all the same whether the gates were closed or opened. He could never have gone away had they been left open before him, not even if the lady were to give him leave and forgive him freely for the death of her husband, so that he could depart in safety. Shame and Love, who opposed him on both sides, held him back: on the one hand, if he left he would be shamed, for Kay and the other knights would never believe that he had accomplished what he had; on the other hand, he was so eager at least to see the beautiful lady, if he could not have any further favor, that he didn't mind imprisonment: he would rather have died than leave.

The damsel, who wished only to keep him company, soon returned to comfort and amuse him and to seek and bring him whatever he desired. She found him obsessed and weak from Love that had entered him and said to him: "My lord Yvain, what sort of a time have you had today?"

"Such," he replied, "as greatly pleased me."

"Pleased you? For God's sake, are you telling the truth? How can anyone have a good time when he sees that they are seeking to kill him? Such a man must desire his own death!"

"Indeed," said he, "my sweet friend, I have no desire at all to die, and yet what I saw pleased me greatly, as God is my witness, and pleases me now and will please me evermore."

"Let's let this be for now," said she, "for I am well aware where these words are leading; I'm not so simple or foolish that I can't understand plain words. But follow me now, for I'll soon make arrangements to get you out of prison. I'll see you to safety tonight or tomorrow, if it please you. Come along, I'll lead you."

"You can be sure that I'll not leave secretly like a thief," he replied. "When the people are all gathered outside there in the streets, then it will be more honorable for me to leave than in the dark of the night."

With these words he followed her into her little room. The damsel, who was clever and eager to serve him, lavished upon him everything he needed. And when the occasion arose, she reminded him of what he had told her: how pleased he had been to see the people who bore him mortal hatred seeking him throughout the room.   [1592]

The damsel was in such favor with her lady that there was nothing she was afraid to tell her, no matter what it might concern, for she was her adviser and confidante. And why should she be afraid to console her lady and instruct her for her own good? At the first occasion she told her in secret: "My lady, I'm astonished to see you behave so foolishly. Do you think your grief will bring your husband back to you?"

"Not at all," she answered, "but I wish I had died of sorrow."

"Why?"

"In order to go after him."

"After him? May God forbid, and may He send you as good a husband as it is in His power to do."

"Don't tell such a lie, for He could never send me such a good one."

"He'll send you a better one, if you'll take him; I'll prove it."

"Go away! Hush! I'll never find another like him!"

"Indeed you will, my lady, if you agree. But tell me now, if it's not too painful, who will defend your lands when King Arthur comes? He is due to arrive at your stone and spring next week. Have you not received word from the Savage Damsel, who sent you a message about this? Ah, what a fine deed she did for you! You should be seeking advice now about how to defend your spring, yet you cannot stop weeping! There's no time to delay, if you please, my dear lady; all your knights, as you are well aware, are not worth a single serving girl; even the proudest among them would never take up his shield and lance to defend your spring. You have a lot of worthless men: there's not a one of them bold enough to mount his horse, and the king is coming with such a large army that he'll take everything without a fight."

The lady reflected and well understood that she was receiving good advice; but she had in her the same folly that other women have: nearly all of them are obstinate in their folly and refuse to accept what they really want.   [1648]

"Go away!" she said, "leave me alone. If I ever hear you speak of this again, you'll be sorry you didn't run away: you talk so much you weary me."

"Very well, my lady," she said, "it's obvious you're the sort of woman who gets angry when anyone gives her good advice."

Thereupon she departed and left her lady alone. And the lady recognized that she had been very much in the wrong; she was eager to learn how the damsel could prove that one might find a knight better than her husband had been: she would gladly hear her tell it, but she had forbidden her to speak. She mulled over these thoughts until the damsel returned; she paid no heed to her lady's injunction, but spoke to her at once: "Ah! my lady, is it fitting that you kill yourself with so much grief? For God's sake, compose yourself and cease this sorrow, if only out of shame: it's not proper that such a highborn lady should persist in her mourning for so long. Remember your rank and your great gentility. Do you think that all valor died with your husband? A hundred just as good or better remain throughout the world."

"May God confound me if you're not lying! Just name me one man who demonstrates as much valor as my husband did throughout his life!"

"You'll not be happy with me; instead you'll become angry again and threaten me once more."

"I won't, I promise you."

"Then may it advance your happiness, which will soon come to you if you are willing to accept it. And may God grant that it please you! I see no reason to remain silent, for no one can overhear us. You will consider me presumptuous, but I should speak my mind, I think: when two armed knights come together in battle, which one do you think is worth more, when the one has defeated the other? As for me, I give the prize to the winner. And what would you say?"

"It seems to me you're setting a trap and want to catch me by my answer."

"By my faith, you can clearly understand that I'm following the line of truth and am proving to you irrefutably that the one who defeated your husband is more worthy than he was: he defeated him and pursued him boldly as far as this place and imprisoned him within his own house."

"Now I've heard sheer nonsense, the greatest ever spoken. Go away, you creature filled with evil! Go away, you foolish and meddlesome hussy! Don't ever say such mad things again, and never come back into my presence if you're going to speak of him."

"Indeed, my lady, I was certain that you wouldn't be happy with me, and I told you so before I spoke. But you promised me that you would not get angry and wouldn't be displeased with me. You've kept your promise to me poorly, and now it's come about that you've spoken your mind to me; I'd have done better to have kept quiet."   [1730]

Then she returned to her chamber, where my lord Yvain was staying, and attended to his every comfort; but nothing could please him as long as he couldn't see his lady, and he didn't have any suspicion of what the damsel was undertaking on his behalf. All night long the lady struggled within herself, for she was very worried as to how to protect her spring. So she began to feel sorry for having reproached the girl for having insulted and mistrusted her, because now she was totally convinced that the damsel had not brought up the knight's name in hope of any payment or reward, or out of any affection for him. And she fully realized the damsel loved her more than him and would never give her advice that would bring her shame or trouble, for she was too loyal a friend to her.

You can see how the lady's changed already: she feared that the girl to whom she'd spoken harshly could never again love her in her heart; and the knight, whom she'd refused, she had now truly pardoned in righteousness and by force of argument, since he had never done her any wrong. So she spoke with him just as if he had come into her presence and began to plead the case with him:

"Do you seek to deny," she asked, "that my husband died at your hands?"

"That," he said, "I cannot deny, and I fully grant it."

"Then tell me why you did it. To hurt me, or out of hatred or spite?"

"May I never have respite from death if ever I did it to hurt you."

"Then you have done no wrong to me; nor did you wrong him, for had he been able he would have killed you. Therefore it seems to me I've given a just and rightful judgment."

In this manner she herself found good cause and reason for not hating him. She spoke in a manner conforming to her wishes and by her own efforts kindled her love, like the log that smokes as soon as the flame is put to it, without anyone blowing or fanning it. And if the damsel were to return now, she would win the quarrel that she'd so avidly argued and for which she'd been so bitterly reproached.

The damsel did return in the morning and took up the matter just where she'd left it off; and the lady kept her head lowered, because she felt guilty for having spoken ill of her; but now she wanted to make amends and ask her the knight's name, rank, and lineage. So she humbled herself wisely and said: "I want to beg your forgiveness for the insults and prideful words that I foolishly spoke to you; I shall always abide by your advice. But tell me, if you know, about the knight of whom you spoke to me at such length: what sort of man is he, and of what lineage? If he is of a rank suitable for me and does not hold himself aloof, I promise you that I will make him my husband and lord of my land. But he must behave in such a way that people will not blame me and say: 'That's the woman who took the man who killed her husband.'"

"In God's name, my lady, it will be so. You will have the noblest and the finest and the fairest lord who ever came from Abel's line."

"What is his name?"

"My lord Yvain."

"In faith, he's not baseborn, but of the highest nobility; of this I'm sure, since he is the son of King Urien."

"By my faith, my lady, you are right."

"And when can we have him here?"

"In five days."

"That's too long, for I wish he were here already. Have him come tonight or tomorrow at the latest."

"My lady, I don't think a bird could fly so far in one day. But I shall send one of my servants who is swift of foot, who will make it to the court of King Arthur, I should think, no later than tomorrow evening, for he cannot be found before then." [1835]

"This delay is much too long: the days are long. But tell him he must be back here tomorrow evening and that he must go more swiftly than ever, for if he chooses to push himself hard, he can make two days out of one. Moreover the moon will be out tonight, which will turn the night into day. Upon his return I will give him whatever he wants me to give."

"Leave this task to me and you will have him in your hands within three days at the latest. Meanwhile you must summon your people and seek their counsel concerning the imminent arrival of the king. In order to maintain the custom of defending your spring, it behooves you to seek good advice; and there's none of them haughty enough to dare boast he would go there. Therefore you can properly say that you must remarry. A very renowned knight has sought your hand, but you dare not take him unless they all accept him. And I can promise you this much: I know they are all so cowardly that, so as to burden another with the charge that would be too heavy for them, they will all fall at your feet and be grateful to you, for they will no longer be in fear. Because whoever's afraid of his own shadow will gladly avoid, if he can, an encounter with lance or javelin, for to a coward such games are unwelcome."

"By my faith," the lady replied, "this I wish, and to this I consent; and I had already thought it out just as you have stated it, and we shall do it just so. But why are you tarrying here? Be off with you! Don't delay any further! Do what you must to bring him here, and I shall assemble my people."

Thus ended their conversation. The damsel pretended to send for my lord Yvain in his own land; and each day she bathed him, and washed and brushed his hair; and in the meantime she prepared for him a red woolen robe, lined in fur with the chalk still upon it. Whatever he needed to adorn himself, she was able to provide for him: a golden clasp at his neck, worked with precious stones, which makes one look quite fashionable, and a belt and purse made of a fabric trimmed with gold. When she had outfitted him fully, she told her lady that her messenger had returned, having carried out his task properly.

"What?" said she. "When will my lord Yvain come?"

"He's already here."

"He's here? Then have him come at once, secretly and privately while there is no one here with me. See to it that no one else comes, for I would hate to see a fourth person."

The damsel departed at once. She returned to her guest, but did not betray on her face the joy that her heart felt; instead she said that her lady knew that she had been keeping him there, adding: "By God, my lord Yvain, there's no use hiding any more, since word of you has spread so far that my lady knows you are here. She's reproached me harshly and has quarreled sharply with me over it, but she's given me her word that I can bring you into her presence without hurting or endangering you. And she will not harm you in any way, I believe, except that—and I mustn't lie to you about this, for I would be betraying you—she wants to have you in her prison, and she wants you imprisoned in such a way that not even your heart would be free."

"Indeed," he said, "I am fully in accord. This would not hurt me at all, for I very much want to be in her prison."

"And you shall be, I swear by this right hand that I now place upon you. Come along now, but remember my advice and behave so humbly in her presence that she will not imprison you harshly. Yet you needn't trouble yourself about this: I don't believe you'll find such imprisonment too unpleasant."

Thus the damsel led him along: troubling him, then reassuring him, and speaking in veiled words of the prison in which he'd be put, for no lover is without imprisonment; so she is right to call him a prisoner, for anyone who loves is a prisoner.   [1946]

The damsel led my lord Yvain by the hand to where he was much cherished; yet he feared he would be unwelcome, and it is no wonder that he was fearful. They found the lady seated upon a large red cushion. I assure you that my lord Yvain was very fearful as he entered the room where they found the lady. She spoke not a word to him; and this caused him to be more terrified, and he was frozen with fear because he was sure he'd been betrayed. He stood a long while there until the damsel spoke up and said: "Five hundred times accursed be the soul of the one who brings into a fair lady's room a knight who won't approach her and hasn't tongue or words or sense enough to introduce himself!"

Thereupon she pulled him by the arm, saying: "Come over here, sir knight, and don't be afraid that my lady will bite you! Now ask her for peace and accord, and I too will beg her to pardon you for the death of Esclados the Red, who was her husband."

My lord Yvain immediately clasped his hands, fell to his knees, and spoke as a true lover: "My lady, in truth I'll not seek your mercy, but will instead thank you for whatever you may choose to do with me, for nothing could displease me."

"Nothing, sir? And if I should kill you?"

"My lady, great thanks be to you, you'll never hear me say otherwise."

"Never before," said she, "have I heard such a thing: so you freely place yourself wholly in my power without my even compelling you?"

"My lady, it is no lie to state that there is no power so powerful as the one that commands me to consent to your will in everything. I am not afraid of doing anything that it may please you to command of me, and if I could make amends for the slaying, in which I did no wrong, then I would make it good without question."

"What?" she said. "Now tell me, and be forgiven the punishment, how you did me no wrong when you killed my husband?"

"My lady, if you please," he said, "when your husband attacked me, was I wrong to defend myself? If someone who tries to kill or capture another is himself killed by the other in self-defense, tell me, does that man commit any wrong?"

"He doesn't at all, if one judges rightly; and I think it would gain me nothing if I were to have you killed. Now I would gladly know what gives you the power to consent to my wishes without question. I absolve you of all wrongs and misdeeds; but sit down now and tell me what has over-powered you."

"My lady," he said, "the power comes from my heart, which is set on you; my heart has given me this desire."

"And what controls your heart, fair sir?"

"My eyes, my lady."

"And what controls your eyes?"

"The great beauty I see in you."

"And what wrong has beauty done?"

"My lady, such that it makes me love."

"Love, then, whom?"

"You, my dear lady."

"Me?"

"Indeed yes."

"In what way?"

"In such a way that it cannot be greater; in such a way that my heart does not quit you, and I never find it elsewhere; in such a way that I cannot think of anything else; in such a way that I give myself entirely to you; in such a way that I love you more than myself; in such a way that, should it please you, I would gladly live or die for you."

"And would you dare undertake to defend my spring for me?"

"Indeed yes, my lady, against all men."

"Know then that we are reconciled."

Thus they were swiftly reconciled. And the lady, who had consulted earlier with her barons, said: "From here we shall proceed to this hall where my people are, who advised and counseled me in view of the need, and authorized me to take a husband, which I will do, given the necessity. Here and now I give myself to you, for I should not refuse to marry a good knight and a king's son."   [2052]

Now the damsel has accomplished all that she had set out to do. My lord

Yvain was not upset, I can certainly tell you, as the lady took him with her into the hall, which was filled with knights and men-at-arms. My lord Yvain was so fair that they all gazed upon him in wonder. They all rose as the two of them entered, and they greeted my lord Yvain and bowed before him, surmising: "He is the one my lady will take; cursed be anyone who opposes him, for he seems exceptionally noble. Indeed the empress of Rome would find in him a worthy spouse. Would that he were already pledged to her and she to him with bare hand, so that she could wed him today or tomorrow."

Thus they all spoke excitedly together. At the head of the hall was a bench where the lady went to sit, where all could see her, and my lord Yvain made as if he wished to sit at her feet, until she raised him up. Then she summoned her seneschal to make his speech loudly enough that all might hear it, and the seneschal, who was neither disobedient nor slow of speech, began:

"My lords," said he, "war is upon us: not a day passes without the king making preparations as fast as he can to come lay waste to our lands. Before these two weeks are over, everything will be laid waste unless a good defender can be found. When my lady married, not even six full years ago, she did so on your advice. Her husband is now dead, which grieves her. He who held all this land and who did very well by it has but six feet of earth now: it's a great pity he lived such a short while. A woman does not know how to bear a shield or strike with a lance; she can help and improve herself greatly by taking a good husband. Our lady was never in greater need; all of you must urge her to take a husband before the custom is ended, which has been observed in this town for more than sixty years past."

On hearing these words they all agreed that it seemed a proper thing to do. They all fell at her feet, urging her to do what she already desired; and she let herself be begged to do her wish, until, as if it were against her will, she agreed to what she would have done even if they had all opposed her. "My lords," she said, "since it pleases you, this knight who is seated here beside me has ardently implored me and asked for my hand; he wishes to devote himself to my honor and my service, and I thank him for it, as you should likewise thank him. Indeed I did not know him before, but I have heard much said in his praise: he is of such nobility, know it well, as to be the son of King Urien. In addition to being of high lineage he is such a valiant knight and is so possessed of courtesy and wisdom that no one should discredit him before me. I believe that you have all heard tell of my lord Yvain: it is he who has asked for my hand. On the appointed day I shall have a nobler knight than I deserve."

"If you are to act wisely," they all said, "this day will not end before the marriage has taken place, for one is very much the fool to delay a single hour doing what is to his advantage."   [2140]

They implored her so much that she agreed to do what she would have done anyway, for Love commanded her to do that for which she asked their advice and counsel. But she took him with greater honor by having the consent of her people, and their urgings were not unwelcome; rather they moved and stirred her heart to do what pleased it. The running horse quickens its pace when it is spurred. In the presence of all her barons the lady gave herself to my lord Yvain. By the hand of one of her chaplains he took Laudine of Landuc, the lady who was daughter of Duke Laududez, of whom they sing a lay. That very day, without delay, he became engaged and they were wed. There were many miters and croziers there, for the lady had summoned her bishops and her abbots. There were many people of the highest nobility, and there was much happiness and pleasure, more than I could relate to you even were I to contemplate it for a long while; I prefer to keep silent rather than describe it poorly.

So now my lord Yvain is lord of her land and the dead knight is fully forgotten; he who killed him is married: he has taken his wife and they have slept together, and the people love and esteem more the living knight than ever they did the dead. They served him well at the wedding feast, which lasted until the evening before the king came to the marvel of the spring and stone.

King Arthur arrived with all his companions, for everyone in his household was in that troop of horsemen, and not a single knight had stayed behind.

Suddenly my lord Kay began to speak in this manner: "By God, now what has become of my lord Yvain, who hasn't come along, though he boasted after eating that he would go avenge his cousin? It's clear he spoke after the wine! He's fled, I can guess, because he wouldn't dare have come for anything. He boasted out of overweening pride. A man must be terribly bold to commend himself for something others don't praise him for, especially when he has no proof of his valor, unless it's through false flattery. There's a big difference between the braggart and the brave: the braggart tells tall stories about himself around the fire, thinking all his listeners are fools and that no one really knows him. But the brave man would be very upset if he heard his own valiant deeds being told to another. Nonetheless I can understand the braggart, for he's not wrong to praise and boast about himself, since he will find no one else to lie for him. If he doesn't say it, who will? The heralds are silent about them; they publicly proclaim the brave and cast the braggarts to the winds."

My lord Kay spoke in this manner, but my lord Gawain said: "Enough, my lord Kay, enough! Though my lord Yvain is not yet here, you cannot know what difficulty he's encountered. In truth he never so lowered himself as to speak basely of you, so steeped is he in courtesy."

"Sir," replied Kay, "I'll say no more, and you'll not hear me speak more about this today, since I see that it upsets you."   [2221]

Then the king, in order to behold the deluge, poured a full basin of water upon the stone beneath the pine, and it began at once to rain furiously. It was not very long before my lord Yvain rushed out fully armed into the forest and came riding faster than a gallop upon a tall and powerful horse, strong and hardy and swift. And it was my lord Kay's resolve to ask for the battle because, no matter what might be the outcome, he always wanted to begin the melees and skirmishes, or else he would become very angry. In front of everyone he came to the foot of the king and asked to be accorded the battle.

"Kay," said Arthur, "since it pleases you and since you have requested it in the presence of all, it must not be denied you."

Kay thanked him and then mounted. If my lord Yvain can cause him a little shame, he'll be delighted and will gladly do it, for he recognized him at once by his armor. He grasped his shield by the loops and Kay took his; they charged one another, spurred their steeds, and lowered the lances that each held tightly gripped. They thrust them forward a little until they held them by the leather-wrapped hilt; and as they rushed together they each struck with such mighty effort that both lances shattered and split right up to the handle. My lord Yvain gave Kay such a powerful blow that he somersaulted from his saddle and struck the ground with his helmet. My lord Yvain didn't wish to cause him further injury, so he dismounted and claimed his horse.

Some among them were pleased by this, and many were able to say: "Ha! Ha! Look at how you, who mocked the others, are lying there now! Yet it's only right that you be pardoned this time, because it's never happened to you before."

In the meantime my lord Yvain came before the king, leading Kay's horse by the bridle, because he wished to present it to Arthur. "Sir," said my lord Yvain, "accept this horse, for I would do wrong to keep anything of yours."

"And who are you?" asked the king. "It's impossible to recognize you unless I hear your name or see you without your armor."

When my lord Yvain stated his name, Kay was overcome with shame, dejected, speechless, and confounded for having said that he had run away. And the others were very happy and rejoiced in his success. Even the king was overjoyed; but my lord Gawain felt a hundred times more joy than anyone else, for he preferred Yvain's company to that of all the other knights he knew. And the king requested and begged him to tell them, if he did not mind, about his exploits; for he was most eager to know all about his adventure. He kept urging him to tell them truly, so Yvain told them all about the service and kindnesses the maiden had shown him; he didn't skip a single detail and forgot nothing.

Afterward he begged the king to come with all his knights and take lodging with him, for they would bring him honor and happiness if they would stay with him. The king said that for a full eight days he would gladly share his love, joy, and company; and my lord Yvain thanked him. They did not delay there any longer but mounted at once and rode straightway to the town. My lord Yvain sent his squire, who was carrying a cranefalcon, in advance of the company in order that they not catch the lady by surprise, and to give her people time to bedeck their houses for the king.

When the lady received word that the king was coming, she was delighted. Indeed everyone who heard the news was happy and elated by it. And the lady summoned all her subjects and urged them to go to greet him; and they didn't argue or complain, for everyone wished to do her will. They all set out upon great Spanish horses to welcome the king of Britain, and in loud voices they greeted first King Arthur and then all his company. "Welcome," they said, "to this company that is so full of noble men. Blessed be he who leads them and brings us such fine guests."

The town resounded with joyous preparations for the king. Silken cloths were brought forth and stretched out for decoration, and tapestries were used for pavement and spread out through the streets in anticipation of the king's arrival. And they did something else; because of the heat of the sun they stretched awnings over the streets. Bells, horns, and trumpets made the town reverberate so that God's thunder couldn't have been heard. Where they dismounted, maidens played flutes and pipes, snares, tambourines, and drums; for their part agile gymnasts performed their tricks; all sought to express their delight, and amidst this joy they welcomed their lord, exactly as they should receive him.

The lady also came forth, dressed in an imperial material, a robe of new ermine, with a diadem upon her head all studded with rubies. Her face showed no trace of sullenness but instead was so cheerful and radiant that, to my mind, she was more beautiful than any goddess. All around her the crowd was milling, and everyone kept repeating: "Welcome to the king, the lord of all kings and lords in the world." It was not possible for the king to answer them all, for he saw the lady approaching to hold his stirrup. But he didn't wish to await this, so he hurried to dismount and was off his horse as soon as he saw her. She greeted him and said: "Welcome a hundred thousand times to my lord the king, and blessed be my lord Gawain, his nephew."

"To your fair self and countenance, beautiful creature," replied the king, "may God grant happiness and good fortune."

Then King Arthur clasped her around the waist in a courteous and friendly manner, and she received him with open arms. I'll not speak of how she made the others welcome, but never afterward have I heard tell of a people welcomed so happily, shown such honor, or served so well.

I could tell you much about the joy, were it not a waste of words; but I wish only to make brief mention of the meeting that occurred in private between the moon and the sun. Do you know of whom I would speak? He who was chief of the knights and who was acclaimed above them all ought surely to be called the sun. I speak of my lord Gawain, for by him knighthood is made illustrious just as the sun in the morning shines down its rays and lights up wherever it touches. And I call her the moon, for there can be only one like her, in true fidelity and assistance. And yet I do not say it only for her great renown, but because she is called Lunete.   [2418]

The damsel was named Lunete and was a winsome brunette, very sensible, clever, and attractive. She made herself known to my lord Gawain, who esteemed her highly and loved her dearly; and he called her his sweetheart. Because she had saved his companion and friend from death, he offered her his service. And she described to him with what difficulty she had contended with her lady, to the end that she took my lord Yvain as her husband, and how she protected him from the hands of those who were seeking him: though he was in their midst they didn't see him. My lord Gawain was delighted at what she told him and said: "Young lady, I place myself in your service, such a knight as I am, whether you need me or not. Do not trade me for another unless you think you can do better; I am yours and you will be, from this day forth, my lady fair."

"I thank you, sir," said she.

Thus these two became acquainted; and the others gave themselves to one another, for there were some ninety ladies present, each one beautiful and fair, noble, attractive, prudent, and sensible, gentle ladies and of good lineage. There the knights could pass a pleasant moment embracing and kissing them, conversing with them, gazing upon them, and sitting beside them; this much pleasure at least they had.

Now my lord Yvain feted the king, who stayed with him; and the lady so honored him and his knights, one and all, that some fool among them might have thought that the favors and attentions she showed them came from Love. But we can consider simpleminded those who believe that when a lady is polite to some poor wretch, and makes him happy and embraces him, she's in love with him; a fool is happy for a little compliment and is easily cheered up by it. They devoted the entire week to splendid entertainment: the hunting and fishing were excellent for those who tried their hands at them; and those who wanted to see the land that my lord Yvain had acquired along with the lady he had married could go for a pleasant ride of six leagues, or five, or four to the neighboring towns.

When the king had stayed as long as he wished, he had preparations made for travel; but all week long his people had implored and begged him as persuasively as they could to be allowed to take my lord Yvain with them.

"What! Would you be one of those men," said my lord Gawain to my lord Yvain, "who are worth less because of their wives? May he who lessens his worth by marrying be shamed by Holy Mary! He who has a beautiful woman as wife or sweetheart should be the better for having her, for it's not right for her to love him if his fame and worth are lost. Indeed you would suffer afterward for her love if you were to lose your reputation, because a woman will quickly withdraw her love, and she's not wrong to do so, if she comes to hate a man who loses face in any way after he has become lord of the realm. Now, more than ever, your fame must grow! Break the leash and yoke and let us, you and me, go to the tourneys, so no one can call you a jealous husband. You shouldn't hesitate; rather you should frequent tournaments, engage in combat, and joust vigorously, whatever it might cost you. He who hesitates never acts! Indeed you must come along, for I'll fight under your banner. See to it that our friendship does not end, fair companion, because of you, for it will never fail on my account. It's strange how one hopes for a life of ease that never comes. Pleasures grow sweeter when delayed, and small pleasures are more delightful when postponed than great ones are enjoyed today. The joy of love that comes later is like the green log burning, for it gives off more heat and burns longer, since it is slower to get started. One can get used to something that then becomes very difficult to forsake; and when one wants to forsake it, he cannot. I don't say this lightly, for if I had as beautiful a lady as you have, fair sweet friend, by the faith I place in God and the saints, I'd be very reluctant to leave her! I know I'd be infatuated myself. But a man can give good advice to another who cannot heed such advice himself, much like those preachers who are sinful lechers, but who teach and preach the good that they have no intention of practicing themselves!"   [2542]

My lord Gawain spoke at such length about this matter and so implored him that my lord Yvain agreed to speak with his wife and to accompany him if he could obtain her leave. Whether it was a wise or foolish choice, he would not stop until he had permission to return to Britain.

He then conferred in private with his lady, who had no idea he wished her leave. "My most dear lady," he said to her, "you who are my heart and soul, my wealth, my joy, and my well-being, grant me one favor for your honor and mine."

The lady unhesitatingly granted it, for she was unaware of what he intended to ask. "Fair sir, you may ask me for whatever favor you please."

My lord Yvain immediately requested leave to accompany the king and frequent the tourneys, lest he be called a coward. And she said: "I grant you leave until a date I shall fix. But the love I have for you will become hatred, you can be sure of that, if you should stay away beyond the period I shall set for you. Be assured that I'll not break my word; if you break yours, I'll still be true to mine: if you wish to have my love and if you cherish me in the least, remember to return promptly, and no later than one year at most, eight days after the feast of St. John, for today is the octave of that feast. You will be banished from my love if you are not back here with me on that day."

My lord Yvain wept and sighed so deeply that he could hardly say: "My lady, this period is too long. If I could be a dove, as often as I wished I would be back with you. And I beg God that it please Him not to let me overstay my leave. Yet a man may intend to return promptly and not know what the future holds. And I don't know what will happen to me, whether illness or imprisonment will detain me; you are too exacting if you do not make exception at least for physical hindrances."

"Sir," she said, "I do make this exception; nonetheless I truly swear to you that, if God keeps you from death, no physical impediment awaits you as long as you remember me. Now put this ring of mine upon your finger and let me tell you all about the stone: no true and faithful lover, if he wears it, can be imprisoned or lose any blood, nor can any ill befall him; but whoever wears and cherishes it will remember his sweetheart and will become stronger than iron. It will be your shield and hauberk; in truth I have never before lent or entrusted it to any knight, but out of love I give it to you."

Now my lord Yvain has his leave; he wept profusely upon taking it. And the king did not wish to delay any longer despite anything one might have said to him; rather he was eager to have all their palfreys brought forward, equipped and bridled. His wish was no sooner expressed than done: the palfreys were led forth and there was nothing to do but to mount. I don't know how much I should tell of my lord Yvain's departure, or of the kisses showered upon him, which were mingled with tears and flavored with sweetness. And what should I tell you of the king? How the lady escorted him with all her maidens and all her knights as well? It would take too long. Since the lady was weeping, the king urged her to stop and to return to her manor; he urged her so insistently that in great distress she turned back, leading her people with her. [2642]

My lord Yvain left his lady so reluctantly that his heart stayed behind. The king might take his body with him, but there was no way he could have the heart, because she who remained behind clung so tightly to that heart that he had no power to take it with him. Once the body is without the heart, it cannot possibly stay alive, and no man had ever before seen a body live on without its heart. Yet now this miracle happened, for Yvain remained alive without his heart, which used to be in his body, but which refused to accompany it now. The heart was well kept, and the body lived in hope of rejoining the heart; thus it made for itself a strange sort of heart from Hope, which often plays the traitor and breaks his oath. Yet I don't think the hour will ever come when Hope will betray him; and if he stays a single day beyond the period agreed upon, he will be hard pressed ever again to make a truce or peace with his lady.

Yet I believe he will stay beyond it, for my lord Gawain will not let him leave his company; both of them frequented the tournaments wherever there was jousting. The year passed swiftly and my lord Yvain did so splendidly all year long that my lord Gawain took great pains to honor him; and he caused him to delay so long that the entire year passed and a good bit of the next, until it reached mid-August, when the king was holding court at Chester.

The previous evening they had returned there from a tournament where my lord Yvain had fought and carried off all the glory. The story tells, I believe, that neither of the two companions wanted to take lodgings in the town but had their tent set up instead outside the town and held court there; they never came to the king's court, but instead the king attended theirs, for with them were the finest knights and the greatest number of them. King Arthur was seated in their midst when Yvain suddenly began to reflect; since the moment he had taken leave of his lady, he had not been so distraught as now, for he knew for a fact that he had broken his word to her and stayed beyond the period set. With great difficulty he held back his tears, but shame forced him to hold them.

He was still downcast when they saw a damsel coming straight toward them, approaching rapidly on a dappled black palfrey. She dismounted before their tent without anyone helping her, and without anyone seeing to her horse. And as soon as she caught sight of the king, she let fall her mantle and without it she entered the tent and approached the king. She said that her lady sent greetings to the king and my lord Gawain and all the others, except Yvain, the liar, the deceiver, the unfaithful one, the cheat, for he had beguiled and deceived her. She had clearly seen through his guile, for he had pretended to be a true lover but was a cheat, a seducer, and a thief. "This thief has seduced my lady, who had not experienced such evil and could never have believed that he would steal her heart. Those who love truly don't steal hearts, but there are those who call true lovers thieves, while they themselves only pretend to love and in reality know nothing about it. The true lover takes his lady's heart but would never steal it; instead he protects it so that those thieves who appear to be honorable men can't steal it. Such men are hypocritical thieves and traitors who strive to steal the hearts of those they don't really care about; but the true lover cherishes his lady's heart wherever he goes and returns it to her. My lord Yvain has slain my lady, for she thought he would keep her heart and bring it back to her before the year had passed. Yvain, you were most negligent not to remember that you were to return to my lady within one year; she gave you leave until the feast of St. John, yet you cared so little that you never again thought of her. My lady marked in her room each day and each season, for one who loves truly is troubled and can never get a good sleep, but all night long counts and reckons the days as they come and go. This is how true lovers pass the time and seasons. Her complaint is not unreasonable, nor is it premature; I am not bringing it up to cause a scene but am simply stating that the one who married you to my lady has betrayed us.   [2770]

"Yvain, my lady no longer cares for you, and through me she orders you never again to approach her and not to keep her ring any longer. By me, whom you see here before you, she orders you to send it back to her: return it, for return it you must!"

Yvain could not answer her, for mind and words failed him; the damsel stepped forward and took the ring from his finger; then she commended to God the king and all the others, except him whom she left in great anguish. And his anguish grew constantly, for everything he saw added to his grief and everything he heard troubled him; he wanted to flee all alone to a land so wild that no one could follow or find him, and where no man or woman alive could hear news of him any more than if he had gone to perdition. He hated nothing so much as himself and did not know whom to turn to for comfort, since he was bringing on his own death. But he would rather lose his mind than be unable to take revenge upon himself, who had taken away his own happiness.

He slipped out from among the barons, because he was afraid of going mad in their presence. No one took particular notice of this, and they let him go off alone: they were well aware that he did not care for their conversation or company. And he went on until he was far from the tents and pavilions. Then such a great whirlwind arose in his head that he went mad; he ripped and tore at his clothing and fled across fields and plains, leaving his people puzzled and wondering where he could be. They went seeking for him right and left among the knight's lodgings and through the hedgerows and orchards, but they were seeking him where he wasn't to be found.

And he ran on and on until he encountered, beside a park, a youth who had a bow and five barbed arrows, whose tips were broad and sharp. Yvain approached the youth, from whom he took the bow and arrows he was holding; yet afterward he didn't remember anything he had done. He stalked wild animals in the forest and killed them and ate their flesh raw. [2830]

He lived in the forest like a madman and a savage, until one day he came upon a hermit's abode, very small and cramped. The hermit was working his land; when he saw the naked stranger he was certain beyond any doubt that the man did not have all his senses; of this he was absolutely certain. From the fright it gave him he dove into his little hut. The good man in his charity took some bread and clear water and placed it outside his house upon a narrow window ledge; and Yvain, who was eager for the bread, came up; he took and bit into it. I don't believe he'd ever tasted such hard and bitter bread; the measure of barley kneaded with straw, from which the bread was made that was sourer than yeast, had not cost twenty sous; and moreover it was moldy through and through and as dry as bark. But hunger so tormented and afflicted him that the bread tasted to him like gravy. For hunger is a gravy that blends well and is suited to all foods. My lord Yvain quickly devoured the hermit's bread, which seemed good to him, and drank cold water from the pitcher.

After he had eaten, he plunged again into the woods and hunted stags and does. And the good man in his hut, when he saw him leave, prayed to God to protect the stranger and keep him from ever returning this way. But no one, no matter how mad, would fail to return very gladly to a place where he has been kindly received. Not a week passed during Yvain's period of madness that he didn't bring to the hermit's door some wild game. This was the life he led from that day on; and the good man undertook to skin the game and put a sufficient amount of the meat on to cook; and the bread and the pitcher of water were always at the window to nourish the madman; thus for food and drink he had venison without salt or pepper, and cool spring water. And the good man was at pains to sell the skins and purchase unleavened bread of barley and oats.

From then on Yvain always had his fill of bread and meat, which the hermit provided for him, until one day he was discovered sleeping in the forest by a lady and two damsels from her household. One of the three ran and dismounted beside the naked man they had seen; she examined him closely before she could find any mark upon him by which he could be recognized; yet she had seen him so often that she would have recognized him immediately had he been as richly attired as he had been many times before. She was slow to recognize him, but she kept looking until in the end she realized that a scar he had upon his face was like a scar that my lord Yvain had upon his; she was sure of this, for she had often noticed it. She recognized him by the scar and was certain beyond doubt that it was he; but she had no idea how it had happened that he was found here destitute and naked. She crossed herself repeatedly in amazement; she didn't touch or awaken him, but took her horse, remounted, and came to the others and told them with tears in her eyes what she had seen.   [2921]

I don't know whether I should waste time telling of all the sadness she displayed, but weeping she said to her mistress: "My lady, I have found Yvain, the most accomplished knight in the world, and the most virtuous; but I do not know what misfortune has befallen the noble man; perhaps some grief has caused him to behave in this manner; one can certainly go mad with grief. And one can clearly see that he is not in his right mind, for truly nothing could have made him behave so basely if he had not lost his mind. Now may God restore his wits as good as they were before, and then may it please him to remain in your service, for Count Alier, who is making war on you, has wickedly invaded your lands. I can foresee the war between you ending to your advantage, if God so favored him that he were restored to his senses and would undertake to help you in this need."

"Now don't worry," the lady said, "because if he doesn't run away I feel sure that with God's help we can remove all the madness and turmoil from his head. But we must set off at once, for I recall an ointment given me by Morgan the Wise; she told me that it could drive away any madness, however great, from the head."

They set off at once toward the town, which was so close by that it was not more than half a league away, measured in the leagues of that land, for measured against ours, two of their leagues make one of ours, and four make two. Yvain remained sleeping alone while the lady went to fetch the ointment. She unfastened one of her cases and withdrew a flask that she entrusted to the damsel, urging her not to be too liberal with it, to rub only his temples and forehead, for there was no need to use it elsewhere. She should apply the ointment only to his temples and forehead and conserve the rest of it carefully, for he didn't suffer anywhere else, only in his brain. She sent along a bright-colored shift, a coat, and a mantle of red-dyed silk. The damsel brought this for him, and also led by her right hand a fine palfrey; and from her own belongings she added a shirt and soft breeches, and black, fine-spun stockings.

With all these things she returned so swiftly that she found him still sleeping there where she had left him. She placed the two horses in a clearing, tying and tethering them well; then with the gown and ointment she came to where he was sleeping, and she showed real courage in approaching the madman close enough to touch and treat him. She took the ointment and rubbed it over him until there was none left in the box, for she was so eager to heal him that she applied the ointment everywhere; she lavished it all upon him, not heeding her mistress's warning, nor even recalling it. She applied more than was necessary; but she used it to good purpose, so she thought: she rubbed his temples and his forehead and his entire body down to his toes.

She rubbed his temples and his whole body so vigorously under the hot sun that she expelled the madness and melancholy from his brain; but she was foolish to anoint his body, for it was of no avail to him. Had there been five measures of the ointment she would have done the same, I believe. [3013]

She hurried off carrying the box and hid herself near her horse, but she didn't take the gown with her because, if he awakened, she wanted him to see it there ready for him, and to take it and put it on. She stayed behind a large oak until he had slept enough and was healed and rested and had regained his senses and memory. But then he saw that he was as naked as an ivory statuette; he was ashamed and would have been more so had he realized what had happened to him; but he didn't know why he was naked. Before him he saw the new gown; he wondered greatly how and by what chance this gown had come to be there; he was disturbed and embarrassed at seeing his own bare flesh and said that he would be dead and betrayed had anyone who knew him found or seen him in this state.

Quickly he dressed himself and looked out into the forest to see if anyone was approaching. He attempted to rise and stand upright, but didn't have strength enough to walk. He needed to find a helper to aid and lead him, because his grave malady had so weakened him that he could barely stand upon his feet. Now the damsel didn't wish to delay any longer but mounted her palfrey and rode by him as if she hadn't noticed him. In desperate need of help of any kind to lead him to a hostelry until he could regain his strength somewhat, he made a great effort to call to her. And the damsel began looking about her as if she didn't realize what was the matter with him. Feigning fright, she rode back and forth, since she didn't want to go directly to him. And he began to call her again: "Damsel, this way! this way!"

Then the damsel directed her ambling palfrey toward him. By behaving in this manner she led him to believe that she knew nothing about him and had never seen him before, and in doing so she behaved wisely and courteously. When she came before him, she said to him: "Sir knight, what do you want, calling to me in such distress?"

"Ah!" said he, "prudent damsel, I have found myself in these woods, but I don't know by what misfortune. In the name of God and your faith in Him, I beg you only that you lend or give me outright this palfrey that you are leading."

"Gladly, sir, but come along with me where I'm going."

"Which way?" he asked.

"Out of these woods, to a town I know of nearby."

"Fair damsel, now tell me if I can be of service to you."

"Yes," she said, "but I don't think you are at all well just now; you'll have to remain with us at least two weeks. Take the horse I'm holding and let's go find you lodgings."

And he, who asked nothing better, took it and mounted. They rode until they came to the middle of a bridge over a swift and roaring stream. The damsel threw the empty box she had been carrying into the stream, because in this way she hoped to excuse herself to her mistress for the ointment. She would tell her that in crossing the bridge she had accidentally dropped the box into the water: the box slipped from her grasp when the palfrey stumbled beneath her, and she herself had nearly fallen in after it, which would have been even worse. She intended to use this lie when she came before her mistress.

They rode along together until they reached the town; there the lady welcomed my lord Yvain cheerfully. When they were alone, she asked the damsel for her box of ointment, and the damsel told her the lie just as she had worked it out, for she dared not tell her the truth. The lady was terribly upset and said: "This is a dreadful loss, for I'm quite certain that it will never again be found. But once something has been lost there is nothing to be done but do without it. One often thinks things will turn out well that later turn out ill; so I, who thought this knight would bring me wealth and joy, have now lost the most precious and best of my possessions. Nonetheless I want to urge you to serve him above all others."

"Ah, my lady, you speak wisely now, for it would be a terrible thing to turn one misfortune into two."   [3134]

Then they spoke no more of the box and proceeded to look to my lord Yvain's comfort in every way they could: they bathed him, washed his hair, and had him shaved and trimmed, for one could have plucked a whole fistful of beard from his face. Whatever he wished they did for him: if he wanted armor, it was laid out for him; if he wanted a horse, a large and handsome, strong and hardy one awaited him. Yvain remained there until one Tuesday when Count Alier approached the town with men-at-arms and knights and set fires about it and pillaged the land. Those within the town straightway mounted their horses and donned their armor; some armed, but others yet unarmed, they sallied forth until they met the plunderers, who, not deigning to flee before them, awaited them at a pass. My lord Yvain, having now rested long enough to have had fully recovered his strength, struck into the thick of the press. He hammered a knight's shield so forcefully that I think he knocked knight and horse together in a heap: this knight never arose again, for his back was broken and his heart burst within his breast.

My lord Yvain backed off a little and recovered his breath; covering himself completely with his shield, he rushed to clear the pass. More quickly and more easily than you could count one, two, three, and four, you could behold him dispatch four knights. And those who were with him took courage from his example; for a man with a poor and timid heart, when he sees a brave man undertake a bold deed before his very eyes, will be overcome at once with disgrace and shame, and will discard the weak heart within his body; in this way he receives steadfastness, bravery, and a good man's heart. Thus these men grew bold and each stood his place bravely in the melee and battle.

The lady, who had climbed high into her castle tower, saw that the melee had succeeded in capturing the pass, and she saw many dead and wounded lying upon the ground, both friends and foes, but more of the enemy than her own, for the courtly, brave, and good Sir Yvain had forced them all to cry mercy just as the falcon does the teal. And all those men and women who had remained in the town and were watching from the battlements said: "Ah, what a valiant warrior! See how he makes his enemies bow before him! How fiercely he attacks them! He strikes among them like a lion among the fallow deer when hunger besets and assails it. And our knights are all bolder and braver than before; and were it not for him alone, no lances would have been broken nor swords drawn for fighting. One must love and cherish a valiant man whenever he is found. See now how he proves himself; see how he rises up in the battle line; now see how he stains his lance and naked sword with blood; see how he pursues them; see how he drives them back, how he charges them, how he overtakes them, how he gives way, how he returns to the attack! But he spends little time in turning and much in renewing the attack. See what little care he has for his shield when he comes into the fray: how he lets it be slashed to pieces; he doesn't take the least pity upon it, but he is most eager to avenge the blows that are rained upon him. If the whole Argonne Forest were felled to make lances for him, I don't believe he'd have a single one left this night; one could not place so many in his lance-rest that he'd not split them all and call for more. And see how he wields his sword when he draws it! Roland never caused such devastation with Durendal against the Turks at Roncevaux or in Spain. If Yvain had in his company a few good comrades like himself, the villain we deplore would leave defeated or remain a captive in disgrace." [3246]

And they added that she to whom he granted his love was born in a lucky hour, for he was mighty in arms and as renowned above all others as a torch among candles, and the moon among the stars, and the sun above the moon. And he so won over the hearts of every man and woman there that all of them wanted him to marry their lady and rule over their land because of the prowess they perceived in him.

Thus they praised him one and all and spoke the truth in doing so, for he had so beset their enemies that they had fled in disorder. But he and all his companions after him pursued them hotly, for beside him they felt as safe as if they were enclosed by a high thick wall of hard stone. The chase lasted a long time, until finally those who were fleeing grew weary and their pursuers cut down and eviscerated all their horses. The living rolled over the dead, killing and slaying one another; they came together violently.

Meanwhile Count Alier fled with my lord Yvain, who did not hesitate to follow him, in hot pursuit. He gave chase until he overtook him at the foot of a steep hill, quite near the entrance to one of his mighty fortresses. The count was caught at this spot, and nothing could help him now. Without much discussion my lord Yvain accepted his surrender, for once he had him in his hands and they were alone, one against one, there was no escaping, no evasion, no means of defense. Instead the count swore to surrender himself to the lady of Noroison, to place himself in her captivity, and to make peace on her terms. And when Yvain had accepted his oath, he had him uncover his head, remove his shield from about his neck, and tender him his naked sword. His was the honor of leading off the captured count; he turned him over to his enemies, whose joy was boundless.

As soon as the news reached the town, everyone, man and woman alike, came forth to meet them, with the lady of the castle leading the way. My lord Yvain, who held the prisoner by his hand, presented him to her. The count acceded fully to her wishes and demands, and assured her of his faith with promises, oaths, and pledges. He gave her his pledge and swore that he would hold peace with her from that day forth, that he would make good all losses that she could prove, and would build anew the houses that he had razed to the ground. When these things had been arranged to the lady's satisfaction, my lord Yvain asked for leave, which she would not have given him had he agreed to take her as his mistress or his wife.

He would not allow anyone to follow or accompany him, but left immediately in spite of all entreaties. Now he returned along the road from which he'd come and left the lady, to whom he had brought great joy, much chagrined. And the greater the joy he had brought her, the more now it disheartened and grieved her that he refused to stay, for now she wished to do him honor and would have made him, had he agreed, the lord of all she had, or would have given him generous payment for his services, as much as he wished to take. But he refused to listen to anything anyone might say; he left the lady and her knights, though it pained him that he could remain there no longer.   [3344]

My lord Yvain rode pensively through a deep wood until he heard from the thick of the forest a most dolorous and loud cry. He headed immediately toward the place where he had heard the cry, and when he arrived at a clearing, he saw a dragon holding a lion by the tail and burning his flanks with its flaming breath. My lord Yvain did not waste time observing this marvel; he asked himself which of the two he would help; then he said that he would take the lion's part, since a venomous and wicked creature deserves only harm, and the dragon was venomous, and fire leapt from its mouth because it was so full of wickedness. Therefore my lord Yvain determined that he would slay it first; he drew his sword and came forward with his shield before his face, so as not to be harmed by the flame pouring from the dragon's mouth, which was larger than a cauldron. If the lion attacked him later, he would not lack for a fight, but with no heed to the consequences Yvain was determined to help him now, since pity summoned and urged him to aid and succor the noble and honorable beast. He pursued the wicked dragon with his trenchant sword; he cut it through to the ground and then cut the two parts in half again; he struck it repeatedly until it was hacked into tiny pieces. However, he was obliged to cut off a piece of the lion's tail, that the wicked dragon was still clutching in its teeth; he cut off only as much as he had to and could not have taken off less.

Once he had rescued the lion, he still thought that it would attack him and he would have to do battle with it; but the lion would never have done that. Listen to how nobly and splendidly the lion acted: he stood up upon his hind paws, bowed his head, joined his forepaws and extended them toward Yvain, in an act of total submission; then he knelt down and his whole face was bathed in tears of humility. My lord Yvain recognized clearly that the lion was thanking him and submitting to him because he had slain the dragon and delivered him from death; these actions pleased him greatly. He wiped the dragon's poisonous filth from his sword, which he replaced in his scabbard, and set off again upon his way. Yet the lion stayed by his side and never left him; from that day on he would accompany him, for he intended to serve and protect him. The lion went along ahead of Yvain until, from his vantage point, he scented on the wind some wild beasts grazing; hunger and natural instinct summoned him to begin to prowl and hunt in order to procure his food; Nature intended him to do so.

He set out upon the trail enough to show his master that he had caught the scent of wild game. Then he stopped and looked at Yvain, for he wished to do his will in serving him; he did not want to go anywhere against his master's will. Yvain perceived by the lion's behavior that he was awaiting his permission. He clearly understood that if he held back, the lion too would hold back, and if he followed him, the lion would capture the game that he had scented. So he called to him and ordered him as one would a hound. The lion immediately put his nose in the air to catch the scent; and it had not deceived him, for he had not gone a bowshot's distance when he saw in a valley a roe-deer grazing all alone. He'd catch it at once, if he could, and did so with his first spring, and drank its still warm blood. After he had killed it, he tossed it over his back and carried it until he came before his lord, who afterward cherished him more because of the great devotion within him.   [3457]

Since it was now near nightfall, Yvain chose to spend the night there, where he could strip as much from the deer as he wished to eat. Then he began to carve it: he split the hide above the ribs and cut a roast from its loin; he struck a spark from a piece of flint and started a fire in some dry wood; then he straightway placed his roast on a spit over the fire to cook; he roasted it until it was done, but it was not a pleasure to eat, for he had no bread or wine or salt, no cloth, no knife, nor anything else. While he ate, his lion lay at his feet without moving, gazing fixedly at him until he had eaten as much of his roast as he wanted. Then the lion ate what was left of the deer, down to the bones. And while Yvain laid his head all night upon his shield and got what rest he could, the lion showed such sense that it stayed awake and took care to watch over his horse, which was grazing on grass that provided it some little nourishment.   [3486]

In the morning they set off together and when evening came, it seems to me, they did as they had done the preceding night; and this continued for nearly two weeks, until chance brought them to the spring beneath the pine tree. There my lord Yvain nearly lost his mind again as he neared the spring, the stone, and the chapel. A thousand times he sighed, and he was so grief-stricken that he fell in a faint; and his sword, which was polished, slid from the scabbard and pierced through the mail of his hauberk at his neck, below his cheek; the chain links separated and the sword cut the flesh of his neck beneath the shining mail, causing blood to gush forth. The lion thought he saw his companion and master lying dead; you've never heard tell of any greater grief than he began at once to show, for he twisted and clawed and bellowed and wanted to kill himself upon the sword, which he thought had slain his master. With his teeth he took the sword from Yvain;

he laid it over a fallen tree and propped it against a trunk behind, so that it wouldn't slip or fall when he ran his breast against it. His intention was nearly fulfilled when Yvain awoke from his faint; the lion, which was running headlong toward death like the mad boar that pays no heed to what he runs into, stopped his charge.

My lord Yvain had fainted, as I've told you, by the fountain's stone; when he came to, he bitterly reviled himself for having overstayed the year and earned his lady's hatred. "Why does the wretch who's destroyed his own happiness not kill himself?" he asked. "Why do I, wretch that I am, not kill myself? How can I stay here and behold my lady's possessions? Why does my soul remain in my body? What good is a soul in such a sad body? If it had flown away, it would not be suffering so. It is fitting that I despise and blame myself greatly, as indeed I do. He who through his own fault loses his happiness and his comfort should feel a mortal hatred for himself. Truly he ought to despise himself and seek to end his life. And what keeps me from killing myself now when no one is watching? Have I not observed this lion so disconsolate just now on my behalf that he was determined to run my sword through his breast? And should I, whose joy has changed to grief, fear death? All happiness and comfort have abandoned me. I'll say no more, because no one could speak of this; I've posed a foolish question. Of all joys the greatest was the one assured to me; yet it lasted such a little while! And he who loses such joy by his own mistake has no right to good fortune!"   [3564]

While he was lamenting in this fashion, a poor, sad prisoner who was locked within the chapel overheard this lament through a crack in the wall. As soon as Yvain had recovered from his faint, the prisoner called to him: "Heavens!" said she. "What do I see there? Who is lamenting so bitterly?"

"Who are you?" he queried.

"I," said she, "am a prisoner, the saddest creature alive."

"Hush, foolish creature!" he replied. "Your grief is joy and your suffering bliss compared to those that I endure. The more a man has learned to live in happiness and joy, the more does grief, when he suffers it, upset and destroy his senses than another man's. A weak man can carry a weight, when he is accustomed and used to it, that a stronger man could never manage to carry."

"In faith," said she, "I know well that what you say is true; but that is no reason to think that you suffer more than I. Therefore I don't believe it, because it seems to me that you can go anywhere you please, while I'm imprisoned here. And moreover I am doomed to be taken from here tomorrow and put to death."

"Ah, God!" said he, "for what crime?"

"Sir knight, may God never have mercy on the soul in my body if I've deserved it in the least! Yet I shall tell you the truth and never lie about it: I am imprisoned here because I am accused of treason and I cannot find anyone to defend me from being burned or hanged tomorrow."   [3608]

"Now to begin with," he said, "I can say that my grief and my misery surpass your suffering, for anyone can save you from death. Am I not right?"

"Yes, but I don't yet know who will. There are only two men left who would dare engage in battle for me against three men."

"What? In God's name, are there three of them?"

"Yes, sire, by my faith: there are three who accuse me of treason."

"And who are the two knights who love you so dearly that either one would be brave enough to face three men singlehanded in order to defend and rescue you?"

"I shall tell you without falsehood: one is my lord Gawain and the other my lord Yvain, for whose sake I shall be unjustly handed over tomorrow to death."

"For whose sake did you say?" asked Yvain.

"Sire, so help me God, for the son of King Urien."

"Now I've understood you clearly; yet you shall never die without him. I myself am that Yvain for whom you are in these straits. And you are she, I believe, who protected me in the entry hall; you saved my life and my body between the two portcullises, where I was downcast, sad, anxious, and distressed. I would have been captured and killed had it not been for your good help. Now tell me, my sweet friend, who those men are who have accused you of treason and have imprisoned you in this remote place."

"Sire, since you wish me to tell you, I'll not hide it from you any longer. It is true that I did not hesitate to aid you in good faith. Through my urgings my lady took you as her husband; she accepted my advice and counsel, and by our Holy Father in Heaven I intended it then and still think it more to her benefit than yours. This much I confess to you now: I sought to serve her honor and your desire, as God is my help. But when it happened that you overstayed the year after which you should have returned here to my lady, she grew angry with me at once and felt very much deceived for having trusted me. And when the seneschal—a wicked, dishonest, disloyal man, who was extremely jealous of me because my lady trusted me more than him in many things—heard of this, he saw then that he could foment a real quarrel between us. In front of everyone assembled at court he accused me of betraying her for you. I had no aid or counsel except myself alone, and I said that I had never conceived or committed treason against my lady. In my confusion I replied, hastily and without advice from anyone, that I would have myself defended by one knight against three. The seneschal was not courtly enough to think of refusing this challenge, nor could I get out of it or change it for anything that might happen. So he took me at my word, and I had to offer assurances to produce one knight prepared to fight three within forty days. Since that time I have been to many courts: I was at King Arthur's court but found no one there to advise me, nor did I find anyone who could tell me anything encouraging about you, for they had heard no news." [3699]

"Pray tell me," queried my lord Yvain, "where was the noble and kind lord Gawain? He never failed to help a damsel in distress."

"He would have made me joyful and happy if I had found him at court: I could never have asked anything of him that would have been refused me; but a knight has carried off the queen, they tell me, and the king was assuredly mad to send her off with him. And Kay, I believe, escorted her to meet the knight who has carried her off; and now my lord Gawain, who is seeking her, has embarked upon a difficult task. He will never rest a single day until he has found her. I have told you the entire truth about my situation. Tomorrow I shall die a hideous death and be burned without pity because of your shameful crime."

"May it never please God that anyone harm you on my account!" he replied. "As long as I'm alive, you shall not die! Tomorrow you can look for me, outfitted in accord with my rank, to place myself at your command, as it is fitting for me to do. But you mustn't tell anyone who I am; no matter what happens in the battle, be careful that I am not recognized!"

"Indeed, sire, no amount of torture could compel me to reveal your name: I will suffer death first, since you wish it so. And yet I beg you not to return there on my account; I don't want you to undertake such a desperate fight. I thank you for promising to do it so willingly, but consider yourself free of your oath, for it is better that I alone die than see them delight in your death. Were they to kill you, still they'd not spare me; so it's better that you remain alive than for both of us to die."

"It pains me to hear what you've said," answered my lord Yvain. "Fair friend, either you do not want to be delivered from death, or else you scorn the favor of my offer to help. I don't want to argue with you further, for you have done so much for me, indeed, that I must not fail you in any need that you might have. I know that you are distraught; but, if it please God in whom I trust, all three of them will be put to shame. No more of this now; I must go to seek what shelter I can in this wood, for I don't know of any lodging near to hand."

"Sire," said she, "may God grant you both good lodging and a good night, and may He protect you from anything that might do you harm."

My lord Yvain left at once, accompanied as ever by his lion. They traveled along until they neared a baron's stronghold that was enclosed all about by a thick, strong, and high wall. The town, which was extremely well fortified, feared no assault by mangonel or catapult. Outside the walls the entire area had been cleared so that no hut or house remained standing. You will be told the cause for this later, when the time comes.

My lord Yvain made his way straight toward the stronghold; as many as seven squires appeared, lowered a drawbridge for him, and advanced toward him. But they were very frightened by the lion they saw accompanying him, and they asked him to please leave his lion at the gate so it wouldn't attack or kill them. "Say no more about it," he replied, "for I'll not enter without him: either we will both be given lodging or I shall remain out here, for I love him as much as myself. Yet you needn't be afraid of him, for I shall watch him so carefully that you need have no fears."

"Well then, let it be!" they replied.   [3804]

Then they entered the town and rode until they encountered knights, ladies, men-at-arms, and charming damsels approaching, who greeted him, helped him dismount, and saw to removing his armor. They said to him: "May you be welcome, sire, among us here, and may God grant you to stay until you can leave with great happiness and honor."

Everyone, from the highest to the lowest, did his best to make him feel welcome; amid great rejoicing they showed him to his lodgings. Yet after they had shown their gladness, grief overwhelmed them and made them forget their joy; they began to cry out, to weep, and to tear at themselves. So for a long while they continued in this manner, alternating joy and weeping: in order to honor their guest, they acted joyful in spite of themselves, for they were upset about an adventure they were expecting the next day; and they were all convinced and certain that it would come to pass before midday. My lord Yvain was troubled to see them changing moods so often, for they showed both joy and grief. He addressed himself to the lord of the town and castle: "In God's name," he said, "fair dear sweet sir, would it please you to say why you have honored me and welcomed me with joy and then wept?"

"Yes, if you really wish to know; but you should much prefer that it be kept quiet and hidden; if it were my choice, I would never tell you anything that might cause you to suffer. Let us bear our own grief, and don't you put any of it upon your heart."

"There is no way that I could see you grieving so and not take it to heart; no, I am very eager to know, whatever trouble it might cause me."

"Then," said he, "I shall tell you. I have suffered greatly because of a giant who wishes me to give him my daughter, who is more beautiful than all the maidens in the world. The wicked giant, may God curse him, is named Harpin of the Mountain; never a day passes that he doesn't take everything of mine he can get to; no one has more cause than I to complain, to lament, and to grieve. I am about to go out of my mind with grief, for I had six sons who were knights, fairer than any I knew in this world; the giant has taken all six of them. He killed two of them as I watched and tomorrow will kill the other four unless I either find someone to face him in battle and rescue my sons, or agree to hand my daughter over to him. And when he has taken her, he'll turn her over to the vilest and filthiest stable-boys he can find in his household for their sport, since he would scorn to take her for himself.

"Tomorrow this sorrow awaits me, unless God Almighty brings me help. And therefore it's no wonder, fair dear sir, if we are weeping; but on your account we force ourselves insofar as we can at this time to assume a cheerful countenance; for a man is a fool to receive a worthy man and not show him honor, and you seem a worthy man to me. Now, sire, I have told you the sum of our great distress. The giant has left us nothing in town or in the castle except what you see here; you must have seen for yourself, if you paid any heed this night, that there's not a board standing, except for these bare walls; he has leveled the whole city. After he had carried off everything he wanted, he set fire to the rest; thus he's done me many a wicked deed." [3900]

My lord Yvain listened to everything that his host told him, and after he had heard it all he was pleased to answer him. "Sire," said he, "I am very upset and distressed by your troubles, but I am surprised you have not sought help from the court of good King Arthur. No man is so mighty that he couldn't find at Arthur's court some who'd like to measure their own strength against him."

Then the wealthy man explained to Yvain that he would have had good help had he known where to find my lord Gawain. "He would not have taken this request lightly, for my wife is his sister; but the queen has been carried off by a knight from a foreign land, who came to court to fetch her. However, he would never have been able to carry her off by his own devices if Kay had not so misled the king that he placed the queen in his keeping and entrusted her to him. He was a fool and she imprudent to trust to Kay's escort; and I am the one who stands to suffer and lose the most in this, for it is quite certain that the brave Sir Gawain would have come here in all haste had he known of the danger facing his niece and nephews. But he doesn't know, which so grieves me that my heart is nearly bursting; instead he has gone after the knight, to whom God should cause woe for having carried off the queen."

My lord Yvain couldn't stop sighing when he heard this; out of the pity he felt for him, he answered: "Fair dear sweet sir, I will gladly face this perilous adventure, if the giant and your sons come early enough tomorrow not to cause me too great a delay, for I must be somewhere else tomorrow at noon, as I have given my oath."

"Fair sir, I thank you one hundred thousand times for your willingness," replied the noble man. And all the people in the household thanked him in like manner.   [3958]

Then from a chamber came the maiden with her graceful body, and her fair and pleasing face. She was miserable, sad, and quiet, with her head bowed toward the earth as she walked, for her grief was neverending; and her mother walked beside her, since the lord had summoned them to meet their guest. They approached with mantles wrapped about to hide their tears; and he bid them open their mantles and raise their heads, saying: "What I am asking you to do should not be difficult, for God and good fortune have brought us a very high-born gentleman, who has assured me that he will do battle against the giant. Don't let anything keep you from falling at his feet at once."

"May God never let me see that day," said my lord Yvain at once. "It would not be at all fitting for the sister or niece of my lord Gawain to fall at my feet for any reason. May God keep me from ever being so filled with pride as to allow them to fall at my feet. In truth, I'd never get over the shame it would cause me. But I would be grateful to them if they would take comfort until tomorrow, when they will see if God wishes to help them. There is no need to beg me further, as long as the giant arrives early enough that I won't have to break my promise elsewhere, for nothing will prevent me from being tomorrow at midday at what is truly the greatest undertaking that I could ever have."

He did not want to give them absolute assurance, because he was afraid that the giant might not come early enough for him still to return in time to rescue the maiden who was imprisoned in the chapel. Nonetheless he gave them enough assurances that they were quite hopeful; and they thanked him one and all, for they placed great trust in his prowess and thought he must be a fine man because of the lion accompanying him, who lay as gently beside him as would a lamb. They took comfort and rejoiced for the hope they found in him, and were never afterward sad.

When the time came, they led him to bed in a well-lighted room, and both the damsel and her mother accompanied him, for already they held him very dear and would have held him a hundred thousand times dearer had they known of his courtliness and his great prowess. Both he and the lion lay down and rested there, since no one else dared lie there; instead they locked the door so tightly that they could not come out until dawn the next day. After the room was unlocked, Yvain arose and heard mass and, to fulfill the promise he had made them, waited until prime.   [4035]

Then he summoned the lord of the town and spoke to him in the presence of all: "Sire, I can delay no more; I hope you will not object to my leaving, because it is impossible for me to stay longer. Yet I assure you that

I would gladly stay a bit longer, for the sake of the nephews and niece of my beloved Sir Gawain, if I did not have pressing business such a long way from here."

All the maiden's blood quaked and boiled with fear, as did the lady's and the vavasor's. They were so afraid Yvain would leave that they were about to fall at his feet in spite of their majesty, when they suddenly realized that it would neither satisfy nor please him. Then the lord offered to share his wealth with Yvain, if he would accept either land or some other goods, if he would only wait a little longer. "God forbid that I should accept anything!" Yvain replied.

And the grief-stricken maiden began to weep aloud and beg him to stay. Distressed and anguished, she prayed him in the name of the glorious Queen of Heaven and the angels, and in God's name, not to leave, but to wait just a bit longer. She begged him also in the name of Gawain, her uncle, whom he knows and loves and esteems. And he felt great compassion when he heard that she implored him by the man he most loved, and by the Queen of Heaven, and by God, who is the honey and sweetness of pity. He sighed deeply in his anguish, because on the one hand he would not want to see her whom he'd sworn to help be burned to death for all the wealth of Tarsus; his life would reach its end or he would go completely mad if he could not arrive in time to save her. Yet on the other hand, memory of the great nobility of his friend my lord Gawain caused him such distress that his heart nearly burst in two since he could stay no longer.

Yet he didn't move, but delayed and waited until the giant arrived of a sudden leading the captive knights. From his neck there hung a large, squared stave, pointed in front, with which he prodded them frequently. They weren't wearing anything worth a straw, only filthy, dirty shirts; their feet and hands were tightly bound with ropes, and they were seated upon four thin, weak, and worn-out nags that limped along. They came following the edge of a wood; a dwarf, ugly as a puffed-up toad, had tied the horses' tails together and was walking beside the four of them; he was beating them constantly with a six-knot whip to show how brave he was. He beat them until they were covered with blood. In this manner they were led shamefully along by both knight and dwarf.   [4113]

On a level spot before the gate the giant stopped and cried out to the worthy man that he intended to kill his sons if he did not give him his daughter. He intended to turn her over to his lackeys to be their whore, for he didn't love or prize her enough to deign to abase himself for her. She would have a thousand knaves with her constantly, all covered with lice and naked like tramps and scullery-boys, who'd all use her shamefully. The gentleman nearly went mad when he heard the giant saying that he would debauch his daughter, or else before his eyes his four sons would be killed. He suffered the agony of one who would prefer to be dead than alive. He kept bemoaning his sad fate and wept profusely; and then my lord Yvain began to speak, with noble and comforting words: "Sire, this giant, who's boasting so out there, is most vile and conceited; but may God never grant him power over your daughter: he despises and insults her so! It would be too terrible if such a truly beautiful creature, born of such noble parents, were abandoned to his knaves. Bring me my horse and my armor! Have the drawbridge lowered and let me cross over it! One or the other of us—I don't know which—will have to be defeated. If I can force this cruel and wicked man, who's caused you so much misery, to humble himself to free your sons and make amends before your people for the insults he has spoken, then I could commend you to God and be about my other business."

Then they went to lead forth his horse and brought him all his arms; they were eager to arm him well and soon had him properly outfitted; they made no more delay in arming him than was absolutely necessary. When they had equipped him properly, there was nothing to do but lower the drawbridge and see him off; it was lowered and off he rode, but nothing could keep the lion from accompanying him. Those who remained behind commended his soul to the Savior, for they were very afraid that the wicked devil, their enemy, who had slain many a good man before their eyes in the square, would do the same to him. They prayed God to protect him from death, to return him to them alive and well, and to grant him to slay the giant. Each prayed this silent prayer to God in his own manner.

The giant with fierce bravado came toward Yvain, threatening him and saying: "Whoever sent you here didn't care much for you, upon my eyes! Indeed he couldn't find a better way to avenge himself on you. He'll be well avenged for whatever wrong you did him!"

"You're wasting your breath," said Yvain, who was unafraid of him. "Now do your best, and I'll do mine, for such idle chatter wearies me."

Immediately my lord Yvain charged him, for he was eager to be off. He aimed his blow at the giant's breast, which was protected with a bearskin; the giant came racing toward him from across the way, with stave raised high. My lord Yvain struck him such a blow to the breast that it ripped his bearskin; he moistened the tip of his lance in his body's blood, instead of sauce. The giant hit Yvain so hard with his stave that he doubled him over. My lord Yvain drew his sword, which he wielded well. He found the giant unprotected, for he had so much confidence in his brute strength that he refused to wear any armor; and Yvain, with his sword drawn, rushed upon him. With the sharp edge, not the flat side, he struck him and sliced from his cheek enough flesh for a meal. And the giant in turn struck Yvain a blow that made him fall forward onto his horse's neck.   [4220]

At this blow the lion bristled and prepared to help his master; he sprang in anger, and with great force he clawed and stripped like bark the giant's hairy bearskin, ripping off at the same time a huge hunk of the giant's thigh; he tore away both nerves and flesh. The giant turned to face him, bellowing and roaring like a wild bull, for he had been sorely wounded by the lion. He raised his stave with both hands and tried to hit the lion but failed when the lion jumped aside; he missed his blow, and it fell harmlessly to one side of my lord Yvain, without touching either of them. Then my lord Yvain took aim and struck him two quick blows: before the giant could recover, Yvain had severed his shoulder from his chest with his sword's sharp blade; with his second blow my lord Yvain ran his blade beneath the giant's breast and through his liver. The giant fell; death embraced him. And had a mighty oak fallen, I don't believe it would have made a greater thud than did the giant. All those on the castle walls were eager to behold this blow. Then it was made clear who was the swiftest among them, for they all ran to grab the spoils of the hunt, like the hound that pursues the game until he's caught it. In this same manner all the men and women ran unabashedly and excitedly to where the giant lay upon his back.

The lord himself ran there, and all the members of his court; so did his daughter, so did his wife. Now the four brothers, who had suffered many hardships, rejoiced.

They knew that nothing in this world could detain my lord Yvain a moment longer, so they begged him to return and celebrate as soon as he had completed his task where he was going. He answered that he did not dare promise them this; he could not guess whether it would end well or not. But he did say to the lord that he wanted his four sons and his daughter to take the dwarf and go to my lord Gawain as soon as they learn of his return, to tell him how he had acquitted himself on that day, for a good deed is wasted if one doesn't wish it to be made known.

And they replied: "This deed will not be kept secret, for that is not right. We shall be pleased to do as you wish, but we would like to ask, sire, whom we are to praise when we come before Sir Gawain, if we do not know your name?"

"This much you may say, when you come before him: that I told you that I was called the Knight with the Lion. I must also beg you to tell him for me that he knows me well and I, him, though he will not recognize me. I ask nothing more of you. Now I must leave here; and nothing upsets me more than having tarried here so long, because before midday has passed I have much to do elsewhere if I can get there in time."

Then he departed without further delay, but not before the lord had begged him, as insistently as he could, to take his four sons with him: each would do his utmost to serve him, if he would have them. But it did not please or suit him to be accompanied by anyone; he left them and went away alone. [4314]

As soon as he departed he rode as fast as his horse could carry him toward the chapel, for the road was straight and clear, and he knew it well. But before he could reach the chapel, the damsel had been dragged forth and the stake prepared to which she was to be tied, clad in nothing but her chemise. Those who falsely accused her of something she had never contemplated held her bound before the fire. When he arrived, my lord Yvain was greatly anguished to see her before the fire into which she was about to be thrown. Anyone who doubted his concern would not be courteous or sensible! It is true he was greatly upset, but he was convinced that God and justice would aid him and be on his side: he had faith in God's aid and did not disdain his lion either. He charged at full speed into the crowd, shouting: "Release her! Release the damsel, you wicked people! It's not right she be burned at the stake or in a furnace, for she's done no wrong."

The people scattered to every side and made way for him, and he was eager to see with his own eyes the one his heart beheld everywhere she went.

He sought her until he found her, and this so tested his heart that he had to restrain it and rein it in just as one restrains with great difficulty a restive horse with a strong rein. Sighing, he looked gladly upon her, yet he did not sigh so openly that one could hear it but stifled his sighs with much effort.

And he was seized by great pity when he heard and saw and understood the poor ladies making a curious lament and saying: "Ah, God! How you have forgotten us! We will not know what to do when we lose our good friend, who gave us such counsel and such aid and took our part at court! At her urging our lady dressed us in her finest robes; things will be very different for us, for we will have no voice at court. May God curse him who takes her from us! May He curse him who causes us to have such a great loss! There'll be no one to say or urge: 'Give this mantle and this cloak and this robe, dear lady, to this good woman, for truly, if you send them to her they will be well used, since she is in great need of them.' Such words will not be spoken, for there is no one left who is generous and good, and everyone asks only for himself and never for anyone else, even when he himself has no needs."   [4386]

The women lamented in this fashion. My lord Yvain was among them and clearly heard their complaints, which were not false or insincere, and saw Lunete kneeling stripped to her chemise; she had already made her confession, asking God's pardon for her sins and offering her amends. And Yvain, who had loved her deeply, approached her, lifted her to her feet, and said: "My damsel, where are those who condemn and accuse you? I shall challenge them to immediate battle, if they dare to accept it."

And she, who had not seen or noticed him before, answered: "Sire, God has sent you to me in my great need! Those who bear false witness against me are right here waiting; had you come just a little later I would have been dust and ashes. You have come to defend me, and may God grant you the strength to do so, in proportion as I am innocent of the charges brought against me."

These words had been heard by the seneschal and his brother. "Ha!" said he, "woman, miserly in telling the truth, and generous with lies! One's a fool to take on such a weighty task at your words! The knight who's come to die on your account is crazy, for he's alone and we are three. So I advise him to turn away before things get bad for him."

Angered by these words, Yvain replied: "Whoever's frightened, let him flee! I'm not so afraid of your three shields that I'd go off defeated without a blow. I'd be most ungallant were I to abandon the lists and field to you while I was yet hale and healthy! Never, as long as I'm alive and well, will I flee in the face of such threats. But I advise you to have the damsel released, whom you have so wrongly accused; for she tells me, and I believe her and she's given me her word and sworn upon peril of her soul, that she never committed, or spoke, or conceived treason against her lady. I fully believe everything she has told me, and I shall defend her if I can, for in her righteousness I find my strength. And if the truth be told, God himself takes on the cause of the righteous, and God and righteousness are as one; and since they are on my side, therefore I have better companions than you, and better aid."

In his folly the seneschal replied that Yvain could set against him whatever pleased and suited him but that the lion must not harm them. And Yvain said that he had not brought his lion to be his companion and that he needed no one but himself; but if his lion were to attack them, they should defend themselves well, for he could pledge them nothing on this score. They responded: "No matter what you say, you've no cause to remain here if you don't discipline your lion and make him stand aside peacefully. And you would be smart to leave, for everyone in this land knows how this damsel has betrayed her lady; it's only right that she pay for it in the fire and flames."

"May it not please the Holy Spirit!" said he who well knew the truth. "May God not permit me to leave before I have delivered her!" [4473]

Then he ordered the lion to withdraw and lie quietly; and it withdrew as he commanded. The discussion and taunts between the two ended at once, and they separated. The three charged toward Yvain together and he came slowly to meet them, for he did not intend to be turned back or injured by their first charge. He let them shatter their lances and kept his intact: he made a quintain of his shield, and each broke his lance against it. And he rode off until he'd put about an acre's ground between himself and them; but then he returned swiftly to the fray, for he did not care for long delays. Upon his return he reached the seneschal before his two brothers: he broke his lance upon his body, driving him to the ground against his will. Yvain gave him such a mighty blow that he lay there a long while stunned, unable to do him any harm. The two others sprang to the attack: with bared swords brandished they both struck mighty blows but received more powerful yet from him, for a single one of his blows was easily worth two of theirs. He defended himself so well against them that they could gain no advantage until the seneschal himself arose and renewed the attack with all his might; the others joined in until they injured him and got the upper hand.

Seeing this, the lion delayed no longer in coming to his aid, for it seemed to him that Yvain was in need. And all the ladies, who dearly loved the damsel, called repeatedly upon God, begging him with all their hearts never to allow the one who was suffering for her cause to be defeated or killed. With their prayers the ladies brought him aid, since they had no other weapons. And the lion brought such aid that at his first attack he struck the seneschal, who was back upon his feet, so ferociously that the chain-links flew from his hauberk like so many pieces of straw in the wind. He dragged him down with such violence that he ripped the cartilage from his shoulder and all down his side. Everything he touched he stripped away, leaving his entrails exposed. His two brothers sought to avenge this blow. Now they were all even on the field: the seneschal, who was struggling and writhing in the red stream of blood that flowed from his body, could not escape death. The lion attacked the others, and nothing my lord Yvain could do by way of threats or striking could drive him back. Though he tried his best to chase him off, the lion no doubt recognized that my lord Yvain was not at all displeased by his aid but rather loved him the more for it. The lion struck them ferociously until they had cause to complain of his blows, and they in turn wounded and maimed him. [4550]

When my lord Yvain saw his lion wounded, the heart in his breast overflowed with wrath, and rightly so. He struggled to avenge his lion, striking the brothers so hard that they were completely unable to defend themselves against him, and they submitted to his mercy because of the succor brought him by his lion, which was now in dreadful pain, for he'd received so many wounds that he had good cause to be distressed. And for his part my lord Yvain was far from being well, for he had many wounds upon his body; but he was not as concerned with these as with his lion, who was suffering.

Now, just as he had desired, he has freed his damsel, and her lady has quite willingly made her peace with her. And those who had been eager to burn her were themselves burned upon the pyre, because it is right and just that those who wrongfully condemn another should die by the same death to which they have condemned the other.

Now Lunete was happy and joyful to be reconciled to her lady, and the two of them were happier than anyone had ever been before. Everyone there offered to serve their lord, as was proper, without knowing who he was; even the lady, who possessed his heart but didn't know it, implored him repeatedly to be pleased to remain there until both he and his lion were restored to health. And he replied: "Milady, I cannot remain a single day in this place until my lady has ceased her anger and displeasure toward me. Only then will my task be ended."

"Indeed," said she, "this troubles me; I don't consider the lady who bears you ill will to be very courteous. She should not close her door to a knight of your renown unless he had greviously offended her."

"Milady," said he, "however much it may hurt, I am pleased by whatever she desires. But do not question me about this, for nothing can force me to tell the cause or the offense to anyone except those who are already well aware of it."

"Does anyone except you two know of it?"

"Yes, to be sure, milady."

"Tell us your name, if you please, fair sir; then you may leave without obligation."

"Without obligation, milady? Indeed not, for I owe more than I could repay. Nonetheless I should not conceal from you the name I have chosen for myself: whenever you hear reports of the Knight with the Lion, it is I; I wish to be called by this name."

"For God's sake, sire, how is it that we have never before seen you nor heard your name mentioned?"

"Milady, in this way you can know that I am not of great renown."

Then the lady replied without hesitation: "Once again, if it would not trouble you, I would like to urge you to stay."

"Indeed, milady, I could not until I were certain I possessed my lady's good will."   [4628]

"Go then in God's favor, fair sir, and may it please Him to turn your grief and sorrow into joy!"

"Milady," said he, "may God hear your prayer!" Then he added softly, under his breath: "Milady, you carry the key and have the locket in which my happiness is enclosed, yet do not know it."

Then he left in great sorrow, and there was no one who recognized him except Lunete alone. Lunete accompanied him a long while, and he begged her still never to reveal who had been her champion.

"Sire," said she, "it won't be told."

Afterward he begged her to remember him and to speak a good word for him in her lady's presence, should the occasion arise. She said for him to say no more about that, for she would never forget him and would not be unfaithful or idle. And he thanked her a hundred times and departed, downcast and distraught on account of his lion, which he had to carry since it was too weak to follow him. Upon his shield he made a litter of moss and ferns; after he had made a bed for him, he laid him upon it as gently as he could and carried him along all stretched out on the inner side of his shield.

He bore him along in this fashion until he came before the gate of a very strong and beautiful manor. He found it locked and called out, and the porter opened it before he had had the chance to call out more than once. The porter reached for his reins, saying: "Fair sir, I offer you free use of my lord's lodging, if it please you to dismount here."

"I wish to accept this offer," he said, "for I am in great need of it and it is time to find a lodging."

Next he passed through the gateway and saw the assembled household, all coming to meet him. They greeted him and helped him dismount: some placed his shield, still bearing the lion, upon a raised stone; others took his horse and put it in a stable; others, just as they should, took and removed his armor. As soon as the lord heard this news, he came into the courtyard and greeted Yvain; and his wife came after him, along with all his sons and daughters; there were crowds of other people, who all happily offered him lodging. They placed him in a quiet room because they found he was ill, and they gave proof of their good nature by putting his lion with him. Two maidens who were skilled in medicine set themselves to healing Yvain, and both were daughters of the lord of the manor. I don't know how many days they stayed there, before he and his lion were healed and were obliged to continue onward.

Meanwhile it happened that the lord of Blackthorn had a quarrel with Death; and Death so overwhelmed him that he was forced to die. After his death it happened that the elder of his two daughters claimed that she would keep all of his lands as her own as long as she was to live and that her sister would have no share. The younger sister said she would go to King Arthur's court to seek help in defending her lands. And when the elder saw that her sister would not concede to her the entire inheritance without contest, she was extremely vexed and determined that, if possible, she would reach court before her.   [4724]

She readied herself at once; without delay or hesitation she rode until she came to court. And the other set off after her and hastened as fast as she could; but her journey and steps were wasted, for her elder sister had already presented her case to my lord Gawain, and he had granted everything she had requested. But Gawain had insisted that if she were to tell anyone, he would never again take up arms in her cause; and she had agreed to this condition.

Just afterward the other sister arrived at court, wrapped in a short mantle of fine wool lined with ermine. Only three days previously Queen Guinevere had returned from the prison where Meleagant had kept her and all the other captives; and Lancelot, betrayed, remained locked within the tower. And on the very day that the maiden arrived at court, news reached there of the cruel and wicked giant that the Knight with the Lion had slain in battle. My lord Gawain's nephews greeted their uncle in the name of the Knight with the Lion, and his niece told him all about the great service and bold deeds he had done for them for his sake, and said that Gawain was well acquainted with him, although he didn't recognize who he was. This conversation was overheard by the younger daughter of Blackthorn, who was bewildered, distraught, and confused, fearing that she would not find help or good counsel at court, since the best had failed her—she had tried in every way, by pleading and by cajoling, to persuade my lord Gawain, and he had said to her: "My friend, you are begging me for what I cannot do, since I have accepted another cause and will not abandon it."

The maiden withdrew at once and came before the king. "My lord," she said, "I came to you and to your court to seek help, yet have found none, and I am surprised that I cannot find help here. Yet it would be ill-mannered of me to depart without obtaining leave. Moreover I would like my sister to know that she could have what is mine out of love, if she wished it; but I will never surrender my inheritance by force, if I can obtain help and counsel."

"What you say is proper," asserted the king, "and while she is still here I urge, pray, and beg her to leave you your rightful portion."

But the elder sister, assured of having the best knight in the world as her champion, answered: "Sire, may God strike me down if I share with her one castle, manor, field, forest, meadow, or anything whatever. But if any knight at all dares to bear arms on her behalf and fight for her rights, let him come forth at once!"

"Your offer is unfair," said the king, "for she needs more time; if she wishes, she can seek a champion for up to forty days, in accord with the practice of all courts."

"Fair sir king," replied the elder sister, "you may establish your laws as you desire and as you please, and it would not be right or proper for me to disagree with you. Therefore I must accept the delay if she requests it."

Her sister replied that she did request, desire, and ask for it. She immediately commended the king to God and departed from the court, determined that she would spend all her life seeking through every land for the Knight with the Lion, who devoted himself to helping women in need of aid.   [4822]

Thus she set out upon the quest and traveled across many lands without learning any news, which so upset her that she fell ill. But she was very fortunate to arrive at the house of an acquaintance to whom she was very close and who could tell just by looking at her that she was not at all well. They insisted that she remain with them, and when she told them her situation, another maiden took up the search that she had been pursuing and continued the quest in her stead.

So while the one remained behind, the other rode rapidly along all alone all day long, until the shadows of night fell. She was frightened by the night, but her fright was doubled because it was raining as heavily as God could make it pour, and she was in the depths of the forest. The night and the forest frightened her, but she was more upset by the rain than the night or the forest. And the road was so bad that her horse often sank to its girth in the mud. A maiden in the forest alone with no escort might easily be frightened by bad weather and the black night, so black that she could not make out the horse upon which she was seated. Therefore she implored incessantly, first God, then His mother, and then all the saints in heaven; and that night she offered many prayers that God might show her the way to lodging and lead her out of this forest.   [4862]

She prayed until she heard the sound of a horn, which greatly cheered her, for she felt that she might find lodging, if only she could reach it. She headed in that direction until she entered upon a paved road that led her directly toward the sound of the horn, which had been blown loud and long three times. And she made straight for the sound, until she came to a cross set up to the right of the road; she thought that the horn and the one who had blown it might be there. She spurred on in that direction until she neared a bridge and saw the white walls and barbican of a round keep. Thus by good fortune she had headed toward the town and reached it, because the sound had led her there. The horn blasts that had attracted her had been sounded by a watchman who had climbed up onto the ramparts. As soon as the watchman saw her, he shouted greetings to her and descended. He took the key to the gate and opened it, saying: "Welcome, maiden, whoever you may be. This night you will be well lodged."

"I ask nothing more this night," said the maiden, and he led her within. After the hardships and trials she had undergone that day, she was fortunate to find such comfortable lodgings there. After supper her host addressed her and inquired where she was going and what she was seeking. She answered him at once: "I am seeking one whom I have never seen, I believe, and have never known; but he has a lion with him, and they say that if I find him I can place all my trust in him."

"I can testify for my part," said he, "that when I was in most desperate need God led him to me some days ago. Blessed be the paths that led him to my manor, for he avenged me on one of my mortal enemies and made me so glad when he killed him before my very eyes. Tomorrow outside this gate you can behold the body of a huge giant that he killed so easily he hardly worked up a sweat."

"For God's sake, sire," said the maiden, "now tell me in all truthfulness if you know where he was headed or if he stopped at any place."

"I don't," said he, "so help me God! But tomorrow I can start you along the road upon which he set off."

"And may God lead me to where I might hear a true report," said she, "for if I find him I shall be overjoyed." They talked in this manner for a long while before finally going to bed.   [4932]

As soon as dawn broke, the damsel arose, for she was very eager to find what she was seeking. When the lord of the manor and all his companions had arisen, they set her upon the proper path that led straight to the spring beneath the pine. She rode swiftly along the road until she arrived at the town, where she asked the first people she encountered whether they could inform her concerning the knight and the lion who were traveling together. And they told her that they had seen them defeat three knights right on this very spot. "In the name of God," she insisted at once, "since you have told me so much, don't hold anything back, if you have more to tell me!"

"No," they said, "we don't know anything except what we have told you. We have no idea what became of him. If she for whose sake he came here can't give you any information, there will be no one to tell you. However, if you wish to speak with her, you need go no farther, because she has gone into this church to hear mass and pray to God, and she has been in there long enough to have finished all her prayers."

Just as they were saying this to her, Lunete came out of the church. "There she is," they said. The maiden went toward her and they greeted one another. The damsel immediately asked about Yvain and the lion.

Lunete said she would have one of her palfreys saddled, for she wished to go with her and would take her to an enclosed field to which she had accompanied him. The damsel thanked her wholeheartedly. In no time at all they brought her the palfrey and she mounted. As they were riding along, Lunete told her how she had been accused and charged with treason, how the pyre had been lit upon which she was to be placed, and how he had come to her aid when she was in the greatest need. Conversing thus, she accompanied her as far as the path where my lord Yvain had parted from her. When she had accompanied her that far, she said: "Keep on this road until you come to a place where, if it pleases God and the Holy Spirit, you will be given news of him more accurate than any that I know. I well remember that I left him quite near here, or at this very place; we have not seen one another since, nor do I know what he has done since then, for he was in great need of healing when he left me. From here I send you after him, and may it please God that you find him healthy today, rather than tomorrow. Go now. I commend you to God; I dare not follow you farther, for my lady might get angry with me."   [5009]

They separated at once. Lunete returned, and the other left and rode until she found the manor where my lord Yvain had stayed until he was restored to health. She saw people before the gate: ladies, knights, and men-at-arms, as well as the lord of the manor. She greeted them and asked if they could give her information about a knight that she was seeking.

"Who is he?" they inquired.

"One who they say is never without a lion."

"Upon my word, maiden," said the lord, "he has just now left us; you can catch up with him today if you can follow his trail, but be careful not to tarry!"

"Sire," said she, "God forbid! But tell me now which direction to take." "This way, straight ahead," they told her. They begged her to greet him on their behalf; but this was to little avail, for she did not pay them any heed. Instead she set off at a full gallop, for a trot seemed to her too slow, even though her palfrey's gait was rapid. So she galloped through the mire as fast as over the smooth and level road, until she caught sight of the knight with his lion beside him. She was full of joy and said: "God help me! Now I see the knight I've pursued so long; I've followed his tracks well. But if I pursue him and return emptyhanded, what good will it be to catch up with him? Little or nothing, to be sure; yet if he does not return with me, then all my efforts will have been wasted."

As she spoke these words, she hastened her palfrey so that it was bathed in sweat. When she caught up to him, she hailed him, and he replied at once: "May God be with you, fair one, and keep you from cares and woe."

"And you, too, sire, for I hope that you'll be able to help me!" Then she came up beside him and said: "Sire, long have I sought you. Word of your great prowess has kept me on a wearying search through many lands, yet I've continued my search, thank God, until finally I've caught up with you. And if I have suffered any hardship, it doesn't matter to me, nor do I complain or remember it; all my limbs are lightened, for the pain was lifted from me as soon as I encountered you. It is not I who need you: someone who is better than I, a more noble and worthy woman, sends me to you. And if you disappoint her hopes, then your reputation has betrayed her, for no one else will help her. With your aid the maiden, who has been disinherited by her sister, expects to win her suit completely. She doesn't want anyone else to intervene, and no one can convince her that another could help her. You can truly rest assured that if you triumph in this cause you will have redeemed the landless girl's inheritance and added to your own glory. She herself was seeking you to defend her inheritance, because of the good she expected from you; and she would have let no one come in her place had she not been detained by an illness that forced her to her bed. Now tell me, if you please, whether you dare to come, or whether you'll remain idle here."

"No," said he, "no one gains a reputation by idleness; and I'll not rest a moment but will gladly follow you, my sweet friend, wherever you please. And if she on whose behalf you have sought me has great need of me, you ought never to despair, for I shall do everything in my power for her. Now may God grant me the courage and grace that will enable me, through His good help, to defend her rights." [5110]

So the two of them rode along talking until they approached the town of Dire Adventure. They did not wish to pass it by because the day was growing late. They drew near to this town, and the people who saw them coming all said to the knight: "Beware, sir, beware! You were shown this place of lodging to cause you shame and suffering; an abbot would swear this to you."

"Ah!" he said, "foolish, vulgar people, full of every wickedness and lacking every good quality, why have you accosted me so?"

"Why? You'll know it well enough if you ride on just a little farther! But you'll never know anything until you have stayed in this high fortress."

Immediately my lord Yvain headed toward the tower, while all the people cried out in loud voices: "Hey! Hey! wretch, where are you going? If ever in your life you've encountered anyone who's shamed and vilified you, in there where you're headed they'll do much worse by you than you could ever tell!"

"Dishonorable and unkind people," said my lord Yvain as he heard them, "meddlesome and foolish people, why do you assail me? Why attack me? What do you ask of me? What do you want of me that you growl so after me?"

"Friend, do not get angry," said a lady somewhat advanced in years, who was very courteous and sensible, "for indeed they mean no harm by what they say, and are only warning you not to go and take lodging up there, if you would only heed their words. They dare not tell you why, but they chastise and warn you because they want to arouse your fears. Custom ordains that they do this to everyone who approaches, to keep them from entering there. And the custom in this town is such that we dare not offer lodgings in our homes, under any circumstances, to any gentleman who comes from outside. Now it is up to you alone: no one is standing in your way. If you wish, you can ride up there, but I would advise you to turn around."

"Milady," said he, "I believe it would be to my honor and benefit to accept your advice; but if I did, I don't know where else I could find lodging for this night."

"In faith," said she, "I'll say no more, for this is none of my concern. Go wherever you wish. However, I would be very happy to see you come back out without having suffered too great shame within. But this could never happen!"

"Milady," he replied, "may God bless you for your words of warning! But my pure heart draws me there, and I shall do what my heart desires."

Immediately he headed for the gate, with his lion and the maiden. The porter called him aside and said: "Come quickly, come, for you have arrived at a place where you will be held fast; and cursed be your arrival!"   [5188]

Thus the porter warned him and hastened up the stairs; but his warning was most unpleasantly delivered. And my lord Yvain, without reply, passed in front of him and discovered a large hall, lofty and new. Before it was a meadow enclosed with huge round pointed staves; and by peering through the staves he could make out up to three hundred maidens doing various kinds of needlework. Each one sewed as best she could with threads of gold and silk; but they were so poor that many among them wore no belts and went ungirded. Their coats were worn through at the breasts and elbows, and the blouses at their necks were filthy; their necks were gaunt and their faces pale from the hunger and deprivation they'd known. He observed them, and as they caught sight of him they lowered their heads and wept; and for a long while they remained there without doing anything, because they felt so miserable they could not raise their eyes from the ground.

After my lord Yvain had watched them for a while, he turned around and headed straight for the gate; but the porter sprang up before him and shouted: "It's no use; you can't escape now, fair master. You'd like to be outside again now, but, by my head, you can't do it: before you escape you'll have suffered so much shame that you couldn't suffer more. It wasn't at all clever of you to enter here, for there's no question of leaving."

"Nor do I want to, fair brother!" said he. "But tell me, on the soul of your father: where do the damsels I saw in this meadow, who were weaving cloths of silk and gold, come from? Their needlework pleases me, but I was very distressed to see that their faces and bodies are so thin and pale and sad. I'm sure that they would be very beautiful and elegant if they had what they desired."

"I will never tell you," said he; "find someone else to answer that question."

"So I shall, since there's no better way."

Then he searched until he found the door to the meadow in which the damsels were working. He came before them and greeted them all, and he saw teardrops trickling down from their weeping eyes. He said to them: "May it please God to lift from your hearts this sadness, whose origin I do not know, and turn it into joy."

"May God, whom you've invoked, hear your prayer!" one maiden answered him. "Who we are and from what land will not be hidden from you; I believe this is what you wish to ask."   [5258]

"I've come for no other reason," said he.

"Sire, it happened long ago that the king of the Isle of Maidens went looking for news through courts and countries. Like a naive fool, he continued until he fell into this peril. He came here in an evil hour, for we captives, who are here now, must bear the shame and suffering without ever having deserved it. And know well that you yourself can expect great shame here if they refuse your ransom. At any rate, it happened that my lord came to this town, inhabited by two sons of the Devil (and don't think this is made up, for they were born of a woman and a demon!). And these two were about to do battle with the king, which was a most unhappy thing, for he was not yet eighteen. They could easily have run him through like a tender lamb, so the terrified king saved himself as best he could: he swore that he would send here each year, as long as he lived, thirty maidens from his land; he was released for this payment. And it was decreed by oath that this tribute was to last as long as the two demons prevailed, unless some knight could vanquish them in battle, and then he would no longer have to pay this tribute and we would be free from shame, grief, and misery. Never again will anything please us. But I'm babbling on like a child when I speak of freedom, for we can never escape this place; we shall weave silk cloth all our days, yet never be better dressed than now.

"We shall remain poor and naked forever and shall always be hungry and thirsty; no matter how hard we try, we'll never have better to eat. Our bread supply is very meager: little in the morning and less at night, for by the work of our hands we'll never have more to live on than four deniers in the pound; and with this we cannot buy sufficient food and clothing, for though our labor is worth twenty sous a week, we have barely enough to live on. And you can be sure that there's not a one of us whose work doesn't bring in twenty sous or more, and that's enough to make a duke wealthy! Yet here we are in poverty, while he for whom we labor grows rich from our work. We stay awake much of the night and all day long to earn his fare, for he has threatened us with torture if we rest; therefore we dare not rest. But what more should I tell you? We are so shamed and ill-treated that I cannot tell you the fifth of it. And we are wracked with sorrow whenever we see young knights and gentlemen die in combat with the two demons. They pay most dearly for their lodgings, as you must do tomorrow, for alone and unaided you must, whether you wish to or not, do battle and lose your reputation against these two devils incarnate."

"May God, our true spiritual King, protect me," said my lord Yvain, "and restore you to honor and joy, if it be His will! Now I must go and see what welcome will be shown me by those within."

"Go now, sire. May He who gives and bestows all gifts watch over you!" [5350]

Yvain and the maiden continued until they reached the main hall, without having encountered anyone, good or evil, to speak with them. After passing through the manor, they came out into an orchard. They never had to inquire or worry about stabling their horses; why should they, since those who thought they'd win them stabled them well? But I think they were overconfident, for their owner was still in perfect health. The horses had oats and hay, and fresh litter belly-deep.

Then my lord Yvain entered the orchard, followed by his retinue. He saw a wealthy man lying there, propped up on his elbow on a silken cloth; and a maiden was reading to him from a romance. (I don't know who composed it.) And to listen to the romance, a woman too had sat down there. It was the maid's mother, and the gentleman was her father. It gave them pleasure to watch and listen to her, for she was their only child. She was not yet sixteen but was so very beautiful and elegant that the God of Love would have sought to serve her, had he seen her, and would never have let her love anyone but himself alone. To serve her he would have become a man, abandoned his divinity, and struck his own body with the dart whose wound never heals, unless an unfaithful doctor tends it. It is not right for anyone to be healed until he meets with unfaithfulness, for he who is healed in any other way does not love truly. I could tell you so much about these wounds that it would take all day, if you were pleased to hear it; but there are those who'd be quick to say that I speak of idle tales, for people no longer fall in love, nor do they love as once they did, nor even want to hear love spoken of.

So listen now in what manner, with what hospitality and good cheer, my lord Yvain was given lodging. All those who were in the orchard sprang to their feet to greet him, and as soon as they saw him they addressed him in these words: "This way, fair sir, and may you and all that you have be called blessed in every way that God can bring about or decree!"

I don't know whether they were feigning, but they welcomed him most joyfully and acted as if they were very pleased for him to be comfortably lodged. The daughter of the lord herself served and paid him great respect, as one should to a noble guest: not only did she remove all his armor, but with her own hands she washed his neck and face and forehead. Her father wished him to be paid every due respect, just as she did. She brought forth a pleated chemise and white breeches from her wardrobe; with needle and thread she laced up his sleeves as she clothed him. May God grant that this attention and service not cost him too dearly! To wear over his chemise she offered him a new surcoat, and around his neck she placed an unworn mantle of bright-hued wool. She was so diligent in serving him that he was embarrassed and troubled, but the maiden was so courteous, so guileless, so well-mannered, that she still didn't feel she was doing enough, for she well knew that her mother wanted her guest to lack for nothing that she could do to honor him.

That evening he was served so many courses at dinner that there were far too many: just carrying in the many courses tired the serving-men. At night they paid him every honor and put him comfortably to bed; the lion slept at his feet as was its custom. Once he was in his bed, no one went near him again. In the morning, when God, by whose command all is done, had relit His light throughout the world as early as was fitting, my lord Yvain arose at once, and he and the maiden went to a nearby chapel to hear mass, which was speedily said for them in honor of the Holy Spirit.   [5460]

After mass, when my lord Yvain felt it was time to leave and that nothing would prevent it, he heard baleful news: it was not to be as he chose. When he said: "Sire, if it please you, I should like your leave to depart," the lord of the manor replied: "Friend, there is a reason I cannot yet give you my leave: in this town a most wicked devilry has been established that I am compelled to maintain. Shortly I shall summon here before you two tall and powerful men of mine, against whom, right or wrong, you must take up arms. If you can hold your own against them and defeat and kill them both, my daughter desires you for her spouse, and this town and everything that goes with it awaits you."

"Sire," replied Yvain, "I want none of your wealth. May God grant me no share here, and may your daughter remain with you. In her the emperor of Germany would find a good match, were he to win her, for she is beautiful and well-bred."

"Enough, fair guest!" said the lord. "I don't have to listen to your refusal, for you cannot escape. The knight who can defeat the two demons who are about to attack you must take my town, wed my daughter, and rule over all my lands. The combat cannot be averted or postponed in any manner. But I am convinced that cowardice makes you refuse my daughter's hand: in this way you hope to avoid the combat altogether. Yet you cannot fail to fight, because no knight who has slept here can possibly escape. This is a custom and fixed payment that will last for a long time to come, because my daughter will not be wed until I see them dead or vanquished."

"Then I must fight them, though it's against my will; but I would very gladly pass this by, I assure you! So now, though it pains me, I'll do battle, since it cannot be avoided." Immediately the two black and hideous demon's sons came forth. Each had a spiked club of cornel wood, which had been covered with copper and wound with brass. They were in armor from their shoulders to their knees, but their heads and faces were left unarmed, and their stocky legs were likewise left uncovered. Thus armed they came, holding in their hands round shields, wieldy but strong for fighting. [5529]

The lion began to tremble as soon as he saw them, for he well knew by the arms they carried that they had come to fight his master; he bristled and snarled, shaking with rage in his eagerness to fight and beating the earth with his tail, for he was determined to rescue his master before they killed him. When they saw the lion, they said: "Vassal, take your lion away from here, for he's threatening us! If you are not willing to acknowledge defeat, I swear to you that you must put him somewhere where he cannot undertake to help you or harm us. You must deal with us alone, for the lion would be glad to help you if he could."

"If you are afraid of him, take him away yourselves," said my lord Yvain, "for I'd be quite pleased and satisfied if he did you harm, if he could, and I am grateful to have his help."

"In faith," they said, "this cannot be, for you must have no help from him! Do the best you can alone with no help from anyone else. You must face the two of us alone; if the lion were here with you and were to attack us, then you wouldn't be alone: it would be two against two. So I swear to you, you must take your lion away from here, though you may soon regret it."

"Where do you want him to go?" he asked. "Where would it please you for me to put him?"

"Lock him in there," they said, showing him a little room.

"It shall be done as you wish." [5572]

Then he took him and locked him in. At once the people went to fetch Yvain's armor and help him don it. Next they led forth his horse and handed it to him, and he mounted. The two champions charged Yvain to injure him and bring him shame, for they were unafraid of the lion, which was locked within the room. With their maces they struck him such blows that his shield and helmet afforded him little protection, for when they hit

his helmet they bashed and knocked it awry, and his shield shattered and
dissolved like ice; they made such holes in it that you could put your fist
right through. Both of them were greatly to be feared. And how did he
handle the two demons? Sparked by shame and fear, he defended himself
with all his strength; he exerted himself and strove to land mighty and
powerful blows. He was not sparing in his gifts to them, for he doubled
their own generosity.

Now the lion, still locked within the room, had a sad and troubled heart,
for he recalled the great kindness shown him by this noble man who now
stood in dire need of his aid and service. The lion would render him full
measure and copiously repay his kindness; his payment would not be
discounted if he could get out of that room. He searched in every direction,
but couldn't find any escape. Hearing the blows of the fierce and mortal
battle, he began to roar so mightily that he was beside himself with rage. He
searched until he discovered that the threshold was rotten near the ground;
he scratched until he could squeeze under just up to his haunches. My lord
Yvain was by this time hard-pressed and bathed in sweat, having found the
two fellows to be strong, cruel, and persistent. He had suffered many a
blow and returned them as best he could, but he had not succeeded in
wounding them at all, for they were too skilled in swordplay, and their
shields could not be dented by any sword, no matter how sharp or well-
tempered.   [5628]

So my lord Yvain had every reason to fear for his death; but he was able
to hold his own until the lion clawed beneath the threshold enough to work
himself completely free. If the demons aren't defeated now, then they'll
never be, because the lion will allow them no respite as long as he knows
they're alive. He pounces upon the one and throws him to the ground like a
tree-trunk. Now the demons fear for their lives, and there's not a man there
who doesn't rejoice within his heart. The demon who was dashed to the
earth by the lion will never rise again if he's not rescued by the other.

His companion ran over to bring him aid but also to save himself, so the
lion wouldn't charge him as soon as it had killed the demon he'd thrown to
the ground. Indeed he was much more afraid of the lion than of its master.

Once the demon has turned his back to Yvain, who can see his bare neck
exposed, Yvain would be a fool to let him live any longer, for he was
fortunate to get such an opportunity. The fiend has offered him his neck
and head exposed, and Yvain struck him such a blow that he severed head
from trunk so swiftly that he never knew it. Then Yvain quickly dismounted to rescue the demon held down by the lion, for he intended to
release and spare him. But to no avail, because the lion in his wrath had so
wounded him in pouncing that he was hideously disfigured and was now so
far gone that no doctor could arrive in time to save him. When Yvain drove
back the lion, he saw that it had ripped the demon's shoulder from its place.
Yvain had no more reason to fear him, for his club had fallen to the ground
and he lay there like a corpse, without moving or twitching.

But he was still able to speak and said with what little strength he had:
"Please take away your lion, fair sir, so he'll harm me no more, for from this
moment on you may do with me whatever you wish. Only a man without
pity would refuse to show mercy to another who's begged and pleaded for
it. I will defend myself no longer; since I'll never rise up from here by my
own strength, I place myself in your power."

"Say then," said Yvain, "whether you acknowledge that you are vanquished and defeated?"

"Sire," said he, "it is obvious: I am vanquished in spite of myself, and I acknowledge that I'm defeated."

"Then you have no need to fear either myself or my lion."

Immediately all the people ran up and gathered around him. Both the lord and lady embraced the knight in their great joy and spoke to him of their daughter, saying: "Now you will be lord and master over us all, and our daughter will be your lady, for we shall give her to you to be your wife."

"And I," he replied, "return her to you. Let whoever wants her have her! I don't want her, but I'm not saying this out of disdain: don't be upset if I don't take her, for I cannot and must not do so. However, if you please, release to me the captives you are holding; you are well aware that it is time for them to be set free."   [5715]

"What you say is true," the lord answered, "and I release them to you, for there is no longer anything to prevent it. But you would be wise also to accept my daughter with all my possessions, for she is beautiful, rich, and sensible. You will never make a better marriage than this one!"

"Sire," said Yvain, "you are unaware of my difficulties and my duties, and I don't dare explain them to you; but rest assured, when I refuse what no one would refuse who could devote his heart and mind to a fair and lovely maiden, that I would gladly take her if I could or should take her or any other. Yet I cannot—and this is the truth—so leave me in peace, because this other damsel, who came here with me, awaits me now; she has kept me company, and I wish now to go with her, no matter what the future may bring me."

"You wish to leave, fair sir? But how? Unless it meets with my approval and I order it, my gate will never be opened for you; you will remain my prisoner here instead. You are mistaken and full of pride when you disdain my daughter, whom I have begged you to accept."

"Disdain, sire? Indeed not, upon my soul; but I cannot marry any woman nor remain here, whatever the penalty. I must follow the damsel who is leading me, for it cannot be otherwise. But, if it please you, with my right hand I will swear, and you must believe me, that if I am able I will return just as you see me here now and take your daughter's hand whenever it may seem good to you."

"Cursed be anyone," he replied, "who would require an oath or a pledge or a promise! If my daughter pleases you, you'll return soon enough; no oath or vow, I believe, would make you come back sooner. Go now, for I relieve you of all pledges and promises. If you are detained by rain or wind, or by anything whatsoever, it doesn't matter to me! I will never hold my daughter so cheap that I would force her upon you. Now go about your business, for it makes no more difference to me whether you return or stay away."   [5774]

Immediately my lord Yvain turned away and remained no longer in the town. He took away with him the captives who'd been released; although the lord delivered them to him poor and shabbily garbed, it seemed to them now that they were rich. Two by two they all left the town, walking before my lord Yvain; I don't believe they'd have expressed any more joy for this world's Creator, had He come from Heaven to earth, than they showed for

Yvain. All these people who'd insulted him before in every way they could imagine came now to beg his forgiveness; they walked beside him asking mercy, but he insisted he didn't understand. "I don't know what you're talking about," he said, "so I bear no grudge against you, for I cannot remember that you ever said anything that would have hurt me."

Everyone rejoiced at what he heard and praised him greatly for his courtliness. When they had accompanied him a long while, they all wished him Godspeed and begged his leave. The damsels, too, took their leave and as they did so they all bowed low before him, praying that God would grant him happiness and health and let him fulfill his desires wherever he might go. And he, who was troubled by the delay, asked God to watch over them. "Go," he said, "and may God bring you safe and happy into your own lands." They went on their way at once and left rejoicing greatly.

And my lord Yvain immediately set off in the opposite direction. He did not stop riding hard all the days of that week, following the lead of the maiden, who knew the way well to the remote place where she had left the disinherited maiden, wretched and woebegone. But when she heard that the maiden and the Knight with the Lion were approaching, no happiness could surpass that which she felt in her heart; for now she was convinced that her sister would leave her a portion of her inheritance, which pleased her. The maiden had lain sick a long while and had only recently recovered from her illness, which had gravely weakened her, as was apparent from her face. Yet she was the first to go to meet him, which she did without delay; she greeted him and paid him honor in every way she could. There is no need to speak of the joy that prevailed that night at the hostel: nothing will be told of it, for there would be too much to relate. I omit everything until they remounted their horses the next day and left.   [5845]

Then they rode until they saw a town where King Arthur had been residing two weeks or more. There too was the damsel who had disinherited her sister, for she had kept close to court in expectation of the arrival of her sister, who even now was approaching. But this thought scarcely crossed her mind, for she was convinced that it was impossible for her sister to find a knight to withstand my lord Gawain in combat, and only a single day of the forty set was left. The dispute would be settled fully in her favor by right and by judgment if this one day were to pass. Yet she would soon be faced with much more than she had anticipated.

That night Yvain and the younger sister spent outside the town in small and uncomfortable lodgings, where no one recognized them; for if they had slept in the town, everyone would have recognized them, and this they did not desire. At daybreak they left the lodging furtively, keeping well concealed until the day was bright and full.

I don't know how many days had passed since my lord Gawain had left court, and no one there had had any news of him, with the sole exception of the maiden for whom he had agreed to fight. He had been in hiding some three or four leagues away and arrived at court equipped in such a way that even those who had known him always could not recognize him by the armor he wore. The damsel, whose injustice toward her sister was manifest, presented him at court before everyone, for by his help she intended to win the dispute in which she was in the wrong. "Sire," she said to the king, "time is passing; today is the last day and soon it will be early afternoon.

Everyone can clearly see how I am prepared to defend my rights; if my sister were about to return, there would be no choice but to wait for her. Yet, praise God, since she is not going to return, it is obvious she cannot better her situation. So my efforts have been for naught, though I have stood ready every day right to this very last to defend what is mine. I have won everything without a battle, so it is quite right that I go now to rule over my inheritance in peace. I will owe no accounting for it to my sister as long as I live: she will live wretched and forlorn."

And the king, who was well aware that the maiden had faithlessly wronged her sister, said: "My friend, at royal courts one must wait, by my faith, as long as the king's justice is seated in deliberation. You must not attempt to rush things, for I believe that your sister will still arrive in time."

Before the king had finished these words, he saw the Knight with the Lion and the younger sister beside him; the two of them were approaching alone, for they had slipped away from the lion, who was still where they had spent the night.   [5928]

The king saw the maiden and recognized her immediately; he was pleased and delighted to see her, for he sided with her in this dispute, as he wished to do what was right. In his delight he said to her, as soon as she was near enough to hear: "Come forward, fair one, and may God save you!"

When her sister heard these words, she was startled and turned around. Seeing her sister with the knight she had brought to fight for her rights, she turned blacker than the earth. The younger sister was warmly greeted by everyone. When she caught sight of the king, she came before him and said: "God save the king and his court! Sire, if my rights in this dispute can be upheld by a knight, then they will be defended by this knight who in his kindness has followed me here. Although this good and well-born knight had much to do elsewhere, he has felt such pity for me that he has put all his other affairs behind him to help me. Now my lady, my very dear sister whom I love as much as my own heart, would do the proper and courteous thing if she were to concede me my rights so that there would be peace between us, for I ask for nothing that is hers."

"Nor, in truth, do I ask for anything of yours," said she. "You have nothing and never will! You can talk on as much as you like, but words won't get you anything. You can just dry up with all this whining!"

And her younger sister, who was very sensible and courteous, and knew what was seemly, replied at once. "Indeed," said she, "it troubles me that two brave men such as these will have to fight for the sake of the two of us; though the dispute is quite minor I cannot abandon my claim, for I have great need of it. Therefore I would be grateful to you if you would grant me my rights."

"One would surely have to be a real fool," said she, "to accede to your request. May the flames of Hell consume me if I give you anything to ease your life! The Saone and the Danube rivers will sooner join their banks than I spare you the battle!"

"May God and the right that is mine, in which I have always trusted and trust still to this very day, aid this knight, who out of love and generosity has offered himself to my service, though he does not know who I am. He does not know me, nor I him."   [5994]

So they argued until nothing remained to be said. Then the knights were led to the middle of the courtyard; and everyone hurried there, just as people are wont to rush up when they are eager to see swordplay and the blows of battle. Those who were to fight did not recognize each other at all, though they'd always loved one another.

And did they not love one another now? Yes, I answer you, and no. And I'll prove that each reply is correct. My lord Gawain truly loves Yvain and calls him his companion; and Yvain loves him, wherever he might be. Even here, if he recognized him, he would rejoice at once to see him and would give his head for Gawain, and Gawain his for Yvain, before he'd let any harm be done him. Is this not true and total love? Indeed yes! And the Hatred, is it not fully in evidence? Yes, for it is certainly clear that each would like to cut off the other's head, or at least shame him enough to destroy his reputation. By my word, it's a real miracle that Love and mortal Hatred can be found so close together! Heavens! How can two such contrary things dwell together in the same lodging? It doesn't seem to me that they could live together, for one couldn't stay a single evening in the same place as the other without there being a quarrel and fuss, as soon as one knew the other was there. Yet in a single building there are different sections, for there are public rooms and private chambers; this must surely be the case here. Perhaps Love is locked within some secret inner nook, and Hatred's on the balcony above the street, because she wants the folk to notice her. Now Hatred's in the saddle, for she spurs and charges and tramples over Love as hard as she can, while Love doesn't stir.   [6048]

Ah, Love! Where are you hidden? Come out and you'll see what an army the enemies of your friends have brought and set against you. The enemies are those very men who love one another with a sacred love; for a love that isn't false or feigned is a precious and holy thing. But now Love is wholly blind and Hatred likewise can't see a thing; for Love, if she had recognized them, must surely have prevented them from striking one another or doing anything to hurt the other. Therefore Love is blind, vanquished, and confused, for those who by right are hers she doesn't recognize, though she looks right at them. And Hatred can't say why the one hates the other yet wants to start a wrongful fight, so each feels a mortal hatred for the other. You can be sure that the man who wishes to shame another and seeks his death does not love him.

What? Does Yvain wish to slay his friend, my lord Gawain? Yes, and the desire is mutual. Then would my lord Gawain wish to kill Yvain with his own hands, or do even worse than I have said? Not at all, I swear and pledge to you. Neither would want to shame or hurt the other for all that God has done for man, nor for all the Roman Empire. But I've told a horrible lie, for it is perfectly obvious that the knight with his lance raised on its brace is ready to attack his adversary, who in turn wants to wound the knight and bring him shame, and both are perfectly intent upon this. Now tell me, when one has defeated the other, of whom will the one who receives the worst of the blows complain? For if they come to blows, I'm quite afraid that they'll continue to fight until one or the other surrenders. Can Yvain rightfully say, if he gets the worst of it, that the man who's hurt and shamed him has counted him among his friends and has never called him anything but "friend" and "companion"? Or should it happen by chance that Yvain wounds or overwhelms him, will Gawain have the right to complain? Not at all, for he won't know whom to blame. [6109]

The two knights drew back for the charge because they didn't recognize each other. When they met, their lances broke, although they were stout and made of ash. Neither knight spoke to the other, for had they spoken their meeting would have been different! There would have been no lance or sword blows struck at that encounter: they would have come running to embrace and kiss each other rather than attack. But now the two friends were striking and injuring one another. Their swords gained no value, nor did their helmets or shields, which were dented and broken. Their sword-blades were nicked and dulled, for they dealt such mighty swipes with the sharp edge, and not the flat part, and struck such blows with the pommels on noseguards, necks, foreheads, and cheeks, that they were all black and blue where the blood gathered beneath the skin. And their hauberks were so torn and their shields so battered that neither knight escaped unharmed; they struggled so hard that both were nearly out of breath. The combat was so heated that all the jacinths and emeralds that decorated their helmets were knocked loose and crushed, for they pummeled their helmets so hard that both knights were stunned and had their brains nearly beaten out. Their eyes glistened, as with square and mighty fists, strong nerves, and hard bones they dealt wicked blows to the face as long as they could grip their swords, which were most useful as they hammered hard. [6152]

Wearied after a long struggle, with helmets bashed in and hauberks ripped asunder from the hammering of their swords, and with shields split and broken, they both withdrew a little to let their muscles rest and catch their breath again. But they did not stop long, and soon one rushed upon the other more fiercely than before, and everyone said they'd never seen two more courageous knights: "They're not fighting in jest, but in deadly seriousness. They'll never receive the merits and rewards they've both earned on this field." The two friends overheard these words as they were fighting and understood that they were speaking of reconciling the two sisters, but that they could find no way to persuade the elder to make peace. Although the younger had agreed to accept without opposition whatever the king decided, the elder was so obstinate that even Queen Guinevere and all the knights, and the king, the ladies, and the townspeople, sided with the younger sister. They all came to beg the king to give a third or quarter of the land to her, despite her elder sister, and to separate the two knights, for both were so valiant that it would be a terrible thing if one were to injure the other or reduce his honor in the least. And the king replied that he would never attempt a reconciliation, for the elder sister was such a wicked creature that she'd have no part of it.

The two knights, whose blows were so bitter that it was a marvel to behold, overheard this whole discussion. The battle was so even that there was no way to determine who was getting the better or who the worse. Even the two who were fighting, purchasing honor by their suffering, were amazed and astounded; they fought on such equal terms that each one wondered greatly who could withstand his onslaught with so much courage. They had fought so long that day was fading into night, and both knights had weary arms and sore bodies. Their warm blood bubbled out from many wounds and flowed beneath their hauberks; it was no wonder if they wished to rest, for both were in great pain.   [6218]

At last the two stopped to rest, each realizing that, although it had been a long time coming, he had finally met his match. They both rested for a long while, for they didn't dare resume the combat. They had no more desire to fight, both because dark night was nearing and because each had developed great respect for the other; these two reasons kept them apart and summoned them to make peace. But before leaving the field, they would learn each other's identity and feel both joy and pity. My lord Yvain, who was very brave and courteous, spoke first. Yet his good friend still did not recognize him by his voice, for he was suffering so that he could not speak loudly and his voice was broken, weak, and hoarse, because all his blood was trembling from the blows that he'd been dealt.

"Sire," said Yvain, "night is falling; I don't believe we'd be blamed or reproached if night were to part us. And I can state, for my part, that I respect and esteem you greatly, and that I have never in my life suffered so much in any fight or encountered any knight I'd rather meet and know. I have every admiration for you, because you had me on the brink of defeat. You know how to strike good blows and make them count! No knight I've ever met knew how to pay out such blows; I'm sure I've never before received as many as you've lent me today! Your blows have totally exhausted me."

"By my word," said my lord Gawain, "I am even more stunned and weakened than yourself! And if I acknowledged my debt, you would perhaps not be displeased: if I've lent anything of mine, you've paid back the account, both capital and interest; for you were more generous in paying back than I was in accepting the payment. But however it may be, since you'd be pleased for me to tell you how I'm called, the name will not be hidden: I'm called Gawain, son of King Lot."

When my lord Yvain heard this news, he was both shocked and dismayed; in anger he cast to the earth his bloody sword and broken shield; he dismounted from his horse and said: "Alas! What misfortune! A most dreadful misunderstanding has brought on this combat, when we didn't recognize one another. If I had recognized you, I swear I would never have fought against you, but would have declared myself defeated before the initial blow."

"What!" said my lord Gawain. "Who are you?"

"I am Yvain, who loves you more than any man in this whole world round; for you have always loved me and shown me honor in every court. But I would like to honor you and make amends in this affair by declaring myself utterly defeated."

"You would do this for me?" asked the gentle Sir Gawain. "I'd be presumptuous indeed if I accepted such a settlement. This honor will not be mine, but yours, for I leave it to you."

"Ah, fair sir! Say no more, for this could never happen. I can't stand upright any longer, for I am wounded and overcome."

"Surely you have no cause to say this," replied his friend and companion. "It is I who am wounded and defeated; and I don't say this just to flatter you, for there's not a man in this world to whom I'd not say as much rather than endure more blows."   [6314]

Thus speaking they dismounted; each threw his arms around the other's neck, and they embraced; but even this did not prevent each from claiming to have been defeated. The quarrel did not desist until the king and the barons all came running up; they saw the two rejoicing together and were very eager to discover what this could mean, and who these knights were who had such joy in each other.

"My lords," said the king, "tell us who has so suddenly brought about this friendship between you, for all day long I have witnessed such enmity and discord."

"Sire, the misfortune and ill luck that brought on this combat shall not be hidden from you," replied his nephew, my lord Gawain. "Since you are waiting here now to learn the cause of it, there will certainly be someone to tell you the truth. I, who am your nephew Gawain, did not recognize my companion, my lord Yvain here present, until he, as fortunately it was pleasing to God, asked my name. We told each other our names, and after a long battle we've recognized one another. We fought hard, and had we battled just a little longer it would have been too much for me because, by my head, his strength and the evil cause of her who engaged me as her champion would have killed me. But I would rather have my companion defeat me in battle than slay me."

Thereupon all my lord Yvain's blood stirred and he said to my lord Gawain: "Fair dear lord, so help me God you are quite wrong to say this! Let my lord the king understand clearly that I am the one who was overwhelmed in this battle and utterly defeated."

"It was I."

"No, I!" they both declared. They were both so honest and noble that each bestowed and granted the wreath of victory to the other. Neither wished to accept it, and each tried to impress upon the king and his people that he was overcome and defeated.

The king ended the quarrel after he had listened to them a while; what he had heard pleased him, and also that he had seen them embrace one another, although each had given the other many ugly wounds.   [6377]

"My lords," said Arthur, "your great love for one another is manifest when each claims to have been defeated. But now rely on me, for I believe that I can effect a reconciliation that will bring honor to you both, and for which everyone will praise me."

Then the two knights swore that they would do his will exactly as he stated it, and the king said that he would settle the dispute faithfully and justly. "Where," he said, "is the damsel who has thrown her sister off her own land, and has forcibly and maliciously disinherited her?"

"Sire," said she, "here I am."

"Are you there? Then come here! I have known for a long time that you were disinheriting her. Her rights will no longer be denied, for you yourself have just acknowledged the truth to me. It is right that you renounce all claims to her share."

"Ah, sir king! If I've given a foolish answer, you shouldn't hold me to my word! In God's name, sire, don't be hard on me! You are the king and should protect me from all wrong and error."

"That is why," said the king, "I wish to restore to your sister her rightful share, for I've never wished to be party to any wrongdoing. And you have clearly heard that your knight and hers have submitted to my mercy. What I shall say may not please you, for your wrongdoing is well known. Each so wishes to pay honor to the other that he claims he's been defeated. There is no need to delay further, since it has been left to me: either you will do everything I ask exactly as I ask it, without deceit, or I will proclaim that my nephew has been defeated in battle. That would be much the worse for you, but I am prepared to say it against my inclination." [6425]

In fact he would never have said it at all, but he told her this to see whether he could frighten her enough to get her to restore her sister's inheritance to her out of fear, because he had clearly seen that only force or fear, and no amount of pleading, would ever convince her to restore it. Because she was afraid and frightened, she said: "Fair sir, I am compelled to do as you desire, but it grieves my heart. Yet I'll do it, although it hurts me: my sister will have what is rightfully her portion of my inheritance; I offer her you yourself as my pledge, so that she may be more assured of it."

"Restore it to her outright," said the king, "and let her be your vassal woman and hold it from you; love her as your vassal woman, and let her love you as her liege lady and as her blood-born sister."

Thus the king arranged the matter, and so the maiden was invested with her lands and thanked him for it. The king told his brave and valiant nephew to allow himself to be disarmed and asked my lord Yvain, as well, if it pleased him to have his armor removed, for they had no further need of them. Thereupon the vassals took off their armor and embraced one another as equals. And as they were embracing, they saw the lion running toward them, seeking its master. As soon as the lion saw Yvain, it began expressing its joy; then you could see the people drawing back, and even the bravest among them fled.

"Stay still, everyone," said my lord Yvain. "Why are you fleeing? No one is chasing you! Don't be frightened that this lion you see will do you any harm. Please believe this, for he is mine, and I am his; we are companions together."

Then everyone who heard tell of the adventures of the lion and his companion knew for certain that it could have been none but he who had killed the wicked giant. My lord Gawain addressed him in these words: "Sir companion, so help me God, you've covered me with shame this day: I've repaid you poorly for the service you did me in killing the giant to save my niece and nephews! I had thought about you for a long time, and I was particularly anxious because they told me there was love and friendship between the two of us. There's no doubt that I thought often about this, but I couldn't figure it all out, for I had never heard tell of any knight I knew in any land where I had been who was called by the name of the Knight with the Lion." [6498]

While they were still speaking, their armor was removed, and the lion was not slow to come to where his master was seated. When it reached him, it showed its joy as far as a dumb beast could. Both knights had to be taken to sickrooms in the infirmary, for they needed a doctor and ointments to heal their wounds. The king had them brought before him, for he loved them dearly. Then King Arthur summoned a physician, who knew more than anyone about the art of healing and who ministered constantly to them until he had healed their wounds as quickly and as well as he could.

When he had cured them both, my lord Yvain, who had his heart set fast on love and was dying of it, saw that he could not endure and that in the end he'd die unless his lady took pity upon him. And he determined that he would leave the court all alone and go to do battle at her spring; and there he'd cause so much thunder and wind and rain that she would be compelled to make her peace with him, or else there would be no end to the storm at her spring and to the rain and high winds.

As soon as my lord Yvain felt that he was sufficiently healed, he left without anyone's noticing; but he had with him his lion, who would never leave him as long as he lived. Then they journeyed until they saw the spring and caused the rain to fall. Don't think I'm lying to you when I say that the storm was so violent that no one could tell the tenth part of it, for it seemed that the whole forest was about to fall into Hell! The lady was fearful that her town might collapse too; the walls trembled, the tower swayed and was on the point of crumbling. The boldest of her knights would rather have been captured by the Turks in Persia than be there within those walls. They were so afraid that they cursed their forefathers, saying: "Damn the first man to settle in this country, and those who built this town! In all the world they couldn't find a more hateful place, for a single man can invade and torment and beleaguer it."

"You must take counsel in this matter, my lady," said Lunete. "You won't find anyone willing to help you unless you seek far afield. Truly we'll never again have a moment's peace in this town, nor dare to pass beyond its walls and gate. Even if all your knights were assembled for this affair, you know full well that even the very best among them would not dare step forward. So the fact is that you have no one to defend your spring, and you will be shamed and ridiculed; it would be a pretty honor for you indeed if the knight who's attacked you leaves without a battle. Surely you are in a dreadful situation if you don't come up with something."

"You who are so clever," said her lady, "tell me what I should do about it, and I'll follow your advice."

"Indeed, my lady, if I had a solution I would gladly offer it; but you need a much wiser counselor than I. Therefore I don't dare interfere, and I'll endure the rain and wind along with everyone else until it pleases God to show me some brave man at your court who'll take upon himself the burden and responsibility of this combat. But I don't believe it will be today, which bodes ill for your situation."

And the lady answered her at once: "Mademoiselle, speak of something else! There's no one in my household I can expect to defend the spring or the stone. But if it please God, let us hear your advice and suggestion, for they always say that in time of need one can best test his friend." [6607]

"My lady, if someone thought he could find the man who slew the giant and defeated the three knights, he would do well to seek him out. Yet as long as he suffers the wrath and displeasure of his lady, I don't believe he'd follow any man or woman in this world, unless that person swore and promised to do everything in his power to alleviate the great enmity that his lady feels toward him, for he's dying of sadness and grief."

"I am prepared," her lady replied, "to pledge to you my word of honor before you set out upon this quest that, if he comes to my rescue, I will do everything he desires, without guile or deception, to reconcile them if I am able."

"My lady," Lunete answered her then, "I have no doubt that you can very easily make his peace, if you so desire. As for the oath, I hope you won't mind if I take it before I set off on my way."

"I've no objection," said her lady.

With consummate courtesy Lunete had a very precious reliquary brought to her at once, and the lady knelt before it. Lunete very courteously caught her in the game of Truth. As she administered the oath, she left out nothing that it might be useful to include.   [6644]

"Raise your hand, milady!" she said. "I don't want you to blame me in the future for this or anything, because you are not doing me a favor. What you're doing is for your own benefit! If you please, swear now that you will do all that you can to see that the Knight with the Lion will be assured of having his lady's good favor, just as he once had it."

The lady then raised her right hand and spoke these words: "As you have said, I say it too, that, so help me God and the saints, I will never be faint of heart or fail to do all that is within my power. I shall restore the love and good will that he once enjoyed with his lady, insofar as I have the strength and ability."

Now Lunete has succeeded. She had never desired anything as much as what she had just accomplished. A gently paced palfrey had already been led forth for her. Merrily and with a smile on her face Lunete mounted and rode until she found beside the pine tree the man she had not thought to find so near at hand. Instead she thought she'd have to search widely before coming upon him. Because of the lion she recognized him as soon as she saw him; she rode swiftly toward him, then dismounted upon the hard earth. And my lord Yvain recognized her as soon as he caught sight of her. He greeted her, and she him, saying: "Sire, I am very happy to have found you so nearby!"

"What?" my lord Yvain replied. "Were you looking for me, then?"

"In truth, yes, and I haven't felt so happy since the day I was born, for I have gotten my lady to agree, unless she wants to perjure herself, that she will be your lady again as she once was, and you her lord. I can tell you this in all truthfulness."

My lord Yvain was overjoyed at this marvelous news he thought he'd never hear. He couldn't show his gratitude enough to the girl who'd arranged this for him. He kissed her eyes and then her face, saying: "Indeed, my sweet friend, there is no way I could ever repay you for this. I fear that I don't have strength or time enough to pay you all the honor and service due."

"Sire," said she, "don't be concerned or let that worry you, for you'll have strength and time enough to help both me and others. If I have rendered what I owed, then I am due no more gratitude than the person who borrows another's goods and then repays him. And even now I don't believe I've paid back all I owed."

"You have indeed, as God's my witness, more than five hundred thousand times! Let's be off as soon as you're ready. And have you told her who I am?"

"No, upon my word; and she doesn't know you except as the Knight with the Lion."   [6722]

Thus they went off in conversation, with the lion faithfully following, until they all three reached the town. They spoke not a word to man or

woman they met in the streets. When they came before the lady, they found
her overjoyed at having heard that her maiden was approaching, bringing
with her the lion and the knight whom she was most eager to meet, to
know, and to see. My lord Yvain let himself fall at her feet in full armor; and
Lunete, who was beside him, said: "Milady, have him rise and use your
power, efforts and wisdom to procure that reconciliation and pardon that no
one this whole world over can procure except for you."

The lady had him rise at once and said: "All my resources are his. I wish
only to do his will and bring him happiness, so far as I am able."

"Indeed, milady, I wouldn't say it," replied Lunete, "if it weren't true:
you have much more power in this matter than I've said. So now I'll tell
you the whole truth, and you'll realize that you've never had and never will
have a better friend than this knight. God, who desires that there be perfect
peace and perfect love unending between you and him, caused me to find
him today quite nearby. To prove the truth of all this, there's but one thing
more to say: Milady, do not be angry with him further, for he has no other
lady but you. This is my lord Yvain, your husband."

At these words the lady trembled and said: "So help me God Almighty,
you've caught me neatly in your trap! In spite of me you'll make me love a
man who doesn't love or esteem me. What a fine thing you've done! What a
great way to serve me! I'd rather have put up with the storms and high
winds all my life; and if it weren't such an ugly and wicked thing to break
one's oath, this knight would find no peace with me no matter what his
efforts. Every day of my life I would have harbored, as fire smoulders under
the ashes, a pain that it is no longer fitting to mention, since I must be
reconciled to him."   [6782]

My lord Yvain heard and understood that his cause was proceeding so
well that he would have his peace and reconciliation. "Milady," he said,
"one should have mercy on a sinner. I have paid dearly for my foolishness,
and I am glad to have paid. Folly caused me to stay away, and I acknowledge my guilt and wrong. I've been very bold to dare to come before you
now, but if you would keep me I'll never do you wrong again."

"Indeed," said she, "I do agree to this, because I'd be guilty of perjury if
I did not do everything I could to make peace between us. So if you please, I
grant it to you."

"Milady," said he, "five hundred thanks! And as the Holy Spirit is my
help, nothing in this mortal life that God could give would have brought
such happiness!"

Now my lord Yvain is reconciled, and you can be sure that he'd never
before been so happy for anything. Although he has been through suffering, now everything has turned out well, for he was loved and cherished by
his lady, and she by him. He didn't recall any of the troubles, because the
joy he felt for his sweet love made him forget them all. And Lunete, too,
was very happy: she lacked for nothing now that she had made unending
peace between the noble Sir Yvain and his dear and noble lady. Thus
Chrétien brings to a close his romance of the Knight with the Lion. I've not
heard any more about it, and you'll never hear anything more unless one
adds lies to it.   [6824]

Explicit the Knight with the Lion.

Tintagel Castle in Cornwall, the birthplace of King Arthur. The ruins look out from a steep cliff over the Atlantic Ocean. (Courtesy of the British Tourist Authority)

chapter VI

BÉROUL:
THE ROMANCE OF TRISTAN

Norris J. Lacy

The love story of Tristan and Isolde is one of the most famous in literature. It tells of a passionate and illicit love born of a potion that the two drank by mistake. Because Isolde was pledged to marry Tristan's uncle, King Mark of Cornwall, their love could bring the young couple no happiness; instead it condemned them to suffering, guilt, exile, and a tragic end. This tragedy, throughout the centuries, has inspired countless authors, as well as painters, sculptors, and composers. Two of the greatest retellings of the Tristan and Isolde legend are among the earliest, dating from the second half of the twelfth century; they are the French texts of Béroul (translated here) and of Thomas of Britain in Chapter VIII.

In the medieval tradition the Tristan texts can be divided into two groups, known as the courtly and the primitive (or common) versions. The former, strongly influenced by court culture and by the spirit of courtly love, is a "refined" version, which gives a good deal of attention to the analysis of emotional and psychological states. The so-called primitive tradition includes texts that are less introspective and analytical and often more violent than the courtly version. Thomas's work is a representative of the courtly group, while Béroul's poem belongs to the primitive version. Béroul's work is known to us only in a single long fragment of nearly 4,500 lines of octosyllabic verse, preserved in one manuscript.

The term "primitive" should not be taken as an indication either of date (since Thomas may well predate Béroul) or of quality. Béroul's romance is in fact a highly effective work, composed by a poet of considerable talent. It offers a lively and engaging text. The many problematical or awkward passages (and internal contradictions, as when one of Tristan's enemies is killed, only to reappear later in the text) are no doubt due, not to authorial ineptitude, but to errors or changes introduced when the manuscript was copied—and perhaps, as some would contend, to dual authorship.

The narration is cyclical in form, as King Mark repeatedly becomes suspicious of the lovers and acts on those suspicions by threatening or punishing Tristan and Isolde, only to be somehow persuaded that his wife and nephew are guiltless; he then pardons them, and the cycle begins anew. A number of such cyclical episodes lead up to the long and remarkable scene at Mal Pas, where Isolde swears the equivocal oath that establishes her innocence in all eyes except ours. Béroul prepares that scene elaborately and with careful attention to its dramatic effect: King Arthur and his knights are summoned to witness the trial; Tristan disguises himself as a leper and deceives everyone who passes, taking childlike pleasure in his trickery and even bantering with Mark about the remarkable resemblance Isolde bears to the leper's own lady; and Isolde is depicted almost as a saint—but as a saint who has time for some suggestive asides to her lover. The entire scene is played out in a festive spirit of rollicking fun and mock-seriousness, rather than in the atmosphere of suspense and foreboding that we might expect when Isolde's reputation and life are at stake. The explanation, of course, is that they are *not* at stake. Isolde's vindication has been ensured by four allies: Tristan, Béroul, God, and herself. If we should doubt that God is on the side of the lovers and against their enemies, Béroul intervenes directly and frequently throughout the text, either to reassure us explicitly of that fact or to comment in his own voice on the events of the story.

Throughout the text Tristan and Isolde remain (for most readers) thoroughly sympathetic and likable characters, despite the fact that, technically, they are both traitors and unabashed sinners. But if they are sinners, they have an excuse: they drank a love potion and cannot escape its power for three years. However, even after the potion's power wanes, they feel regret rather than repentance—regret, not for having loved each other, but for the poverty and isolation to which their love has reduced them. Their concerns are far more material than moral. Eventually the hateful dwarf and other enemies of the lovers are punished, and Tristan and Isolde (at least temporarily) are free to see each other. Unfortunately the text breaks off in mid-sentence, leaving us to guess the ending from related texts.

The Béroul who composed this version of the legend identifies himself twice, in the third person, but we know nothing at all about him. Some have suggested in fact that the poem was the work of two authors, the second of whom took up the writing at the point where Tristan returns Isolde to King Mark, or perhaps when Isolde agrees to defend herself by oath. That conclusion, although rejected by a good many scholars, is based on considerations of style and versification and on the fact that the narrative content of the first part closely parallels a related German version of the story (the *Tristrant* of Eilhart von Oberge), while the second division diverges significantly from the German text. Yet, despite undeniable differences between the earlier and later portions of the text, the questions of Béroul's identity and of dual authorship remain unsettled.

Béroul—whoever he or they may have been—wrote during the last quarter of the twelfth century. While we cannot conclusively situate the text much more precisely than that, the mention of the *mal d'Acre* (*dagres* in the manuscript, line 3849) may well be a reference to an epidemic that struck the Crusaders at Acre in 1190 or 1191, suggesting that Béroul's *Tristan* dates from the final decade of that century. The manuscript that preserves the text (Paris, Bibliothèque Nationale, fr. 2171) dates from the middle or end of the following century.

Bibliographic note: The present translation is based on Muret's fourth edition; see Béroul, *Le Roman de Tristan,* edited by Ernest Muret (Champion, 1947). In some cases I have restored manuscript readings that Muret, perhaps needlessly, emended. I have been guided in the interpretation of numerous passages by two textual commentaries: A. Ewert, *The Romance of Tristan by Béroul,* Vol. II: Introduction, Commentary (Blackwell, 1970); and T. B. W. Reid, *The "Tristan" of Béroul: A Textual Commentary* (Blackwell, 1972). In addition I occasionally consulted two translations in Modern French, the line-for-line translation (*Le Roman de Tristan*) by Herman Braet (Gand, 1974) and the freer prose rendering by J. C. Payen: *Tristan et Yseut* (Garnier, 1974).

My translation follows the manuscript closely but not slavishly. I have made minor interpolations (rarely more than a few words) where transitions were needed for clarity. In only one case—a passage containing obviously and frequently corrupt readings—have I significantly altered the order of lines. I have retained the poet's addresses to his readers (although without his frequent *seigneurs,* "lords"). Lacunae in the original are indicated by [. . .]; when I have, infrequently, provided a hypothetical reading to remedy a textual difficulty, I have enclosed my suggestions within brackets; the bracketed material at the beginning of the text summarizes from other sources the events leading up to the opening of Béroul's fragment. Throughout the translation I have periodically inserted line numbers to facilitate comparison with the Old French edition of Muret.

The Romance of Tristan

[*The young Tristan, trained by his tutor and squire Governal on the Continent, had distinguished himself at Mark's court in Cornwall by defeating the Irish giant Morholt, who had demanded that Cornish youths be delivered to him as tribute. A fragment of Tristan's sword remained embedded in Morholt's skull and was found by the giant's niece Isolde. Later, when Tristan was sent to find a wife for King Mark, he came to Ireland, where he killed a dragon but was overcome by its poison. Isolde took care of him until, discovering the notch in his sword, she realized that he had killed Morholt. She spared his life only to avoid marriage to a dishonest seneschal, and she agreed to marry Mark. On the trip back to Cornwall she and Tristan unintentionally drank a love potion and fell hopelessly in love with each other. To conceal the loss of Isolde's virginity, her servant Brangain sacrificed her own by taking Isolde's place in the nuptial bed. Following the marriage Tristan and Isolde saw each other often, and Mark periodically became suspicious (often at the urging of barons who were jealous of Tristan). Béroul's text begins as Mark, warned by the dwarf that Tristan and Isolde intended to meet, had hidden in a tree in order to entrap them. The lovers saw his reflection in a fountain; Isolde, unsure whether Tristan had seen the king, spoke first, while taking care . . .*]

. . . not to give any indication that she was aware of Mark's presence. She approached her friend. Listen how she warned him: "Tristan, for God's sake, it is wrong of you to send for me at this hour!" Now she pretended to weep. [. . .] "In the name of God, the Creator of the heavens and the sea, never send for me again. I warn you, Tristan, I will not come. The king thinks I have slept with you, Tristan; but I affirm my fidelity before God, and may He punish me if anyone ever made love to me except the man who took my virginity. Yet the slanderous barons of this land, for whose sake you fought and killed Morholt, apparently make him believe the worst about us. Sir, I know you have no such desire; nor, in God's name, is there a shameful passion in my heart. I would rather be burned alive and have my ashes scattered in the wind than live a single day in love with anyone but my lord. Oh, God, he does not believe me! How far I have fallen! Sir, Solomon told the truth: whoever saves thieves from the gallows earns their hatred. If the traitors of this land [. . .] they should hide. You suffered greatly from the wound you received in your battle with my uncle. I cured you, and it is hardly astonishing that you became my friend as a result! And they have made the king believe that you love me sinfully. If they were to come before God for judgment, they would be damned! Wherever you may be, Tristan, do not send for me again for any reason. I would not be so daring as to come to you. In fact I'm staying here too long. If the king even suspected that I were here, he would kill me without hesitation, and it would be such a terrible injustice! I'm sure that he would kill me. Surely, Tristan, the king does not realize that he himself is the reason I have affection for you: I loved you because you were his relative. I recall that my mother loved my father's family a great deal, and she told me that a wife does not love her husband much if she does not also love his relatives. I know she was telling the truth. Sir, I loved you for his sake, and I thereby lost his favor." [. . .]

"Surely he is not entirely at fault," replied Tristan. "So his men made him believe something false about us."

"Can you doubt that, Tristan? The king, my husband, is honorable. He would never have suspected us of his own accord. But a man can be misled and made to do wrong. That is what they have done to my husband. Tristan, I am leaving now; I have stayed too long."

"My lady, for God's sake, have mercy on me. I sent for you; now you are here. Listen to my request. I have held you in such high esteem!"

When he heard his mistress speak, he knew that she was aware of the king's presence. He gave thanks to God and knew they would escape without harm: "Oh, Isolde, noble and honorable daughter of a king, several times have I sent for you in good faith. Since I am not permitted in your chamber, this is the only way I can speak with you. Lady, I now implore your mercy, and ask that you not forget this unhappy man who suffers pain and sorrow; and the fact that the king ever thought badly of us saddens me so much that there is nothing left for me to do but die. [. . . If only he] had been so wise as not to believe the liars who urged him to send me away! The traitors from Cornwall laugh and joke about it. Now I understand: they would not want anyone of his lineage around him. His marriage has caused me a great deal of pain. God! why is the king so foolish? I would let myself be hanged by the neck from a tree before I would be your lover! He does not even permit me to defend myself. Those traitors make him angry with me. He is wrong to believe them: they have deceived him, and he doesn't see that! When Morholt came here, I noticed that they never opened their mouths; nor was there a single one of them who dared take up arms. My uncle was very worried then. He would rather have been dead than alive. But I armed myself in order to defend his honor, I did battle, and I won. My uncle should not have believed what his informers say. I am enraged by it! Does he think himself guiltless in this? Surely he cannot fail to see it. Lady, in the name of God, the son of the Virgin Mary, tell him to have a fire made, and I will enter it; if even a single hair is singed on the hair-shirt I will be wearing, then let him have me burned to death; for I know that there is no one at court who will dare do battle with me. Lady, in your generosity, will you not take pity on me? Lady, I implore your mercy. Intercede for me with the king. When I came here to him from across the sea, [I came as a nobleman, and] I want to go back as a nobleman."

"Sir, it is wrong of you to ask me to speak to him about you and to urge him to pardon you. I am not ready to die! He suspects you of being my lover, and you expect me to speak on your behalf? That would be far too rash! I will not do it, Tristan, and you should not ask me to. I am all alone in this land. Because of me he has denied you admission to his chambers. It would be foolish of me to speak to him now about you. Indeed I will not say a word about it; but I will tell you this: I want you to know that if he did pardon you, I would be very happy. But if he knew of this meeting, Tristan, there is no way I could escape death. I am leaving, but I will not rest easy. I am afraid someone may have seen you come here. If the king heard that we met here, it would surprise no one if he had me burned alive. I must leave because I am afraid; I have stayed here too long."

Isolde turned away, and he called her back: "Lady, in the name of God, who to save the world took human form in the Virgin, have compassion and advise me! I know that you don't dare stay longer, but I have no one to turn to except you. I know the king hates me. My equipment has been confiscated. Have it returned to me, and I will flee, for I don't dare stay. I know my worth, and I know that there is no court in the world where I would not be welcomed. And I swear, Isolde, that before the year is up, my uncle will dearly regret having suspected that I ever had anything that belonged to him. I am telling you the truth. Isolde, in God's name, think of me and settle my debt to my host."

"Tristan, I am astonished at what you are asking! You are trying to ruin me. Those are not the words of a loyal friend. You know my husband's suspicions, however unjustified they may be. In the name of God, who created heaven and earth and us, too, if Mark heard that I had settled your debt, he would take that as proof of our guilt. I don't dare do that! And you can be assured that I am not refusing out of avarice."

Then Isolde turned and left, and Tristan, weeping, gave a gesture of farewell. Leaning against a stone, Tristan lamented all alone: "Oh, God! By St. Ebrulfus, I never thought I would suffer such a loss and have to flee in such poverty. I will not even have arms or a horse, nor any companions except Governal. O, God, no one respects a poor man! When I am in another country, if I hear a knight speak of war, I will have to hold my tongue: an unarmed man has no right to speak of battle. I will have to tolerate what fate has brought me, and it has done me an injustice. Good uncle, whoever suspected my conduct with your wife did not know me well! I had no desire to commit such folly."

[. . .] The king, who was up in the tree, had witnessed the meeting and heard the conversation. He was so overcome by pity that nothing could keep him from crying. His sorrow was great, and he hated the dwarf of Tintagel. "Alas," cried the king, "now I see that the dwarf deceived me! He has made me climb this tree and has shamed me completely. He made me believe a lie about my nephew, and for what he did I will have him hanged! He stirred up my anger and made me hate my own wife. I was a fool to believe him. He will pay for it. If I get my hands on him, I will have him burned to death! He will meet a worse fate at my hands than that inflicted on Segoncin, whom Constantine had castrated when he found him with his wife. He had crowned her in Rome, and she was served by many. He loved and honored her, but later he mistreated her and eventually regretted it."

Tristan had left earlier. The king came down from the tree. He told himself that he now believed his wife and doubted the barons, for they had made him believe something he knew to be untrue, something now proved false. With his sword he would give the dwarf what he deserved. Never again would he speak evil words! And never again would Mark suspect Tristan's intentions concerning Isolde. They could meet at will in the chamber. "Now I know the truth. If the rumors were true, this meeting would not have ended this way. They had enough time here; if they were lovers, I would have seen them kiss each other. But I heard them lamenting and know they are innocent. Why did I believe such outrageous rumors? I regret it now and repent: he is a fool who believes what everyone says. I should have established the truth about the two before accepting this foolish notion. This evening was a fortunate one for them: listening to them taught me never again to be suspicious of them. Tomorrow morning Tristan will be reconciled with me, and he will have permission to be in my chamber whenever he wishes. And he will not have to flee tomorrow, as he planned."

The hunchback dwarf Frocin was outdoors, looking up at Orion and Venus. He knew the course of the stars and observed the planets. He knew the future, and when a baby was born he could foretell its entire life. The malicious dwarf Frocin had taken great pains to deceive the king, who one day would kill him. Observing the ascent of the stars, he bristled with rage, for he knew that the king was threatening him and would not give up until he had killed him. The dwarf reddened, then turned pale. He fled as quickly as he could to Wales. The king looked everywhere for the dwarf but, to his great sorrow, could not find him.   [338]

Isolde came into her room. Brangain saw that she was pale and knew that she had heard something distressing; she asked her what it was. Isolde answered: "My dear lady, I have good reason to be pensive and sad. Brangain, I will not lie to you: I don't know who wants to betray us, but King Mark was in the tree, near the marble stone. I saw his shadow in the fountain. God gave me the presence of mind to speak first. I said not a word about what brought me there, I assure you: just sighs and laments. I blamed Tristan for sending for me, and he begged me to reconcile him with his lord, who had false suspicions about us. I told him that his request was foolish, that I would never meet him again and that I would not speak to the king. I don't think I need to tell you more. There were many laments. The king never saw or suspected the truth, and I escaped from the trap."

Brangain rejoiced at these words: "Isolde, my lady, God had mercy on us when he let you conclude the conversation without going further, for the king saw nothing that could not be interpreted in your favor. God has performed a great miracle for you. He is our great Father, and He does not want harm to come to those who are good and true."

Tristan, too, told Governal everything that had happened. When he finished the story, he thanked God that he and Isolde had not done more.

The king, unable to find his dwarf (God! that does not bode well for Tristan!), returned to his chamber. Isolde saw him and said fearfully: "Sir, where have you been? What makes you come here alone?"

"My queen, I have come to speak with you and to ask you a question. Do not conceal anything from me, for I want to know the truth."

"Sir, I have never lied to you. May I be struck dead if a single word of what I say is not true."

"My lady, have you seen my nephew?"

"Sir, I am telling you the truth. You will not believe it, but I will tell you the truth, without deceit. I saw him and spoke with him. I was under the pine tree with your nephew. Go ahead and kill me, king, if you wish. Yes, I saw him. It is a great pity that you think I am Tristan's mistress, and that grieves me so much that I don't care if you kill me. But have mercy on me this time! I told you the truth; if you do not believe me, but instead believe a foolish lie, my faith will protect me. Tristan, your nephew, asked me to meet him under the pine in the garden. He said nothing else, but I could not treat him cruelly: it is because of him that I am your queen. Certainly I would willingly show him proper respect, were it not for those who tell you lies. Sir, you are my husband, and he is your nephew; it is for your sake that I have loved him. But those who are evil and jealous, who want him gone from the court, make you believe lies. So Tristan is going away. May God cover them with shame! I spoke with your nephew yesterday evening. He desperately implored me to reconcile him with you, sir. I told him to leave and never to send for me again; for I would never again come to meet him, and I would not intercede for him. I assure you that nothing else happened. Kill me if you wish, but it would be unjust. Tristan is going away because of this dissension; I know he is leaving the country. He wanted me to pay for his lodging; I did not want to do that or to talk with him any longer. Sir, now I have told you the whole truth. If I have lied, you can cut off my head. Sir, I would gladly have paid his debt if I had dared, but because of your slanderous entourage I did not even want to slip four besants into his purse. He is going away poor; may God care for him! You are wrong to make him flee. Wherever he goes, God will be his true friend!"

The king knew she was telling the truth, for he had overheard the conversation. He embraced her and kissed her repeatedly. She wept, and he comforted her. Never again would he mistrust them because of what a slanderer said; and they could come and go at will. What was Tristan's would be his, and what was his would belong to Tristan. Never again would he believe Cornishmen. Then the king told the queen how the evil dwarf Frocin had informed him of the meeting, and how he had climbed the tree to spy on them.

"What! You were in the tree, sir?"

"Yes, my lady. I heard every word that was said. When I heard Tristan talk about the battle that he fought for me, I felt great pity for him. I almost fell out of the tree! And when I heard you recount his suffering at sea, because of the dragon's wound from which you cured him, and the care you took of him; and when he asked you to pay his debts—you did not wish to do so, and neither of you approached the other—I felt great pity up there in the tree. I smiled to myself, but did nothing else."

"Sir, I am very happy. Now you know that we had enough time. If we were lovers, you would have seen evidence of it. But you didn't see him approach me or make any advances or kiss me. That proves that he does not love me improperly. Sir, if you had not seen it for yourself, you would surely not believe it."

"That is true," replied the king. "Brangain, go to the inn and bring back my nephew; and if he hesitates or does not want to come with you, tell him I command it."

Brangain told him: "Sir, he hates me! God knows he is wrong! He says that it is my fault that he has quarreled with you. He desperately wants to see me dead. I will go; and perhaps, because of you, he will not harm me. Sir, for God's sake, reconcile him with me when he arrives!"

Listen to the cunning woman! She was being deceitful and lying when she complained about Tristan's hatred. "King, I am going for him," said Brangain. "Reconcile us; that will be a noble act."

The king answered: "I will do my best. Go now and bring him back."

Isolde smiled at this, and the king too. Brangain left at once. Tristan was waiting by the wall and had heard them talk with the king. He seized Brangain by the arm, embraced her, and gave thanks to God. From now on he could be with Isolde whenever he wished.

Brangain told Tristan: "Sir, there in his chambers the king spoke at length about you and your dear lady. He has pardoned you, and now he hates those who oppose you. He asked me to come to you; I told him you were angry with me. Pretend that I had to beg you to come with me and that you were reluctant. If the king intercedes for me, pretend to be angry."

Tristan embraced and kissed her. He was happy because now he would again be able to live as he wished. They entered the room that was decorated with murals. The king and Isolde were there, and when Tristan entered, the king said: "Nephew, come in! Forgive Brangain, and I will forgive you."

"Uncle, good sir, listen to me. You are taking this too lightly, for you have brought this upon me, and my heart is breaking! What an injustice! If we were guilty, I should be damned and disgraced. But God knows, we never had any sinful thoughts. And you should know that anyone who makes you believe such a thing surely hates you. From now on I advise you not to be angry with the queen or with me, your own relative."

"I will not, dear nephew, I assure you."

Tristan was reconciled with the king. Mark gave him permission to be in the royal chamber, and now he was happy. Tristan was free to come and go at will, and the king saw no harm in it.   [572]

God! Who could keep love secret for any period of time? For love cannot be hidden. Often one lover nods to the other, or they meet to speak together, in private or in public. They cannot easily postpone their happiness, and they cannot resist frequent trysts.

There were at the court three barons—never have you seen such evil men!—who had sworn that, if the king did not banish his nephew, they would no longer tolerate it; rather, they would withdraw to their castles and make war on Mark. The other day, in a garden, under a tree, they had seen the fair Isolde with Tristan in a compromising position; and several times they had seen them lying naked in King Mark's bed, for whenever Mark went into the forest, Tristan would say: "Sir, I'm leaving." But then he would stay behind, enter Isolde's chamber, and remain a long time with her.

"We will tell him ourselves. Let's go to the king and talk to him. Whatever he may think of us, we want him to banish his nephew." Together they decided on this course. They took the king aside and spoke to him. "Sir," they said, "there is trouble. Your nephew and Isolde love each other. It is obvious to anyone who cares to look, and we will no longer tolerate it!"

The king heard them, sighed, and bowed his head. He paced back and forth, not knowing what to say.

"King," said the three barons, "we will not permit this any longer, for we know for a fact that you are fully aware of their crime and that you condone it. What are you going to do about it? Think about it carefully. If you do not send your nephew away permanently, we will no longer remain loyal to you and will never leave you in peace. We will also persuade others to leave your court, for we cannot tolerate this any more. We have now offered you a choice; tell us your decision."

"Sirs, you are my faithful servants. May God help me, I am shocked that my nephew has tried to shame me; he certainly has a strange way of serving me! Please advise me. That is your duty, and I do not want to lose your services. You know that I am not proud!"

"Sir, send for the dwarf who foretells the future; he is versed in many arts. Let his advice be heard. Send for him, and let this matter be settled."

The hunchback dwarf—may he be cursed—came quickly. One of the barons embraced him, and the king explained his dilemma to him. Alas! Listen to the deceitful and evil advice the dwarf Frocin gave the king! May all such diviners be damned! Who could even imagine such villainy as the cursed dwarf conceived? "Order your nephew to go tomorrow to Arthur, at the fortified city of Carlisle. Have him take Arthur a message, closed and sealed with wax. King, Tristan sleeps near your bed. I know he will want to speak with Isolde tonight, before he has to leave. King, leave the room early during the night. I swear by God and the Church of Rome, if Tristan is her lover, he will come to speak with her. And if he does so without my knowing it or without you and all your men seeing him, then kill me. Otherwise their guilt will be obvious. King, let me take care of things and do what is necessary, and do not tell him of his mission until bedtime."

The king answered: "Friend, it shall be done." Then they separated, and each one went his own way.

The dwarf was crafty, and he did a terrible thing. First he went to a bakery and bought four deniers' worth of flour, which he hid in his apron. Who could have imagined such treachery! That night, when the king had eaten and the others had gone to bed, Tristan went into the king's chamber. "Good nephew," said Mark, "I want you to do me a service. Ride to King Arthur, at Carlisle, and deliver this letter to him. Nephew, give him my greetings, but stay only one day with him."

Tristan heard the message and told the king that he would deliver it: "Sir, I will leave early tomorrow—yes, before the night is through."

Tristan was very distressed. His bed was a lance's length away from the king's. Tristan had a foolish plan: he decided that he would speak to the queen, if he could, after the king was asleep. God! What a shame that he was so foolhardy!

The dwarf was in the room that night. Here is what he did during the night: he sprinkled flour between the two beds, so that footprints would be visible if one of the lovers joined the other that night. The flour would preserve the form of the prints. Tristan saw the dwarf busily spreading the flour. He wondered what was happening, for this was most unusual behavior. Then he thought: "Perhaps he is spreading flour on the floor in order to see our tracks if one of us should go to the other. I'd have to be a fool to take that chance now; he'll certainly see if I go to her."

The day before, in the forest, Tristan had been wounded in the leg by a large boar, and the wound was very painful and had bled heavily. Unfortunately it was unbandaged. Tristan, of course, was not sleeping. The king arose at midnight and left the room, and the hunchback dwarf left with him. It was dark in the room; there was no lit candle or lamp. Tristan stood up. God! he would regret this! Listen: he put his feet together, estimated the distance, jumped, and fell onto the king's bed. His wound opened, and the blood flowing from it stained the sheets. Although the wound was bleeding, he did not feel it, for he thought only of his pleasure. And the blood accumulated in several places.

The dwarf was outside. By the light of the moon he clearly saw the two lovers lying together. He trembled with joy and told the king: "If you can't catch them together now, you can have me hanged!"

The three evil barons, who had conceived this plot, were there. The king came back to the room. Tristan heard him coming; he got up, frightened, and quickly jumped back into his bed. But when he jumped, the blood (alas!) dripped from his wound into the flour. Oh, God! What a pity that the queen did not remove the bedsheets; if she had, nothing could have been proved against them. If she had thought of that, she could have protected her honor.

God performed a great miracle, which saved their life according to his will. The king came back to the room; the dwarf, holding the candle, came with him. Tristan pretended to be asleep and snored loudly. He was alone in the room, except for Perinis, sleeping soundly at his feet, and the queen in her bed. The warm blood could be seen in the flour. The king noticed the blood on the bed: the white sheets were red, and blood from Tristan's leap was visible on the floor.

The king threatened Tristan. The three barons, who were now in the room, angrily seized Tristan in his bed. They hated him because they were jealous of his great prowess, and they hated the queen too. They vilified and threatened her; they would not fail to see justice done. They saw Tristan's bleeding leg. "This is conclusive evidence; your guilt is proved," said the king. "Your denials are worthless. Tristan, tomorrow you will be put to death."

Tristan cried out: "Sir, have mercy! In the name of God, who was crucified, sir, take pity on us!"

The barons said: "Sir, avenge yourself!"

"Good uncle, I do not care about myself; I know I am doomed. If it were not for fear of angering you, this condemnation would be paid dearly. Never would it have occurred to them to lay a hand on me. But I bear you no ill will. Now, for better or for worse, do what you will with me. I am ready to suffer punishment at your hands. But sir, in God's name, take pity on the queen!" Tristan bowed to him and added: "And anyone at your court who accuses me of being the queen's lover should have to face me immediately in armed combat."

The three barons had Tristan and the queen seized and bound: hatred had triumphed. If Tristan had known that he would not have the opportunity to defend himself, he would have let himself be torn limb from limb before allowing either of them to be bound. But his faith in God was so strong that he was convinced that if he were permitted to defend himself, no one would dare take up arms against him; he knew he could defend himself well on the battlefield. For that reason he did not want to take any action in the king's presence; but if he had known how this had come about and what was still to come, he would have killed all three of them, and the king could not have saved them. Oh, God! Why did he not kill them? Justice would have been better served.   [826]

News spread quickly through the city that Tristan and the queen Isolde had been found together and that the king wanted to have them put to death. The people wept and said to one another: "Alas, we have good reason to weep! Oh, Tristan, you are such a worthy knight. What a pity that these villains betrayed and trapped you. Oh, good and honored queen, what land will ever have a princess who is your equal? Ah, dwarf, this is the result of your divination! May anyone who has an opportunity to kill the dwarf be damned if he does not do so! Oh, Tristan, dear friend, we will mourn bitterly when you are put to death. Alas, what grief! When Morholt came to this land and demanded our children, our barons remained silent, for not one of them was courageous enough to oppose him. You undertook the battle for us, the people of Cornwall, and you killed Morholt. He wounded you with a lance, sir, and you nearly died. We should not allow you to be put to death now."

The noise and confusion increased, and people came running to the palace. The king was furious; there was no baron so strong or courageous that he dared urge the king to pardon this crime. The night passed, and day broke. The king gave orders for thorny bushes to be gathered and a trench to be dug. Then he commanded that vine-shoots be found and piled up with hawthorns and blackthorns that had been pulled up by the roots. It was already early morning. A proclamation that was announced throughout the land summoned everyone to court. People came as quickly as they could; the people of Cornwall were all gathered there. There was great noise and commotion, and everyone grieved—except the dwarf of Tintagel.

The king announced that he intended to have his nephew and wife burned to death. All his subjects cried: "King, it would be a terrible injustice to put them to death without trying them first. Sir, have mercy!"

The king angrily responded: "Even if I should be disowned by God, the Creator of the world and everything in it, I am determined to have them burned, regardless of what anyone says. Now let all of my orders be carried out."

He commanded that the fire be lit and that his nephew be brought there: he wanted to burn him first. They went to get him, and the king waited. They led him back—God, this is too disgraceful! He wept, but to no avail; they took him away shamefully. Isolde wept, almost beside herself with despair: "Tristan," she said, "what a shame for you to be bound! I would willingly die if you were spared, dear friend; you would be able to avenge us."

Now hear how great is God's pity; He does not want a sinner to die. He heard the poor people's cries and pleas for the condemned couple. On the road they were taking there stood a chapel, built on the edge of a cliff, beside the sea, facing north. The part of the chapel called the chancel was on the edge of the rock; there was nothing beyond, except the cliff. The hill was of slaty stone. If a squirrel had jumped from it, it would certainly have been killed. In the apse was a purple window, the work of a pious man.

Tristan spoke to his guards: "Lords, here is a chapel; in God's name, let me go in. My life is about to end; I will pray to God that He have mercy on me, for I have sinned greatly. Lords, there is only this one door, and I see that each of you has a sword. It is obvious that I cannot escape, for I have to come out this way. And after I pray to God, I will return to you immediately."

They said to each other: "We can surely permit him to go in."

They untied him, and he entered. Tristan wasted no time, but went past the altar and came to the window. He opened it and jumped out. Jumping was better than being burned alive in public! Now, halfway down, a large flat rock extended out from the cliff, and Tristan landed nimbly on it. The wind caught in his clothes and broke his fall. In Cornwall the stone is still called "Tristan's Leap."

The chapel was filled with people. Tristan jumped down and fell to his knees in the soft sand. The guards were waiting in front of the church, but in vain: Tristan was gone, and God had generously granted him mercy. He ran away along the shore. He could hear the fire crackling, and he had no desire to go back; he ran as fast as he could.

But now listen to what Tristan's master Governal did. Armed, he rode out of the city. He knew that if he were caught, he would be burned in Tristan's place; fear made him run away. He did Tristan a great service by not leaving his sword behind; he picked it up where it lay and brought it with him, along with his own. Tristan saw his teacher and recognized him; he called to him, and Governal approached.

Tristan exclaimed joyfully: "Master, God had mercy on me! I escaped, and now here I am. But alas! What good is that? Since I do not have Isolde, nothing matters to me. I am so miserable! Why was I not killed when I jumped? I will surely regret having survived! I escaped—but, Isolde, they are going to burn you! Surely there was no reason for me to escape. They will burn Isolde because of me, and I will then die because of her!"

Governal said: "Good sir, in God's name, take comfort; don't despair. Here is a thicket surrounded by a trench. Sir, let's conceal ourselves in there. Many people pass here, so we should be able to hear news of Isolde. And if they burn her, then take to your saddle immediately to avenge her! You will have ample help. Never, in the name of Jesus, the son of Mary, will I rest until the three villainous barons who destroyed your lady Isolde have met their deaths. And if you should be killed, sir, before vengeance is taken, I could never be happy again!"

Tristan answered: "You are making too much of this, good master, for I do not even have a sword."

"Yes, you do, for I brought it."

Tristan said: "That pleases me, master, and now I fear nothing, except God."

"I also have something else that you will find most useful: a strong and light hauberk. You will surely need it."

"Give it to me," said Tristan. "By God, if I can get there before my lady is thrown into the flames, I would rather be torn limb from limb than fail to kill her captors."

Governal said: "Do not hurry. God will give you a better way to take vengeance. Then you will not have the obstacles you now face. I see nothing you can do now, for the king is angry with you, and he controls all the inhabitants of the city. He swore that he would hang anyone who passed up a chance to capture you. Everyone is more concerned about himself than about you: if you were accused, there are many who would like to save you but would be afraid even to consider it."

Tristan wept bitterly. If his master had not urged him not to go, he would have returned in spite of all the people of Tintagel, without fear for his life.

A messenger ran into Isolde's room and told her not to cry, for her friend had escaped. "Thanks be to God," she said; "now I do not care if they kill me, or whether I am bound or free."

The king, at the urging of the three barons, had her bound, and she was tied so tightly that her wrists were bleeding. She said: "If I felt pity for myself, now that my friend—thank God!—has escaped from his enemies, I would not be deserving of respect. I know that the evil dwarf and the jealous barons, who want to have me killed, will some day get what they deserve. May they be damned!"

The news came to Mark that his nephew, whom he was to burn, had escaped through the chapel. His face darkened with rage; he could hardly control himself. He angrily commanded that Isolde be brought to him. She left her room, and the clamor increased in the street. When they saw that the queen's hands were shamefully bound, the people were shocked. You should have heard them grieving and imploring God's mercy: "Oh, noble and honorable queen, what grief has been spread throughout the land by those who are responsible for this scandal! And a very small purse would hold all the profit they have gained. May they be cruelly pun-ished!"   [1082]

The queen was brought to the pyre. Dinas, the lord of Dinan, who loved Tristan dearly, fell at the king's feet. "Sir," he said, "listen to me. For a long time I have served you honestly and loyally; you will not find anyone in this kingdom, not even a poor orphan or an old woman, from whom I have profited because of my position as seneschal, a position I have held my whole life. Sir, have mercy on the queen! You want to have her burned without a trial; that is not honorable, since she has not confessed the crime. It will be a tragedy if you have her burned. Sir, Tristan has escaped. He knows the plains, the forests, the trails, and the fords, and he is to be feared. You are his uncle, he your nephew. He would not attack you directly, but if he captured or assaulted the barons, your land would be ravaged. Sir, I can assure you: if a king who ruled over seven countries killed or burned even one of my squires, all his kingdoms would be endangered before I would have fully settled accounts. Do you think Tristan will simply stand by and permit the death of such a noble woman, whom he brought here from a distant kingdom? No, there will be serious trouble. King, entrust her to me, in recognition of my long service to you."

The three who had arranged all this had fallen silent and left; they knew that Tristan was free and were afraid that he was lying in wait for them. The king took Dinas by the hand; angrily he swore by St. Thomas that he would not fail to see justice done and the queen thrown into the flames. Hearing that, Dinas was very sad, because he did not want her to die. He rose, his head bowed: "King, I am going back to Dinan. In the name of God, who created Adam, I would not watch her being burned for all the wealth of all the richest men who have lived since the glory of Rome." Then he mounted his horse and turned away, sad and bereaved, with his head bowed.

Isolde was led to the fire. She was surrounded by people who screamed, cried, and cursed the traitors who had advised the king. Tears flowed down her face. She was dressed in a tunic of dark silk, finely stitched in gold. Her hair reached to her feet and was held by a golden net. One would have to have a very hard heart to see her and not feel pity for her. Her arms were tied very tightly.

There was a leper named Ivain, from Lantyan, and he was terribly deformed. He had come to witness the punishment. With him were a hundred of his companions, with their crutches and staffs. Never have you seen people so ugly, tumorous, and deformed! Each one carried a rattle to warn people of his approach. Ivain cried out to the king in a shrill voice: "Sir, you want to see justice done and have your wife burned! That is cruel punishment, of course, but it would not last long. The fire would quickly consume her, and the wind would scatter her ashes. The fire would die out soon, and the punishment would not outlast the embers. But if you will take my advice, you can punish her in such a way that she will live on in disgrace and will wish to be dead, and everyone who hears about that will respect you all the more. King, would you like to do that?"

The king heard him and answered: "If you tell me how she can live and be dishonored, I assure you I will be grateful to you, and I will reward you if you wish. In God's name, he who can select the worst and most painful punishment of all will have my eternal gratitude."

Ivain answered: "I will tell you my idea. Just look, I have a hundred companions here. Give Isolde to us, and she will be our common property. No woman ever had a worse fate. Sir, our desire is so strong that no woman in the world could bear a whole day with us. And see how our ragged clothes stick to our bodies? With you she was accustomed to luxury: furs, festivities, fine wines, and spacious marble chambers. If you give her to us lepers, when she sees our 'court,' when she lives in our small huts and eats out of our dishes and has to sleep with us, and when, instead of your fine food, she has only some of the scraps that are given to us, then she will despair and will prefer death to such a life! That viper Isolde will then know how terrible her actions were, and she will wish she had been burned."

The king listened to him and then stood there a long time without moving. He understood what Ivain had said. Then he ran to Isolde and took her by the hand. She cried: "Sir, have mercy! Don't give me to them! Have me burned here!"

The king gave her to Ivain, and he took her. There were fully a hundred lepers, and they all crowded around her. Everyone who heard their cries and wails was filled with pity. But if others were sad, Ivain was delighted! He immediately led her away down the hill. All the lepers, on their crutches, were heading directly toward the place where Tristan was lying in wait.

Governal cried loudly: "My son, what will you do? There is your lady!"

"God," said Tristan, "what good fortune! Oh, beautiful Isolde, you who were to die for me, as I for you! Your captors can be sure that if they do not release you immediately, I will make them regret it." He spurred his horse and rode out of the thicket. He cried at the top of his voice: "Ivain, that's far enough. Let her go, or I will cut off your head with this sword!"

Ivain, taking off his cloak, cried loudly: "Attack with your crutches! Show me who is on my side!"

You should have seen the lepers panting and tearing off their cloaks! They all brandished their crutches, threatening and cursing Tristan. He had no desire to injure them, but Governal, attracted by the shouts, came running with a green limb in his hand and struck Ivain, who was holding Isolde. Ivain started bleeding heavily. Tristan's master served him well; he recovered Isolde. Storytellers say that they drowned Ivain, but they are wrong; they do not know the true story, and Béroul remembers it better than they. Tristan was too valiant and courtly to kill lepers!

Tristan went away with the queen. They left the plain and, along with Governal, passed through the woods. Isolde was very happy. They were in the forest of Morrois, and that night they slept on a hill. Now Tristan was as safe as he would have been in a fortified castle. [1278]

Tristan was an excellent archer, skilled with the bow. Governal had taken one from a forester, and he had brought two feathered and barbed arrows. Tristan took the bow and set out through the woods. He saw a buck, drew his bow, and shot, striking the animal directly in the right side. It cried out, leapt up in the air, and fell back to the ground. Tristan brought it back with him.

He prepared his shelter, using his sword to cut branches and making a bower. Isolde spread leaves around thickly; Tristan and the queen settled in it. Governal, who was a skilled cook, made a fire of dry wood. They were certainly well equipped for cooking: they had no milk or salt in their lodging! The queen was exhausted from the fear she had experienced. She became drowsy and wanted to sleep; she wanted to go to sleep beside her lover. Thus they lived deep in the forest; they remained in the wilderness for a long time.

Now hear how the dwarf served the king! The dwarf knew a secret about the king, and no one else knew it. He foolishly revealed it, and as a result the king cut off his head. The dwarf was drunk one day, and the barons asked him why he and the king spoke together so often in private, and what they said. "I have always loyally concealed one of his secrets. I see that you want to know it, but I don't want to betray my word. I will take the three of you to the ford called the Gué Aventuros. There is a hawthorn there, with a hollowed-out trench underneath the roots. If I put my head in there, you can overhear me from outside, and what I say will be about the secret that only I share with the king."

The barons followed the dwarf to the hawthorn. The dwarf was short, but he had a large head, so they enlarged the hole and then stuck his head and neck into it. "Now listen, lords! Hawthorn, I am talking to you, and not to any man: Mark has ears like a horse!" They heard the dwarf.

It happened that, one day after dinner, King Mark was talking with his barons, and in his hand he had a bow of laburnum. The three to whom the dwarf had told the secret came to the king and said to him: "King, we know your secret."

The king laughed and said: "It is the fault of that diviner that I have horse's ears; believe me, this will be the end of him!" He drew his sword and cut off the dwarf's head. That pleased many people who hated the dwarf Frocin for what he had done to Tristan and the queen.

You have heard how Tristan had jumped down on the rocky ledge, and how Governal had fled on horseback, because he feared he would be burned if Mark captured him. Now they were together in the forest, and Tristan fed them with venison. They remained in the woods, but every morning they left the place where they had spent the night. One day, by chance, they came to the hermitage of Brother Ogrin. They were leading a hard and painful life, but their love was so strong and true that both of them were oblivious to their suffering.

The hermit recognized Tristan and, leaning on his staff, addressed him: "Sir Tristan, throughout Cornwall it has been sworn that whoever delivers you to the king will receive a reward of one hundred marks. There is not a baron in the land who has not pledged to turn you over to him dead or alive." Then Ogrin told him kindly: "By my faith, Tristan, whoever repents of his sin through faith and confession will be pardoned by God."

Tristan answered him: "Sir, by faith, you do not know why she loves me deeply. If she loves me, it is because of the potion. I cannot leave her, nor can she leave me, I tell you truly."

Ogrin said: "And what comfort could be given to a dead man? For any man is as good as dead who lives for a long time in sin and does not repent. Absolution cannot be given to a man who does not repent." The hermit

Ogrin preached to them at length and urged them to repent. He explained to them the prophecies of scripture and spoke often of their isolation. He said fervently to Tristan: "What will you do? Think about it carefully!"

"Sir, I love Isolde so much that I cannot sleep! My mind is made up. I would rather be a beggar with her and live on grasses and acorns than to have the kingdom of King Otrant. There is no point in even talking about leaving her, because I cannot do it."

Isolde, at Ogrin's feet, was weeping. The color drained from her face, and she repeatedly implored him to grant them mercy: "Sir, by omnipotent God, we love each other only through the power of a potion we drank. That was our tragedy, and that is why the king drove us away."

The hermit answered: "May God, Creator of the world, lead you to repent."

For their sake Ogrin gave up the hermit's life that night, and the couple spent the night at the hermitage. In the morning they left. Tristan stayed in the woods and avoided the open fields. They lacked for bread, and life was hard. He managed to kill enough stags, does, and bucks to keep them alive. Wherever they stopped, they made a fire and cooked, and they never stayed more than a single night in the same place.

The king had a warrant issued for Tristan: in every corner of Cornwall the terrible news is spread that whoever finds Tristan must turn him in.   [1436]

Anyone who would now like to hear a story that shows the benefits of training an animal should listen to me well. You will hear about Tristan's good hunting dog. No king or count ever had one like it. He was fast and alert; he was beautiful and he ran well, and his name was Husdent. He was leashed, and he kept watch from the dungeon. He was unhappy because he missed his master, and he refused all food. He whined and pawed the ground, tears in his eyes. What pity people felt for the dog! They all said: "If he were mine, I would let him go; it would be a shame if he went mad. Oh, Husdent, there will never be another hunting dog who grieves so much for his master. No animal ever loved anyone so much. Solomon correctly said that his dog was his best friend. You are proof of that, because you have refused to eat since your master was captured. King, release the dog!"

The king, thinking the dog was going mad because he missed his master, said to himself: "This dog is most discerning, for in all of Cornwall I do not think that in our time we could find a knight the equal of Tristan."

The three barons of Cornwall urged the king: "Sir, unleash Husdent. Then we will see whether he is grieving for his master; for if he is mad, he will bite somebody or something as soon as he is free, and his tongue will hang out of his mouth."

The king called a squire to have Husdent released. Everyone climbed up on benches and stools for fear of the dog. Everyone said: "Husdent is mad!" But he paid no attention to them. As soon as he was released, he ran past them without hesitation; he raced out the door and ran to the house where he used to meet Tristan. The king and the others watched him. The dog barked and whined and appeared to be very sad.

Then he picked up his master's trail, and he followed every step that Tristan had taken when he was captured and was to be burned. Everyone urged the dog on. Husdent entered the room where Tristan had been betrayed and arrested; he bounded out of the room, barking, and ran toward the chapel, with the people close behind. Now that he was finally free, he did not stop until he reached the church built on the cliff. The faithful Husdent ran into the chapel without pausing; he jumped onto the altar and, not seeing his master there, jumped out the window. He fell down the cliff and injured his leg. He sniffed the ground and barked. At the edge of the woods where Tristan had taken refuge Husdent paused briefly, then plunged into the forest. Everyone who saw him felt pity for him. The knights said to the king: "Let's stop following the dog. We might not be able to get back easily from where he is leading us."

They left the dog and turned back. Husdent found a trail, and the sound of the happy dog barking filled the woods. Tristan was deep in the forest, with the queen and Governal. They heard the sound; Tristan listened and said: "I am sure that is Husdent I hear." They were frightened. Tristan jumped up and grabbed his bow, and they hid in a thicket. They were afraid of the king and thought he might be with the dog. Husdent, following the trail, wasted no time. When he saw Tristan and recognized him, he raised his head and wagged his tail. Anyone who had seen him weep with joy would have said that no one had never witnessed such happiness.

Husdent ran to the blonde Isolde, and then to Governal. He was happy to see all of them—even the horse. Tristan felt pity for the dog. "Oh, God," he said, "it is unfortunate that the dog followed us. People in hiding have no need for a dog that will not remain silent in the forest. We have to stay in the woods, hated by the king. Lady, Mark has people searching for us on the plains, in the forest, everywhere! If he found us and captured us, he would have us burned or hanged. We don't need a dog. We can be sure that if Husdent stays with us, he will bring us nothing but trouble. It is better to kill him than to let ourselves be captured because of his barking. I regret that such a noble animal came here only to die; it was his noble nature that made him do it. But what else can I do? It grieves me that I have to kill him. Help me make the decision; we have to protect ourselves!"

Isolde told him: "Sir, take pity on him! A dog barks while hunting as much from training as from instinct. After Arthur became king, I heard of a Welsh forester who had trained his hunting dog so that when he wounded a stag with an arrow, the dog would follow the stag anywhere without barking or making any sound. Tristan, it would be wonderful if we could train Husdent not to bark while hunting."

Tristan stood and listened to her. He took pity on the animal; he thought a moment and then said: "If I could train Husdent not to bark, he would be of great value to us, and I will try to do it before the week is out. I don't want to kill him; but I am afraid of his barking, because some day when I am with you or Governal, his barking might cause us to be captured. So I will do my best to train him to hunt without barking."

Tristan went hunting in the forest. He was a skilled hunter, and he shot a buck. Blood flowed from its wound; the dog barked, and the wounded buck fled. The barking of the excited dog echoed through the forest. Tristan struck him violently. Husdent stopped by his master's side, ceased barking, and abandoned the chase. He looked up at Tristan, not knowing what to do. Tristan forced the dog forward, using a stick to clear the path. Husdent wanted to bark again, but Tristan continued to train him. Before the month was up, the dog was so well trained that he followed trails without a sound. Whether on snow, on grass, or on ice, he never abandoned his prey, however fleet or agile it might be.

Now the dog was a great help to them, and he served them well. If he caught a deer or buck in the woods, he would hide it carefully, covering it with branches. And if he caught it in the open, as he often did, he would throw grass over it. He would then return to his master and lead him to the place where he had killed the deer. Indeed dogs are very useful animals!

Tristan remained in the forest for a long time, and he suffered greatly. He did not dare remain long in one place. He knew that the king's men were searching for him and that Mark had ordered anyone who found him to capture him. They lacked for food: they lived on meat and ate nothing else. Is it any surprise that they became pale and thin? Their clothes, torn by branches, became ragged. For a long time they fled through Morrois. Each of them suffered equally, but because they were together, neither was aware of pain. The fair Isolde greatly feared that Tristan would repent because of her; and conversely, Tristan worried that Isolde, disgraced on his account, would repent of her irresponsible actions.   [1655]

Listen now to what happened to one of the three whom God has cursed, and through whom the lovers were discovered. He was a powerful man who was highly respected. He loved to hunt with dogs. The people of Cornwall were so afraid of the forest of Morrois that none of them dared enter it. They had good reason to be afraid, for if Tristan could capture them, he would hang them on trees. They were right to avoid the forest!

One day Governal was alone with his horse, beside a stream that flowed out of a little spring. He had unsaddled his horse, and it was grazing on the tender grass. Tristan was lying in his hut, with his arms tightly around the queen, for whom he had suffered such hardship and torment; they were both asleep. Governal was hidden, and by chance he heard dogs that were pursuing a stag at full speed. They were the dogs of one of the three whose advice had incited the king's wrath against the queen. The dogs ran, and the stag fled. Governal followed a path and came to a heath; far behind him he saw the man whom his lord hated more than anything, and he was approaching alone, without a squire. He spurred and whipped his horse sharply, so that it sprang forward. The horse stumbled on a stone. Stopping beside a tree, Governal hid and waited for the baron, who was approaching rapidly but would be slow to flee! The wheel of fortune cannot be turned backward: he was not on his guard against the anger that he had inspired in Tristan. Governal, under the tree, saw him coming and waited resolutely. He told himself he would rather have his ashes scattered in the wind than pass up a chance for revenge, for it was because of this man and his actions that all of them nearly perished.

The dogs were following the fleeting stag, and the man came after them. Governal jumped out of hiding, and thinking of all the evil the man had done, he cut him to pieces with his sword. He took the head and rode away. The hunters, who had flushed out the frightened stag, were still pursuing it when they saw the headless body of their lord under the tree. They fled as quickly as they could. They were sure that this had been done by Tristan, the object of the king's proclamation.

Throughout Cornwall it was known that one of the three who had caused trouble between Tristan and the king had had his head cut off. All the people were afraid, and they avoided the forest, rarely hunting there any more. Anyone who did enter the forest to hunt feared that the valiant Tristan would find him; Tristan was feared on the plains and even more on the heath.

Tristan lay in his bower; the weather was hot, and the bower was covered with leaves. He was asleep and didn't know that the man who had nearly cost him his life had been killed: he would be happy when he learned the truth. Governal approached the hut, holding the dead man's head in his hand. He tied it to a forked limb by the hair. Tristan awoke, saw the head, and jumped up, frightened. His master cried out: "Stay there; don't be alarmed! I killed him with this sword. You see that it is your enemy." Tristan was happy at what he heard: the man he feared most was dead.

Everyone in the country was so terrified of the forest that no one dared enter it. The lovers had the woods to themselves. While they were there, Tristan invented the Unfailing Bow. He set it up in the woods in such a way that it killed everything that came in contact with it. If a deer came through the woods and touched the branches where the bow was set up and drawn, the bow shot high if the animal touched it high, low if it touched it near the ground. Tristan rightly called it the Unfailing Bow, for it never failed to strike anything, low or high. It served them very well, and enabled them to eat a good many stags. They had to live on wild game in the forest, since they had no bread, and they did not dare show themselves outside the woods. This exile lasted a long time. Tristan provided well for them, and they had an abundance of venison.

It was a summer day, during the harvest season, soon after Pentecost. It was early morning, and the birds were greeting the dawn. Tristan, girding on his sword, left the hut alone to go to the Unfailing Bow. He went hunting through the woods. Before going, he was in great distress—did anyone else ever suffer so much? But because of their pleasure together, both were oblivious to pain. Never, since they had come to the forest, had two people ever tasted such sorrow. Nor, according to the story that Béroul has read, did two people ever love each other so much or pay so dearly for their love.

The queen came to meet him. The heat was oppressive. Tristan kissed her and said: [". . ." She asked:] "Where have you been?"

"I have been hunting a stag, and I am tired. I chased it until I was exhausted. Now I want to sleep."

The bower was made of green branches, with foliage added here and there, and the floor was covered with leaves. Isolde lay down first. Then Tristan lay down, drew his sword, and placed it between them. Isolde was wearing a chemise—if she had been naked, tragedy would have befallen them that day!—and Tristan had his trousers on. The queen wore her emerald wedding ring, but her finger had become so thin that the ring would scarcely stay on.

Notice how they were lying: she had one arm under Tristan's head, and the other one lay over him, so that she was embracing him closely; and he also had his arms around her. Their love was not feigned! Their mouths were close together, but not touching. No breeze was blowing, and the leaves were motionless. A ray of sunshine fell on Isolde's face, which shone brightly. Thus the lovers were sleeping and were not expecting trouble. There were only the two of them, for Governal had ridden down into the woods to see the forester.

Now listen to what happened: they had a narrow escape! A forester had found the bowers where they had stayed, and now he followed their trail until he came to the thicket where Tristan had made his shelter. He saw them sleeping and recognized them. He turned pale and left quickly, trembling with fear: he knew that Tristan, if he should wake up, would take no hostage except his head. It is no wonder that he fled! He ran out of the woods at full speed. [1850]

Tristan and Isolde slept on: they barely escaped death! The place where they slept was two leagues away from where the king was holding court. The forester ran quickly to the king, because he had heard the proclamation about Tristan: whoever gave the king news of him would be handsomely rewarded. The forester knew it, and that was why he ran so swiftly.

King Mark was holding court with his barons in his palace; the hall was filled. The forester ran down the hill and rushed into the palace. Do you think he even paused before coming to the steps in the room? He ran up the stairs. The king saw the forester run in and called to him: "Are you in such a hurry because you have some news? You are running like a man pursuing an animal with his dogs. Are you here to lodge a complaint against someone at court? You give the impression of being in trouble and of having come a long way. If you have something to say, tell me. Did someone refuse to pay a debt or drive you out of my forest?"

"King, please listen to me! Throughout the land it has been announced that whoever finds your nephew should risk his life to capture him or to come and inform you. I have found him! But I am afraid of angering you. If I tell you, will you kill me? I will lead you to the place where he and the queen are sleeping. I saw them together, just now, and they were sound asleep. I was terrified when I saw them."

The king heard him. He sighed, then became agitated and angry. He asked the forester privately: "Where are they? Tell me."

"They are sleeping together in a hut in the forest of Morrois. Come quickly, and we will have our revenge. King, if you do not take cruel vengeance, you have no rightful claim on this land."

The king told him: "Leave here. If you value your life, tell no one what you know, whether he be a stranger or one of my men. Go to the red cross, at the fork in the road by the cemetery. Don't leave there; wait for me. I will give you all the gold and silver you want, I swear it."

The forester left the king, went directly to the cross and remained there. May God curse him, who so wanted to destroy Tristan! He would have been better off leaving, for he would die a terrible death, as you will hear later.

The king entered the room; he convened his retinue and forbade them to be so bold as to follow him. Everyone said: "King, are you serious about going somewhere alone? Kings never travel without an escort. What news have you heard? Don't act on the word of a spy!"

The king answered: "I know nothing. But a maiden asked me to come and speak with her and not to bring anyone with me. I will go by myself, on horseback, without any companion or squire; I will be completely alone."

They answered: "This worries us. Remember, Cato ordered his son to avoid deserted places."

He replied: "I know that, but let me do what I must do."

The king had his horse saddled; he girded on his sword, all the while lamenting the evil Tristan had done by abducting the beautiful, fair Isolde, with whom he had fled. If he found them, they would not be safe: he would not fail to kill them. The king was bent on destruction—what a pity! He left the city, saying to himself that he would rather be hanged than fail to avenge himself on those who had sinned so against him.

He came to the cross, where the man was waiting for him. The king told him to go quickly and lead him to the lovers. They entered the shadowy woods, the spy leading the king. Mark followed him, trusting in the sword at his side, for it had served him often and well. But he was too presumptuous; for if Tristan awoke and the nephew and uncle fought, one of them would surely have died before the battle was over. King Mark said to the forester that he would give him twenty marks of silver to lead him to the right place, as he had promised. The forester (may he be shamed!) said that they were near their destination. The spy held the king's stirrup and had him dismount from his good Gascon horse, and they tied the horses' reins to a green apple tree. They had advanced only a short distance when they saw the bower they were seeking.

The king opened the golden clasps of his cloak and took it off, revealing his strong body. He drew his sword and advanced angrily, telling himself that if he didn't kill them he himself deserved to die. With his sword drawn he entered the bower. The forester had been following closely behind the king, but Mark signaled for him to leave.

The king raised his sword in anger, but then hesitated. He was on the point of striking them; what a tragedy it would have been if he had killed them! Then he saw that she was wearing her chemise, and he saw that there was a space between them, and that their lips were not touching; and when he saw the naked sword separating them and the trousers that Tristan wore, he said: "God, what can this mean? Now that I have seen how they behave together, I do not know what to do. Should I kill them or leave? They have been in the woods a long time. Surely, if they were lovers, they would not be dressed, and they would not have a sword between them. They would be lying together in quite a different way! I wanted to kill them; I won't touch them, but will calm my anger. They have no illicit desires. I won't strike either of them. They are asleep. It would have been terrible if I had touched them; and if I awoke Tristan and either of us killed the other, people would condemn my actions. Before they awaken, I will leave them proof that they were found asleep and that I took pity on them. I do not want them killed, either by me or by any of my men. I see on the queen's finger the fine emerald ring I gave her. I have another one that was once hers. I will take mine off her finger. I have with me some fur gloves which she brought with her from Ireland; I will use them to block the sunlight falling on her face and making her hot. And when I am ready to leave, I will take the sword that now lies between them, and with which Morholt was beheaded."

The king took off his gloves. He looked at the two sleeping together and gently placed the gloves so as to block the sun's ray from Isolde's face. The ring was visible on her finger; he pulled at it without disturbing her. Although it had once been very tight, her fingers were now so thin that it came off easily. The king took it from her without difficulty. Then he gently removed the sword that was between them and replaced it by his own. He then left the bower, mounted his horse, and told the forester to leave immediately; and he did so. The king departed also, leaving the lovers asleep. On that occasion he did nothing more: he returned to the city. Everyone asked him where he had been for so long, but the king lied to them, not admitting where he had been, what he had been seeking, or what he had done.

Now we return to the sleeping couple, whom the king had left in the forest. The queen was dreaming that she was in a rich pavilion in a large wood. Two lions approached her, intending to devour her; she was about to beg for mercy when each of the famished lions took her by the hand. Her fear made Isolde cry out, and she woke up. The gloves, trimmed in white ermine, had fallen on her breast. Her cry awoke Tristan. With his face flushed he sprang to his feet and grabbed the sword like a man enraged. Looking at it, he saw that there was no notch in the blade; he then noticed the golden hilt and recognized the sword as the king's.

The queen saw on her finger the ring he had left her, and saw that he had taken the other one. She cried: "Alas, sir, the king has discovered us!"

He answered: "That is true, my lady. Now we must leave Morrois, for he is surely convinced of our guilt. He has taken my sword and left me his. He could easily have killed us!"

"Sir, I agree with you."

"My love, there is nothing for us to do except flee. He left us only to come back and capture us later. He was alone, and he has now gone back for help. I'm sure he plans to capture us. Lady, let us flee toward Wales. I am faint!" He became pale.

At that moment their squire was returning with the horse. He saw that his lord was pale and asked him what was wrong. "Alas, master, Mark found us sleeping here. He left his sword and took mine. I'm afraid he is arranging a violent punishment. He took the beautiful ring from Isolde's finger and left her his. Master, from those actions we can only conclude that he means us harm. He was alone when he found us; he was afraid, and he went back for help, for he has many courageous and able men. He will bring them back, and he wants to destroy the queen Isolde and me. He wants to capture us, burn us in public, and scatter our ashes to the wind. Let's flee; we cannot stay any longer."

It is true that they could not stay; they could not help being afraid, for they knew the king was of a violent and angry nature. Fearing him because of what had happened, they left quickly. They passed through Morrois, and their fear kept them going day after day; they fled toward Wales. Love has caused them great pain. For three full years they have suffered, and they have become pale and weak. [2132]

*   *   *

You have heard about the wine they drank, which caused them so much torment; but you may not know how long the love potion was supposed to last. Isolde's mother, who brewed it, made it to be effective for three years of love. She made it for Mark and for her daughter; someone else drank it and suffered because of it. For the full three years the wine so dominated Tristan, and the queen too, that neither was unhappy.

On the day after the feast of St. John the three years of the potion's effect were ended. Tristan got up, leaving Isolde in her bower. He saw a stag and shot an arrow at it, wounding it in the side. The stag fled, and Tristan followed it; he pursued it until evening. As he was running after it, the hour came that was the exact anniversary of his drinking the love potion.

Suddenly he repented, saying to himself: "Oh, God, I am suffering so much; for three full years I have had nothing but pain, day in and day out! I have forgotten chivalry, court life, and baronage. I am in exile, deprived of furs and fine clothes, no longer living at court with other knights. God! My uncle would have loved me so much if I had not betrayed him! Oh, God, I am so miserable! I should be at the royal court, attended by a hundred young men who serve me in order to become knights themselves. I should be leading profitable missions to foreign lands. And it distresses me that I have given the queen a hut in the woods instead of a rich chamber at court. She lives in the forest, when she with her attendants could be in beautiful rooms decorated with silk. Her life has been ruined, and it is my fault. I ask mercy from God, ruler of the world. May He give me strength to leave my uncle and his wife in peace! Before God I swear that I would do it if I could, so that Isolde might be reconciled with King Mark, who married her—alas!—publicly and in accordance with the rites of the Christian religion."

Tristan leaned on his bow, regretting the king's enmity, which he had caused by coming between Mark and his wife. That evening Tristan was still lamenting; and Isolde kept repeating to herself: "Alas, I am so miserable! I have wasted my youth, living in the forest like a serf, with no one to wait on me. I am a queen, but I have lost that title because of the potion we drank at sea. That was Brangain's fault; she was in charge of it, and she was so careless! But there was nothing she could do after I had drunk so much of it. I should be surrounded by well-bred young women, the daughters of worthy vassals, and they would serve me in my chambers, and I would arrange for them to marry noble men. Dear Tristan, she who brought us the love potion to drink led us astray, and we could not have been more cruelly betrayed."

Tristan told her: "Noble queen, we are wasting our youth. My dear, if only I could reconcile us with Mark, so that he would forget his anger and accept our assurance that never, by act or word, did we do anything to disgrace him! Then if any knight between Dinan and Durham claimed that my love for you was less than honorable, he would have to face me on the battlefield. And if Mark admitted me to his household, once you are cleared of the charge, I would serve him faithfully as my uncle and my lord; he would have no soldier who would serve him better in war. But if he wished to take you back and refuse my services, I would go to the king of Dumfries, or to Brittany, with no companion except Governal. Good queen, wherever I may be, I will always be yours. I would never leave you, if we could stay together without the deprivation that I have made you endure so long in the wilderness. Because of me you have lost the title 'queen.' You could be living honorably in the palace with your lord, if it had not been for the potion given to us at sea. Noble, beautiful Isolde, tell me what we should do!"

"Sir, thanks be to God that you wish to repent of your sin! Friend, remember the hermit Ogrin, who preached to us about the scriptures and spoke to us at length when you visited the hermitage at the edge of the forest. Dear friend, if you decided to repent, it could not come at a better time. Sir, let's hurry back to him. I trust him completely; he will give us honorable advice, which will let us spend our lives in happiness."

Hearing her, Tristan sighed and said: "Noble queen, we will go back to the hermitage tonight or early tomorrow. With the advice of Master Ogrin let's write to Mark to tell him of our intentions."

"Tristan, I agree. And let us implore our great heavenly King to have mercy on us, dear Tristan."

The lovers set out through the woods, walking until they came to the hermitage. They found Ogrin there, reading. When he saw them, he greeted them warmly. They sat down in the chapel. "Poor outcasts, love has caused you so much suffering! How long will you continue your sinful ways? You have led this life too long; I beg you to repent."

Tristan said to him: "Listen to me. It has been our fate to live this way. We have suffered constantly for three years. If we could only find a way to reconcile the queen with King Mark, I could accept my own exile from his court; I would go away to Brittany or Lothian. But if my uncle will permit me to serve him at court, I will do it faithfully. [. . .] Sir, my uncle is a powerful king. Give us the best advice you can about what you have heard, and we will do your will."

Now the queen threw herself at the feet of the hermit and urgently implored him to reconcile them with the king, assuring him: "Never again will I even think of yielding to sinful desires. Please understand that I am not regretting having loved him honorably and as a friend; but we have both rejected carnal love."

The hermit listened to her and wept. He praised God for what he had heard: "O God, great omnipotent King, I give thanks to You with all my heart for having let me live long enough for these two to come to me for advice about their sin. May You be forever praised! I swear on my faith that I will give you both good counsel. You have come here for advice; now listen to me, Tristan, and you, queen, hear me well, and take my words to heart. When a man and a woman sin with each other and then leave each other and sincerely repent, God will forgive them, however horrible and ugly their crime may have been. Tristan and Queen Isolde, now listen to me carefully: in order to avoid shame and conceal evil, it is often useful to lie a bit. Since you asked me for advice, I will give it to you without delay. I will give you parchment for a letter. First you will greet the king; you will address it to him at Lantyan. Tell the king, with due respect, that you are in the forest with the queen, but that, if he wants to take her back and forget his anger, you will then do the same and will return to his court. Tell him that if anyone, however wise or foolish, accuses you of an illicit love, may

Mark have you hanged if you do not defend yourself in battle. Tristan, I can give you that advice, because you have no equal at court who would dare stand up to you. I am advising you in good faith.

"Mark cannot deny this: when he wanted to burn you to death because of the dwarf, everyone—nobles and commoners alike—saw that he refused to permit a trial. When God had mercy on you and let you escape, as everyone has heard, only His power kept you from perishing in disgrace. The leap you took would have terrified any man alive. You fled because of fear; you rescued the queen, and since that time you have lived in the wilderness. You brought her from her native land and gave her to him in marriage. All that is true, and he knows it. She was wedded at Lantyan. You did not want to leave her in trouble, so you thought it better to flee with her. If he will hear your defense, you will offer to present it in court, so that everyone will witness it. And if it seems proper, once your loyalty to him is established, he should take back his noble wife on the advice of his barons. And if he agrees, you will be his willing and faithful servant; but if he does not want your service, you will leave for Scotland to serve another king. That is what should be in the letter." [Tristan said:] "And I approve. But with your permission, good Ogrin, I wish to add something, because I do not dare trust him: he issued a warrant for me. I therefore ask him, as a lord whom I love and respect, to have another letter prepared to make his pleasure known. He is to have the letter left at the red cross in the middle of the heath. I don't dare tell him where I am, for fear that he will harm me. I will be reassured only when I have the letter, and then I will do whatever he wishes. Master, let my letter be sealed now, and write a greeting on the ribbon: *Vale!* I have nothing more to add."   [2426]

Ogrin the hermit got up; he took pen and ink and parchment, and wrote the letter. When he had finished, he took a ring and pressed the stone into the wax seal. When it was sealed, he handed it to Tristan, who took it gratefully. "Who will deliver it?" asked the hermit.

"I will."

"Don't say that, Tristan!"

"Yes, sir, I will do it. I know Lantyan. Kind sir, with your permission, the queen will stay here. Soon, when it is dark and the king is sleeping, I will mount my horse and take my squire with me. There is a hill outside the town; I will dismount there and continue on foot. My master will hold my horse for me."

That evening, after sunset, when the sky began to darken, Tristan set out with his master. He was familiar with the area. They rode until they came to Lantyan, where they dismounted and entered the city. Guards sounded the alarm. Ducking into a trench, Tristan kept going until he reached the great hall. Anxious and frightened, he came to the window where the king was sleeping and called to him softly—for he certainly had no desire to speak loudly! The king awoke and said: "Who are you, coming here at this hour? What do you want? Tell me your name!"

"Sir, I am called Tristan. I am bringing a letter, and I will leave it here in the window. For a long time now I have not dared speak with you. I am leaving the letter for you, and I don't dare stay any longer."

Tristan turned away, and the king jumped up, calling to him aloud three times: "In God's name, dear nephew, wait for your uncle!"

The king picked up the letter. Tristan left without pausing: he was eager to be gone! He returned to his master, who was waiting for him. He jumped nimbly on his horse. Governal said: "Hurry now; let's escape by taking the side-roads!"

They rode through the wilderness until they reached the hermitage at dawn. Ogrin was fervently praying that God would protect Tristan and Governal, his squire. When he saw him, he was overjoyed, and thanked his Creator. There is no need to ask how Isolde reacted when she saw them: from the time they left at night until she and the hermit saw them again, she had not stopped crying. The wait had seemed interminable to her. When she saw him arriving, she asked them what had happened [. . .]: "Friend, tell me, for God's sake, did you go to the king's court?"

Tristan told them everything: how he was in the city and how he spoke with the king, how the king called to him to come back, and how he had left the letter and the king had found it.

Ogrin said: "May God be praised! Tristan, you can be sure that you will soon hear from King Mark." Tristan dismounted and put down his bow.

They stayed on at the hermitage. Meanwhile the king had his barons awakened. First he sent for his chaplain and handed him the letter he was holding. The chaplain broke the wax seal and read the letter. At the top he saw the name of the king, to whom Tristan sent greetings. He read the whole letter and explained the contents to the king. The king listened attentively; he was overjoyed, because he loved his wife so much. The king awoke his barons and sent for those he valued most; and when they were all there, the king spoke, and they listened quietly:

"Lords, I have received this letter. I am your king; you are my vassals. Let the letter be read and listened to, and when that is done, I ask you to advise me, as it is your duty to do."

Dinas arose first and said to the others: "Lords, listen to me, and heed my advice only if you consider it wise! Anyone who can give better counsel should do so: let him do good and shun foolishness. We do not know from what country this letter came to us. Let it be read first, and then, depending on what it says, whoever can give sound advice should do so. I want to remind you that the worst offense anyone can commit is to give bad advice to his rightful lord."

The men of Cornwall told the king: "Dinas has spoken nobly. Chaplain, read the letter to all of us, from beginning to end."

The chaplain arose, untied the letter, and, standing before the king, said: "Now listen, and hear me well. Tristan, our lord's nephew, first sends greetings and love to the king and all his barons. Then he writes:

'King, you know how the marriage of the daughter of the king of Ireland came about. I went to Ireland by sea; by my prowess I won her, by killing the great crested dragon; and as a result she was given to me. I brought her to your country, king, and you took her as your wife in the presence of your knights. Hardly had you married her when malicious gossips in your kingdom made you believe a lie. If anyone should make accusations against her, I am prepared to take up arms and defend her on foot or on horseback, to prove that she never loved me dishonorably, nor I her. If I cannot establish her innocence and my own, then have me judged before your barons—all of them. Any one of them who wanted to destroy me could have me condemned or burned. Sir, dear uncle, you know that in your rage you wanted to have us burned. But God took mercy on us, and we praise the Lord. Fortunately the queen escaped. That was only just, because (God help me!) you were wrong to want to put her to death. I too escaped, by leaping from the top of a high cliff. Then, as punishment, the queen was given to the lepers. I rescued her from them, and since that time we have not ceased to flee. I could not fail her, since she nearly died, unjustly, because of me. Since then I have remained with her in the woods, for I was not so daring as to show myself on the plain. You ordered that we be captured and delivered to you. You would have had us burned or hanged, and thus we had to flee. But if it should now be your wish to take back the fair Isolde, no baron in the country would serve you better than I. However, if anyone should convince you not to accept my service, I will go to the king of Scotland. I will go abroad, and you will never hear from me again. Consider these matters carefully, king. I can no longer bear such torment. Either I will be reconciled with you, or I will take the king's daughter back to Ireland, and she will be queen in her own country.'"

The chaplain said to the king: "Sir, the letter ends there."

The barons had heard that Tristan was willing to do battle with them for the daughter of the king of Ireland. Every baron of Cornwall said: "King, take back your wife. No sensible person could ever have said about the queen what we have heard. But I cannot advise you to let Tristan stay in this country. Let him go serve the powerful king in Galloway, on whom the Scottish king is waging war. He can remain there, and you will have occasional news of him. If you send for him, he can come back; otherwise we will know nothing about him. Send him a letter telling him to bring the queen back to you immediately."

The king called his chaplain: "Write this letter quickly; you have heard what you are to put in it. Hurry now! I am impatient, for I have not seen the noble Isolde for such a long time. She has suffered too much in her youth! And when the letter is sealed, hang it upon the red cross. Do it tonight. Add my greetings to the letter."

When the chaplain had written it, he attached it to the red cross. Tristan did not sleep that night. Before midnight he had passed through the Blanche Lande, carrying the sealed letter. He knew the Cornwall countryside well. He came to Ogrin and gave him the letter. The hermit took it and read it. He learned of the generosity of the king, who was willing to forget his anger against Isolde and take her back, and he learned when the reconciliation was to occur. Then he spoke as his duty and his faith dictated: "Tristan, what joy has come to you! Your plea has been heard, and the king is taking his wife back. All his men advised him to do so. But they do not dare advise him to retain your services. Instead, go spend a year or two serving a foreign king who is involved in a war. If the king wishes, you will then come back to him and Isolde. The king will be ready to receive her three days from now. The meeting will take place at the Gué Aventuros. There you will give her up, and he will take her back. That is all the letter says."   [2680]

"God," said Tristan, "what a painful separation! He who loses the woman he loves is unhappy indeed! But it must be done, because of the suffering you have endured on my account. You do not have to suffer any more. When we have to separate, we will pledge our love to each other, dear one. As long as I live, in war or peace, I will not fail to send messages to you, and dear friend, send me news of yourself."

With a great sigh Isolde said: "Tristan, listen to me. Leave me Husdent, your hunting dog. No one ever cared for a dog as well as I will for him, dear friend. When I see him, he will remind me of you. However sad I may be, the sight of him will make me happy again. Never in the world will an animal have such fine shelter or such a rich bed. Dear Tristan, I have a ring, a green jasper with a seal. Sir, for love of me, wear the ring, and if you wish to send me a message, send the ring as well, for unless I see the ring, I assure you I will not believe the message. But if I do see it, no king's command can prevent me from doing anything the messenger tells me, as long as it is honorable. And I promise that with all my heart. Friend, will you give me Husdent as a gift?"

And he answered: "My dear, I will give you Husdent as a sign of my undying love."

"Sir, thank you for giving him to me. Take the ring in exchange." She took it off her finger and placed it on his. Tristan kissed the queen, and she kissed him, to symbolize their agreement.

The hermit went to the Mount, because of the rich market held there. He bought various furs, silk, rich scarlet, and cloth whiter than lilies; and he bought a gentle riding-horse with a harness of brightest gold. By cash, credit, and trade, he acquired precious cloth and furs until he had enough to dress the queen richly.

Throughout Cornwall it was announced that the king was to be reconciled with his wife: "Our reconciliation will take place at the Gué Aventuros." The news spread everywhere, and every knight and lady came to the gathering. They had long desired the queen's return, for she was loved by all (except the evil ones—may God curse them!). All four of them later got what they deserved. Two were killed with swords, the third by an arrow; they died a violent death in their own country. And the forester who denounced the lovers did not escape a cruel death, either, for the valiant Perinis killed him in the forest with his sling. God, who wanted to subdue their sinful pride, took vengeance on all four of them.

On the day of the assembly King Mark was surrounded by a great crowd. Many pavilions and barons' tents had been raised there, as far as the eye could see. Tristan, with his lady, rode toward the place until he saw the stone marking the ford. Under his tunic he had worn his hauberk; he feared for his safety because he had wronged the king. He caught sight of the tents on the meadow, and he recognized the king and the men with him. He spoke gently to Isolde:

"Lady, in God's name I ask you to keep Husdent and care for him well. If you ever loved me, love him now. There is the king, your lord, and his subjects with him. We have very little time left to talk. I see knights approaching, and the king and his soldiers are coming to meet us. In the name of God, our great glorious King, if at any time I should make a request of you, lady, do my will."

"Listen to me, dear Tristan. By the faith I owe to you, I will believe what I am told only if you send me the ring that is on your finger. But as soon as I see the ring with my own eyes, no tower or wall or castle could hold me and prevent me from doing the bidding of my lover, if it is honorable and good, and I know it is your will."

"Lady," he said, "may God bless you." He drew her to him and pressed her in his arms.

Isolde spoke thoughtfully: "Friend, listen to what I have to say."

"I am listening."

"You are bringing me back to give me to the king, on the advice of the good hermit Ogrin; I beg you, dear sweet friend, not to leave the country until you know whether the king is angry or reasonable with me. As your true love, I ask you, once the king has taken me back, to go stay at the home of Orri the forester. Please do that for me. We spent many a night there in a bed made for us. [. . .] My friend, go into the cellar under the cabin. I will send you news of the royal court by Perinis. May God keep you, my friend! Please don't refuse to stay there. My messenger will come to you often; by way of my servant and your master, I will send you news of myself. [. . .] I know the three who wanted to destroy us will some day pay for their actions. Their bodies will be found lying in the forest. But until then, dear friend, I am afraid of them. May Hell open up and swallow them! I fear them because they are completely evil."

"My love, whoever accuses you of impropriety should beware and consider me his enemy!"

"Sir," said Isolde, "thank you. Now I am happy, for you have put my mind at ease."

They rode on, and the others approached them; they exchanged greetings. The king, along with Dinas of Dinan, rode well ahead of his men. Tristan held the reins of Isolde's horse and led her forward. He greeted the king respectfully: "King, I am returning the fair Isolde to you. No one ever gave up anything so precious. I see here the men of your land; and in their presence, I ask your permission to establish my innocence and prove before your court that never in my life have she and I been lovers. You have been made to believe a lie; but, as God is my witness, there was no trial. Let me do battle in your court, on foot or otherwise, sir. If I am thus condemned, then burn me in sulphur. But if I can survive unharmed, let no one [accuse me again]. Now keep me with you, or I will go away to Lothian."

While the king was speaking with his nephew, Andrew, a native of Lincoln, urged him: "King, keep him with you, and you will be more respected and feared because of him." Mark was tempted to grant this request, for his heart had softened toward his nephew. The king took him aside, leaving the queen with Dinas, who was true, loyal, and faithful. Dinas chatted and joked with the queen and helped her remove her rich scarlet cape from her shoulders. She was wearing a tunic over a silk chemise. What can I tell you of her mantle? The hermit who bought it never regretted the expense! The robe was rich, and Isolde was beautiful. Her eyes were green, her hair golden.

The seneschal obviously enjoyed her company, to the great displeasure of the three barons (may they be cursed for their viciousness!). They drew near the king and said: "Sir, listen to us, and we will give you sound advice. The queen was accused and fled from your. country. If they are together again in your court, it is our opinion that people will say you condone their crime. Everyone will say so! Send Tristan away from your court, and after a year, when you are certain that Isolde is true to you, you can send for him. We are advising you in good faith."

The king answered: "Whatever anyone else may say, I will not fail to heed your advice." The barons moved away and, in the name of the king, announced his decision.

When Tristan heard that he would not be pardoned, and that the king wanted him to go away, he took leave of the queen. They looked at each other tenderly. The queen blushed, embarrassed before all those gathered there. Tristan then rode off, and many hearts were saddened that day.

The king asked Tristan where he was going and told him he would give him anything he wanted: gold, silver, furs, or anything else. Tristan replied: "King of Cornwall, I will not accept anything from you. As soon as possible I will happily go offer my services to the great king who is embroiled in war."

Tristan had an impressive escort composed of Mark's barons and the king himself. The young man set out toward the sea. Isolde saw him go, and she did not move until he was out of her sight. Tristan left, and those who had accompanied him returned. Dinas, who was still with him, embraced him again and again and begged him to return safe and sound. The two swore fidelity to each other, and Tristan said: "Dinas, listen to me. I have to leave here; you know why. If I send word by Governal that I need something, look after it properly."

They embraced over and over. Dinas told him not to fear: he would do whatever Tristan asked. He lamented their separation, and he promised to look after Isolde—not for the king's sake, but for his love of Tristan. Thereupon Tristan left him, and both of them were sad.

Dinas returned to the king, who was waiting on a heath. The barons all rode quickly back to the city. More than four thousand people—men, women, and children—rushed out of the city, all rejoicing for Isolde and Tristan. Bells rang throughout the city. But when they learned that Tristan was leaving, there was not a one who did not feel bitter grief. They rejoiced about Isolde, however, and all wished to serve her; and every street was hung with brocaded cloths in celebration. Wherever the queen went, the streets were strewn with flowers.

The queen and all the barons went down the road to the monastery of St. Samson. Bishops, clerics, monks, and abbots all came out to greet her, dressed in cassocks and copes. The queen, dressed in dark blue, dismounted; the bishop took her by the hand and led her into the church, up to the altar. The valiant and noble Dinas brought her a garment worth a hundred silver marks, a rich cloth embroidered in gold, such as no count or king ever owned. Queen Isolde took it and placed it reverently on the altar. Later on it was made into a chasuble, which never left the treasure except on feast days; and those who have seen it say it is still at St. Samson.

Then Isolde left the church. The king, the princes, and the counts accompanied her to the palace, where there was great rejoicing. No one was forbidden to enter; anyone who wanted to come in was fed, and no one was refused. Isolde was greatly honored that day, more than at any time since her wedding day. The king freed one hundred serfs and dubbed twenty young men as knights and gave them arms and hauberks.

Now listen to what Tristan did. Having made restitution to Mark, he went away. He left the road and set out on a small path; he followed trails and paths until he came to the forester's lodging by a secret way. Orri led him into the cellar, and there he had everything he needed. Orri was extremely generous. He caught boars and took wild sows in his nets, and trapped stags and does, deer and bucks. He unselfishly gave much of it to his servants. Tristan lived there secretly with him, in his cellar, and he received news of his mistress from Perinis, the queen's kind young servant.

[3027]

* * *

Now you will hear about the three barons—may God curse them!—who tormented the king so much. Before a month had passed, Mark went out hunting, accompanied by the traitors. Now listen to what they did! The peasants had burned part of the underbrush on a heath. The king was standing in the burned area, listening to the cries of his dogs. The three barons came and spoke to him: "King, listen to us. The queen has never proved by oath that she remained faithful to you, and people condemn you for that. Your barons have often asked you to require her to clear herself of the charge that Tristan was her lover. She must prove that people were lying. Make her undergo a trial; demand it as soon as you are alone with her tonight. If she is not willing to be judged, banish her from your empire."

The king listened, and his face reddened. "For God's sake, lords, will you never stop denouncing the queen? She is again being accused of something that should have been put to rest. If you want me to exile the queen to Ireland, tell me so! What do you want of her? Didn't Tristan offer to defend her? But you did not dare take up arms against him. It is your fault he is gone; it was your idea! I sent him away; shall I now send my wife away too? Cursed be the one who persuaded me to make him leave! By the martyr St. Stephen, you are going too far, and I am angry. I am astonished at your persistence. If he did wrong, he is suffering for it. You care nothing for my happiness; I can no longer have peace with you. By St. Trechmor of Carhaix, I warn you: today is Monday, and before Tuesday is finished you will see Tristan here!"

The king frightened them so much that they dared do nothing except flee. King Mark said: "May God curse you for trying to bring me shame! It will do you no good: I will summon the man you drove away."

When they saw Mark's rage, the three of them dismounted in a nearby clearing, leaving the angry king in the field. They said to each other: "What can we do? King Mark is very perverse; he will indeed send for his nephew and will not keep his promise or vow. If Tristan returns, we are finished; if he finds any of us in the forest or on the road, he will not leave a drop of blood in our bodies. Let's tell the king he will now have peace, and we will never mention the subject again."

They came back to the king in the field, but he brushed them aside, for he had no desire to listen to them. He swore frequently under his breath: they should never have spoken to him! He told himself that if his men had been there, he would have had all three barons arrested.

"Sir," they said, "listen to us. You are upset and angry because what we say affects your honor. It is our obligation to advise our lord, but our advice offends you. It is proper that someone who hated you and dared speak to you should have to flee! But we, who are your faithful servants, give you loyal counsel. Since you don't believe us, do as you wish; we will say no more. Pardon us for displeasing you!"

The king listened silently. He leaned on his saddle-bow and said, without turning toward them: "Lords, not long ago you heard my nephew's denials in regard to my wife. At that time you had no desire to take up arms or to mount your horses; I will not permit you to cause trouble now. Leave my land! By St. Andrew, for whom pilgrims journey to Scotland, you have caused me great pain, which will last a year; because of you I have banished Tristan."

The traitors came before Mark. They were named Godoine, Ganelon, and the evil Denoalen. In spite of their pleas the king would not change his mind, and he departed without further delay. Resentfully they left the king for their fortified castles, which were surrounded by palisades and built on rocks high in the hills. If something could not be done about it, they would cause their lord serious trouble!

The king did not delay long. Without waiting for anyone, he dismounted at Tintagel, before his tower, and entered alone. He came into their chamber, still wearing his sword. When he entered, Isolde arose, came to meet him, took his sword, and then sat at his feet. He took her hand and raised her up; she bowed toward him. When she looked into his face, she noticed that his expression was fierce and cruel. She saw that he was angry and that he had come alone.

"Alas," she said to herself, "my friend has been discovered, and my lord has captured him!" Her blood rushed to her face, and her heart froze in her breast. She fell back in a faint before the king, and she became pale. Mark lifted her up in his arms and embraced and kissed her; he thought she had fallen ill.

When she regained consciousness, he asked: "My dear, what is wrong?"

"Sir, I am afraid."

"There is no reason for you to be afraid."

When she heard his assurance, her color returned, and she became calm. She was again self-assured. She spoke cleverly to the king: "Sir, I can see by your expression that your hunters have made you angry. You should not get upset because of a hunt."

At that the king laughed, kissed her, and replied: "Friend, I have three evil men who for a long time have been jealous of my accomplishments. If I don't do something about it now, if I don't drive them out of my land, I will never again have any power over them. They have pushed me too far, and I have given in to them too many times. Now my mind is made up. Because of their words—their lies!—I sent my nephew away from me. I no longer want anything to do with them; but Tristan will soon return, and he will take revenge on the three traitors for me. They will be hanged by him."

When the queen heard him, she almost cried out, but didn't dare. Wisely, she composed herself and said: "God has worked a miracle, arousing my lord's anger against those responsible for the scandal. I pray to God that they may be shamed." She spoke those words softly, so that they could not be heard.

The fair Isolde, who knew the proper words to use, said to the king:

"Sir, what evil have they said of me? Everyone is free to say what he thinks. Except for you I have no one to defend me, and that is why they continue to attack me. May God, our heavenly Father, curse them! They have frightened me so often!"

"Lady," said the king, "listen to me. Three of my most valued barons have left me in anger."

"Why, sir? For what reason?"

"They made accusations against you."

"Why, sir?"

The king answered: "Because you never established your innocence in regard to Tristan."

"Suppose I do it? [. . .] I am ready to do so."

"When will you do it? Today?"

"Give me a little time."

"A great deal of time has already passed."

"Sir, in God's name, listen and advise me. What does all this mean? Why can they never leave me in peace? May God help me, I will make no defense except one of my own choosing. Sir, if I took an oath in your court, before your men, before three days were up they would say they want some other proof. King, I have no relative in this country who would undertake a war or revolt on account of my troubles. But I don't care, because I no longer take notice of what people say. If they want my oath, or if they demand a trial by judgment, let them choose the date. They cannot think of a judgment so cruel that I will not submit myself to it. However, I want King Arthur and his entourage to be there. If I am declared innocent before him, and if anyone makes accusations against me later, those who witnessed my judgment will defend me, whether it is against a Cornishman or a Saxon. For that reason I want them to be there and witness my defense with their own eyes. If King Arthur is there, and his most noble nephew Gawain, and Girflet and Kay the seneschal, and a hundred other vassals of the king, they will not shrink from doing battle to defend me from my accusers. King, for that reason, my defense should take place before them. The Cornishmen are liars and deceivers! Choose a date and ask everyone, poor and rich alike, to come to the Blanche Lande. Announce that you will confiscate the inheritance of anyone who does not come; that way you will have no trouble with them. And I am sure that King Arthur will come as soon as he receives my message, for his compassion is well known to me."

The king answered: "You are right." Then the date, set for two weeks from that time, was announced throughout the country. The king also sent the word to the three who had left the court in anger: whatever the outcome might be, they were happy to hear the news.

Now everyone in the country knew the date chosen for the trial, and they knew that King Arthur would be there, accompanied by most of the knights of his court. Isolde wasted no time. She had Perinis tell Tristan of the pain and suffering she had endured on his account. She asked him to repay her for that suffering; for if he were willing, he could save her from further torment: "Tell him to remember a marsh at the end of the bridge, at Mal Pas, where I once soiled the hem of my dress. There is a small hill near the ford, just this side of the Blanche Lande. He is to go there, dressed as a leper, and take with him a leper's wooden goblet with a bottle tied to it by a leather thong. In his other hand he should have a crutch. And here is our scheme: he will be sitting on the hill at the appointed hour. Have him make his face appear tumorous and hold the goblet in front of him; from those who pass by, he is to ask for alms—nothing more. They will give him gold and silver. He is to keep the money for me, until I can see him alone, in a private room." [3312]

Perinis said: "Lady, I will tell him all that, in confidence." He left the queen and went into the forest, passing through it all alone. At evening he came to Tristan's refuge in Orri's cellar. They had just finished eating. Tristan was happy to see Perinis, for he knew that the noble man had brought him news of his mistress. They grasped each other by the hand, and they sat together. Perinis related the queen's message. Tristan bowed his head and swore by all the saints that those responsible for this could not fail to lose their heads. They would hang high from the gallows! He said: "Tell the queen this, word for word: I will go at the appointed time; she should have no doubt about that. Tell her to be happy and not to worry. I will not rest until I have taken revenge with my sword on those who have made her suffer. Their treachery is now exposed! Tell her to have everything arranged to save herself when she swears her oath. I will see her soon. Go, and tell her not to worry. She cannot doubt that I will go to the trial, disguised as a beggar. King Arthur will see me seated at the entry to Mal Pas, but he will not know me, and I will make him give me alms if I can. You can tell the queen what I have related to you here, in this place she herself had so beautifully constructed. Take her more greetings from me than there are buds on a branch in spring."

"I will tell her," replied Perinis. Then he left by the stairs, saying: "Sir, I am going to King Arthur, for I have to ask him to come to hear the oath and to bring with him a hundred knights who can defend the lady if the traitors ever again question her loyalty. Do you approve?"

"God be with you!"

Perinis ran up the stairs, jumped on his horse, and rode directly to Caerleon. All his efforts to carry out his duty were not well rewarded, for at Caerleon he was told that the king was at Stirling. So the servant of fair Isolde set out for that city. Meeting a shepherd who was playing pipes, he asked: "Where is the king?"

"Sir," the shepherd answered, "he is sitting on his throne. There you will see the Round Table, which rotates like the earth. And his men are seated around it."

Perinis said: "Let us go find him." When he got there, the young man dismounted and went in. There were at court many counts' and vassals' sons, who served others in order to earn their armor. One of them left the others and came running to the king, who said to him: "Where have you come from?"

"I bring you news. Out there is a rider who is urgently looking for you."

Then, watched by many nobles, Perinis came in and stepped up before the king at the dais where all his knights were seated. The young man said in a firm voice: "May God save King Arthur and all his company. That is the wish of his friend, the fair Isolde!"

The king arose and said: "And may God save and protect her, and you

too, friend. I have wanted to hear from her for so long! Young man, here in
the presence of my barons, I grant her whatever she may request. And I will
knight you, along with two others, for bringing me a message from the
most beautiful woman from here to Tudela."

"Sir," he said, "thank you. Now hear why I have come. And may these
barons hear it too, and Sir Gawain in particular. The queen was reconciled
with her lord, as everyone knows. Sir, all the barons of the kingdom were
present at the reconciliation. There Tristan offered to defend his honor and
prove the queen's fidelity before the king. No one cared to take up arms to
dispute her loyalty. But now, sir, they have convinced Mark that she must
take an oath. But there is no one of her lineage at court, neither Frenchman
nor Saxon, who could defend her. A proverb says that a person can swim
easily if someone holds up his chin! King, if I am lying about all this, you
can punish me for slander. The king constantly changes his mind, now
believing one thing, now another. The fair Isolde answered him that she
would take an oath before you. She asks you to take pity on her, as your
dear friend, and come to the Gué Aventuros, with one hundred of your
friends, at the designated time. She knows that your court is loyal and
your company sincere; she will be proven innocent before you, and may
God protect her from misfortune. If she ever asks you to defend her, you
will surely not fail her. The date has been set for a week from now."

Those who heard this wept bitterly; there was not a one of them who did
not shed tears of pity for her. They all said: "God! What do they want from
her? Mark does whatever they wish, and Tristan has left the country. May
no one enter Heaven who does not go to the trial and help her, if that is the
king's will."

Gawain stood up and said graciously: "Uncle, if you give me your
permission, the trial that is to take place will turn out badly for the three
traitors. The worst of them is Ganelon; he and I know each other well.
Once, during a violent joust, I knocked him into a mudhole. If I could get
my hands on him again, by St. Richier, there would be no need for Tristan
to be there! I would make him suffer, and then I would have him hanged on
the highest hill!"

Girflet stood up and took Gawain by the hand. "King, Denoalen and
Godoine and Ganelon have hated the queen for a long time. May God not
preserve me, and may I never again have the pleasure of a woman's private
embrace, if I ever meet Godoine and the point of my lance does not pierce
his body!"

Perinis listened, his head bowed. Yvain, the son of Urien, said: "I know
Denoalen well. He is interested only in slander, and he knows how to
manipulate the king, repeating his accusations until they are believed. If our
paths ever cross, as they did once before, may I be cast out of our faith if I
have the power to hang him with my own two hands and do not do so!
Traitors deserve to be punished. And the king is easily manipulated by
those hypocrites."

Perinis said to King Arthur: "Sir, I am confident that the traitors who
caused trouble for the queen will be properly punished. Threats made at
your court, against people from whatever land, are never idle; you pursue
the matter, and those who deserve it are eventually punished."

The king was pleased; he blushed a little and said: "Young man, let us go eat. My knights will make plans to avenge her."

In his heart the king felt great joy. He spoke so that Perinis would hear him: "Noble and honored company, take care to see that, on the day of the trial, your horses are well fed, your shields new, your clothing rich. We will joust before the fair lady whose message you have all heard. Anyone who shrinks from bearing arms is lacking in pride and self-respect!"

The king had summoned all of them, but they regretted that the day was still so far off; they would have preferred it to be the next day! When Perinis asked permission to leave, the king mounted his horse, Passelande, for he wanted to escort the young man. They rode along, deep in conversation about the beautiful woman for whom many a lance would be splintered. Before leaving Perinis, the king offered him all the equipment a knight should have, but Perinis did not want to accept it.

The king rode with him a while longer, in honor of the beautiful, blonde, noble, and virtuous Isolde; they spoke of her at length. The young man had a fine escort, made up of the king and his knights. They separated with regret, and the king said to him: "Good friend, go now; do not stay any longer. Greet your lady on behalf of her faithful servant, who will come to make peace for her. I will zealously do her will, and I will gain glory by serving her. Remind her of an incident that occurred once, when a lance that was thrown remained stuck in a post; she will know where that was. I want you to tell her that."

"King, I will do it, I promise." Then he spurred his horse, and the king turned back. Perinis left; he had taken pains to serve the queen well, and he had delivered his message. He rode on at full speed, returning to the queen without a day's rest. He told her about his journey and about Arthur and Tristan, and she was happy. They spent that night at Dinan.   [3562]

It was the tenth night of the moon, and the day of the queen's trial was approaching. Tristan, her friend, was not idle: he had devised a strange costume and was dressed in rough wool, without a shirt. His tunic was of ugly coarse cloth, and his boots were pieced together from patches. He had made a cloak of coarse, threadbare wool. He had a marvelous disguise, and he looked exactly like a leper. However, he had his sword girded tightly around his waist.

He secretly left his lodging, accompanied by Governal, who gave him instructions: "Tristan, conduct yourself wisely. Pay close attention to the queen, for she will make no sign to you."

"Master," he said, "I will do as you say. Now take care to do what I want. I am afraid of being recognized. Take my shield and lance; bring them to me, Master Governal, and saddle my horse. In case I need them, you should be at the ford, hidden but nearby. You know which ford, for you have been familiar with it for a long time. Since the horse is as white as flour, cover him all over so that he cannot be seen or recognized by anyone. Arthur and his entourage will be there, and Mark too. Knights from foreign lands will joust to win praise; and for the love of my Isolde, I may do something reckless. Attach to my lance the pennon given to me by my fair Isolde. Now go, master, and I beg you to do all this discreetly." He picked up his goblet and crutch, and he asked and received permission to leave.

Governal came to his lodging, gathered up his equipment, and set out. Taking care that no one saw him, he rode until he came to Mal Pas, where he concealed himself near Tristan. At the edge of the marsh Tristan sat down on a mound. In front of him was his rattle, suspended from his neck by a cord. There were mudholes around him. As he climbed the hill, he did not appear to be sick, for he was large and solidly built; he was certainly not a dwarf, an invalid, or a hunchback! He heard the noise of the people approaching, and he sat down. He had lumps and sores on his face, and whenever someone passed him, he moaned: "I am so miserable! I didn't want to be a beggar and spend my life this way. But what else can I do?"

Tristan's laments made them all take out their purses and give him something. He accepted the alms without comment. Even a man who had been another man's minion for seven years could not have been so successful in extracting money! With his head bowed, Tristan asked for alms in God's name, even from servants and disreputable vagabonds. Some of them would give him something; others would strike him. Unsavory people passed by and taunted him, calling him parasitic and worthless. Tristan listened but did not respond, except to say that he forgave them in God's name. Insolent young men insulted him, but he behaved prudently. He responded to some of his tormentors by helping them on their way with his crutch. At least fifteen of them went away bleeding profusely.

Well-bred young men gave him farthings and silver half-pennies, and he accepted them. He told them that he would drink to them; he explained that he had such a burning in his body that he could not relieve it. All who heard that were moved to tears; they could have no doubt that the man they were looking at was a leper.

Servants and squires hastened to find lodgings for themselves and to set up their lords' tents and pavilions of many colors. Every wealthy man there had his own tent. Knights arrived by all the roads and paths, and there was a great crowd on the marshy ground. The mud there was soft, and the horses sank up to their flanks; many of them fell and struggled to extricate themselves. Tristan laughed and remained unconcerned about it; instead he told all of them:

"Hold your reins by the knots, and use your spurs. Spur sharply, for there is no mud up ahead." But when they tried to advance, the marshy ground gave way under their feet, and they sank into the mud. Those who had not thought to wear boots regretted their error. When the leper saw someone fall into the mud, he would hold out his hand and shake his rattle. And when he saw them sink further, he would cry: "Think of me, and may God save you from Mal Pas. Help me buy new clothes!" He struck his goblet with the bottle. It was a strange place to beg alms; but he was doing it mischievously: he wanted his lady, the blonde Isolde, to be pleased and happy when she passed by.

There was great tumult at Mal Pas. Those who crossed the ford soiled their clothes, and their cries could be heard from far away. The crossing was dangerous for all of them.

And then Arthur arrived. He and many of his barons looked warily at the ford, fearful that they would be mired in the soft mud. All the knights of the Round Table had come to Mal Pas, with new shields and strong horses, and displaying their coats of arms. They were fully equipped from head to foot. Many silk pennons were raised there, and the knights began to joust near the ford.

Tristan recognized King Arthur easily and called to him: "Good King Arthur, I am sick—a weak, deformed leper covered with sores. My father is poor and never had anything. I came here to seek alms. I have heard many good things about you, and you should not turn your back on me. You are dressed in fine grey cloth from Regensburg and from Reims, I see, and underneath the cloth your skin is white and smooth. Your legs are covered with rich brocade and green net, and you are wearing leggings of scarlet. King Arthur, do you see how I scratch myself? I have chills even when others are hot. In God's name, give me your leggings!"

The noble king took pity on him. He had two young men take off his leggings, and he gave them to the leper. Tristan took them, immediately walked back to the hill, and sat down. The leper spared no one who passed by him, and soon he had many fine clothes, including King Arthur's leggings.

As Tristan was sitting near the marsh, an intense and regal King Mark came riding rapidly toward the ford. Tristan decided that he would try to obtain something of Mark's. He shook his rattle loudly and cried out in a hoarse, nasal voice: "In God's name, King Mark, give me something!"

Mark took off his hood and said: "Here, brother, put this on your head; you have suffered too often from the weather."

"Sir," he responded, "thank you. Now you have protected me from the cold." He put the hood under his cloak, folding it to conceal it from view.

"Where are you from, leper?" asked Mark.

"From Caerleon, sir; I am the son of a Welshman."

"How long have you been an outcast from society?"

"Truthfully, sir, three years. While I was healthy, I had a most courtly lady. Because of her my body is now covered with these ugly sores, and it is because of her that I have to use this rattle day and night, making noise that startles those from whom I seek alms in God's name."

The king said: "Tell me how she made you sick."

"Good king, her husband was a leper, and she transmitted the disease to me when we made love. But there is only one woman more beautiful than she in the world."

"Who is that?"

"The beautiful Isolde! And the two of them even dress alike."

The king, hearing that, laughed as he went away. Arthur, who had been happily jousting, came to meet him and asked him about the queen. Mark replied: "She is coming through the woods, good king. She is with Andrew, who is escorting her and looking after her." Then they said to each other: "I don't know how she will be able to cross Mal Pas. Let's stay here and watch for her."

The three traitors—may they burn in Hell!—came to the ford and asked the leper where those who were least soiled had crossed. Tristan pointed with his crutch to the softest part of the crossing, saying: "See the peat-bog at the end of the marsh? That's the best way: I have seen a good many people cross there."

The traitors entered the marsh, and where the leper had indicated, they immediately sank into mud up to their saddle-bows. All three of them fell off their horses. The leper, on the hill, cried to them: "Use your spurs if you are getting dirty in there! Let's go, lords! Now, by the holy apostle, give me something of yours."

The horses became mired in the soft mud, and the three men began to panic because they could not get their footing or a hand-hold. Those who were jousting nearby came quickly to them. Now listen to the leper's lie! "Lords," he said, "hold on to your saddle-bows firmly. May this soft marsh be cursed! Take off your mantles and paddle through the mud. I tell you, and I am sure of it, that other people have crossed today." He struck his goblet so hard he almost broke it. Brandishing it, he struck the bottle with the thong, while using his other hand to shake his rattle.

Then Isolde arrived. She saw her enemies in the mud and her friend sitting on the hill. That made her happy, and she laughed and rejoiced. She dismounted near the bank. Across from her were the king and the barons who had come with him, and they watched those who were flailing and wallowing in the mud. And the leper was urging them: "Lords, the queen has come to swear her oath; let us go hear the trial." There were few people there who were not happy to hear that.

Now listen to what the poor sick leper did! He said to Denoalen: "Grab this stick in both hands and pull hard." He held it out, and the traitor took hold. But the leper let go, and the other man fell back, sinking into the mud until only his hair could be seen. And when he was finally pulled out, the leper said to him: "I couldn't help it! My nerves and joints are numb, my hands were stiffened by the illness called the Mal d'Acre, and my feet are swollen from gout. Sickness has drained my strength, and my arms are weak and shriveled."

Dinas, who was with the queen, understood the ruse and winked at him; he knew it was Tristan beneath the cloak. He saw the three scoundrels caught in Tristan's trap, and he was delighted to find them so discomfited. The queen's accusers had great difficulty climbing out of the mudholes; it would take a long bath to get them clean! In front of everyone they undressed and put on other clothes.

Now you will hear about noble Dinas, who was on the other side of Mal Pas. He spoke to the queen, saying: "Lady, your silk garment will be heavily soiled. This marsh is full of filth, and I would be sorry to see any of it on your clothes." Isolde laughed, for she was not afraid; she winked and looked at him, and he knew what she had in mind. A little farther down, beside a thorn bush, Dinas and Andrew found a ford, where they crossed without getting dirty.   [3878]

Isolde was now on the other side, alone. There, across the ford, was a great crowd, composed of the two kings and all their barons. Isolde was very crafty. She knew that she was being watched by all those who were on the other bank of the Mal Pas. She walked over to her horse, lifted the fringes of the rich material covering the saddle, and knotted them together above the saddle-bows. No squire or servant could have protected them any better from the mud. Then she tucked the stirrup-strap under the saddle and took off the horse's harness and reins. She lifted the hem of her dress with one hand, holding the whip in the other. She guided the horse to the edge of the ford; then she struck him with the whip, and he crossed over the marsh.

The queen had been watched closely by those on the other side. The two great kings marveled at her, as did all the others who were watching. The queen was wearing clothing of Bagdad silk, trimmed in white ermine. Her mantle and tunic formed a train behind her. Her hair, tied in linen ribbons over a fine gold net, fell softly on her shoulders. Her head was encircled by a golden band, and her face was fresh and fair, with rosy cheeks.

She stepped toward the little bridge and said to Tristan: "I have an affair to discuss with you."

"Noble and worthy queen, I will come to you willingly. But I do not know what you want."

"I do not wish to stain my clothes. You will be my packhorse and carry me carefully across the boards."

"What?" he exclaimed. "Noble queen, don't ask me to do that. I am a sick, deformed leper."

"Hurry up and get in position! Do you think I am going to catch your illness? I assure you I won't."

"Oh, God!" he said. "Come what may, I never tire of talking with my lady." He leaned heavily on his crutch.

"My goodness, leper, you are large! Turn your face away so that your back is toward me, and I will straddle you the way a man rides a horse."

Then the leper smiled. He turned around, and she mounted. Everyone, kings and counts alike, watched them. Her thigh pressed against his crutch. He plodded on, pretending to stumble several times. He made a great pretense of suffering. The beautiful Isolde was riding him like a horse, with one leg on each side of him.

People said to one another: "Just look. [. . .] Look at the queen astride a leper who is sick and limping. With his crutch against her thigh, he is nearly falling off the planks. Let's go meet this leper as he comes out of the marsh."

The young men ran toward him. [. . .] King Arthur and all the others followed them. The leper kept his head down as he reached solid ground. Isolde let herself slide off his back. Preparing to leave, the leper asked Isolde to give him food for that night. Arthur said: "He deserves it. Queen, give it to him."

Beautiful Isolde said to the king: "By the faith I owe you, this scoundrel is strong and has enough to eat. He won't even be able to eat what he already has. I felt what he has under his cloak! King, his pouch is completely full. I felt loaves of bread, and half-loaves and other pieces. He has food and clothing. If he can sell your leggings, he can have five pennies sterling. And with my husband's hood he can buy sheep and become a shepherd, or he can buy a donkey to carry people across this marsh. He is no good; I know it. He made a good profit today, for he found people who are to his liking. But he will not leave here with anything of mine, not even a farthing." The two kings laughed at that. They brought the queen's horse and helped her into the saddle. Then they rode off, while those who had armor engaged once again in jousts.

Tristan left the crowd and returned to his master, who was waiting for him. He had brought two fine Castilian horses, with saddle and bridle, and two lances and two shields; and it was impossible to identify any of them. And what of the riders? Governal had covered his face with a hood of white silk, so that only his eyes were visible. He had a fine, strong horse, and Tristan had his, named Bel Joeor, the best horse there was. He had covered his saddle, horse, shield, and clothes with black wool. His face was covered by a black mask, and his hair too. He had attached to his lance the pennon given to him by his lady.

They both mounted their horses and girded on their steel swords. Thus armed and mounted, they passed through a green meadow between two valleys and rode onto the Blanche Lande. Gawain, the nephew of Arthur, said to Girflet: "Look at those two riding toward us at full speed. I don't recognize them; do you know who they are?"

"I know them well," responded Girflet. "The one with the black horse and black pennon is the Black Knight of the Mountain. I recognize the other by his mottled arms, for there are few like them in this country. I'm sure the two of them are bewitched."

The two strangers rode out of the crowd, shields at the ready, lances raised, pennons fastened to the metal. They wore their equipment as easily as if they had been born in it. King Mark and King Arthur spoke far more of these two than of their own men down on the wide plain. The two knights were seen again and again in the front ranks of knights, and many others watched them. They rode through the front lines, but did not find anyone who would joust with them.

The queen recognized them. She and Brangain stood off to one side. Andrew, fully armed, rode up on his horse, with his lance raised and his shield firmly in his hand. He charged headlong at Tristan and attacked him. He did not recognize Tristan, but Tristan knew who he was. He struck his shield, knocking him off his horse and breaking his arm. Andrew lay on his back, motionless at the queen's feet. Governal saw a knight riding forth from the tents: it was the forester who wanted to have Tristan killed while he was sleeping. Now the forester did not have long to live. Governal attacked him without hesitation, thrusting his lance into his enemy's body so powerfully that it emerged from his back. The forester fell dead so quickly that a priest could not have been summoned. Isolde, who was noble and candid, smiled with satisfaction beneath her wimple.

Girflet, Cinglor, Yvain, Taulas, Coris, and Gawain saw their companions humbled. "Lords," said Gawain, "what can we do? The forester is lying here dead. Those two knights surely have magical powers. We do not know them, but they are making fools of us. Let's attack and capture them." The king added: "Whoever can deliver them to us will have served us well indeed!"

Tristan and Governal rode down to the ford and crossed it. The others did not dare follow them, but stayed where they were. They were afraid, thinking the two were phantoms. They wanted to return to their lodgings, for they had had their fill of jousting. Arthur rode at Isolde's right, and the journey seemed very short to him. [. . .] The road branched off to the right, and they dismounted at their tents. Many tents stood on the heath, and even the tent-cords themselves were very expensive. The tent floors were strewn with flowers instead of reeds and rushes. All the roads and paths were filled with people coming to the Blanche Lande, and many of the knights had brought their ladies. Those who were camped on the meadow had been hunting stags. They spent the night on the heath. Each of the kings held an audience, and all those who were wealthy distributed gifts.

After eating, King Arthur went to visit King Mark in his tent, and he took his closest associates with him. Very few of them were wearing woolen clothes; most were dressed in silk. What else is there to say of their clothing? What wool there was had been dyed a rich scarlet color. There were many finely dressed people there. Never had anyone seen two richer courts; they could have satisfied any need. There was much celebration in the pavilions, and that night everyone talked about what was to come: how the noble lady was about to exonerate herself before the kings and all their barons.

King Arthur, his barons, and his friends retired for the night. Anyone who had been in the woods that night would have heard the music of pipes and trumpets coming from the pavilions. Before dawn it began to thunder, no doubt because of the heat. The sentinels announced the new day, and people arose without delay.

The sun shone hot soon after daybreak. The fog and the dew had disappeared. The Cornishmen gathered in front of the two kings' tents, every knight accompanied by his lady. On the grass in front of the king's tent they spread out a silken cloth, lined with dark brocaded material and embroidered delicately with figures of animals. The cloth had been bought in Nicaea. All the relics in Cornwall—whether in treasures or phylacteries, in chests or trunks, in reliquaries or jewel-cases or shrines, in gold or silver crosses or maces—were set out on the cloth and arranged in order.

The kings withdrew to one side, for they wanted to render a careful and impartial judgment. King Arthur spoke first, as was his custom: "King Mark," he said, "whoever advised you to take such an outrageous action committed a monstrous and disloyal act. You are easy to manipulate. You should not believe slander! Whoever caused you to convene this gathering made you swallow a bitter pill, and he should suffer and pay for it. The noble and good Isolde is eager to proceed with the trial. All those who have come to witness her defense can be sure that I will hang anyone who, after the trial, accuses her of infidelity. Such a person would be richly deserving of death. Now listen, king: whoever is at fault, the queen will come forward, before everyone gathered here, and she will raise her right hand and swear on relics, to God in Heaven, that never was there any love between her and your nephew which would result in dishonor to her, and that she never yielded to carnal passion. Mark, this has gone on too long; when she has sworn her oath, command your barons henceforth to leave her in peace."

"Alas, King Arthur, what can I do? You are right to reproach me, for only fools listen to accusations made because of jealousy. I believed them in spite of my better judgment. If she is exonerated here, anyone so foolish as to question her honor thereafter will pay dearly for it. Arthur, noble king, I assure you that I did not want this to happen; and from now on, her enemies will have to be on guard!"   [4181]

Their conversation ended there. Except for the two kings, everyone sat down. Isolde stood between the kings, who held her by the hand. Gawain was beside the relics, and the rest of Arthur's most prized knights surrounded the cloth on which they were arranged. Arthur, who was closest to Isolde, spoke first:

"Listen to me, beautiful Isolde. This is why you are summoned: you must swear that Tristan's love for you was never debauched or carnal, but only the kind of love owed to an uncle and his wife."

"Lords," she said, "praise be to God; I see many holy relics here. Now hear my oath, which I am swearing to reassure King Mark. In the name of God and of St. Hilaire, and on these relics and this reliquary and all the relics anywhere in the world, I swear that no man has ever been between my thighs, except the leper who turned himself into a beast of burden to carry me over the ford, and my husband King Mark. I exclude these two from my oath, but no one else. I cannot swear it about those two: the leper and my lord, King Mark. The leper was between my legs [. . .] . If anyone should require further proof from me, I am ready to provide it here and now."

All who heard her swear the oath could bear it no more, and they cried: "God! Who could doubt her oath! She has thoroughly justified herself! She did far more than she was asked to do, and more than the traitors demanded: she has no need to swear any oath other than the one you have heard, concerned with the king and his nephew. She swore and vowed that no one has ever been between her legs except the leper, who carried her across the ford yesterday morning, and her husband, King Mark. May anyone be cursed who ever again doubts her!"

King Arthur arose and spoke to King Mark in the hearing of all the barons: "King, we have seen and heard the defense. Now let the three traitors Denoalen, Ganelon, and the evil Godoine see to it that they never speak of this again. As long as they live, whether I am at peace or war, nothing can prevent me from coming immediately to defend Isolde, if I learn that she needs me."

She said: "Thank you, sir." The three villains were now detested by everyone. The two courts separated, and the people left. The beautiful, blonde Isolde repeatedly thanked King Arthur.

"Lady," he said, "I guarantee you that as long as I am alive and healthy, no one will ever speak to you disrespectfully. The traitors will regret their actions. With respect and affection I ask the king, your husband, never to believe slander about you."

Mark replied: "If I ever do again, you should punish me for it."

They separated, and each one returned to his kingdom, King Arthur going to Durham, King Mark remaining in Cornwall. Tristan stayed where he was, his mind at ease.

* * *

The king now had peace in Cornwall, and he was respected by all, from far and near. He included Isolde in all his activities and took care to show his love for her. But in spite of this harmony the three villains had not abandoned their malicious schemes. A spy, hoping for a handsome profit, came to talk with them. "Lords," he said, "listen to me, and may I be hanged if I am lying. The king was resentful and angry with you the other day about his wife's trial. I am ready to be hanged or tortured if I cannot lead you to Tristan and let you see him with your own eyes as he waits to speak to his dear mistress! He is hidden, but I know where. When the king's activities take him elsewhere, Tristan is as sly as a fox; he goes into the royal chamber to say farewell. You can have me burned to death if you go to the back window on the right side and do not see Tristan come in, wearing his sword, holding a bow in one hand and two arrows in the other. You can see him tomorrow morning before dawn."

"How do you know this?"

"I have seen him."

"Tristan?"

"Yes, and I recognized him clearly."

"When was that?"

"Yesterday morning."

"And who was with him?"

"His friend."

"What friend? Who?"

"Lord Governal."

"Where are they staying?"

"They have fine lodgings."

"With Dinas?"

"Perhaps."

"They certainly aren't staying there without his knowledge!"

"Surely not."

"Where will we see him?"

"Through the bedroom window, and I am telling you the truth. If I show him to you, I will expect to be richly rewarded."

"Name your price."

"One silver mark."

"Agreed! And you will have much more than that: if you show him to us, you will add handsomely to your wealth."

"Now listen to me," said the scoundrel. "In the wall of the queen's chamber there is a small opening covered by a curtain. Outside the room there is a wide stream, and rushes grow thickly beside it. One of you three should go there early in the morning. Take the path through the new garden, and go directly to the opening; let no one pass by the window. Cut a stick and sharpen it. Use it to pull the curtain back carefully from the opening—it's always left unfastened—so that you will be able to see clearly when he comes to talk with her. If you keep watch that way, may I be burned to death if, in three days or less, you do not see what I have described."

Each of them said: "I promise that we will keep our agreement." Then they sent the spy on his way. They discussed which one of them would go first to witness Tristan's passionate encounter with his mistress. They agreed that Godoine would go first. Then they separated and went their own ways. By the next day they would know about Tristan's conduct. Alas! The noble lady was not on her guard against the villains and their scheme. She had sent word by Perinis, one of her servants, that Tristan should come to her the following morning: the king was going to St. Lubin.

Now listen to what happened! The next night was very dark. Tristan had set out through a thicket, and as he emerged from it, he looked around and saw Godoine coming out of his hiding place. Tristan lay in wait for him, hiding in the grove. He said: "O God, look after me; and may the man coming this way not see me until he is upon me."

Tristan waited with his sword drawn. But Godoine turned off on another path, leaving Tristan there, distressed and angry. He came out of the brush and ran toward the other road, but it was in vain, for the man who had evil intentions was already far away. Only a few minutes later, in the distance, Tristan saw Denoalen coming toward him with two enormous hounds. He hid behind an apple tree. Denoalen rode down the path on a small black horse. He had sent his dogs to flush out a wild boar in a thicket. But before they could do it, their master would receive a blow from which no physician could cure him!   [4380]

The noble Tristan had removed his cloak. Denoalen was riding along fast, suspecting nothing. Tristan jumped out of hiding. Denoalen wanted to flee, but could not: Tristan was right in front of him. Tristan killed him. What else could he have done? The man would have killed him, but he was on his guard, and he cut off his enemy's head before the traitor could say: "I am hurt!" With his sword Tristan cut off the dead man's hair and put it in his pocket. He wanted to show it to Isolde to convince her that the villain was dead.

Tristan left the place without delay. "Alas," he said, "what became of Godoine, who was coming this way so quickly and then just disappeared? Where did he go? Is he gone? If he had waited for me, he would have met the same fate as the traitor Denoalen, whose head I cut off."

Tristan left the bloody body lying on its back on the heath. He wiped his sword and replaced it in his scabbard. He picked up his cloak and put his hood over his head. He covered the corpse with a large branch and left for his mistress's chamber. Now hear what happened to him!

Godoine rode hurriedly and arrived before Tristan. He had pierced the curtain so that he could see into the room. He looked at everything in the room, and Perinis was the only man he saw. The maid Brangain came in. She had just combed Isolde's hair, and she still had the comb in her hand. The traitor, pressed against the wall, looked and saw Tristan enter, holding a laburnum bow. The good man held his two arrows in one hand, and two long braids of hair in the other. He removed his cloak, revealing his handsome body.

The beautiful blonde Isolde came toward him and greeted him, and then, through the window, she saw the shadow of Godoine's head. The queen trembled with rage, but reacted wisely. Tristan spoke to her: "May God protect me, here is Denoalen's hair. I took revenge on him for your sake. He will no longer be buying or using shields and lances!"

"Sir," she said, "what is that to me? But I ask you to stretch your bow and see how well it bends." Tristan drew it and then hesitated. He gathered his thoughts, made a decision, and drew the bow. He asked news of King Mark, and Isolde told him what she could. [. . .] If Godoine could escape from there alive, he would incite a deadly war between King Mark and his wife Isolde. But Tristan (may God grant him honor!) would prevent him from escaping.

Isolde, intensely serious, said: "Friend, put an arrow in your bow, and be sure that the cord is not twisted. I see something that disturbs me greatly. Tristan, stretch your bow as far as possible."

Tristan stood thinking for a moment. Knowing that she had seen something that displeased her, he looked around. He was trembling with fear.

Against the light, through the curtain, he saw Godoine's head. "O God, true King, I have made wondrous shots with bow and arrow; grant that this one not fail! I see one of the three villains of Cornwall, hiding outside treacherously. God, whose most holy body was put to death for all people, let me take vengeance for the evil these traitors have directed at me."

Then he turned toward the wall, drew the bow, and shot. The arrow flew so swiftly that nothing could have moved quickly enough to avoid it. It struck Godoine squarely in the eye, piercing his head and brain. Neither merlins nor swallows could fly half as fast; nor would the arrow have passed any faster through a ripe apple. The man fell back against a post and did not move again. He did not even have the time to cry out: "I am injured! God! Confession [. . .]"

chapter VII

MARIE DE FRANCE:
THE LAY OF CHIEVREFUEIL
(THE HONEYSUCKLE)

Russell Weingartner

The lay entitled *Chievrefueil* is next-to-last in the unified group of lays found in Manuscript Harley 978 of the British Museum. Because this group of lays contains a number of references to its author, Marie, the consensus of scholars has been to declare *Chievrefueil* a work of Marie de France, a noblewoman of French origin who wrote three works in England during the last half of the twelfth century. From a statement of one of her contemporaries and from the fact that her lays exist in a number of manuscripts, we know that Marie was a popular poet in her day. Understandably she was quite proud of her reputation, and, in addition, she was something of a feminist, revealing a strong sympathy for neglected and unloved wives.

Of the twelve lays of Marie, *Chievrefueil* is the shortest. Apparently it is Marie's contribution to the long legend of Tristan and Isolde, which was extremely popular in her lifetime. Where she encountered the tale is unknown and probably undiscoverable, although she informs us that many persons had related it to her and that she had found a written text of it. In saying this, she is probably referring to the entire Tristan narrative, not merely the tale she is relating. This tale is not found in any of the various fragmentary manuscripts that scholars have used to reconstruct a hypothetical original of the Tristan legend. Possibly Marie's tale had been part of the oral tradition and had simply escaped the notice of poets who recorded this material. If so, the *Chievrefueil* incident probably was found in what is called the second division of the *roman*, a segment in which Tristan was temporarily banished from the court of King Mark.

Marie has summarized the longer tale in a brief eight verses, certain that her audience could fill in the details. She can therefore arrive very quickly at the beginning of her own contribution to the legend. In much the same way that she identified her lay *Lanval* with the Arthurian tradition (see the Introduction to *Graelent*), she seems once again to be assuring herself an audience by her use of the Tristan story. We see her utilize the same device, that of stating the irrelevant presence of a well-known character in order to give a kind of legitimacy to the tale. Just as, in *Lanval*, we notice "Yvain" among a group of knights, in *Chievrefueil* the queen stops the procession along the road and calls to her maid "Brangain," about whom we hear nothing more, but whose loyalty to Isolde was known to every reader.

The Tristan story was no doubt interesting to Marie because it is one more example of lovers who are kept apart by society's laws. But she must also have been charmed by the central symbol of the work, the honeysuckle entwined with the hazel tree. She may even be responsible for this traditional way of describing the two lovers.

Bibliographic note: For a good edition of all the Harleian lays, giving the Old French text, see Jean Rychner's edition, *Les Lais* (Champion, 1981). All the Harleian lays have been translated into English by Robert Hanning and Joan Ferrante, *The Lais of Marie de France* (Dutton, 1978), which contains a good selective bibliography.

Chievrefueil (The Honeysuckle)

It pleases me greatly and I truly wish
To tell you the truth
About the lay that they call *Chievrefueil*,
Why it was composed and about whom.
Several persons have recounted and told it to me,
And I found it written down,
About Tristan and the queen,
About their love that was so tender,
From which they had much suffering,
Then died from it on the same day.   10

King Mark was angry;
He was furious with his nephew Tristan.
He banished him from his kingdom
Because of the queen, whom Tristan loved.
He went off to his native land;
In South Wales, where he had been born,
He remained for an entire year;
He could not return.
But then he cast aside all restraint,
Heedless of death and destruction.   20
Don't be at all surprised at this:

For one who loves loyally
Is very sad and melancholy
When his wishes are denied.
Tristan was sad and dejected;
For that reason he left his country;
He went straight to Cornwall,
Where the queen lived.
He stationed himself in the forest, all alone,
Wanting no one to see him.   30
In the evening he emerged
When it was time to seek lodging.
With the peasants, with the poor people,
He took shelter for the night.
He asked them for news of the king
And what he was doing.
They told him that they had heard
That the barons were being convened;
They were to come to Tintagel;
The king wanted to hold his court there.   40
At Pentecost they would all be there;
There would be much joy and merriment,
And the queen would be there too.

Tristan heard this; he was overjoyed.
She would surely not be able to go there
Without him seeing her pass by.
The day on which the king set out,
Tristan returned to the wood
On the road that he knew
The procession was to take.   50
He cut a hazel tree in half,
Split it so that it was squared.
When he had peeled the bark from the stick,
He wrote his name with his knife.
If the queen noticed it,
If she gave it her full attention,
She would understand well, when she saw it,
That the stick was from her beloved—
It had happened to her once before,
And she had indeed noticed it.   60
This was the meaning of the message
That he had imparted and told to her:
That he had been there a long time,
Had waited and remained
To keep watch and to find out
How he could see her,
For he could not live without her.
It was exactly the same with the two of them
As it was with the honeysuckle
That has attached itself to the hazel tree: 70

When it has so entwined itself and taken hold
And completely surrounded the trunk,
Together they can survive quite well;
But if someone then tries to sever them,
The hazel tree quickly dies,
And the honeysuckle as well.
"My beloved, it is the same with us:
Neither you without me, nor I without you!"

The queen came riding along.
She looked a bit ahead;   80
She saw the stick, noticed it well,
Recognized all the letters on it.
She ordered the knights who were accompanying her
And who were traveling with her
To stop immediately:
She wished to dismount and rest.
The knights obeyed her command.
She went far away from her party;
She called her servant,
Brangain, who was very loyal.   90
She moved a little distance off the road;
Inside the woods she found the one
She loved more than anything living;
Together they knew very great joy.
He spoke to her with great freedom,
And she told him whatever she wished.
Then she explained to him how
He would be reconciled with the king,
That it had greatly saddened the king
That he had banished Tristan in that way: 100
He had done it because of the accusation.
Then she pulled herself away, she left her love,
But when it came time to separate,
They began to weep.
Tristan returned to Wales
To wait until his uncle summoned him.

For the joy that he had known,
For his beloved whom he had seen,
And for what he had written down
Just as the queen had said it,
In order to commemorate these words,   110
Tristan, who knew well how to play the harp,
Composed a new lay about it.
I shall name it quite briefly:
In English they call it *Gotelef*,
The French call it *Chievrefueil*.
I have told you the truth about it,
About the lay that I have here recounted.

chapter VIII

THOMAS OF BRITAIN: TRISTAN
("The Death Scene")

James J. Wilhelm

Thomas of Britain is important because the ending of his version of the Tristan and Isolde love story (which he would have titled *Tristran*) has survived, unlike those of Béroul or the German poet Gottfried von Strassburg. But even though Thomas's *Tristan* has supplied an ending, it has not supplied a beginning. The work is unfortunately fragmentary, consisting of only a handful of segments that make up no more than one-sixth of the total story. To get the whole Tristan tale, we have to piece these fragments together. Here, at the ending, we have used the Douce Manuscript from Oxford University for lines 1487 to 1815, and the Sneyd Part 2 from Oxford for the last few lines of the conclusion.

As for Thomas himself, we have no idea who he really was. Even his name is taken largely from his German successor, Gottfried von Strassburg, who says, in writing his own *Tristan*, that he followed "Thomas von Britanje"; "Britanje" could refer to either Britain or Brittany, since the Plantagenet kings like Henry II (whom Thomas probably knew) had bound the Normandy–Brittany area with the British Isles. In any case, it seems evident that Thomas knew the Celtic legends well, was sympathetic to the English (as he shows in a description of London preceding the part where this selection begins), and had mastered the art of writing French romances in a sophisticated but marvelously artless way.

Thomas is often considered the initiator of the "courtly," as opposed to the "heroic," school of romances. He concentrates on the psychology of love and plays down the role of the warrior in medieval narrative. There are long monologues in his work, and some of them are rhetorical almost to the point of foolishness, as when Isolde says in the following selection that she hopes that some sea creature may devour her body and Tristan's so that they may be found together and then placed in a common grave. Despite these "unnatural" flourishes, there is a vigor in Thomas's writing that captures some of the powerful force that has kept this story alive for many centuries. It is obvious that Richard Wagner was inspired by Thomas in writing the "Love-Death" or *Liebestod* final scene of his opera *Tristan und Isolde*. As a result Thomas (quite unknown to himself) serves as an important link between medieval romance and nineteenth-century romanticism.

Bibliographic note: The text translated here is that of Bartina H. Wind (Droz, 1960). For criticism see Joan M. Ferrante, *The Conflict of Love and Honor* (Mouton, 1973), and Gertrude Schoepperle, *Tristan and Isolt: A Study of the Source of the Romance* (2nd ed. R. S. Loomis: Franklin, 1959). Other translations have been made by A. T. Hatto (Penguin, 1967), R. S. Loomis (Dutton, 1951), and Dorothy Sayers (Benn, 1929).

Tristan

[*After finally deciding that he cannot remain in Cornwall, Tristan (Tristran, as Thomas calls him) returns to Brittany, where he was born. He soon becomes involved in local warring, siding with the young heir of a neighboring duchy whose name is Caerdin (Kaherdin). This young man has a lovely sister named Isolde (Ysolt) of the White Hands, who proceeds to fall in love with the hero. Although he is still very much in love with Isolde of Cornwall, Tristan decides finally to marry this girl; he will never consummate the marriage, however. He tells the girl on her marriage night that he has been castrated, and so he preserves his chastity toward all women other than the "true" Isolde.*

Back in Cornwall an evil knight named Cariado tells Isolde that her erstwhile lover has now taken a wife, and she is consumed with jealousy. Tristan meanwhile builds a special hall where he sculpts a statue of the absent Isolde so that he can commune directly with her figure.

When Caerdin learns that his sister is still a virgin despite her marriage, he is infuriated and confronts Tristan with this fact. Tristan calms him down and then shows him his statue of his beloved; Caerdin is overcome by Isolde's beauty. Soon the two vow to return to Cornwall, where Tristan introduces his brother-in-law to Brangain, Isolde's confidante. After several amatory misadventures Tristan and Caerdin decide to return to Brittany, where they immediately are involved in a variety of heroic exploits. A certain Tristan-the-Dwarf pleads with the hero to help him against a giant, but when Tristan aids him, the giant inflicts a poisoned wound upon him. Languishing helplessly, Tristan remembers Isolde's cure of him in the past when he was wounded by her uncle, and so he calls on Caerdin to go to London to beg Isolde to return and heal him. Tristan allows Caerdin forty days for this mission, telling him to hoist a white sail if he is successful and a black one if he is not.]

When Isolde had heard this message,   1487
She felt anguish in her heart
And pain and sympathy and sorrow—

Never had she felt any greater.
Now she thinks deeply, now she sighs;
She longs for Tristan, her dear friend,
But knows not how to reach him.
She goes to speak with Brangain.
She tells her about the misadventure
By which he got the poisoned wound,
About all his pain and his suffering,
And how and by whom he sent for her—
Otherwise his gash won't be healed.   1500
She revealed all of his torments,
Then asked her friend what she should do.
Now there are numerous sighs between them,
And lamentations and tears,
And pains and heaviness,
And grieving and depression.
In the talk they have together,
They express their sadness for him,
And thus after their conversation
They arrive at this decision: 1510
They will make the journey together;
They will go and see Caerdin first
To learn some more about Tristan's plight
And to help him in his hour of need.
Toward vespers-time they prepared themselves,
Taking with them everything they needed
While everyone else was sleeping;
And on the sly they crept carefully
In the pitch darkness with auspicious luck
Through a secret gate in the fortifications   1520
That loomed over the River Thames
Just as the rising tide swept in.
A little boat was waiting for them there,
And the two women quickly got aboard.
Rowing, drifting as the tide now ebbed,
Quick on the winds, they floated away,
Bending every effort to achieve their end.
They never ceased from steady rowing
Until they reached the flagship.
Then they raised the sails, and off they went.   1530
As long as the wind could billow them,
They scoured over the languorous deep,
Then followed the coastline abroad
On which the port of Wissant stands;
Then past Boulogne, past Treport.
The wind was brisk and beneficial,
And the ship that bore them nimble.
They sailed in front of Normandy,
Drifting with joy and gaiety,
Since the breeze was at their beck and call.   1540

Tristan meanwhile tossed with his wound,
Languishing gravely on his bed,
Finding no comfort in anything offered.
No medicine could help him—
Nothing anyone did was of avail.
He was longing for Isolde's arrival,
With no appetite for anything else;
Without her, he found nothing good;
He lived only with the thought of her.
So he languished there on his bed   1550
In the hope that she would come
And would remedy his illness;
He was sure he couldn't live without her.
Every day he sent someone down to the shore
To see if Caerdin's ship was coming back;
He had no other thought upon his mind.
Often he had himself carried down
On a litter to the side of the sea,
Where he waited to see if the ship
Was coming and what sails it bore.   1560
His heart was set on nothing else
Except for her arrival;
Toward this all his thoughts were aimed,
His longing and his will.
All that the world offers he counted
As nothing if the queen did not come.
Then he would have himself carried back
Because of the inner doubts he feels,
Since he's afraid that she may not come,
That she may prove disloyal to him;   1570
And he prefers to hear this from someone else
Rather than to see it with his own eyes.
He wants to keep a lookout for the ship,
But does not want to hear that he's failed.
He feels anxious deeply inside himself
Yet is still very passionate to see her.
He often complains to his wife, Isolde,
But never tells her about his longing—
Only about Caerdin, who isn't coming.
The longer Caerdin's absent, the more he fears   1580
That his friend has failed him at his task.
Ah, you should hear his terrible torment,
The profundity of his suffering,
Which is pitiful to all who love.
Never have you heard of a greater grief
From such a love, from such a longing.

Meanwhile as Tristan awaited Isolde,
The lady herself was anxious to land
After drawing in sight of the Breton coast,

So that she could survey the whole coastline.   1590
How happy all are, how gaily they sail—
Till suddenly a swell leaps from the south
And strikes the middle of the mainsail,
Making the whole ship stop in its course.
The crew rush to turn the sails around,
But despite their effort it starts to move back.
The wind grows stronger, kicking up waves;
The waters from the deep are welling up;
The sky is turbulent, the air is dense;
Swells are surging, the water's black.   1600
It rains, it hails, a storm is raging.
Bowlines break and staylines snap.
They lower the mainsail and run adrift,
Dipping on waves battered by winds.
They send out the landing-boat on the brink
Because they seem close to the friendly shore,
But this is done inauspiciously,
For the waves soon smash the boat to bits.
By this time they have lost so much
And the tempest has risen to such a pitch   1610
That no skipper—not even the ablest—
Can steady himself upon his feet.
All the crew are sobbing and wailing
And venting their sorrow out of fear.
Then said Isolde: "Alas, poor me!
God does not mean for me to live
To cast my eyes on my beloved Tristan.
He wants to drown me here in the deep!
Tristan, if I could just talk with you,
It wouldn't bother me if I died.   1620
Dearest lover, when you learn of my death,
I know you'll never again be happy.
You'll feel so desolate about my demise
That you'll lapse into deep, deep suffering,
And you'll never again be cured.
My arrival lies beyond my hands.
If God so wills it, I shall come,
And I'll nurse you out of your illness,
Since I don't think you have other pains,
Except that now you don't have the right help.   1630
This is my only sorrow and grief,
And in my heart I feel such distress
Because, my love, you'll never be able,
Once I am dead, to ward off your death.
I don't care a thing about dying myself.
Whenever God wills it, I will it too;
But as soon as you learn of my fate,
I know that you shall also perish;
Such is the nature of our love:

I can't feel any sorrow unless you're there;   1640
You can't die unless I die too,
And I can't perish without your loss.
If I have to face my end here at sea,
Then you will have to drown on land.
Since you can't drown there on the land,
You'll have to join me out at sea.
I foresee your death looming before me,
And I know that soon I shall have to die.
Lover, I'm failing in my desire.
I wanted very much to die in your arms   1650
And to be buried with you in the same tomb,
But we have not succeeded in this at all.
Yet—it still might happen—
For if I should drown out here
(Since you, I am sure, will drown then too),
Some sea creature might devour us both
And so, by sheer chance, we could enjoy
A single grave, my dearest love,
For someone might catch that creature
And recognize our bodies inside,   1660
And then join us in great honor,
As is appropriate for our love.
But this is nonsense that cannot be—
Unless, O God! You make it so!
Lover, what could you do here on the sea?
I know that you can never come here.
Yet I am here, and here I'll die—
Drown without you, Tristan my love,
And to me, it's a very great comfort, darling,
That you won't even know about my death.   1670
From this point on it will not be heard;
I don't know, dearest, who could report it.
You will survive me by a long time
And keep on expecting my sudden arrival
If it pleases God that He may heal you—
And that is the only thing I pray for.
I'm more anxious now about your health
Than I am about my own coming to shore
Because of my fine, true love for you.
But, friend, after my death I fear   1680
That, once you are cured,
You'll drop me completely from your memory,
Finding some comfort in another woman,
Tristan, my dear, after my death.
Surely I fear or at least I suspect
Isolde of the White Hands, my love.
I don't know if I should be so distressed,
But if death should come to me first,
I wouldn't live very much longer than you.

Ah me, I don't know what to do! 1690
But above all else, I love you.
I pray that God wills that we shall meet
And, my beloved, that I can cure you;
Otherwise let us both perish of grief!"
As long as the tempest lasts,
Isolde complains and loudly laments.
The winds and the brutal weather
Endure on the ocean for about five days;
Then the winds yield to fairer weather.
The crew hoists up the sail of white, 1700
And they skim along with rapid grace
Until Caerdin again sees his Brittany.
Everyone's happy, gay, and glad;
They raise the mainsail on high
So that all on the coast can perceive
Whether the color is white or black.
Caerdin wants to show off the color white
Because it was now the very last day
Of the forty-day period Tristan had set
For them to return to their native land. 1710
But just as they were skimming gaily,
A hot swell hit and the wind died down,
And suddenly they couldn't sail any more.
The sea was all calm and glassy smooth.
Their ship didn't budge an inch,
Except with the bobbing of the tide,
And they didn't have their landing boat.
Now they all suffered terrible misery.
They could see the shoreline up ahead,
But they had no wind to push them there. 1720
So up and down they bobbed on the waves,
Drifting forward and drifting back.
They couldn't advance their voyage a bit
Because they were so impeded.
Isolde was now bitterly distressed;
She could see the land she coveted,
And yet she couldn't disembark;
Desire impelled her to the brink.
Everyone on ship yearned for the land,
But the wind was too weak to project them. 1730
Often poor Isolde let out a shriek.
Everyone on the shore yearned for the ship,
Which they still hadn't exactly spied.
The delay made Tristan sad and depressed;
Often he was moaning, and often he sighed
For Isolde, whom he desired with all his heart.
Some tears trickle down; he twists his body,
Almost driven to death by desire.
While he suffers this anguish and pain,

His wife Isolde appears before him   1740
Carefully contriving a clever ruse;
She says: "My love, Caerdin's coming now.
I've spied his ship out on the sea,
And I assume that it has trouble sailing;
And yet I can see it with my own eyes,
And I'm certain that it is his.
God grant that he may bring the news
That will give some comfort to your heart!"
Tristan leaped up on hearing this
And said to Isolde: "My lovely wife,   1750
Are you absolutely certain it's his?
If so, then describe the mainsail."
Isolde replied: "I know it for sure.
I can tell you frankly the sail is black.
They've hoisted it up very high
Because the wind is failing them."
Then Tristan suffered a complete collapse—
Greater than any past or to come;
Turning his face now toward the wall,
He whispered: "God save us, Isolde!   1760
Since you won't be coming to see me,
My love for you forces me to die.
I can't hold on any longer to life.
For you I die, Isolde, my love,
Though you feel no pity for my suffering,
But you'll feel grief about my death.
My friend, it's a very great comfort to me
That you'll feel pity about my death."
Three times he uttered: "My love Isolde,"
And on the fourth, he gave up the ghost.   1770

Then all his knights and companions
Ran wailing around the castle.
Their cries were loud, their passion great.
Knights and sergeants leapt to the task
And bore him nobly from his bed,
Laying him out on a cloth of silk,
Covering him with a shroud that's striped.
The wind then rose up on the sea
And billowed out the middle of the sails,
Bearing the ship at last to shore.   1780
Isolde clambered down from the bark
And heard the wailing in the streets
And the bells clanging in churches and chapels.
She asked some people what had happened:
Why all this clamor of the bells
And for whom everyone was weeping?
An aged man replied to her then:
"Milady, may the Good Lord help me!

We've suffered such an awful loss
That no people will ever suffer more.   1790
Tristan the valiant, the grand, lies dead.
He was the mainstay of all our realm.
He was generous to those in need
And helpful to those under stress.
He has died just now in his bed
From a wound he received in battle.
Never has such a catastrophe
Fallen upon our kingdom."
As soon as she heard this news,
Isolde was rendered mute with grief.   1800
She was so stricken by his death
That she ran up the street in disarray
Ahead of the others into the palace.
Never in their lives had the Bretons seen
A lady of such stunning beauty.
All were wondering throughout the city
Where she came from, who she was.
Isolde went inside to view the body
And, turning toward the Orient,
She prayed for him in a pitiful way: 1810
"Dear lover, Tristan, as I see you dead,
Reason tells me I can't live any more.
You died out of your great love for me,
And I'll die, darling, out of compassion,
Since I was unable to come here in time
And cure your body of its wound.
Dearest, dearest, because of your death
I'll never know any comfort again—
Any joy or happiness or delight.
Curses on that storm that made me   1820
Delay so long out there at sea
So that I couldn't come to see you!
If I had only come here in time,
I could have given you back your life;
I could have spoken to you very softly
About the great love we once shared;
I could have bemoaned our current fate,
Mentioning our happiness and ecstasy,
Our pain as well as the sorrow
That we've had throughout our affair;   1830
I could have reminded you of all this
And kissed you and embraced you.
If I couldn't cure you entirely myself,
Then we might have died together!
But since I couldn't come in time
And didn't know the true outcome,
Arriving only to find you dead,
I'll now take solace from the same drink.

You surrendered your life because of me,
And now I'll do the same for my beloved;   1840
For you I want to die the very same way."
Lying beside him, she hugged him tightly,
Pouring kisses over his mouth and face,
And drawing him closely to her breast;
Body to body, mouth to mouth,
She rendered up her spirit completely
And suffered death there at his side
Out of her sorrow for her true love.
Tristan perished because of his love,
And Isolde because she did not come in time;   1850
Tristan perished from his deep passion
And Isolde from her compassionate love.

[*According to popular mythology, the two lovers were buried side by side, and out of Tristan's grave there sprang a rose bush, while out of Isolde's came an entwining vine; others claimed that the two plants were a hazel tree and a honeysuckle vine.*]

chapter IX

THE PROSE MERLIN
and the
SUITE DU MERLIN

Samuel N. Rosenberg

The great seer of western Europe is a creature of Celtic legend, to whom Geoffrey of Monmouth gave literary life in his Latin *Historia regum Britanniae* (*History of the Kings of Britain*) and *Vita Merlini* (*Life of Merlin*). He then appeared in a mid-twelfth-century French adaptation of the *Historia*, Wace's *Roman de Brut*; but as a fully developed figure in vernacular literature he emerged only around 1200, in the poem *Merlin*, composed by the Burgundian cleric Robert de Boron. Robert had already written a lengthy verse narrative on Joseph of Arimathea and the origin of the Grail. His Merlin poem was intended as a continuation of the story, to be followed in its turn by a Grail romance built around the figure of Perceval. How far Robert actually succeeded in his endeavor is not quite clear, for the surviving *Merlin* is a mere fragment consisting of the five hundred opening verses, and there is no remnant of the Perceval poem. In both instances, however, as in the case of the Joseph poem, we have prose "translations" that may have been prepared by Robert himself and seem, in any event, to constitute a realization of his great plan for a Grail trilogy.

Among the versions of the Prose *Merlin* is one joined to a sequel known as the *Suite du Merlin*, an anonymous work over twice as long as Robert's, dating from the second quarter of the thirteenth century. The *Suite* makes mention of Robert de Boron as its author, but the claim is surely spurious. Together, these works were apparently envisaged as forming part of an even greater, more complex Romance of the Grail than Robert had conceived. Merlin—to a great extent reinvented in comparison with the models in Geoffrey—is the dominant character in the combined narrative, which opens with the demonic circumstances of his conception in pre-Arthurian times and leads, through many episodes, to his death at the hands of the Lady of the Lake. At the same time that he participates importantly in the action, he stands back and shapes it, influencing the behavior of characters and the course of events through his special powers. Dominant at a still further remove from the action itself, he is all the while concerned to have the events chronicled in an abiding written record. Yet the two-part narrative extends its scope beyond Merlin and makes it clear that the limits of his life are insufficient to define the work's purpose or coherence. Certainly the countless characters and sometimes bewildering adventures bespeak an intention that surpasses an interest in Merlin himself. Thus Robert concludes his story with the accession of Arthur to the royal throne; the *Suite*, moreover, pursues its tale past the death of Merlin and explicitly reminds the reader in its final sentence, as elsewhere, that the subject of overarching and continuing significance is the Grail. However different the two parts may be—and they are—they share that vision.

The selection of excerpts presented here, accounting for about one-fifth of the original, concentrates on the intriguing and commanding figure of Merlin. Spanning his whole life, it includes material from both Robert de Boron and the *Suite*, and allows their different conceptions and emphases to be seen: the prophetic Merlin of the first giving way to the sorcerer of the second; the historical and political interest of the one contrasting with the chivalric and supernatural bent of the other.

The translation attempts to convey the texture as well as the message of the original. It deliberately relies on a rather colorless, restricted vocabulary, along with the considerable repetition and limited syntactic variation that reflect the formative stage of French literary prose at the beginning of the thirteenth century.

Bibliographic note: The text translated here was edited by Gaston Paris and Jacob Ulrich (Firmin Didot, 1886). For the *Merlin* proper I found occasional clarification in the texts edited by Alexandre Micha (Droz, 1980) and Bernard Cerquiglini (Bibliothèque Médiévale, 1981). For both parts I consulted the Modern French translation by Emmanuèle Baumgartner (Stock, 1980). Useful bibliographic references are included in all these volumes. In addition one might consult Chapters 19, 23, and 24, among others, in *Arthurian Literature in the Middle Ages*, edited by R. S. Loomis (Oxford University, 1959).

From the Prose Merlin

1. The Plot to Create Merlin

According to the tale, the Enemy was very angry when our Lord went down into Hell and freed Adam and Eve and as many others as He wished. When the demons found out, they were astonished; they gathered together and said: "Who is this man who has crushed us and smashed our defenses so that we can hide nothing from him and he can do whatever he likes? We never thought that a man could be born of woman and yet escape our grasp. This one, though, was born independent of us, and batters and torments us as much as he likes. If he was born of woman, how is it that we have no earthly pleasure in him and he ruins us so?"

Then one of the demons answered: "Lords, we have been ruined by what we thought would benefit us most. Remember the words of the prophets, who said that the son of God would come down to earth to save the sinners descended from Adam and Eve. And we went and seized those who said that the man who would come to earth would deliver them from the torments of Hell. Everything the prophets said has now come true. He has taken away all those that we had taken hold of, and we are powerless against him. He has taken away from us all those who believe in his special birth, who believe he was born of woman in such a way that we had no part in the event and were not even aware that it was going to happen."

"Don't you know, then," said another, "that he has them washed in water in his name? They are washed in the name of the Father, of the Son, and of the Holy Spirit, so that we can never again have them as we used to. We have now lost them all through this washing, so that we have no power over them unless they choose to come back to us. Thus the man who has taken them away has reduced our power. Moreover he has left ministers on earth who will save them, no matter how great a part they have had in our works; they have but to repent and renounce our works and do as the ministers say. We have thus lost them all. Our Lord has offered them a great spiritual gift: to save mankind, he came to earth and deigned to be born of woman and suffer all the torments of the world; and he was born of woman unbeknownst to us and without committing any sin of the flesh. When at last we came along, we tried and tested him in every way we knew, but he resisted all our efforts and chose instead to die in order to save mankind. He must surely love all men, if he was willing to suffer such great pain to take them away from us. We now have to seek a way to win them back so that they cannot repent or even speak to the ministers who could grant them the pardon that he paid for with his death."

Then all together they said: "We have lost everything, since he can pardon sinners up to the last moment. Whoever embraces him will be saved. Even someone who has always performed our works is now lost to us if he repents. We have now lost them all."

They went on: "Those who have harmed us most are those who kept predicting his coming to earth. Those are the ones from whom the greatest harm has come. The more insistent they were, the more we tormented them; so it seems he hastened to their rescue, to deliver them from the torments we were making them suffer. But how can we now find a spokesman of our own who could speak to men and tell them of our intelligence and our achievements and everything we do and how we have the power to know all things that have ever happened? If we had a man with such power, a man who could relate all that and live with all other men on earth, he could certainly help us with his teachings like those sorcerers and wizards who used to be with us, whose prophecies we knew were false. He would thus reveal everything said and done both long ago and recently, and he would be believed by many people."

Then they all said together: "It would be a great accomplishment to father such a man, for he would be widely believed."

Then one of them said: "I do not have the power to make a woman pregnant, but if I had, you could count on me: I know a woman who says and does whatever I want."

Another said: "There is one among us who is able to take on the appearance of a man and make a woman conceive. But he has to do it as discreetly as possible."

In this way the demons decided that they would engender a man who could lead the others astray. What fools, though, to think that our Lord would remain unaware of their scheming! But thus the Enemy undertook to create a man in his image, using his memory and his intelligence to deceive both mankind and Jesus Christ. (You can see how foolish the Devil is, to think that he can deceive the One who is master over him and all the world.) With that agreement, then, the council ended. The demon who claimed power over a woman did not delay in coming to the place where she lived and making her do his will. And everything that she and her husband possessed she dedicated to the Enemy.

[*The Devil gradually destroys the woman and most of her family. A surviving daughter, despite her virtuous behavior, falls victim to him one night in her sleep and conceives a child, whose father she is clearly at a loss to identify. She faces being burned at the stake for fornication. A worthy priest befriends her and persuades her judges to let the young woman live at least long enough to give birth. The judges agree, confining her to a tower with two women there to guard her.*]

2. Merlin's Birth and the Defense of His Mother

She remained for a long while in the tower. The judges had prepared whatever was needed and delivered it to the two women who were with her. There she remained, as you have heard, and gave birth when God wished. When the child was born, he had the intelligence and the power of the Enemy, whose offspring he was. But the Enemy had been senseless to father him, for our Lord had redeemed with His death those who repent truly, and He had pardoned their sins, while the Enemy had seduced the young woman with a trick. She, though, as soon as she realized that she had been deceived, begged mercy of the One who mattered and then placed herself under the authority of God and the Holy Church, and she obeyed all the orders of her confessor. Nevertheless God did not want the Devil to lose what he had desired and what he had created the child for, and so, as the Devil wished, the child received his ability and his power to know all things said and done in the past. But our all-knowing Lord knew that the mother had confessed and repented and had done so sincerely, that she had not, moreover, been to blame for what had happened, and that in any case she had been washed pure by baptism. He did not wish the sin, then, to harm the child, and so God gave him the power to know all things to come. In this way the boy knew the things of the past through the Devil, and the knowledge of the future came to him from God, who thus wanted to counterbalance the other's work. Let the boy, then, decide which way to turn: to choose the Devil's path or our Lord's! For the Devil creates only the body, while our Lord confers the breath of life and, according as it pleases him to grant intelligence and memory, the ability to see and hear and understand; and more than to any other he gave the ability to this child, whose need was greater. We shall soon see which side the boy would choose.

When the two women saw the child and picked him up, they were both frightened, because he was all covered with hair, more than any other child they had ever seen. They showed him to his mother, who, seeing him, crossed herself and said: "This child frightens me!"

The other women said: "He does us, too. We can hardly hold him."

The mother said: "Send him down from the tower and have him baptized."

They asked: "What name do you wish to give him?"

She said: "I want to name him Merlin, for my father."

After the baptism Merlin was entrusted to his mother for nursing, which she did for nine months. At that point the boy looked as if he were a year old.

When he reached the age of eighteen months, the two women said to his mother: "Lady, we would like to leave here and go back to our families. It seems to us we have been here for a long time, and we cannot stay forever."

She answered: "Of course. I cannot stop you." But she began to weep and to beg them, for the love of God, to remain a bit longer. With her child in her arms she went over to a window and kept crying. She said: "Dear son, I am going to die because of you, though I have done nothing to deserve it. No one knows who your father was, and I cannot be believed, whatever I say. I am doomed to die."

As she was bemoaning her death and the torment she expected, the child looked at his mother and said: "Dear mother, do not be afraid; you will never die on my account."

When his mother heard him speak, her heart almost failed her; her arms suddenly dropped from the child, and she let him fall to the floor. The women, sitting near a window, heard the noise and jumped up, convinced that she was trying to strangle him. "What are you doing to your child? Do you want to kill him?" they said.

She answered, stunned: "No. I was just stunned by the incredible thing he said to me, and my heart and my arms failed me."

They asked: "What did he say to you?"

"He said," she answered, "that my death will never come because of him."

The women said: "He is going to say something else." They picked up the child and listened closely for any further words, but he gave no sign of speaking any more.

After a long wait the mother said to the two women: "Threaten me, and you'll see if he tries to speak again." Then the mother took him in her arms and began to weep; she would truly have liked him to speak in front of the women.

They said right away: "Lady, what a horror that a beautiful woman like you should be burned at the stake because of such a creature! It would have been much better if he had never been born."

The child then spoke: "That's a lie. My mother made you say it."

The women were startled to hear him speak and said: "This is no child, but a devil! He knows what we have said and done!"

And they spoke to him and put many a question to him, but he said only: "Let me be! You are fools, and greater sinners than my mother."

The women were astonished and said: "This can't be kept hidden! Let's tell it to the people down below." The two women then went to the window and told the crowd what the child had said.

At this remarkable news they agreed it was time to let the mother face her punishment, and a letter was written summoning her to punishment forty days later. When the mother received the summons and learned the date of her ordeal, she was filled with fear and sent word to her good confessor. Many days passed, until only seven were left before she was to go to the stake. Whenever she thought of that day, she felt bewildered and terrified and burst into tears. The child, though, moving around in the tower and seeing his mother crying, began to laugh and look delighted. The women said to him: "You have no thought for what is on your mother's mind. She is going to be burned at the stake this week, because of you! What a curse that you were ever born, for thanks to you—unless God puts it right—she is going to suffer a dreadful end."

The child answered: "Dear mother, that is not the truth. As long as I live, no man will dare to kill you or touch you or deliver you to the stake, unless God wishes."

Hearing these words from the boy, the mother and two women were overjoyed and said: "A child who can say such things will be a wise and virtuous man, God willing."

That is where matters stood until the appointed day. That day the two women were released and the mother appeared before the judges with the child in her arms. But the judges first spoke in private to the women who had been with her, asking whether it was true that the child had spoken as reported. When the women related everything they had heard him say, the judges were greatly surprised and said that he would need to know a good many words if he were to save his mother from death. Then they came back. Meanwhile the good man who was the mother's confessor had arrived.

One of the judges said: "Young woman, have you any final request? Prepare yourself now, for your end is near."

She answered: "My lord, if you please, I should like to speak with this good man." She was allowed to do so and went into a side chamber, leaving the child outside. Many people put questions to him, but to no effect.

Meantime the woman spoke to her confessor, shedding bitter tears all the while. When she had finished, the good man asked: "Is it true, then, that your child speaks as they claim?"

She answered: "Yes, my lord" and recounted what she had heard him say.

The good man said: "Something extraordinary is going to come of this."

Then they left the chamber, and the woman picked up her child and stood once more before the judges. Seeing her, they said: "Young woman, will you state who the father of this child is? Beware of keeping it a secret."

She answered: "My lords, I see clearly that I am doomed. May God show me no mercy if I ever saw the father or ever even let a man come close enough to make me pregnant."

The judges answered: "We do not believe that that can be true, but we will ask other women if what you claim is possible, for we have never heard such an extraordinary thing."

With that the judges went aside to speak to a number of women about the young woman's claim. "Ladies," said one of the judges, "has any of you, or anyone you know of, ever been able to conceive a child and give birth without first having relations with a man?"

The women said it was impossible. Then the judges returned to Merlin's mother and told her what they had heard from the other women. "And now it is right that justice be done."

Then Merlin, angered by these words, jumped in front of the judges and said: "Lords, such justice is not about to be done! If you put to death all the men and women who have been guilty of adultery, you would have to burn two-thirds of all the people present here! I know everyone's secrets, and if I wanted to reveal them, I could make them all confess. You may be sure that many have behaved worse than my mother. In fact she is not guilty as charged. Or if she is, this good man here has taken the guilt upon himself. If you don't believe me, ask him."

The judges called up the priest and asked him if Merlin had just stated the truth. The good man then retold word for word everything that Merlin's mother had said to him. Asked whether everything had truly happened as she claimed, he answered: "I told her that she need fear neither God nor man and that justice would be done. She herself has told you how she was seduced and how she bore this extraordinary child without knowing who had fathered him or how; she came to confess and repent, and I ordered her penance."

The boy then said to the good man: "You wrote down the night and the hour I was conceived, and you can easily find out when I was born. In that way you can be sure of much of what my mother says."

The good man answered: "That is true, but I cannot tell where your knowledge comes from. Somehow you know more than all the rest of us."

Then the women were called up who had been in the tower with Merlin's mother. They compared the length of the pregnancy and the date of birth with the confessor's note on the time of conception, and it all fitted together.

One of the judges said: "Nevertheless she shall not be acquitted unless she states who the father is."

That angered the boy, and he said: "I know my father better than you do yours. And your mother knows who fathered you better than mine knows who fathered me."

That angered the judge, and he said to Merlin: "If you have any charge to make against my mother, I shall examine it."

Merlin answered: "I could readily say that, if you sent her to the stake, her death would be more justified than my mother's. If I make her admit that to you, acquit my mother, because she is not guilty as charged and everything she has said about my conception is true."

The judge was much annoyed by Merlin's words and said: "Merlin, if you are right, your mother will be spared the stake. But understand this: if you cannot prove your charge against my mother well enough to persuade me and save your own, you too shall be burned at the stake."

Then the judge and Merlin agreed to adjourn for two weeks. The judge sent for his own mother, while he had Merlin and his placed under guard; and he himself stayed with the guards all the time. The boy was often questioned about his mother and other persons, but throughout the two weeks no answer could be drawn from him.

On the appointed day the judge's mother arrived, and Merlin and his mother were led out of their prison. Before all the people the judge said: "Merlin, here is my mother, against whom you have an accusation to make. Say to her what you wish to say."

The child answered: "You are far from being as wise as you think. Go take your mother to a secluded house and take along your closest supporters, and I shall call upon my mother's supporters: all-powerful God and her confessor."

The people who heard these words were so dumbfounded that they could hardly respond, but the judge realized that there was wisdom in them. The child turned to the other judges: "Lords, if I can convince this man of my mother's innocence, will you all acquit her?"

They answered: "If she is deemed innocent by him, she will have no further problem."

As proposed, then, Merlin and the judge went off to a private place. The judge took his mother and two of his most upright friends, and the child took along his mother's confessor. When they were all gathered, the judge said: "Now you can tell my mother what you will in order to win your mother's release."

"My wish," said Merlin, "is less to champion my mother against a wrong than it is to defend the right, both God's and hers. You may be sure that my mother did nothing to deserve the death you want to put her to, and if you listen to me, you will acquit her and give up any inquiry concerning your own mother."

The judge answered: "You can't get by with that. You will have to say more."

Merlin said: "Are you assuring my mother and me that, if I can defend her successfully, you will release her?"

The judge answered: "That is true."

Merlin answered: "You want to send my mother to the stake because she gave birth to me without knowing who my father was. But if I wished, she could more easily say whose son I am than you can say who your father was, and your mother can more easily say whose son you are than my mother could now say whose son I am."

The judge said: "Dear mother, am I not the son of your true husband?"

"Yes, dear son," said the judge's mother.

Merlin responded: "My lady, you will have to tell the truth if your son does not acquit my mother and me. But if he were willing to do so with no further discussion, I would gladly keep quiet."

The judge answered: "I will do nothing of the sort."

"In that case you shall have the advantage of learning from your mother's testimony who your father was!" Those present were astonished at

Merlin's words and crossed themselves. Merlin said to the judge's mother: "My lady, you must tell your son whose son he is."

And the lady said: "You devil! Haven't I told him?"

Merlin answered: "You know perfectly well that he is not the son of the man he thinks."

The lady was frightened and said: "Of whom then?"

He answered: "You know that he is the son of your priest. The first time you had relations with him, you told him that you were afraid you would become pregnant, and he told you that you wouldn't be, and he said that every time he went to bed with you he would make a note of it, because he was afraid you might go with some other man as well—though not with your husband, since the two of you had a falling out in any case. When the child was conceived, you were quick to complain to the priest that you were pregnant. If what I am saying is true, admit it. Otherwise I shall have to go on."

The judge was angry and asked his mother: "Is it true, what he says?"

In her fright the mother answered: "Dear son, do you really believe what this devil is saying?"

Merlin said: "If you do not admit it, I will tell you something else that you know to be true." The lady kept silent. Merlin went on: "I know everything that happened. The truth is that when you realized you were pregnant, you asked your priest to reconcile you with your husband, because you wanted to disguise the fact that you were with child by him. He managed to reconcile the two of you, and you went to bed together. In that way you gave the good man to understand that the child was his. Many other people believe so, too. And this very man here firmly believes that he is the son of your good husband. Afterward you persisted in such behavior, and you still do. The very night before coming here you were with the priest, and in the morning he escorted you quite far along the way. When he turned back, he whispered to you with a smile: 'Make sure you obey all the wishes of our son.' He knows, thanks to his notes, that this man is his son!"

When the judge's mother thus heard Merlin speak the truth, she felt greatly distressed and sat down. She realized that she would have to confess. Her son looked at her and said: "Dear mother, whoever my father may be, I am your son and will behave as your son. But tell me the truth: is this boy's statement true?"

The mother answered: "Dear son, in the name of God, forgive me! I cannot hide it from you: everything he has said is true."

At those words the judge said: "So the child was telling the truth! And he knew more about his father than I knew about mine! It is not right that I should punish his mother if I am not punishing my own." And he said to Merlin: "Merlin, I ask you for God's sake, so that I can clear your mother's name and your own in public: tell me who your father is."

Merlin said: "I will tell you, more out of love for you than out of fear of your authority. I want you to know that I am the son of a demon who seduced my mother. He is from that race of demons known as Incubi, who live in the air. He gave me the ability to know all things said and done in the past, and that is how I know what life your mother has always led. Our Lord, moreover, wanted me to have that memory because of my mother's virtue and her true repentance; and because of my own submission to the commandments of the Holy Church, He granted me the power to know the things that are to come. Then Merlin took him aside and said: "Your mother will go tell what I have said to the man who fathered you, and when he hears that you know the truth, he will be so frightened of you that he will run away. And the Devil, whose works he has always performed, will lead him to a river, and he will drown there. You can see, then, how well I know the things that are to come."

The judge answered: "Merlin, if what you have told me is true, I will never again fail to believe you."

There ended their private conversation; they reappeared before the crowd, and the judge announced: "This child has saved his mother from the stake. Let all who ever see him know that they have never seen and will never see a man more wise than he."

They all cried: "God be praised if she is saved from death!"

At this point, according to the tale, Merlin remained with the judges. The judge sent his mother home, along with two men who would test the truth of Merlin's prediction. As soon as she was back, the mother spoke in private to the priest about the extraordinary thing she had heard. He was so terrified that he could not utter a word in reply, and it occurred to him that the judge would come to kill him. With this thought in mind he went out of the town and soon came to a river. He thought it would be better to drown himself than to be made to die a horrible death by someone else. Thus did the Devil, whose works he had performed, lead him to jump into the river and drown, which was witnessed by the two men who had accompanied the judge's mother. As the tale says, a man should not flee the company of other people, for the Devil more easily takes hold of a man alone than with a group.

The two witnesses returned to the judge and reported the deed, which had taken place on the third day of their stay, as they had seen it. The judge marveled at their news. He told it to Merlin, who laughed and said: "Now you can see whether I speak the truth!" He added: "Please repeat everything I have told you to Blaise, my mother's confessor."

The judge then related to Blaise the extraordinary fate of the priest. Then Merlin went off with his mother and Blaise, and the judges went on their way.

3. Merlin's Instructions to Blaise

Blaise, now, was a worthy man and had a sharp mind under his tonsure. Hearing such intelligent words from Merlin, who was at that time no more than two and a half years old, he wondered how the boy could be so wise. He probed and tested, until one day Merlin said: "Stop probing. The more you probe, the more you will wonder. Instead do what I ask you and accept everything I tell you, and I will teach you how to receive the love of Jesus Christ."

Blaise said to Merlin: "I heard what you said about being fathered by the Devil, and I believe it. I am afraid, then, that you may lead me astray."

Merlin said: "It is a habit of all faint-hearted people to see their own behavior in everyone else and more readily take note of the bad than the

good. Just as you heard me say that I was a son of the Devil, you heard me
say, too, that God had given me knowledge and awareness of the things
that are to come. With that in mind, if you were wise, you would surely
understand which direction I was bound to take. You may be sure that it is
God who wants me to know these things, because the demons never gained
my allegiance. True, I have not ceased to share their skill in ruse and
trickery, but I have only as much of it as I need to have and I certainly do
not use it for their benefit. Nor were they very wise in choosing a mother
for me, for they put me into a womb that was not meant to be theirs, and
my mother's virtue harmed their cause. If they had placed me instead in my
grandmother, I would not have had the capacity to know God and would
have belonged to them: it was through her that came all the trouble that my
mother inherited from her father, all the disasters that you have heard her
recount. But now believe what I shall tell you about faith in Jesus Christ. I
shall tell what no one else, save God alone, could tell you. Make it into a
book; and many people, hearing it read, will be better for it and save
themselves from sin, and you will thus be performing an act of great
charity."

Blaise answered: "I shall gladly write the book, but I beg you, in the
name of the Father and the Son and the Holy Spirit, in the name of the dear
Lady who bore our Lord, and in the name of all the angels and archangels
and apostles and everything that comes from God, that you should not
deceive me or lead me astray or do anything that is not according to the will
of God."

Merlin answered: "May all the creatures that you have just named speak
ill of me to God, if I ever do anything to you that is not in accordance with
His will!"

"Tell me, then," said Blaise, "whatever you wish for our good, and I
will do it from now on."

Merlin said: "Then go find a good supply of ink and parchment, and I
will tell you many things to write in your book."

When Blaise was prepared, Merlin gave him a faithful account of the love
that Jesus Christ and Joseph [of Arimathea] had shown each other, and told
him the story of Alain and his companions, and how Joseph had relin-
quished the Grail and then died; and he recounted how the demons, after all
these events, realized that they had lost their power over men, and how,
since the prophets had harmed them, they all agreed to engender a man.
"And you have heard from my mother and from others the effort and the
cunning that they put into that. But in their mad excess they never gained
my allegiance."

Merlin thus dictated the whole story to Blaise. Blaise marveled at the
extraordinary things he was hearing, but they seemed right and true to him,
and he wrote them down with great care.

While he was busily at work, Merlin said to him: "What you are writing
down is going to bring me great suffering."

Blaise asked him to explain, and Merlin said: "Men from the west will
come in search of me. They will have sworn to their lord to kill me and take
my blood back to him, but as soon as they see me and hear me speak, they
will no longer want to. When I go off with them, you leave for those parts
where the keepers of the Holy Grail live, and from then on all people will be

eager to hear or read this book, the fruit of your pains. Still, it will have no final authority, since you are not and cannot be an apostle: the apostles never wrote anything about our Lord that they themselves had not seen and heard, while everything that you are writing you can see or hear only through me. Just as I live hidden, and always shall, from those to whom I do not wish to reveal myself, so, too, the book will remain obscure and only rarely will anyone reap all its benefit. You will take it with you when I leave with those who come in search of me. And so the book of Joseph, the book of the lineages that I have told you about, will be put together with your book and mine; your labor will have been completed and you will be worthy of their company. Your book, then, will be joined to that of Joseph, as clear evidence of the work that you and I have done. If they like it, they will show their thankfulness and pray for us to our Lord. The two books together will make a single fine book and will be of equal worth—except in this respect: that I cannot and must not relate the private words that passed between Joseph and Jesus Christ."

[*The throne of England falls into the hands of the usurper Vertiger, or Vortigern, who, trying to build an impregnable tower, finds that the walls keep collapsing. Merlin, coming to be recognized as a seer, offers to solve the problem: under the foundation there are two quarrelsome dragons that need to be released. Brought to light, the white one kills the red one and then dies himself. The tower is completed, but Merlin explains to Vertiger that, as prefigured by the dragons' combat, he, the usurper, will soon be defeated in battle by the sons of the late king. This occurs, and the elder son, Pendragon, accedes to the throne. With the help of Merlin's wizardry Pendragon and his brother, Uther, make progress against the Saxon invaders of their land, killing their king, Hangus, or Hengist. The brothers are happy to have an ally in Merlin.*]

4. The Testing of Merlin's Prophetic Wisdom

Then the two brothers, in the name of God and with the promise that they would defer to him in all matters, appealed to Merlin to remain with them. Merlin answered: "My lords, you must both know that I have all the knowledge of hidden things that I want to have. And you, my lord," he said to the king, "you know, don't you, that I have told you the truth about whatever you have asked me?"

The king answered: "I have never caught you in a lie."

"And you, Uther, did I not tell you the truth about a certain lady when you thought that no one could know it?"

Uther answered: "You have been so open with me that I can never lose my confidence in you. And it is because I know how worthy and how wise a man you are that I wish you would stay with us."

Merlin answered: "I shall gladly stay. But I want to share a secret of mine with the two of you: I am compelled, from time to time, to go off by myself, far away from people. Be assured, though, that wherever I am I shall have you uppermost in my mind, and if I ever learn that you are facing some problem, I shall do everything possible to come to your aid. But if you want to keep my friendship, please do not be disturbed whenever I go away, and every time I come back, give me a warm welcome in public. Worthy men will love me all the more, and the wicked, who will never be friends of yours, will hate me, but if you treat me well, they will never dare let it be seen. Let me add that except for you, in private, I will not disguise my appearance. I shall soon come to your palace, and those who have already seen me will run to tell you of my arrival. As soon as you receive the message, make it obvious that you are delighted, and they will tell you that I am an excellent seer. Then do not hesitate to ask me whatever your counselors suggest, and I shall advise you concerning anything you ask."

At this point, according to the tale, Merlin took leave of Pendragon and Uther and, taking on the appearance by which the people of the land would recognize him, he went to see the men who had been Vertiger's counselors. They were very happy and hurried to tell the king that Merlin had come. The king was delighted by the news and went out to meet him. Those who were well disposed toward Merlin said: "Merlin, here comes the king to meet you!"

The king gave Merlin a joyful welcome and led him to the palace, where his counselors immediately drew him aside and said: "My lord, Merlin here is the best seer alive. Ask him to tell you how you can capture Hangus's castle and how the war between you and the Saxons will end. If he wants to, he will tell you!"

The king agreed, and they then left the matter for the moment because the king wanted to show Merlin proper honor. Two days later, in front of his assembled counselors, he asked Merlin for his advice, as had been suggested: "Merlin, dear friend, I have heard that you are very wise. I beg you to tell me, then, how I can capture Hangus's castle and whether I can drive the Saxons out of our land."

Merlin said: "My lord, now you can see just how wise I am! I can assure you that ever since Hangus died, the Saxons have yearned for nothing better than to run away from this land. In fact your messengers will bring you that news tomorrow, and you will send them back with a peace proposal. Then the Saxons will send word that they are prepared to leave you this land that was your father's, and you will have them escorted away and will give them ships to ensure their departure."

The king said: "Merlin, that is very good. But I will send them a peace proposal beforehand by other means, simply to see how they respond."

He dispatched King Urfin, one of his counselors, along with two other men. They rode to the castle and were met by the Saxons, who asked the knights what they wanted. Urfin answered: "Lords, in the name of the king, we are asking for a three-month truce."

"We shall consider it," said the Saxons. They drew aside to deliberate and agreed: "The death of Hangus has left us sorely pressed, and we do not have enough food to remain here through the king's three-month truce. Let us ask him to lift the siege and leave us the castle as a fief held from him, and each year we shall give him as tribute ten knights, ten damsels, ten falcons, ten hares, and one hundred riding horses."

That was the outcome of their deliberations, which they conveyed in just those terms to the messengers. The messengers relayed it to the king and Merlin and all the barons, whereupon the king asked Merlin what he would do. Merlin answered that he would not intervene, for great harm to the kingdom would come from it. "But send them word right now that they should leave the castle with no delay—since they have nothing to eat, they will do so gladly—and that if they do not leave, they will have no truce. Tell them that you will give them ships and boats to enable them to go and, if they refuse, capture as many of them as you can and put them all to a harsh death. I assure you, though, that they will be only too happy to escape alive, for they now believe that they are going to die."

The next morning the king did as Merlin had said and dispatched his envoys with that message. When those in the castle received it and realized that their lives would be saved, they were overjoyed as never before, because since the death of Hangus they had not known where to turn. Word of it was sent throughout the land, and the king had them escorted to the port and given ships to sail away.

As you have heard, then, Merlin understood what was in the Saxons' hearts, and through his advice the king sent them on their way. Thus the Saxons left Pendragon's kingdom, and Merlin retained the full confidence of the king.

So things remained for a long time, until one day, when Merlin had spoken to the king about an important matter, one of the barons, who felt slighted, came to the king and said: "My lord, it is extraordinary how you rely on that man! All his knowledge, I tell you, comes from the Devil. Allow me to put him to the test, and you will be convinced that I am right."

The king answered: "I agree, provided you do not anger him."

The other said: "My lord, I promise not to do or say anything to displease him."

So the king agreed, and the baron was delighted. A powerful man by reason of fortune and family, he was regarded by everyone as both very wise and treacherous. One day he came up to Merlin at court, made a great display of friendliness, and drew him aside into a conversation with the king and two other men. He said to the king: "My lord, this is one of the wisest men in the world. I have heard that he predicted Vertiger's death to him, that Vertiger would die in a fire set by you, and he did. That is why I ask you all, in the name of God, since you know that I am sick, to ask him to tell you what kind of death I shall have. I am sure that, if he wants, he can say that."

The king and the others put the question to Merlin, but Merlin, who had heard the baron's words and understood perfectly well what envy and ill will they expressed, turned to the king and said: "My lord, you have asked me to predict his death, and I will: on the day of his death he will fall from his horse and break his neck. That is how his life will end."

At those words the man said to the king: "My lord, you have just heard him! May God protect me!" Then he drew the king aside and said: "My lord, remember what he said, for I am going to make a change and put him to another test."

With that he went home and disguised himself; then he returned as quickly as he could and pretended to be sick. He asked the king in secret to bring Merlin to him, but without telling Merlin whom he was going to see. The king agreed and promised not to tell. Then the king came to Merlin and said: "Merlin, come to town with me to visit a sick man."

Merlin answered with a laugh: "My lord, a king must not ride out without an escort of at least twenty men!"

Then the king picked some men to escort him and they went to see the baron. As soon as they arrived, the sick man's wife, as planned, fell to her knees before the king and said: "My lord, in the name of God, have your seer tell me whether my husband will recover!"

The king, with an innocent look on his face, turned to Merlin and said: "Merlin, could you answer this woman's question about her husband?"

"My lord," said Merlin, "please be assured that this man lying here will not die of his illness."

The sick man, pretending to speak with difficulty, asked Merlin: "My lord, how will I die, then?"

And Merlin answered: "On the day of your death, you will be found hanging." With these words Merlin, looking irritated, turned away and walked out of the house, in order to let the sick man speak to the king in private: "My lord," he said, "now you see that Merlin is a madman and tells lies, since he has predicted for me two different deaths that are incompatible. I will test him once more in front of you. I shall go to an abbey and there pretend to be sick. I shall have the abbot ask you to come, saying that I am one of his monks, and that he is extremely fearful that I may die, and he will ask you to bring your seer with you. I assure you that this is the last test."

The king agreed to this plan and then returned home. The baron went to an abbey, proceeded as he had said, and sent the abbot to fetch the king. Together with Merlin the king then rode out to the abbey and, when he had heard mass, the abbot and fifteen monks invited him to come see their sick brother and to bring along his seer. The king asked Merlin whether he would accompany him, whereupon Merlin called both him and his brother Uther before an altar and said to them: "Lords, the better I know you, the more foolish I find you. Do you believe that I do not know how this fool will die? So help me God, I know perfectly well! I shall tell you how, and you will be even more surprised by what I am going to say than by the two predictions I have already made."

The king said: "Merlin, can it be that a man can die in two ways?"

Merlin answered: "My lord, if he does not die as I have predicted, never again believe anything I say! I know for certain how he will die; and when you have seen it happen, you will ask me to foretell your death as well. And let me say to Uther that I shall yet see him king before I go."

With that the king, Uther, and Merlin rejoined the abbot. "My lord," said the abbot to the king, "in the name of God, have your seer tell me whether the monk lying there will ever be able to recover."

The king conveyed the question, and Merlin, looking irritated, said to the abbot: "My lord, he can get up whenever he wishes. There is nothing wrong with him; it is pointless for him to put me to any test, because he is bound to die in the two ways I have already predicted, and in a third, also, even more surprising than the others. After breaking his neck and hanging, he will drown. All three things will happen to him. And now let him put an end to his playacting! I know quite well what evil purposes he harbors in his heart."

The man sat up and said to the king: "My lord, now you can recognize how mad he is and see that he does not know what he is saying! How could he be speaking the truth? He says that on the day of my death I will break my neck and be hanged and drown, and all of that is supposed to happen at the same time! You know as well as I that no one could die like that. You need to wonder, then, whether you are being wise to have confidence in such a man and to let him rule over your counselors and yourself."

The king said: "I will not act before seeing how you die."

The baron was very angry to hear that Merlin would not be ousted from the king's council until after his death. But that is where matters remained, except that everyone learned what Merlin had foretold about the death and was curious to see what would happen.

One day, a long time afterward, the good baron who was supposed to die in three ways was riding along with a great retinue, when he came to a river. There was a wooden bridge over the river, and his horse stumbled and fell to its knees. The man was pitched forward and fell in such a way that his neck broke. He rolled over and fell into the water in such a way that his clothes caught on one of the piles of the old bridge, leaving his body dangling upside down, with head and shoulders immersed in the water. When they saw this, the men in the escort raised a great cry, and the people of the nearby town heard it and hurried over as fast as possible on foot or by boat. The good people said to those who were pulling the body out of the water: "Lords, see whether his neck is broken!"

They looked and said that there was no doubt of it. They all marveled at that, saying: "He really spoke the truth, Merlin did, when he said that this man would break his neck and hang and drown. Anyone who does not trust whatever he says is out of his mind, because it is obvious to us that he tells the truth."

Merlin did not need to be told of the event to know of it. He came to Uther, who held him very dear, and recounted the man's death just as it had occurred, and then told him to report it to the king, which Uther did.

The king marveled at the news and said to his brother, Uther: "Who told you that?"

Uther said: "It was Merlin."

The king sent Uther to ask Merlin when it had happened. Merlin answered: "It happened yesterday, and messengers will come to report it to the king in six days. I, though, am leaving, because I do not want to be here when they come. They would ask me many questions that I would not care to answer. From now on, moreover, I shall speak in public only in veiled terms, so that people will understand what I foretell only when they see it happen."

Now, the tale tells us that, once Merlin had spoken, he left for Northumberland to see Blaise. Uther, for his part, reported to the king what Merlin had said to him, and the king, thinking that Merlin was angry, asked where he had gone. Uther answered: "My lord, I do not know, but he said that he did not want to be here when the news arrived."

At this point the tale takes leave of Pendragon and Uther and speaks of Merlin in Northumberland relating all these events and many others to Blaise as material for his book.

On the sixth day the witnesses to the death of the baron arrived at the king's court and related the extraordinary event just as they had seen it.

Whereupon the king said, and everyone else agreed, that no man was wiser than Merlin, and they decided to put down in writing from then on every prediction that they would hear Merlin make. Thus was begun a book called the *Book of the Prophecies of Merlin*, which contains what he foretold about the kings of England and about later events. Yet the book does not say who Merlin was or where he came from, because they wrote down only what he predicted.

5. The Battle of Salisbury and the Erection of Stonehenge

Merlin remained away a long time. Meanwhile he had won the full confidence of King Pendragon (whom the English called by his baptismal name of Aurelius Ambrosius) and his brother, Uther. When he became aware of their decision to put all his pronouncements down in writing, Merlin told this to Blaise, who asked him: "Merlin, will their book be just like mine?"

Merlin answered: "Not at all. They will write down only what they can understand before the fact." With that Merlin came back to the king's court, where he was given the news of the baron's death, as if he had known nothing about it. Merlin then began to make the veiled statements that were recorded in the book: prophecies that could be truly understood only after the event. Somewhat later Merlin very movingly told Pendragon and Uther how much he loved them and wanted to work for their power, their good, and their fame. They were delighted with this avowal and said to Merlin that he should feel free to tell them whatever he liked and that he should not hide anything of concern to them.

Merlin answered: "I will never hide anything that I should tell you. Moreover I am going to tell you something now that you will find extraordinary. Do you remember the Saxons, whom you drove out of your land after the death of Hangus?"

"Of course," they answered.

"They took home with them the news of Hangus's death. Hangus, now, came from a very noble line, and when the family received the news of his death and the expulsion of the others, they all came together and agreed to seek vengeance, with the idea of conquering this kingdom."

Pendragon and Uther were greatly surprised to hear this and asked Merlin: "Have they so many men under arms that they can think of attacking us?"

Merlin answered: "For every man of yours they will have two, and if you do not behave very wisely, they will destroy you and conquer your kingdom."

They said: "We shall follow your counsel faithfully and do exactly as you say." Then they asked Merlin: "When do you think their army will arrive?"

Merlin said: "The eleventh day of July; and no one here will know it, except you. I ask the two of you not to speak of it but to do as I say. Summon all your men, all your knights, rich and poor, and give them the warmest welcome you can—it is always wise to keep your men happy— and keep them with you at court. Then ask them to do their utmost to spend the last week of June with you at the entrance to Salisbury Plain. There you must assemble all your forces near the river in order to fight off the enemy."

"What!" said the king. "Are we then to let them sail so far inland?"

"Yes, if you listen to me. Let them disembark and then march away from the riverbank, unaware that you have your troops assembled there. Once they are at some distance, you will send men of yours down to the ships to make it clear that you are cutting off their retreat. When they see what has happened, they will be bewildered, and one of you must then pursue them so closely with his troops that they will be forced to camp far away from the river. In that camp they will lack water, and the boldest of them will be panic-stricken. Keep them cut off like that for two days, and attack them on the third day. If you do that, I assure you that your men will win."

The two brothers then said: "For God's sake, Merlin, please tell us, too, whether we are going to die in that battle."

And Merlin said: "My lords, nothing begins that does not come to an end, and no man should fear death if he receives it properly. Everyone living must realize that he will die, and you must realize that you will as well, and that neither nobility nor fortune can spare you from death."

Pendragon said: "Merlin, you once told me that you could predict my death just as you had predicted the death of the baron who was testing you, and you were right about his. Tell me then, please, about mine."

Merlin said: "I should like the two of you to send for the best reliquaries that you possess and to swear, both of you, by the holy relics that you will do whatever I command for your good and your fame. When you have sworn, I shall feel free to tell you what it will profit you to know."

They did as Merlin had stated, and when they had taken the oath, they said: "Merlin, we have followed your order. Now we ask you, please, to tell us why you had us do it."

Merlin answered the king: "You asked me about your death and the outcome of the battle, and I am going to tell you. But do you know what you have just sworn to each other? You have sworn that in the coming battle you will behave honorably and loyally both to God and to each other. And I will show you how. Make your confession, which is more fitting now than at some other time, because you are about to go into combat. If you do as I say, be assured that you will win, for the Saxons do not believe in the Trinity or in the fact that Jesus Christ appeared on earth; besides, you are defending your lawful inheritance, yours by right. One of you will die in the struggle, at peace with Jesus Christ according to the commandments of the Holy Church: he need hardly fear death. I want you to know that never, since the Holy Church was established on this island, has there been so great a battle as the one about to come, nor in your time will there ever be. Each of you has sworn to the other that he will fight for his honor and his fame. I want you to know, even if I do not speak more specifically, that one of you is to depart from this life. On the site of the battle the one surviving will, under my guidance, build the finest and most imposing monument he can. And I promise to offer so much help that this work of mine will last as long as Christendom. I have told you that one of you is to die. Now see that you show your valor!"

After a while the day of the convocation came. The two brothers had

done as Merlin had ordered, and at Pentecost they came to the river to hold
court, and everyone assembled there. They were generous with gifts and
unstinting in their hospitality. There they still were in the first week of
July, when they learned that the enemy ships had arrived. At this news
Uther was convinced that Merlin had told him the truth, and he ordered the
prelates of the Holy Church to see that all the men in the army confessed
their sins and forgave one another their wrongs. Meanwhile the invaders
had disembarked. They remained in their camp for eight days and on the
ninth rode out. King Pendragon, who had spies in their army and knew
what they were doing, told Merlin, and Merlin said that it was indeed true.
Then the king asked him how to proceed. Merlin said: "You will dispatch
Uther tomorrow, together with a large company of men. Once he is sure
that the Saxons are far from their ships, let them bar their way back to both
the river and the sea and force them to camp out in the fields. Let him pull
back then, and in the morning, when the Saxons try to push ahead, let him
attack them and keep so close that they will not be able to ride on their way.
Then they will all regret that they had not stayed at home! Uther and his
men should keep this up for two days. On the third day, as soon as the sky
is bright and clear, you will see a red dragon dashing through the air
between heaven and earth. You must then attack. When you see that sign,
you can fight with no fear, because it will be a sign of your name, and your
side will win."

With that they separated, and Merlin came to Uther and said: "See that
you show your valor, for you need not fear death in this battle." Merlin
then went to join Blaise in Northumberland and related everything that had
happened. Blaise put it into writing, and thanks to his book we know it
today. But here the tale falls silent about him and Merlin and returns to the
deeds of Uther and Pendragon in their battle with the Saxons.

Now, according to the tale, the two brothers did exactly as Merlin had
prescribed. Uther chose a great company of horsemen, the strongest and the
best that he could find, and rode with them until they could see the camp
that the Saxon army had set up on open ground. They spread out between
the ships and the tents and thus forced the enemy to spend that night out in
the fields with no water and far from the ships where their food supplies
were. For two days Uther held them in such a grip that they could not
move in any direction. On the third day King Pendragon came with a great
company of men, whom he commanded to prepare and take their places for
battle. When the Saxons saw the two armies around them, they were panic-
stricken. Uther and his troops attacked them so fiercely that they were
thrust back toward Pendragon's army. There was such noise, such shouting, such clamor, that you couldn't have heard God thundering. Pendragon's men were all prepared to strike as soon as the king ordered, but he was
waiting for the monster to appear, as Merlin had said. And in fact the
monster appeared with almost no delay. They saw a red dragon come
flying through the air, spewing fire and flame through its nose and mouth,
and roaring directly over the army of the Saxons. At the sight the Saxons
were panic-filled and terrified. Pendragon and Uther told their men that
their foe was surely destroyed: had they not just seen the sign foretold by
Merlin? And so Pendragon's troops charged with all the speed their horses
were capable of, and when Uther saw the king's men joined in battle, he and

all his troops charged the enemy as well, and with even greater boldness. They all fought with great violence, and the battle was terrible and fierce. And in that ruthless battle King Pendragon met his death.

The Battle of Salisbury took place as you have just heard: Pendragon died, and Uther won. Many men were killed; and the Saxons all died, without exception, either drowned or slain. So ended the Battle of Salisbury. After the death of Pendragon Uther became king. He had all the bodies of the Christians brought together in the same place for burial; everyone brought bodies of friends, one after another. Uther had the body of his brother buried along with his men; and on each tomb he had the soldier's name inscribed and the name of his lord. Pendragon's tomb he built higher than the others, and he said that he would have no name inscribed upon it, for only fools could ever see that tomb and not understand who lay buried there.

After that Uther went to London with all his men, as did all the prelates of the Holy Church who were his vassals. And there Uther was crowned. Two weeks later Merlin came to court, and the king received him with great joy. Merlin said: "Uther, I want you to tell your people about my prediction that the Saxons would invade, about the agreement that you and Pendragon made with me, and about the oaths that the two of you swore to each other."

Uther reported to his people how he and Pendragon had acted in all matters in accordance with Merlin's words, but he did not speak of the dragon, which he understood no better than anyone else. Merlin, however, went on to reveal the meaning of the dragon. He said that it signified the death of Pendragon and the elevation of King Uther. Uther was then given a surname: to honor his brother, and to remember the appearance of the dragon and its meaning, he was from then on called Uther Pendragon. The barons thus learned with what firmness and steadiness Merlin had guided the two brothers.

Some time then went by. Merlin was on the best of terms with both Uther Pendragon and his counselors. One day, well into the king's reign, Merlin asked him: "What will you do to honor Pendragon, who lies in Salisbury Plain?"

The king answered: "I shall do whatever you wish."

"You swore to me that you would build a monument, and I told you that I myself would help you as much as possible. I now pledge to you that we will create something that will last as long as the world. You keep your word, and I shall keep mine."

The king said to Merlin: "What can I do?"

He answered: "Undertake something never imagined before, and it will be spoken of forever."

The king said: "Gladly."

"In that case send to Ireland for the large blocks of stone they have there; send your ships to fetch them. Whatever their size, they can be lifted with my help, and I will even go along to point out to your men which ones I want brought back."

The king then dispatched a great number of ships. Once they arrived, Merlin pointed out some enormous boulders and said to the men: "These are the stones to take." But at the sight of such size they thought this was sheer madness and said that even all of them together could not roll one of those stones over and that, please God, they were not about to load them onto their ships. Merlin said: "Then you have come here for nothing."

The men returned to the king and told him what an extraordinary thing Merlin had commanded them to do, a feat they were sure no one in the world could perform. The king answered: "Just be patient till Merlin comes."

When Merlin came, the king told him what his men had said, and Merlin answered: "I shall keep my promise even without their help."

Thereupon Merlin brought the great stones from Ireland by magic, and they still stand in the burial ground at Salisbury.

Once they had been transported, the king took a great number of people and went to see that extraordinary accomplishment. Looking at the stones, they said they had never yet seen such large blocks and did not believe that human power could move even one of them. They marveled at Merlin's ability to transport them without anyone's seeing or knowing. Then Merlin said that the stones needed to be set up.

The king said: "Merlin, no one but God could do that, except you!"

And Merlin said: "Leave now, for I am going to honor my promise concerning Pendragon. I shall create something for the king that could never be accomplished by any other mortal man."

Thus Merlin set up the blocks of stone that still stand in the burial ground at Salisbury, and his accomplishment has lasted all this while.

6. The Creation of the Round Table

Merlin had great affection for the king and served him for a long time. One day he drew him aside and said: "Now that I see the whole country is safely under your control, I must reveal to you the greatest secret that I know. I have great love for you, as I showed when I saved you from being killed by Hangus, and you should feel the same way toward me. That is why I want to tell you something."

The king answered: "There is nothing you might want for which I would not do my utmost."

Merlin answered: "If you do it, the benefit will be yours, for I shall show you the way to God's love."

The king answered: "Merlin, don't hesitate to tell me what you want. You cannot ask for anything a man might do that I would refuse."

Then Merlin said: "My lord, what I am going to say will sound very strange to you. Please keep it a secret, as I want the good and the fame that it will bring to be yours alone."

The king promised Merlin never to speak of it. Then Merlin said: "My lord, I wish you to know that I have knowledge of all things done and said in the past and that it comes to me from my demonic origin. Our Lord, who is all-powerful, has also given me the wisdom to know the things that are to come. Through that gift the demons lost their hold over me, so that I shall never carry out their will. Now you know where I find the power to do what I do. Our Lord wants you to know something else as well. When you know it, be sure to carry out His will. Sire, you must believe that our Lord came to earth to save mankind and that at the Last Supper He said to His apostles: 'There is one among you who will betray me.' And the guilty one left His company, just as He had foretold. After that, sire, our Lord suffered death for our sake. Then a knight appeared who asked for the body and removed it from the cross. After that, sir, our Lord was resurrected, and the knight [who was named Joseph of Arimathea] went away to a wilderness with a great part of his family and many other people. A great famine occurred, and they complained to the knight, who was their leader. He asked God to show him why they were enduring such suffering. Our Lord commanded him to build a table, in memory of the table of the Last Supper, and to place on it a certain bowl that he had, from which Jesus and the apostles had eaten at that Supper; the table was to be covered with a white cloth, as was the bowl, except in front of his place. Bron, a brother-in-law of his, then caught a fish, which was put in the center of the table next to the bowl in front of Joseph. Through the power of that bowl the wicked at the table were separated from the good. My lord, whoever could sit at that table had the fulfillment of his heart's desire. Sire, there was always an empty place there, representing the place where Judas had sat at the Last Supper until he heard the words our Lord spoke for him and he withdrew from His company. His place remained empty until our Lord put another man there in order to bring the number of apostles back to twelve. The two tables were thus perfectly matched. And so our Lord fulfills man's heart's desire at the second table. The people who sit there call that bowl, which bears His grace, the 'Grail.' Now, if you trust me, you will establish the third table, in the name of the Trinity, which the three will represent. I assure you that if you do it, much good will come of it to both your body and soul, and things will happen in your lifetime that will make you truly marvel. If you agree, I shall help you, and if you do it, I assure you that it will be one of the things that the world will speak about most. If you trust me, you will do it and, believe me, it will make you very happy." That is what Merlin said to the king.

The king answered: "I do not want our Lord to be deprived of anything on my account, and so I agree to rely upon you completely."

Merlin said: "Consider, then, my lord, where you would best like to have the table."

The king answered: "I want it to be where you would like to have it."

Merlin said: "At Carduel, in Wales. Gather all the people of your kingdom there at Pentecost and prepare to give away many fine gifts; give me men, too, to carry out my orders. When you are ready, I shall choose the knights who are worthy of being seated at the table."

The king then sent out word to everyone, and Merlin went away to have the table made. That is how things remained until Pentecost, when the king went to Carduel. There he asked Merlin how his work had progressed, and Merlin said: "Very well, my lord."

On the day of Pentecost, then, everyone gathered at Carduel. There were many knights and ladies. The king said to Merlin: "Which men are you going to choose to sit at the Table?"

Merlin said: "Tomorrow you will see something you would never have imagined seeing. I shall choose fifty of the most worthy men in this land,

and once they have taken their seats, they will never want to return home from here. Then, too, you will see the meaning of the empty place and of the other two tables reflected in your own."

The king said: "I am eager to see that."

Merlin chose fifty of the most worthy men he could identify and seated them at the Table; he called the king and showed him the empty place; many others saw it too, but only the king and Merlin knew why it was empty and what it signified. Then Merlin said to the king that he should take his seat, but the king declined to sit until he could see the others served, which he ordered to be done before he would take a step toward the Table. Once they had been served, he sat down as well.

In that way a week passed, during which the king gave many beautiful gifts and fine presents to the ladies, young and old. When it came time for the crowd of guests to take their leave, the king came to the worthy knights who were sitting at the Table and asked them what they had in mind to do. They answered: "Sire, we have no wish to move away from here. We would rather send for our wives and children, and live in this town at the pleasure of our lord. That is how we feel."

The king asked them: "Lords, is that how you all feel?"

And they all answered: "Yes, although we certainly wonder how that can be! Some of us had never even seen one another before coming here, and few were acquainted with any of the others; yet now we have as much love for one another as a son has for his father, or even more! We will never willingly separate; only death can part us."

The king marveled to hear them speak like that, as did everyone else who heard them. It made him happy, and he ordered that they be shown as much honor in the town as he himself was shown. Once everyone was gone, the king said to Merlin: "You did indeed speak the truth. I am now convinced that our Lord wanted the Table to be established; but I still wonder about the empty place, and I do wish that you would tell me, if you know, who will one day sit there."

Merlin said: "I can tell you that the place will not be taken in your lifetime. The man who will take it will be born in due time, but to a father who has not yet married and does not know that he is to sire him. It must happen, too, that the man who is to take this place will first occupy the empty seat at the Table of the Grail (something that the guardians of the Grail will have never seen before). It will happen not in your lifetime but during the life of the king who comes after you. Meanwhile I should like you to hold your assemblies and maintain your court in this town, and to live here yourself and gather your people here for the annual feasts."

The king said: "Gladly, Merlin."

Merlin said: "I shall be away, and you will not see me for a long time."

Then the king asked him: "Merlin, where are you going? Do you mean you will not attend all the great gatherings that I shall have here?"

Merlin said: "No, I cannot be present. I want your people to credit everything they are going to see happen, and not simply dismiss it as my work."

At this point, according to the tale, Merlin took leave of Uther Pendragon and went to rejoin Blaise in Northumberland. He told him about the establishment of the Table and all the other things that you have heard or will hear in this book. And for more than two years Merlin stayed away from the king's court.

7. *Uther Pendragon's Desire for Ygerne*

The king had long been in the habit of holding his court at Carduel when one day he decided to summon all his barons and have them bring their wives with them. He sent letters throughout the land summoning them for Christmas, and the barons did as he commanded. There came to court a great number of ladies, maidens, and knights. I cannot name all the people who came, but can tell you about those who are spoken of in my tale. I want you to know, then, that the duke of Tintagel was present, together with his wife, Ygerne. When the king saw her, he fell passionately in love with her, but he never let it show, except that he tended to look at her more than at the other women. She became aware of it and realized that the king liked to look at her. With that knowledge she avoided as much as possible coming into his presence, for she was no less virtuous than beautiful. The king, in order to express his love, but also to keep anyone from noticing it, sent presents to all the ladies, and to Ygerne he sent those that he thought she would like the best. Seeing that he sent presents to all the other women as well, she neither wished nor dared to refuse his gifts.

Before the court dispersed, the king invited all his barons to come back at Pentecost together with their wives, just as they had come to this feast. They all agreed very gladly. When the duke of Tintagel took his leave, the king accompanied him a long way and showed him great honor. Just before turning back, the king whispered to Ygerne that he wanted her to know that she was carrying off his heart with her. She, though, offered no acknowledgment, and with that the two parted.

The king remained in Carduel and saw to the entertainment and comfort of the worthy men at the Table, but his heart was always with Ygerne. He waited like that until Pentecost, when the barons and their ladies returned. The king was very happy when Ygerne came back, and he gave her many presents in the course of those days. When he sat down to dinner, he had the duke and Ygerne sit beside him. So generous were his gifts and his attentions that Ygerne could no longer deny that the king loved her. Everyone, meanwhile, enjoyed the celebration very much, and the king showed his barons great honor. When the feast was over, they all made ready to take their leave and return home. The king urged them to come back when he would invite them, and they all agreed. With that the court dispersed.

The king endured his pain for a whole year. Finally he complained to two of those closest to him and told them what torment he was suffering on account of Ygerne. They said: "Sire, what would you have us do? There is nothing you can order that we will not do if we possibly can."

The king said: "How could I see more of Ygerne?"

They said that if he went to her land, people would suspect something and he would be blamed for it.

"Then what advice," said the king, "would you give me?"

They said: "The best we can. Proclaim a great gathering at the court of

Carduel and make it clear to everyone coming that he is to plan to stay for two whole weeks and that he is to bring his wife. That will allow you to win the love of Ygerne."

The king summoned his barons, and they all came to Carduel. Once again he greeted them with many fine presents. He was very glad to see them all again, but to a counselor of his named Urfin [Ulfin] the king confided that he did not know what to do about his love for Ygerne, which was killing him. He could not go on living without seeing her: when he saw her, his pain grew lighter; yet he could not live without some further remedy for his love and would surely die.

Urfin answered: "There is something wrong with you if desire for a woman can make you think of dying! Has anyone ever heard of a woman who has not yielded when she has been wooed and begged the right way, especially with gifts to her and to the people around her? And you are giving up?"

The king answered: "You are right; you obviously know what is needed in such a situation. Please help me, then, in every way you know. Take whatever treasure of mine you want and give it to the people around Ygerne, and speak to her in whatever way you know will be helpful to me."

Urfin said: "I shall do whatever I can."

That brought their conversation to a close, but then Urfin added: "You be sure to remain on good terms with the duke, and I shall see to speaking with Ygerne."

The king agreed, and they undertook to act. The king behaved very graciously toward the duke throughout the week and gave many a fine gift to his retinue. Urfin spoke to Ygerne, telling her what he believed would please her most, and a number of times he presented her with very beautiful gifts. She protested and did not want to accept any of them, but one day she drew Urfin aside and said to him in private: "Why do you want to give me all these beautiful presents?"

He answered: "Out of admiration for your mind and your great beauty. But I cannot really give you anything, for everything the king possesses is already yours, and his very person awaits your pleasure."

She answered: "You mean . . . ?"

He said: "That you are the sole possessor of his heart and he is utterly yours."

She answered: "Whose heart do you mean?"

And he said: "The king's."

She crossed herself and said: "God! What a traitor the king is, just pretending to be a friend to the duke so that he can disgrace me! Urfin," she said, "do not ever speak to me about this again. You may be sure that I would tell my husband, and once he knew, your death would be sure to follow. I am telling you, I will keep it quiet only this time."

He answered: "My lady, it would be an honor to die for my lord. But what lady has ever before refused to accept the king as her lover! And he does love you more than anyone else. Surely you are fooling? By God, do take pity on the king! Be assured, besides, that you may face great problems if you do not, and that neither you nor the duke can prevail against the king's will."

She answered, with tears in her eyes: "I shall resist him perfectly well, please God. I will never again come near any place where he may be."

With those words Urfin and Ygerne parted. Urfin came to the king and told him everything Ygerne had said. The king answered that that was the way a virtuous lady should respond, but added: "Do not let that stop you from pursuing her."

The next day the king was sitting at the dinner table, with the duke beside him. In front of the king stood a very beautiful gold cup, which Urfin whispered to him he should send to Ygerne. The king raised his head and said to the duke: "My lord, ask Ygerne to take this cup and drink from it for love of me. I shall have one of your knights take it to her filled with good wine."

The duke answered in all innocence: "My lord, thank you very much. She will be glad to accept it." The duke called over one of his knights and said: "Brethel, take this cup to your lady from the king and tell her to drink from it for love of him."

Brethel [Britaelis] carried the cup to Ygerne in the room where she was dining and said to her: "My lady, the king sends you this cup, and my lord asks that you take it and drink from it for love of him."

When Ygerne heard that, she turned red with embarrassment, but she took the cup and drank and then held it out for Brethel to take back. But he said: "My lady, my lord asks that you keep it."

She kept it. Brethel went back to the king and thanked him on Ygerne's behalf, even though she had not said a word about thanks. Then Urfin went to see what Ygerne was doing and found her quiet and thoughtful. At the end of the ladies' meal, once the tables had been removed, she turned to him and said: "Urfin, it was dishonorable for your lord to send me that cup. Have no doubt that I shall tell my husband how you and the king are plotting to disgrace me."

Urfin answered: "My lady, you are surely sensible enough to know that once a woman has said such a thing to her husband, he will never trust her anymore. And for that reason you won't do it."

Ygerne answered: "How wrong you are!"

And with that Urfin left Ygerne.

Dinner was over, and the king was feeling very cheerful. He took the duke by the hand and said: "Let us go see the ladies."

The duke said: "With pleasure, my lord."

The king and duke then went to the room where Ygerne was with all the other ladies, but the king was there to see her alone, and Ygerne knew it. She suffered through his presence until night fell and she could return to her own quarters.

When the duke joined her, he found her in tears. At the sight he was extremely surprised and took her in his arms as any truly loving man would do. He asked her what was wrong, and she said: "I won't hide it from you, for there is no one I love as much as you."

Then she told him, as you have heard, what the king was trying to do and said that all the ladies he invited and all these gatherings at court were simply his way of reaching her. "And now you have made me accept his cup and drink from it for love of him. I tell you, I can no longer hold out against him or against that counselor of his, Urfin. And yet I know that, having told you as much, I can only expect something terrible to happen. Please take me away from here, for I do not want to remain in this town any longer."

When the duke heard these words, he was very upset, as he loved his wife deeply. He sent through the town for all his knights. As soon as they gathered, they realized how angry he was. The duke said to them: "Lords, prepare to leave in total secrecy, and do not ask me why until I am ready to tell you."

They all said: "As you command."

The duke said: "Leave all your baggage and take only your arms and your horses. The rest will follow tomorrow. I do not want the king to know that I am leaving, or anyone else that I can hide it from."

Everything was done as the duke ordered. He had his horses brought for the departure, and he and Ygerne rode off as secretly as they could. And so the duke withdrew to his own land, taking his wife with him.

In the morning word of the departure spread very quickly through the town from those of the duke's men who had remained. When the news reached the king, it pained him greatly, and he was very troubled that the duke had taken Ygerne away. He sent for all his barons and informed them of the shame and scorn to which the duke had subjected him by leaving the court without his permission. They answered that they were all extremely surprised and that the duke had acted very rashly. They did not know, of course, why the duke had left. The king said: "My lords, how shall I get him to make amends? Advise me!"

They said: "Sire, just as you wish."

The king said: "With your agreement I shall send him word to come back and right the wrong that he has done. And he must return just as he went away!"

They all agreed. Two of the king's men rode off to Tintagel bearing the message. When they reached the duke, they told him that the king had sent for him. Hearing that he was to return to the court exactly as he had left it, he understood full well that he was to go back with Ygerne, and he answered the messengers: "You may tell the king that I will not go back to his court, because he has behaved toward me and my household in such a way that I am bound not to trust him and or to go to his court. I will not say anything further, but, as God is my witness, he has made it impossible for me to trust him anymore." At that the messengers turned back toward the king's court.

When the messengers had gone, the duke sent for the worthy men of his privy council and explained to them why he had come away from Carduel and how the king was disloyally pursuing his wife. They responded that, please God, he would never succeed and that a king who so betrayed his own vassal deserved to be punished. Then the duke said: "My lords, in the name of God and because it is your duty, I ask you to help me defend my land if the king attacks."

They answered that they would gladly do so and would help him as fully as they could. Thus did the duke take counsel with his vassals.

The messengers, back at court, gave the king the duke's reply. The king said that he was extremely surprised by the rashness of the duke, whom he had always considered a very wise man. He asked his barons to help him in erasing the shame that the duke had brought upon his court. They answered that they would not refuse him, but they all asked that in loyal fashion he not take action against the duke for another forty days. The king agreed and asked them to be at Tintagel in forty days, ready to do battle. They said that they would be there, and the king then sent his messengers to the duke to issue the challenge. The duke said that he would defend himself if he could and, once the messengers had left, he made ready for the defense. The messengers reported to the king that the duke would defend himself if he were attacked.

The king was very vexed to hear that. Summoning his barons from throughout the land, he met them all at the edge of the duke's estates and from there started to ravage his towns and castles. Then the king heard that the duke was in one castle and his wife in another. He gathered his counselors and asked them which one they thought he should attack first, and they advised him to attack the duke, for if he defeated him, he would have the whole land under his control.

The king accepted their unanimous advice, but as he was riding toward the duke's castle, he said to Urfin: "Urfin, what shall I do about Ygerne?"

Urfin answered: "My lord, we must be patient when it comes to something we cannot have right away. You need to put all your efforts into defeating the duke. Once you have done that, you can see about the other matter."

At this point, according to the tale, the king laid siege to the duke's castle. A long time went by with no success, and the king's spirits sagged. He was heartsick for Ygerne, and all the while he was in his tent he wept. When his men saw him weeping one day, they withdrew and left him alone; but when Urfin, who was outside, heard about it, he came in. He was sorry to find him in tears and asked why he was crying. The king said: "Urfin, you must know why! You know that I am dying of love for Ygerne. It is clear to me that I am bound to die, for I have lost all the peace of mind that a man needs. Without it, all I can do is die. I do not see any remedy."

Urfin said: "My lord, how feeble-hearted you are, if you can think of dying because of a woman! But let me give you some good advice. If you sent word to Merlin to come here, he would surely be able to counsel you. Of course, you would give him whatever he might want."

The king answered: "There is nothing I would not do, but I know perfectly well that Merlin is aware of my distress. I am afraid I must have made him angry when I let someone try to take the empty seat at the Round Table. For a long time he has stayed far away from me. Or else it may disturb him that I love the wife of a vassal of mine. But there is nothing I can do about it! My heart just can't let go! Besides, I remember that he told me I should not send for him."

Urfin answered: "My lord, there is one thing I am certain of: if he is safe and sound and still loves you as he used to, then, knowing what distress you feel, he will not delay in coming to you."

With those words Urfin consoled the king. He added that if he made an effort to show good cheer and spend some time with his men, he would in fact feel much better. The king said that he would gladly follow that advice, but he could hardly forget his love for Ygerne. For a while he did find comfort in that way; and he attacked the castle once again but could not capture it.

One day, as he was riding through the camp, Urfin came upon a man whom he did not know. The man said to him: "Urfin, sir, I should like to speak with you in private."

Urfin said: "And I with you."

Then they both rode out of the camp. Urfin dismounted and asked the man who he was. He said: "I am an old man. I was considered wise when I was young, but now they say I just speak drivel. But I'll tell you in confidence that I was recently in Tintagel and met a good man there who told me that your king was in love with the wife of the duke and that he destroyed the duke's land because the duke had taken her away from Carduel. If you trust me and give me a good reward, I know someone who could arrange a meeting with Ygerne and advise the king about his love."

When Urfin heard the old man speak this way, he wondered, with surprise, where he could have learned such things and he asked him to direct him to the man who could help the king. The old man answered: "I should like to know first what reward the king would give me."

Urfin said: "Can I find you back here once I have spoken with the king?"

The man said: "Yes, me or my messenger."

Urfin bade him goodbye and rode off. He came to the king and told him about the encounter. The king laughed and asked: "Urfin, do you know that man?"

He answered: "My lord, he was an old man."

The king asked: "When are you to meet again?"

Urfin said: "In the morning; and he told me I should be able to say what reward you will give him."

The king said: "I shall go with you."

The next morning the king followed Urfin and, once outside the camp, came upon a cripple. The king rode right past him, and the cripple cried out: "King, give me something I can be grateful for, and may God satisfy your heart with what you love best in the whole world!"

The king laughed and said to Urfin: "Urfin, will you do something for me?"

He answered: "Yes, my lord, whatever I can."

"Then go," said the king, "and hand yourself over to the cripple, and tell him that I have given you to him, since you are the most valuable thing I have with me."

Urfin rode straight back to the cripple and sat down beside him. The man said: "What do you want of me?"

He answered: "The king wants me to be in your service."

Hearing that, the cripple laughed and said: "The king saw right through me! He knows me better than you do! But go back to the king now and tell him that he would be leading you into a serious mistake in order to have his way. Tell him, too, that I realize he recognized me and that that will be to his benefit."

Urfin came back to the king and reported these words. The king and Urfin then galloped back to the spot where they had seen the man, but he was no longer there. The king said to Urfin: "Do you know who the man is who spoke to you yesterday in the guise of an old man? He is the same one you have seen today as a cripple."

Urfin answered: "Can a man really change his appearance like that? Who can he be?"

The other answered: "I tell you, it is Merlin, playing a little joke on us. And when he wants to speak to us, he will let us know!" That is where they let the matter stand. Merlin, meanwhile, went to the royal tent in his normal appearance and asked where the king was. A messenger then came to the king and told him that Merlin was asking for him. Uther Pendragon was delighted to hear this and, along with Urfin, hurried to Merlin as fast as he could. He said to Urfin: "Now you will see what I have been telling you: Merlin has come! I knew it would be pointless to send for him."

Urfin said: "My lord, now it will be clear whether you have ever shown enough respect for his will, for no man alive could be of greater help to you in winning the love of Ygerne."

Then Merlin approached Urfin with these words: "If the king were willing to swear on holy relics that he would grant me what, with no offense to his honor, I would ask of him, I would help him obtain the love of Ygerne. But you must swear this likewise before returning to him."

Urfin answered: "It can't happen too soon!"

The king agreed, and Urfin reported to Merlin: "It is time to bring an end to his suffering."

But Merlin laughed and said: "When the oaths have been sworn, I shall tell you how it can be done." Then the king had the relics brought in, and together with Urfin he swore, as Merlin instructed, that he would give Merlin what he wanted. After swearing the oath, the king said: "Now, Merlin, I ask you please to give me your help. No man in the world needs it more than I do!"

Merlin answered: "My lord, to reach Ygerne you will have to take on a very different appearance, for she is a very virtuous woman and faithful to both God and her husband. But now you are going to see what power I have to help you achieve your goal." He went on: "My lord, I shall make you look like the duke, so that no one will recognize you. The duke, moreover, has two knights, Brethel and Jordan, who are extremely close to him and Ygerne. I shall disguise Urfin as Jordan and myself as Brethel. I shall open the gate of the castle where Ygerne is staying and let you in, and you will be able to share her bed. Urfin and I shall come in after you, thanks to our disguised appearance. But you will have to leave very early the next morning, because, while we are there, we shall receive some very unexpected news. Now give the necessary orders to your troops and barons, and forbid anyone to go near the duke's castle before we have come back. And be sure to tell no one where you are planning to go."

Urfin and the king answered that they would do as instructed, and Merlin said: "Now prepare to leave; I shall change your appearance on the way."

The king hurried to do what Merlin had said and, as quickly as he could, returned and asked: "Are you ready?"

The other answered: "We have only to go!"

With that they set out and rode along until they came close to the castle.

Then Merlin said to the king: "My lord, you stay here, while Urfin and I go off for a moment."

They left, and Merlin disguised himself and Urfin. Coming back, Merlin handed the king an herb and said: "My lord, rub your hands and face with this herb."

The king did so and unmistakably took on the appearance of the duke. Merlin said: "My lord, you remember seeing Jordan, don't you?"

The king said: "Yes, I know him quite well."

Merlin then went to fetch Urfin, disguised as Jordan, and brought him back to the king. Urfin said: "I would not take you for anyone but the duke!" And the king said of Urfin that he looked just like Jordan, and, looking at Merlin, they were both convinced that they were seeing Brethel.

They went on speaking as they waited for nightfall. Then, in the early darkness, they approached the gate of Tintagel. Merlin called to the gatekeeper, who, just like the guards, was sure that he was looking at Brethel and the duke and Jordan. They opened the gate and let the three men in. Once inside, "Brethel" forbade the guards to tell anyone else that the duke had arrived, but there was no question of keeping the news from the duchess. The three men rode up to the palace. When they had dismounted, Merlin and the king spoke in private for a moment, and Merlin reminded the king to show the same cheerfulness as the duke. The three then came to Ygerne's chamber, where they found the lady in bed, and, as quickly as they could, Merlin and Urfin helped the king prepare to join her there.

The king and Ygerne thus spent that night together, and that night they engendered the good king who was to be known as Arthur. The lady received Uther Pendragon with all the passion she felt for her husband the duke, whom she loved very much, and they stayed together until dawn. At that point news came to the town that the duke was dead and his castle taken. The news was not confirmed, but when it reached "Brethel" and "Jordan," who were already awake, they rushed to their lord, still in his bed, and said: "Sir, get up! Hurry back to your castle, because your men think you are dead!"

He answered: "No wonder they think so, since I left the castle without anyone knowing!" In the presence of the others he took leave of Ygerne with a tender kiss, and the three men left the castle as quickly as they could. No one took notice of them, and the king was delighted. Merlin said to him: "My lord, I have kept my promise to you. Now keep yours to me."

The king said: "You have done me the best favor and shown me the greatest friendship a man is capable of, and, God willing, I shall keep my promise faithfully."

Merlin said to the king: "I trust so. Now I can tell you that you have fathered an heir. He will be the gift you have promised me, for you are not to keep him yourself, and you will grant me all your authority over him. We can write down the night and the time when he was conceived, and so you will know whether I have told you the truth."

"I gave you my word," said the king, "and I will do just as you have said. I grant you the child."

They all rode on until they came to a stream. There Merlin had them wash, and they all regained their normal appearance. Then they rode on to the king's camp as quickly as they could. At their arrival the vassals gathered around and reported that the duke was dead. The king asked how it had happened, and they replied that when he had left, the camp was very quiet and calm. "The duke realized that you were not here. He ordered his men armed, and they came out on foot and on horseback, and struck our camp and did much damage before we were armed. But the cry went up, and our men rushed to their arms, counterattacked, and pushed the enemy back to the castle gate. There the duke turned and fought bravely, but his horse was killed and he was struck down, and there the duke died among our foot-soldiers, who did not recognize him. We threw ourselves against the enemy at the gate, but, with the duke gone, there was very little resistance."

The king said that he was grieved by the death of the duke.

And so the duke of Tintagel died, and his castle was taken. The king spoke to his barons and told them how grieved he was by the duke's misfortune, and he asked their help in deciding how to make amends, for, not having hated the duke or sought his death, he did not want to be blamed for what had happened. "I shall make whatever amends I can."

Then Urfin, who was an intimate of the king, said: "My lord, the damage has been done, and we must repair it as well as possible."

Urfin then took aside a number of the barons and said to them: "Lords, how do you advise the king to make amends to the duchess and her family for the death of her lord? He is asking for your counsel, and it is your duty to offer it."

They answered: "We shall gladly counsel him, but you should counsel us about the best recommendation to make, for we know that you are very close to him."

Urfin answered: "Do you think, because I am an intimate of his, I advise him differently in public and in private? Do you take me for a traitor? If, in any case, it were up to me to advise him on settling matters with the lady and her relatives, I would recommend something that you would not even dare imagine."

They answered: "Do tell us. We know that you are a man of good counsel, and we ask you to state what you think."

He said: "I shall tell you what I think, and if you know any better, say so. I would advise the king to summon all the relatives of the duke and duchess to Tintagel, where he could have them appear before him and he could offer them a settlement—such that, if they rejected it, they would receive the blame and he would be praised for his good will."

The barons then came before the king and gave him their counsel, but they did not say that it had come to them from Urfin, since he had forbidden them to do so. The king answered: "Lords, I accept your counsel and will proceed as you have explained."

And so the king sent word throughout his lands that the relatives of the duke should come to Tintagel, because he wanted to make amends for the wrongs that they imputed to him. Then Merlin came to the king in private and said: "My lord, do you know who thought of this plan?"

The king said: "No, only that the barons have recommended it."

Merlin said: "My lord, all of them together would never have been able to devise it. It was wise and loyal Urfin who found in his heart the best and the most honorable way to peace, and he believes that no one knows it. And no one does, except me and now you!"

The king asked Merlin to tell him the plan, which Merlin then did. The king was overjoyed and said: "How do you advise me?"

Merlin said: "I have no better or more loyal counsel to give you than what you have heard. It will let you accomplish everything you most fervently desire. Now I am going to leave, but I want to speak to you in front of Urfin. Once I have left, you can ask him how he came to devise this settlement."

The king agreed. Urfin was called in, and in his presence Merlin said: "My lord, you promised to give me the heir that you have fathered and cannot recognize as your own son. You have in writing the date and hour of his conception, and you know that only through me was it all possible. Yet the sin would be yours if I did not now lend my aid, for his mother might well find the child a source of shame, and by herself a woman is defenseless against a growing problem that she cannot hide. I want Urfin, too, to put down in writing the time of the child's conception. Neither you nor the child will see me before the night he is born. Meanwhile I ask you to trust whatever Urfin tells you. He is utterly devoted to you and will never advise anything that is not to your benefit and your honor. I shall not speak with you for the next six months, but will speak with Urfin between now and then. Trust whatever word I send you through Urfin and act accordingly, if you wish to keep my affection and his, and if you wish to behave in good faith."

And so Urfin noted the time of the child's conception, and Merlin said to the king in private: "My lord, you must take care not to let Ygerne know that you went to bed with her. That more than anything else will put her at your mercy, so that if you ask her about her pregnancy and who the father is, she will not be able to tell you, and she will be very embarrassed. That is how you can best help me to obtain the child."

Merlin thereupon took leave of the king and Urfin. While the king rode off toward Tintagel, Merlin left for Northumberland. There he related all these events to Blaise, who wrote them down, and that is how we know them.

8. The Birth of Arthur

At Tintagel the king gathered his vassals and asked them what he should do. They said: "Sire, we advise you to make peace with the duchess and her family and the family of the duke."

The king told them to go speak with her and tell her that she could not hold out against him but that, if she wanted peace, he would abide by her wishes. As the barons left for the castle, the king took Urfin aside and said: "What do you think of this way of settling the matter?"

The king gave Urfin to understand that he knew that he had devised the plan, and Urfin said: "My lord, the idea was mine. It is for you to say whether you like it."

The king answered: "I like it, and I wish the duchess were already here."

Urfin said: "My lord, do not intervene in the discussion. Leave it in my hands." Their conversation ended there.

At Tintagel Castle the messengers found the duchess and the duke's relatives and told them how the duke had died through his own rashness.

They said that the king was grieved and that he was ready to make peace with the lady and her family, who could no doubt see that it was pointless to resist him, and so the good men advised the lady and all her relatives to accept the royal offer. They answered that they would discuss it, and withdrew. "The messengers are right when they say that we cannot hold out against the king, but let us hear what kind of settlement he would offer us. The king may well propose a peace that we can hardly reject. That, lady, is our view."

The lady answered: "I never declined the advice of my husband, and I shall not decline yours."

They returned to the messengers, and one of the wisest in the group spoke: "Lords, my lady would like to know what amends the king is prepared to make."

The messengers answered: "We do not know the king's wishes, but he has said that he would abide by the recommendations of his barons."

The others answered: "If that is true, the settlement will be a good one. You are such worthy men that, God willing, you will give him good and honorable advice."

They decided that two weeks later the lady and her family would come before the king to hear his offer. The messengers then returned to the king and told him what they had learned, and he said that the lady and all those accompanying her would have safe conduct and should not hesitate to come. During the next two weeks the king and Urfin spoke of many things. Then, on the appointed day, just as the barons had advised, he sent for the duchess. When she reached the camp, the king gathered all her barons together with his own and asked them what peace settlement they wanted to request for the lady. Her advisers answered: "Lord, the lady has not come here to make a request, but to hear what you will offer as compensation for the death of her husband."

The king was struck by the wisdom of these words. He drew his counselors aside and asked them: "Lords, how do you advise me?"

They answered: "Sire, only you can know what sort of settlement you have it in your heart to offer them."

The king answered: "I'll tell you: You are all my vassals and all such worthy men that you will never give me poor counsel. I leave the matter entirely in your hands."

They said: "It is a heavy burden, sire. Order Urfin to join our group, for without his help we could never reach a decision."

When the king heard them ask for Urfin to advise them, he made it clear that he was delighted, and he said to Urfin: "I brought you up, and I have made you a powerful man, and I know how wise you are. Go help them in their deliberations."

Urfin said: "Yes, of course, just as you say. But let me leave you with this word: that no lord can ever be too greatly loved by his vassals and that, if they are worthy men, he can never humble himself too much to win their hearts." With that Urfin went to join the counselors.

Once they were all together, they asked him: "Urfin, what is your advice to us?"

Urfin answered: "You have heard that the king leaves the matter in your hands. Let us now go to the duchess and her relatives and find out whether they agree to do the same."

They all answered that he had spoken well, and then went to see the lady and her advisers. They told them that the king was leaving the matter in their hands and would accept whatever settlement they proposed; they had come, they went on, to ask whether the lady's side would do the same. Her counselors answered: "We need to confer about this."

They conferred and then said that the king could do no better than to leave the matter in the hands of his barons. The lady, her advisers, and the relatives of the duke then agreed to do the same, and the king's counselors acknowledged their decision. Then they withdrew and discussed the question, and when each man had spoken his mind, they turned to Urfin for his views. Urfin said: "I shall tell you what I think. As you know, my lords, the duke did not do anything to deserve to die, and it is the king's fault that he is dead. Isn't that true? His wife remains with children to support, but you know that the king has laid waste to all her lands; moreover she is the best lady in the world—the most beautiful, wise, and virtuous. You know, too, that the duke's death has meant a great loss to his relatives, and it is only right that, in order to win their friendship, the king should compensate them for some part of their loss. Furthermore you know that the king has no wife. I conclude, then, that the only way the king can redress the wrong that he has done is by marrying the duchess. It seems to me that he should do it to repair the harm, to ensure our affection, and for the sake of everyone in the kingdom. Having done that, he should marry off the duke's daughter to King Lot of Orkney, who is here with us, and he should similarly treat the other relatives of the duke, so that they will regard him as their friend, their lord, and their rightful king. Now you have heard my counsel; suggest something else if you are not in agreement."

They all answered: "You have made the best proposal that anyone could imagine. If you actually present it to the king and he accepts, we will all support it."

Urfin answered: "My lords, that is not enough. I must be able to tell the king that the plan already has your full support. I see the king of Orkney here. The settlement depends to a great extent on him. Let him say what he thinks of it."

Lot responded: "Whatever you may once have said about me, I do not want to stand in the way of peace."

Having heard that, the rest all fell into agreement. They returned to the king and sent for the lady and her advisers. When all were assembled, Urfin stated the peace terms as planned and then asked the barons: "Are you in favor of this agreement?"

And they all answered yes. Urfin turned toward the king and said: "My lord, what is your wish? Do you accept the terms proposed by these worthy men?"

The king answered: "I do, provided the lady and her family agree and King Lot is willing to marry the duke's daughter."

Then King Lot spoke: "My lord, for the sake of your friendship and for peace, I shall do whatever you think right."

Then Urfin addressed the lady's spokesman, asking: "Do you accept this agreement?"

And the man answered wisely. He looked around at the lady and her counselors, who were so moved that all had tears in their eyes, and some, from both sadness and joy, were actually weeping. He himself was weeping as he answered: "No lord has ever before made amends with such generosity."

Urfin asked the lady and the duke's family: "Do you accept this agreement?"

The lady remained silent, but her relatives all answered: "There is no one who cannot; we accept it! We consider the king to be so worthy and so honorable a man that we place all our trust in him."

The peace was thus ratified by both sides, and Uther Pendragon took Ygerne as his wife, and gave her daughter to King Lot of Orkney. The wedding of the king and Ygerne took place on the twenty-eighth day after the settlement, which had taken place three weeks after the death of the duke; almost two months had thus passed since the night when the king had been with the duchess in her chamber. The daughter who became the wife of King Lot later gave birth to Mordred, to my lord Gawain, to Agravain and Gareth and Gaheris. Another daughter, a bastard, was married to King Neutre of Sorhaut. Finally, on the recommendation of the whole family, the king sent the daughter named Morgan to school at a convent. She was so gifted that she learned the seven arts and quite early acquired remarkable knowledge of an art called astronomy, which she used all the time. She also studied nature and medicine, and it was through that study that she came to be called Morgan the Fay. The king provided all the other children, too, with good guidance, and he showed the duke's relatives great friendship.

And so Uther Pendragon won Ygerne. After some time her pregnancy became apparent, and the king, lying with her one night, placed his hand on her stomach and asked who had made her pregnant. It was clear that it could not be he, for, ever since they had married, he had written down every time he had gone to bed with her; and it could not have been the duke, for he had been away from her for a long time before his death. When the lady heard the question, she felt ashamed and began to weep. With tears in her eyes, she said: "My lord, I cannot tell you a lie when you already know so much, and I shall not try, but, in God's name, take pity on me! If you assure me that you will not leave me, I shall tell you something extraordinary but true."

He assured her that he would never leave her, whatever she might say. Delighted with his reassurance, she went on: "My lord, I shall tell you an extraordinary story." And she told him how a man looking just like her husband the duke had been to bed with her in her chamber. "And he brought with him two men whom my husband loved most dearly, and right before my servants he came into the room and entered my bed. I had no doubt at all that it was my husband. The man fathered the child that I am now carrying, and I now know that it was the very night my husband died. He was lying with me when the news of the death reached the castle. He let me go on believing he was my husband, saying that his men simply did not know what had become of him, and with that he went away."

When the queen had told her story, the king answered: "My dear love, take care to keep your condition a secret from as many people as you can, because you would be disgraced if it were known. I hope you understand that, when the child is born, we cannot reasonably acknowledge it as ours, and we shall not keep it for ourselves. I am asking you, then, to give it, as soon as it has been born, to a certain person that I shall point out to you, and in that way we shall never hear anything further about it."

She answered: "My lord, you may do as you wish with me and whatever is mine."

Then the king came to Urfin and repeated the conversation he had had with the queen, to which Urfin replied: "My lord, now you know how virtuous and loyal she is, for she did not attempt to lie about that extraordinary occurrence. You have also been of great help to Merlin, since he could not obtain the child in any other way."

That is how matters remained until the sixth month, when Merlin had promised to return. He came and spoke in private with Urfin, asking for news of whatever interested him, and Urfin told him truthfully whatever he knew. After the conversation the king had Urfin bring Merlin to him, and when all three were together, he told Merlin how he had behaved toward the queen and how he had brought about the peace agreement that allowed him to marry her. Merlin answered: "My lord, Urfin is absolved of his sin in bringing you together with the queen. But I am not yet absolved of mine in helping him to deceive her and facilitate the conception of a child whose father she does not know."

The king answered: "You are so wise that you will find a way to free yourself of the sin."

Merlin said: "My lord, you must help me."

The king said that he would help in any way he could and that he was in any case going to give him the child. Merlin said: "In this town lives the most worthy man in the land, and his wife is the most worthy and honorable woman, with the finest qualities imaginable. She has given birth to a son, and her husband is a man of only modest means. I want you to send for him and to give him money on this condition: that he and his wife swear on holy relics that they will raise a child who will soon be brought to them and nourish him with the lady's own milk, and that they will have their son nursed by another woman but treat this child as their very own."

The king said: "Merlin, I shall do everything you say."

Then he said goodbye, and Merlin went back to Master Blaise.

The king sent for the good man and received him very warmly. As the man was greatly surprised by such a warm welcome, the king said to him: "Dear friend, I must reveal to you an extraordinary thing that has happened to me. You are my liegeman; I ask you, then, by the loyalty you owe me, to help me in a certain matter that I shall explain to you and that you must keep hidden as well as you can."

The man answered: "My lord, there is nothing you may command that I will not do if I am at all able; and if not, I will at least keep it a secret."

The king said: "An extraordinary thing happened to me in a dream. A good man appeared to me in my sleep, who told me that you are the most worthy and loyal man in the kingdom. He told me, too, that your wife has just given you a son. Then he ordered that I ask you to remove the boy from your wife's breast and give him over to another woman, so that your wife, for my sake, could nurse another child soon to be brought to her."

The worthy man answered: "My lord, that is quite a lot to ask! But please tell me when this child will be brought to us."

The king said: "So help me God, I am not sure!"

The good man said that he would do as the king wished, and he was then given so generous a gift that he was astonished. He left the king and went back to tell his wife what had been said. It seemed to her a very strange thing, and she said: "How can I give up my own child and start nursing another?"

He said: "There is nothing we can refuse to do for our lord. He has given us so much and promised so much that we must do as he pleases. I insist that you agree."

She said: "I am yours, just as the child is, and you may do as you wish both with me and with him. I agree, then, for I am bound to accept what you want."

The good man was delighted to have the consent of his wife. Then he told her to find a nurse for their child even before the other one was brought to them, and so he took the boy from his mother's breast. Meanwhile the time approached for the queen to give birth. The day before the delivery Merlin came to the court in secret and spoke to Urfin: "Urfin, I am very pleased with the king for having so effectively given my message to Auctor [Hector]. Now tell him to go to the queen and announce to her that she will have the child tomorrow evening after midnight, and let him order her to surrender it right away to the good man who will be waiting just outside the room."

At these words Urfin said: "Merlin, are you, then, not going to speak to the king?"

Merlin said: "Not this time."

Then Urfin came to the king and told him what Merlin had ordered.

The king welcomed the news with delight and said: "Urfin, won't he speak to me before he leaves?"

And Urfin said: "No, but do what he orders."

The king then came to the queen and said: "My lady, listen to what I have to tell you; trust me and do as I say."

The queen said: "My lord, you have all my trust, and I shall do whatever you order."

The king said: "My lady, tomorrow evening after midnight you will give birth, with God's help. I want you, please, as soon as the child has been born, to have one of your personal maids give it to the first man she finds just beyond the door of the room. And order all the women who are present at the birth never to say that it took place, because the news would bring great shame to both you and me: many people would say the child was not mine, and they would apparently not be wrong."

The lady answered: "My lord, what I recounted to you earlier is true. I shall do as you command—but I find it remarkable that you already know the time of my delivery."

The king said: "My lady, please do as I order."

She answered: "My lord, of course I will, please God."

With that the king left the queen. The next day, as God wished, the lady's labor began after vespers and continued until the time the king had predicted; she gave birth between midnight and dawn. As soon as she had delivered, she called over a woman in whom she had especial trust and said to her: "Dear friend, take the child out of the room. At the door, if you find a man who asks for it, give it to him. But try to find out, too, who he is."

The woman did as ordered; she wrapped the child in the finest linens she had and carried it to the door, where she saw a man who looked remarkably decrepit. She said to him: "Good man, what are you waiting for here?"

He answered: "I am waiting for what you bring me."

She asked: "Who are you? To whom can I tell my lady I gave her child?"

He answered: "That is not for you to ask; just do what you have been told."

The woman handed him the child and, once he had taken it, she had no idea of what became of him. She went back to her lady and said: "My lady, I gave the child to an old man; that's all I know about him."

The queen was greatly pained and wept. Meanwhile the man to whom the child had been given went as quickly as he could to Auctor. He found him in the morning just as he was going to mass, called to him and said: "Auctor, I want to speak to you."

Auctor looked at him, thought him a very honorable man, and said: "My lord, what is it you wish?"

The old man said: "Auctor, I have this child to give you. I ask that you bring him up with more care than your own. You may be sure that, if you do so, great good will come of it for you and your offspring, but if anyone were to tell you more now, you would not believe it."

Auctor said: "My lord, is this the child that the king has asked me to raise?"

The man answered: "Yes indeed. Both the king and all good men should ask you to do it. And you may be sure that my request has at least as much weight as that of a powerful baron."

Auctor took the child and saw how beautiful it was; he asked whether the boy had been baptized. The man said no, but that Auctor should have him baptized right away. Auctor gladly agreed and asked what name he should be given. The other answered that he should have the name Arthur. "Now I am leaving, since I have nothing more to do here. Great good will come to you from this child, as you will soon realize. In a short while you and your wife will be unable to say which you prefer, this one or your own."

Auctor answered: "My lord, who shall I tell the king gave me the child? Who are you?"

The man said: "You cannot know any more for the time being."

At this point, according to the tale, Merlin took leave of Auctor. Auctor had the child baptized without delay and gave him the name Arthur. Then he took the boy home to his wife and said: "My lady, here is the child that I asked you to take in."

She answered that he was welcome and took him into her arms. She asked her husband whether the child was baptized, and he answered that he was named Arthur. Then the lady gave him her breast.

[*With Merlin's help Uther Pendragon reigns effectively for many years. When he dies with no apparent heir, Merlin assures the great lords of the realm that God will soon designate his successor. This is Arthur, now grown to manhood, who proves himself the rightful new king by pulling the Sword from the Stone. The* Prose Merlin *concludes with Arthur's coronation. The* Suite du Merlin, *opening one month later, presents a series of important episodes in Arthur's life, which continually bring into play the prophetic and necromantic powers of Merlin. The often intertwined episodes include, among others, the birth of Mordred, the disclosure of Arthur's true parentage, the magical appearance of the sword Exca-*

libur, the fateful tale of Balin and his brother, the combats with Pellinor, the first
hints of the treachery of Morgan the Fay, Arthur's marriage to Guinevere, the
renewal of the Round Table, the adventures of Gawain, and the appearance,
abduction, and rescue of Niviane the Huntress. Meanwhile many years have
passed, and Merlin is now an old man.]

From the Suite du Merlin

---

9. Merlin's Love for Niviane the Huntress

There was great joy at court. The king asked the Huntress, as soon as
she had given him her hounds, her pointer, and the stag's head: "Well, my
young lady, what do you say? Have we kept our word to you?"

"Yes indeed, my lord," she said. "I would never have thought you could
be so successful. And since I am not missing any of the things that I had
when I first came to your court, I shall now take my leave to return to my
country as quickly as I can."

"My lady," said the king, "do stay a while, if you like, together with all
the ladies who are companions to my lady the queen. I assure you that you
will receive as much honor and respect as the noblest lady at court, or even
more. You well deserve it, God knows!"

"Indeed, my lord, as God is my witness!" said Merlin. "And you don't
even know as much as I do!" Then he whispered to him: "I can assure you
that she is extremely worthy and intelligent and has all the nobility of the
daughter of a king and queen. If you do her honor, everyone will be
grateful to you."

The king said that he was quite ready to do her honor, now and as long
as she remained at court. Then he asked the queen to keep her in her
company and to show her greater respect and friendship than any of her
other young ladies. The queen gladly agreed, and so urged the Huntress
that she consented to stay at court for a while. The queen asked her what
her baptismal name was, and she answered that she was named Niviane and
was the daughter of a nobleman in Brittany, but she did not say that she was
the daughter of a king. Let all those who listen to the tale of my lord Robert
de Boron know, however, that this young lady was the one who would
later be called the Lady of the Lake, and would raise Lancelot of the Lake in
her dwelling, just as the great *Story of Lancelot* makes clear. But the present
Story of the Holy Grail does not speak much of that and instead goes on as
follows.

[*Merlin tells Arthur about certain inescapable misfortunes that are to come:
Pellinor's death at the hands of Gawain and the destruction of the realm through
Mordred.*]

Merlin happily spent much time with Niviane the Huntress, so much
time, in fact, that he fell deeply in love with her, for she was extremely
beautiful and was no more than fifteen years old. The girl was very wise for

her age, and she was frightened by Merlin's attention; she was afraid that he might dishonor her by means of a magic spell or take advantage of her during her sleep. He, though, had no such desire, not wishing to do anything that might vex her.

Now, according to the tale, the young lady remained at court for a good four months. Merlin, much in love with her, came to see her every day. Seeing him so taken with her, she said to him: "I won't ever love you unless you swear to teach me some of the spells that you know."

He began to laugh then and said: "There is nothing I know that I would not teach you, because you are the only woman I love or could love."

"Since you love me so much," she said, "I want you to swear with your bare hand that you will never do anything, either by magic or otherwise, that you think might displease me."

He took the oath immediately. So it was that the girl became an intimate of Merlin, although not in the sense that she admitted him to her bed—but he was waiting and hoping to have his way with her, to know her in the flesh and deflower her (for he knew that she was still a virgin); and so he began to teach her sorcery and enchantment, and she learned rapidly.

During that time the king of Northumberland—the Northumberland that borders Brittany—sent a letter to King Arthur, saying: "King Arthur, I greet you as my friend and ask, in friendship and courtesy, that you bid farewell to my daughter Niviane, who, I have been informed, has been staying at your court, and send her back to my country in the company of the messengers that I have sent you. Be assured that I am most grateful to you for the honor and hospitality that you have shown her."

When the king had seen the letter, he sent for the girl and said: "My lady, your father has sent messengers here for you. What do you wish? Will you leave us or stay?"

"My lord," she said, "I will leave, since I have been sent for."

"That is certainly a wise and worthy answer," he said. "Yet I must say that if I did not know the desire of your royal father, I should prefer to have you stay here. I have very much enjoyed your company."

"My lord," she said, "I am very happy to hear that, and if I wished to live away from my father's house, there is no court in the world where I would more gladly stay than at yours, which deserves more praise than any other. But since it is my father's wish that I return home, I cannot fail to do so, even if only out of obedience."

"That is the best decision you can make," said the king, "and I respect you all the more for it."

So it was that the girl had to leave the court to return to her own country. I can tell you that the queen and the other ladies were all saddened by it, since everyone had come to be very fond of her. On the eve of her departure Merlin came to her and said: "Ah, young lady, are you really going?"

"Yes indeed, Merlin," she said; "and what will you do? Won't you come along with me?" (She said that because she could not imagine he might in fact come along!)

"Certainly, my lady!" he said. "I won't let you go without me but will keep you company all the way back to your country. And once there, I shall stay if you wish me to and, if you do not, I shall leave. Whatever you like, I shall be sure to do."

When she heard that he would come with her, she felt struck to the quick, because she hated no one else so much as Merlin. She did not dare let it show, however. She pretended instead to be delighted and thanked him very much for offering to accompany her.

The horses were saddled and the young lady bade farewell to the king and queen; and in the morning, as soon as she had heard mass, she left. Merlin did not tell anyone at court that he too was going, as he well knew that the king would not be pleased to grant him leave, should he ask for it. From Camelot they rode straight down to the sea and there boarded a ship for Brittany. They arrived safely and then rode into the land of King Ban of Benwick. There, if they had not had Merlin with them, the girl and her party would have been frightened, as the war raging between King Ban and King Claudas of the Wasteland left no one safe. That night the girl turned for shelter to a castle of King Ban's that sat high atop a remarkable pinnacle and was one of the strongest castles in the entire land; it was called Trebe. King Ban was not at the time in the castle, being engaged not far away in his war with King Claudas, but the queen, his wife, was there: Helaine, the most beautiful woman in all of Brittany and the most worthy known to either God or man. She and the king had only one child, a boy not yet one year old, but already the most beautiful creature in the world. He was affectionately known as Lancelot, but his baptismal name was Galahad.

Queen Helaine, as soon as she recognized the young lady of Northumberland, gave her a joyous welcome. (You must not think, you who are listening to this tale, that the Northumberland that I mean was the kingdom of Northumberland in Britain, which lay between the kingdoms of Logres and Gorre; that would be a gross mistake, for the one I mean was in Brittany.) Queen Helaine, as I was saying, welcomed the girl with great delight and warm hospitality. When they had eaten, the queen had her son brought in for the girl to see. After a long look the girl said: "Beautiful boy, if you can only live to the age of twenty, you will be the handsomest of all men!"

At that Merlin laughed, together with everyone else who had heard it. He whispered to the girl: "He will live more than fifty years, but he will gain even more fame for his knightly valor than for his beauty. You cannot imagine another knight, either before him or after, who could be his peer."

She answered with thanks to God that He had let her see such a beautiful creature, and she kissed him more than a hundred times. Then the child's nurses took him back to their chambers, and the queen said to the girl: "My lady, it would be of great help to us if the boy were older than he is! There is a relentless war going on every day with a neighbor of ours, who is doing us as much harm and damage as he can."

"My lady," said the girl, "what is the name of this neighbor of yours?"

"He is," she said, "Claudas of the Wasteland, the most treacherous man in the world. I wish God would one day let me have my revenge. I would be overjoyed, because I have never hated any other man as much as I hate him."

"My lady," said Merlin, "you will hate him even more. But you will see the day, well before the death of Lancelot, when Claudas will have no inch of land left in this country and will slink off with just a few followers, defeated and humbled, all his possessions gone, to seek some poor refuge in another land."

"Ah, God!" said the queen, "if I could see that day, I would never ask for any other happiness in this life, for there is nothing I hate as much I do him. And it's no wonder if I hate him: I owe him my poverty!"

"Take heart, my lady," said Merlin. "Be assured that what I have predicted will come true."

"May God grant that!" she said; "I would be very happy."

That, then, is what Merlin said about Claudas, and eveything happened eventually just as he had foretold. The lady did not inquire who he was, as she could never have imagined that Merlin would come near her castle.

The next day, as soon as the girl had heard mass, she and her party left Trebe, riding on until they reached a wood. It was small, but for its size it was the most beautiful and the most delightful in all of France or Brittany; the wood was called En Val, because most of it lay in a valley. When they were in the wood, Merlin said to the girl: "My lady, would you like to see the Lake of Diana, which you have heard of so often?"

"Yes indeed," she said; "I should be very pleased to see it. Nothing about Diana could fail to please me or could leave me indifferent, since throughout her life she enjoyed hunting in the woods just as much as I do, or even more."

"Let us go, then," he said, "and I shall show it to you."

Then they went down through the valley until they found a very large, deep lake. "There," said Merlin, "is the Lake of Diana." And they continued on their way until they came to a place on the shore where there was a marble tomb. "My lady," said Merlin, "do you see this grave?"

"Yes," she said, "of course."

"Here, let me tell you," said Merlin, "is where Faunus, Diana's lover, is buried. He was deeply in love with her, but she was so cruel to him that she brought about his death in the most treacherous way possible. That was his reward for loving her faithfully."

"Really, Merlin," said the girl, "did Diana kill her lover?"

"Really," he said. "There is no doubt of it."

"Do tell me how it happened," she said; "I want to know."

"Of course," said Merlin; "I shall tell you. Diana, as you know, lived in the time of Vergil, a long time before Jesus Christ came to earth to save sinners, and above all else she loved hunting in the woods. She had hunted in all the forests of France and Brittany, but nowhere had she found a wood as pleasing to her as this one, and so she settled here and built her manor on the shore of this lake. In that way she could go hunting in the woods during the day and come back to her lake at night. She spent a long time here, concerned only with the hunt, until one day the son of a king who held this entire country saw her and fell in love with her. He was struck not only by her beauty but also by such courage and swiftness and agility as no man could match. The young man was not yet knighted, but he was very handsome and bright. He pursued Diana so ardently that she at last granted him her love, but on condition that he never return to his father or seek any company but hers. He consented and so remained with her. And she, for his sake and also because the place pleased her so much, built a very beautiful, impressive manor on the shore of the lake. Faunus was thus cut off from the world, separated by his love for Diana from his father, his friends, and all other sorts of companions.

"When he had been with her for two years, Diana met another knight while she was out hunting, just as she had earlier met Faunus, and she fell passionately in love with him. This was Felix, who had been born into a poor and humble family but through his prowess had become a knight. He knew that Faunus was Diana's lover and knew too that if Faunus discovered him, he would leave him in sorry shape or even kill him. He said to Diana: 'You say you love me . . .'

"'It is true,' said Diana; 'more than any other man I have ever seen.'

"'No good,' he said, 'can ever come to me of that. Even if I loved you very much, I would not dare to come near you, because I know that if Faunus found out, he would destroy not only me but my whole family as well.'

"'Don't be concerned by that,' she said. 'You must not let that stop you from coming to me.'

"'On the contrary,' he said; 'either you rid yourself of him once and for all, or I can never stay with you.'

"'I cannot rid myself of him as long as he is sound and fit,' she said. 'He loves me far too much ever to allow it.'

"'You must do it,' he said, 'in one way or another.'

"Diana loved Felix so much that she would have paid with her life to have him in her bed, and so she decided to kill Faunus, either with poison or in some other way. Now this grave that you see here was already in existence at the time; it was ordinarily full of water, and there was a stone slab covering it. An evil sorcerer named Demophon, who lived in this land, had given the water the power to heal the wounds of all those who bathed in it; it was a feat of black magic. One day, then, Faunus came home from hunting with a wound that a wild animal had inflicted on him, and Diana, who could think of nothing but harm and misfortune for him, decided, as soon as she had heard he was wounded, to have the grave drained of its water so that he could not be healed in it. When he came near and saw that the healing water was gone, he felt sudden panic and said to Diana: 'What shall I do? I am very badly wounded!'

"'Have no fear,' she answered. 'I can heal you. Take off all your clothes and lie down in the grave, and I shall put the stone slab back in place over you. Then, through the slit in the slab, I shall strew herbs over your body, herbs of such great power that you will be healed as soon as you have felt their warmth.'

"Faunus, who would never have thought that she intended to betray him, said that he would do whatever she ordered. He lay down naked in the grave, and the stone was placed over him; it was so heavy that he could not possibly have pushed it back without help from above.

"Then Diana, who was determined to be done with him, flooded the tomb with molten lead that she had ready, so that he died instantly, burned to the very entrails. Once she had put Faunus to death, she came to Felix and said: 'I have freed myself of the man whom you have feared,' and she told him how she had done it.

"When she had finished, he said: 'The whole world should hate you for that! No one could love you now, and certainly not I!' With that he drew his sword, seized Diana by her hair, and cut off her head. Because Diana had enjoyed this place so much during her life and because at her death, her body was thrown into the lake, the lake came to be named the Lake of Diana, and it will bear that name as long as the world lasts. Now you have heard how Diana killed her lover and why this is called the Lake of Diana."

The girl said: "You have certainly told the story well, Merlin! But now tell me what became of the buildings that she had built here."

"The father of Faunus," said Merlin, "destroyed them as soon as he learned how Faunus had died; he smashed everything that Diana had built."

"That was wrong of him," answered the girl, "for her manor stood in a very lovely and charming place. I find this place so beautiful and appealing that, so help me God, I will never leave it. I shall have a house built as great and fine as any here before and live here in it for the rest of my life. And I ask, Merlin," she went on, "that, out of love for me, you take charge of the project."

He said that, since she asked him to, he would gladly do it. Merlin thus undertook to build the dwelling beside the Lake of Diana.

The young lady said to the men in her party: "My lords, I should be delighted if you cared to stay here with me, as I could hardly remain in this forest alone. You must understand that I wish never to leave this place but rather spend my whole life hunting here, always coming back to my house to rest for a day or two or more before returning to the hunt."

The men to whom she spoke were noblemen and close relatives of hers; they answered: "If you prefer to remain here rather than go back to our lord your father, we shall remain too. We dare not return home without you."

She said that she was happy with that decision. "Let me add," she said, "that Merlin has given me so much gold and silver that you will have enough to spend for a lifetime."

"Lady, if you had no resources, we would do everything possible to support you ourselves, which would only be our duty."

Then Merlin hired masons and carpenters from throughout the land and had them construct along the shore a great house and outbuildings so fine and so lavish that in all Brittany you could not have found a royal or princely dwelling that was any finer. When the work was finished and the masons and carpenters gone, Merlin said to the young woman: "This manor will be worthless to you if I do not make it invisible to everyone except the people who live in it." Then he cast a spell over all the buildings, so wondrously closing them off from every side that nothing was visible but water. If you stood outside, however closely you looked, all you could see was the lake. When he had accomplished this wonder, Merlin showed it to the girl and said: "Is your manor safe enough? No one will ever see it, no matter how close he comes, unless he belongs to the household. And if anyone who does belong tries, out of envy or hatred, to show it to an outsider, he will immediately fall into the lake and drown."

"My God, Merlin!" said Niviane. "I have never before heard of such clever protection!"

Merlin remained with the young lady. He stayed at the manor night and day, feeling a greater love for her than he had ever felt for anyone or anything else in the world. And because of his great love, he did not dare to seek any favor of her, lest he vex her. All the same, he thought that one day, somehow or other, he would take his pleasure with her. He had already taught the girl so many spells and so much magic that she knew more than anyone alive, apart from Merlin himself, and no one could imagine any game or pleasant distraction that she could not produce through sorcery. There was no one in the world, though, whom she hated as fiercely as she did Merlin, because she was well aware that he was eager to deflower her, and if she had dared attempt to kill him, whether by poison or in some other way, she would have done it with fury. But she did not dare, since she was afraid that he would realize what was about to happen, he who was so much more alert than other people. Nevertheless she had so enchanted him with the very spells that he himself had taught her, that she could say whatever she wanted and he would not grasp her meaning.

10. *The Journey Toward the Perilous Forest*

One day, when Merlin was walking through the manor, he noticed, sleeping in the main hall, a knight who was a relative of the girl's. She, the mistress of the household, was present, and Merlin exclaimed: "Ah, God! He is much more at ease, this knight, than King Arthur has been today!"

"What has happened to Arthur?" said the young lady. "Tell me!"

"Today," Merlin said, "he came so close to death that he was terrified he might not escape; nor would he have, if not for the boldness of Kay, his seneschal, who with two blows killed two kings. That is how King Arthur was saved and his enemies defeated."

"Really," said the girl, "it is wrong of you to let him fall into such danger! You should always be at his court to protect him, not far away as you are."

"The truth is," said Merlin, "that I am staying away from Britain for two reasons. One is that I am so in love with you that I could not possibly live without you. The other reason is that my power as a seer tells me I should no sooner be back there than I would be poisoned or killed in some other way."

"What!" she said. "Can you not protect yourself?"

"No," he answered. "I am already so spellbound that I cannot tell who is planning my death."

"You mean," she said, "that all your claims to see into the future have now come to naught?"

"Apart from my own life and death," he said, "I can still foretell almost everything. But where I myself am concerned, I am so bound by enchantments that I am helpless, for I cannot undo the spells unless I am willing to lose my soul. But I would much rather let my body be destroyed through someone's treachery than let my soul be damned."

This revelation made the young lady very happy, as she longed for nothing else so much as Merlin's death, and now it was clear that, with all the magic she had been practicing against him, he was indeed unable to grasp what she had in mind. One day not long afterward Merlin was sitting beside her at the table and said to her: "Ah! Lady of the Lake, if you only felt some affection for Arthur! If you only knew what is being plotted against him! His sister Morgan, whom he trusts completely, has just stolen his good and trustworthy sword Excalibur, together with the scabbard, and she has replaced it with one that looks identical but is worthless. And tomorrow he is to meet a knight in single combat! That means that his life is in danger, because his sword will fail him when he needs it. The other man, meanwhile, will be using the best sword that a knight could use and will be wearing a scabbard that has the power to keep its wearer from losing any blood."

"How terrible!" said the girl. "What a risk for the king! Now I should very much like the two of us to be present at the combat, for if Arthur is undone, it will surely be the worst thing that could happen in our time."

"He will be defeated and die," said Merlin, "unless our Lord decides otherwise. And it will happen because of a sin that I know he committed after our Lord had raised him to his kingly rank." The young lady asked what the sin was. "I may not reveal that to you," he answered; "it does not concern you or me. It is only for God to take vengeance, as He wishes, for great sins."

"That's right," she said, "and it was very wrong of me to ask. But tell me: could you in any way delay the battle long enough for us to reach Britain?"

"Yes, of course," he answered.

"And how many days," she asked, "would it take us to reach the site of the battle?"

"Twelve days," he said.

"I ask you, please, then," she said, "to delay the combat. Let us leave tomorrow morning and ride straight there without a stop. If it is God's will to let us arrive in time, I am sure that King Arthur will not lose a hair in battle."

"The truth is, Lady of the Lake," said Merlin, "there is nothing I would more gladly do than go to Britain, if I were not fearful of being betrayed and killed."

"You must not have any such fear," she answered. "You may be sure that I will watch over you as carefully as I watch over my very self, for I love you more than any other man in the world—and rightly so, since you have taught me everything I know, and my happiness depends on you."

"My lady," he said, "do you wish me, then, to go to Britain with you?"

"Yes, please," she said.

"Then I shall go," he answered, "since you wish me to. All the same, I believe it is a rash mistake."

Then the young lady decided who would stay at home and who would go with her. The next day, as soon as it was light, she and Merlin set out, together with two knights and four squires. The knights were cousins of hers and knew for a fact that there was nothing she hated more than she did Merlin. When they reached the coast, they set sail and, with a good wind, crossed very quickly to the British side. Once they were off the boat and on their horses, Merlin said: "Let us turn toward the kingdom of Logres. That is where we can find what we have come for."

One of the knights objected: "If we go in that direction, we shall have to pass through the Perilous Forest."

"True," said Merlin, "but that is where our road takes us."

Thereupon they all took the direction that he showed them. That day they rode on in peace, without any incident worth recording. The next morning they left the impressive, well-fortified castle where they had spent the night and continued to ride until the hour of tierce. Then they came to a beautiful, open plain where the only trees that grew were two extraordinary, huge elms. The two elms stood halfway down the road, and a cross stood between them. Near the cross there were a hundred or more graves. Beside it were two thrones beautiful and magnificent enough for an emperor, and each one had an ivory arch over it that protected it from the rain. On each of the thrones sat a man with a harp in his hand, playing whenever he wished. There were also many other instruments lying about, as if the men had nothing to do but play. Now, according to the tale, as the travelers were approaching them, Merlin halted and said to the others: "Do you see the two men who are sitting on those thrones with harps in their hands?" They answered that they did. "And do you know what they are doing?" They said that they did not and asked him to tell them.

"I shall tell you, then," said Merlin, "the most extraordinary thing that you have heard in a long time. The melody coming from those harps has the power to enchant any man or woman who hears it, except the two players. The spell is so overpowering that the hearers immediately lose all control of their limbs, fall down as if dead, and lie on the ground as long as the harpers want them to. Many people have suffered from this enchantment. Besides, if some good man came through here and had with him a wife or mistress of any beauty at all, the sorcerers would force themselves on her in the man's presence and then kill him, whoever he might be, so that he would not talk. That is how the two sorcerers have long behaved, and they have caused the death of many a worthy man and the shame of many a virtuous and beautiful lady. But if I have ever been able to cast a magic spell, I will now make sure that no good man or lady will ever again be subjected to their cruelty."

Then he stopped his ears as best he could in order not to hear the sound of the harps: he acted like the serpent that lives in Egypt, the asp, which stops one of its ears with its tail and presses the other against the ground in order not to hear the sorcerer's incantations. That is how Merlin approached the sorcerers, since he was fearful of their magic; and, protected as he was, the spell had no effect on him. To the girl and to the others, though, it proved so harmful that they could no longer remain in their saddles; they fell to the ground as if dead and lay in a faint. When Merlin saw his lady in such a state, he was not a little upset, and he said: "My love, I promise to take such revenge that no one will ever forget it. And through you all people will benefit who pass by here in the future, for if they are bound by some spell when they arrive, they can free themselves at once simply by touching one of these two trees."

Then he uttered the magic words that he knew to be fitting, and hurried on toward the sorcerers. When he came up to them, he found them already unconscious and stiff-limbed, so that a child would have had enough strength to kill them then and there. They could do nothing but sit and stare at Merlin, and their harps had fallen to the ground. At this point, according to the tale, Merlin looked at them in their helplessness and said: "Ah, evil outcasts that you are! If anyone had stunned you like this in the past, it would have been an act of charity, for you have caused great suffering and been guilty of great treachery ever since you came into this land! But now your wickedness and crimes have come to an end!" Then he returned to the young woman and her party and succeeded with his magic in restoring them to their normal state. He asked them: "What was it like?"

"My lord," they answered, "we felt all the pain and all the dread that a human being can imagine, for we clearly saw the princes and ministers of Hell. They bound up all our limbs so tightly that we were powerless to do anything and thought we were dead in body and soul."

"Now you can put aside your fear," said Merlin. "Once I have finished with these two, no man alive will ever again be tormented by them." Then he had two large pits dug in the ground, one beside each tree. When they were deep enough, he took one of the sorcerers, still sitting as he was on his throne, and lowered him into the first pit; that done, he did the same with the other. Next he quickly took and lighted a great quantity of sulphur and threw it into the pits, so that in no time at all the sorcerers were dead, choked by the hot fumes and the smell of the sulphur. Merlin then asked his fellow travelers: "What do you think of such vengeance? Is it great enough to match the crime?"

"Yes indeed," they all said, "and everyone who ever hears of it, sir Merlin, will bless you for it! You have done a great good deed by freeing the road of those two devils, for they would only go on doing evil as long as they lived."

"Still," said Merlin, "I cannot consider myself satisfied unless my vengeance is known to all the people who come here even long after my death." Then he himself went over to the graves of the good men whom the sorcerers had slain and removed three slabs of stone for each of the pits. These he arranged over the pits in such a way as to let onlookers clearly see the flames that burned within. When he had finished, he showed his work to the girl and her companions and said: "Do you think that this fire can last a long time?"

"Sir," they said, "we don't know, but you do. Tell us, please."

"I shall tell you," he said, "because I want you to know what a wonder this is. I tell you, this fire will burn as long as Arthur reigns, and that will be a long time. All that while it will never fail, but on the very day when Arthur leaves this world the flame, too, will die. And something else will happen here, an even greater wonder: the bodies of the sorcerers will be preserved just as they are right now, without burning up or rotting, as long as King Arthur lives; they will remain as intact as they are today. Nor will the thrones burn or fall apart until Arthur leaves this life. I am doing this so that all good men who live after me, when they see this wonder, can bear witness that I was the greatest wizard of all who ever breathed in the kingdom of Logres. It is true that, if I thought I still had long to live, I would not trouble with such a thing, since I would then have ample time to demonstrate my powers. But I know that I am bound to die soon, and I have done this extraordinary thing for that reason, for I want it to stand after my death as proof of my great craft."

The others answered: "Indeed, my lord, this will make it clear that you are the wisest of the wise, for a greater wonder has never been heard of." At that point they left the spot and took their way straight toward the Perilous Forest. But at this point the tale leaves off speaking of them and returns to Arthur and his court.

[*Here are narrated the adventures that constitute the background of Arthur's imminent battle. They include the king's defeat of an invading army, the seating of several new knights at the Round Table, and, most pertinently, the machinations of Morgan the Fay to destroy her brother Arthur.*]

11. The Death of Merlin

Now, according to the tale, when Merlin left the sorcerers whom he had brought to a dreadful end (as our book has already recounted), he rode on together with his companions for the rest of the day and then spent the night with a very worthy vavasor who offered them all the warmest welcome he could. But Merlin was dying of love for the young Lady of the Lake. He did not dare make any advance to her, because he well knew that she was still a virgin. Nevertheless he did not expect to wait too long before becoming intimate with her and doing what a man does with a woman. He had taught her so much magic, though, that she knew hardly less than he did. She also understood very well that he was only interested in deflowering her; she hated him for it with all her being and sought his death in every way she could. As I told you a while ago, she had already cast so many spells over him that he was by now quite unable to discern what she was plotting. She had revealed to one of the knights in her company, who was a cousin of hers, that she was going to kill Merlin as soon as she saw the right moment. She could not wait any longer! "Even if he made me sovereign over all the riches of the world, I would not be able to find it within me to love him, because I know that he is a son of the Devil and is not like other men."

The Lady of the Lake spoke like that quite often, since she thoroughly hated Merlin for being a son of the Enemy. One day, as they were all riding through the Perilous Forest, night came on rather suddenly while they were in a deep valley full of rocks and boulders and far from any town or castle or people of any sort. The night was so utterly dark that they could not proceed, but had to halt right where they were. With tinder that they had and very dry wood that they could gather, they lit a big fire and prepared food that they had brought with them from a castle where they had stopped earlier that day. After the meal Merlin said to the young lady: "My lady, nearby among the rocks I could show you the most beautiful little chamber that I know of. It was carved entirely out of the rock, and it has iron doors so strong that if anyone were trapped inside, I believe he could never get out."

"What an extraordinary thing you are telling me!" said the girl. "A beautiful and charming room here among the rocks—and I thought there could be nothing here but demons and wild beasts!"

"Yet it is true," said Merlin. "Not a hundred years ago there was a king in this land named Assen, a very worthy man and a fine knight. He had a son, Anastew, who was a knight of great valor and prowess. The young man loved the daughter of a certain poor knight with a love as great as any mortal man could feel for a woman. When King Assen found out that his son loved a girl of such low and poor circumstances, he rebuked him for it and tried to dissuade him. But the young man loved the girl no less for all that, and he went on seeing her. When the king saw that his pleas were in vain, he took the boy aside and said: 'If you do not give her up at once, I will kill you!'

"The other answered: 'I shall never give her up but will love her as long as I live.'

"'In that case,' said the king, 'you may be sure that I shall separate you from her. I will kill her, and then you.'

"When the knight heard these words, he decided to carry off and hide the girl so that his father could not find her. Then he went looking for a remote and hidden place, where no one lived or passed through; there he would withdraw with the young lady and stay for the rest of their lives. He had oftentimes hunted in this forest, so that he knew this valley well. He came here right away, bringing along the companions he loved best and men who knew something about building. Out of the bare rock they carved a beautiful dwelling. When it looked just as he wished, so splendid that you would almost need to see it in order to believe it, he hurried back to where he had hidden his lover and he brought her here. He provided their home in the rock with everything he thought necessary, and there he spent his entire life with his lover, in happiness and joy. They died on the same day and were buried together in the chamber itself. Their bodies are still there and will not decay as long as I am alive, because they were embalmed."

When the young lady heard that story, she was thoroughly delighted and decided immediately that, if she could, she would shut Merlin away in the lovers' room. And if ever spells or incantations could help a woman, she was sure that they would help her. She said to Merlin: "Really, Merlin, those two lovers must have loved each other truly, if they could give up everything and everyone just to enjoy each other!"

Merlin then whispered to her: "That is what I, too, have done, lady. To be with you, I have given up King Arthur and all the great men of the kingdom of Logres, who looked up to me as their master. But I have gained nothing by following you."

She answered quickly: "Merlin, if you could have had your way at the very start, you would no doubt have considered yourself fortunate and fulfilled. So would I, if I could have my way."

"Indeed, my lady," said Merlin, "there is nothing in the world, however difficult, that I am not prepared to do, if only you want it done. I beg you to tell me what it is that you cannot do yourself!"

"I will not tell you now," she said, "but you shall know soon enough. . . . Now that chamber of the two lovers that you told me about—I want to see it. We can spend the night there together. The true love that they filled it with makes me love the place."

Very glad to hear those words, Merlin said that since she wanted to see the room, she would see it; besides, it was not at all far. He told two squires to come along with torches, and they all started down a narrow path that ran off from the road. It was not long before they came to a rocky cliff, where they found a very narrow iron door. Merlin opened it and stepped inside, and the others followed. There they found themselves in a chamber covered with mosaics so splendidly crafted that the best workman in the world might have devoted twenty years to them. "Really," said the girl, "what a beautiful, splendid place this is! It was obviously created for the delight of pleasure-loving people."

"And this is not even their bedroom!" said Merlin. "This is where they often ate, but now I shall show you where they slept together." Then he went over to an iron door and opened it. He stepped inside and called for some light. When the others were at the threshold, he said: "Now you can see the chamber where the two lovers lived and the place where their bodies lie."

With that, they went in and began to look all around. When they had thoroughly examined the room and all the art that it contained, they said that never had there been so beautiful a dwelling in the whole world.

"Truly," said Merlin, "it is beautiful, just as they were who made it this way." Then he showed the girl, on the other side of the chamber, a beautiful, splendid tomb that was covered with a rich, red cloth expertly embroidered in gold with figures of animals. "My lady," said Merlin, "under this stone lid are the bodies of the two lovers whom I have told you about."

She eagerly picked up the cloth and looked closely at the slab that covered the tomb. She recognized it as made of red marble. "Really, Merlin," she said, "this is a beautiful, splendid place. It seems clear that it was planned and built for the delight and enjoyment of cheerful, pleasure-loving people."

"So it was, indeed," said Merlin. "If you knew how much effort and how much care went into it, you would be amazed."

"What about this stone slab?" she asked. "Can anyone lift it?"

"No one," said Merlin, "except me. However, I advise you not to look at the bodies, because bodies that have lain in the ground as long as these have are ugly and horrible, not fit to see."

"Even so," she said, "I want the lid raised."

He agreed and, grasping it at the edge, he raised it on one side. It was so heavy that ten men would have had great trouble moving it, so that we can only believe the power of his mind was of greater avail than the strength of his body. But that was true of everything he did.

Then he laid the slab down on the ground alongside the tomb. The young lady looked in and saw that the two bodies were wrapped in a white shroud, which prevented her from seeing faces or limbs. Realizing that that was all she would see, she said to Merlin: "Merlin, you have told me so much about these two lovers that if I were God for a moment, you can be sure I would unite their souls in everlasting joy. In fact I find it such a pleasure to think about their life together that for their memory's sake I want to stay right here, without moving, all through the night."

"I shall stay with you," said Merlin, "to keep you company."

As she spoke, so she did. The girl ordered her bed to be made in that very room, and as soon as it was done, she lay down to sleep. Merlin did likewise, but in a different bed. That night Merlin had been feeling a great torpor rather than his usual alertness and cheer, and he fell asleep as soon as he had closed his eyes. He was like a man under a spell, and he had indeed lost all the craft and all the knowledge that had always been his. The young lady, who was well aware of his state, left her bed to come over to him and place him under an even greater spell than before. When she had numbed him to such an extent that he would be powerless to move even to save his neck from the ax, she threw open the door to the room and called to her men to come in. She led them over to the bed where Merlin lay and began to turn him over and around in every direction, like a lump of earth. He showed no more response than if his soul had already departed from his body. She then said to the men standing there: "Well, what do you think of him now, my lords? Look how the enchanter is enchanted!"

In their astonishment they crossed themselves and said that they would never in the world have imagined such a thing could happen. "Now tell me," she said, "what shall we do with him? He followed me on this journey not for the sake of my honor but in order to disgrace me and take away my maidenhood. I should rather see him hang than let myself be touched by him, for he is a son of the Devil and I could never, for anything imaginable, love a son of the Devil. I must decide, then, how to free myself of him. If I do not make sure right now that I am free of him forever, I shall never again find as good an opportunity."

"My lady," said one of the squires, "you have no need to wonder or to hesitate. I am ready to get rid of him for you at this very moment."

"How would you do it?" she asked.

"Kill him," he said. "What else is there to do?"

"God never forgive me," she said, "if he is slain in front of me! I could not bear to watch him killed. But I shall find a better way to take revenge than you propose!" At that she told the men to pick him up by the head and feet and throw him into the tomb where the two lovers lay. Then she had them replace the stone slab. When, with great effort, that was done, she began her incantations, and with her spells and magic words she so tightly bound and sealed the slab in place that there was no one afterward who was able to move it or open it or look at Merlin, dead or alive, until she herself returned at the request of Tristan (as is recounted in the true story of Tristan, and the very *Tale of the Cry* speaks of it, though not in detail). Nor was there anyone afterward who heard Merlin speak, except Bademagu, who arrived four days after he had been entombed. At that point Merlin was still alive and spoke out when Bademagu, wanting to know who was in the tomb lamenting so bitterly, attempted to raise the stone slab. Merlin said to him: "Bademagu, do not struggle to raise the slab! Neither you nor anyone else will succeed, until the lady returns who has buried me here. No strength and no stratagem will be of any avail, for I am trapped here by such powerful charms and magic spells that no one could release me except my enchantress herself."

I shall not recount any more of this episode in the present book, because the *Tale of the Cry* recounts it in detail. You may know, though, that the cry that Master Helie has written about is the last cry that Merlin ever uttered in that grave in which he lay trapped. His cry came from the sharp pain he felt when he realized that he was being killed by a woman's cunning and that a woman's craft had defeated his own. The echo of the cry was heard throughout the length and breadth of the kingdom of Logres, and it gave rise to many extraordinary events, as the *Tale* recounts in detail. And since it is all explained there, we shall not speak of it in the present book, but instead go back now to our own story.

When Niviane had sealed Merlin in the tomb, as I have explained, she closed the door to the chamber behind her as securely as she could, though without using any magic spell, and then spent the rest of the night in the front room with her men. In the morning, when day broke, she left the dwelling, closing the door behind her but not in such a way as to bar entry to anyone whom chance might lead to it. Once she and her party were mounted, they rode directly from the rocky cliff toward the site where she understood that Arthur's battle was to take place. She reached it on the appointed day. The tale does not speak of any adventure that may have occurred on the way, but only of the fact that she arrived at the field of combat. With that our tale falls silent about her and turns back to King Arthur, recounting how he achieved victory in his battle and how he learned that that trap had been laid for him by his sister Morgan.

[*Niviane arrives in time to save Arthur from his foe by magically restoring to him his sword Excalibur and its enchanted scabbard. Morgan, undeterred, persists in her efforts to destroy Arthur, but the Lady of the Lake again rescues him. The work ends with the following sentence:*]

Now the tale ceases to speak of the Lady of the Lake and King Arthur and the entire life of Merlin, and goes on to the subject of the Holy Grail, which is the point of this book.

SOME GENERAL BOOKS
FOR FURTHER READING

[*Readers should also refer to the bibliographic notes ending the introduction to each chapter.*]

Alcock, Leslie. *Arthur's Britain*. Penguin, 1971.

Ashe, Geoffrey. *A Guidebook to Arthurian Britain*. Longman, 1980; rev. Aquarian, 1983.

———. *Kings and Queens of Early Britain*. Methuen, 1982.

———, ed. *The Quest for Arthur's Britain*. Praeger, 1968; rev. Paladin, 1982.

Barber, Richard W. *Arthur of Albion*. Barnes and Noble, 1971; rev. as *King Arthur in Legend and History*, Cardinal, 1973.

———, ed. *Arthurian Literature*. 2 vols. Rowman and Littlefield, 1981–82.

Bruce, J. D. *The Evolution of Arthurian Romance*. 2 vols. Johns Hopkins University, 1923; rpt. Peter Smith, 1958.

Chambers, E. K. *Arthur of Britain*. Sidgwick and Jackson, 1927; rpt. Barnes and Noble, 1964.

Darrah, John. *The Real Camelot*. Thames and Hudson, 1981.

Frappier, Jean, and Reinhold R. Grimm. *Le Roman jusqu'à la fin du XIIIe siècle*. (Vol. 4 of *Grundriss der romanischen Literaturen des Mittelalters*). Winter, 1978.

Hanning, Robert W. *The Vision of History in Early Britain*. Columbia University, 1966.

Jenkins, Elizabeth. *The Mystery of King Arthur*. Coward, McCann and Geoghegan, 1975.

Köhler, Erich. *Ideal und Wirklichkeit in der höfischen Epik.* Niemeyer, 1956.

Lacy, Norris, J., et al., eds. *The Arthurian Encyclopedia.* Garland, 1986.

Loomis, Roger Sherman. *The Development of Arthurian Romance.* Harper and Row, 1964.

——, ed. *Arthurian Literature in the Middle Ages.* Oxford University, 1959.

——, and Laura Hibbard Loomis. *Arthurian Legends in Medieval Art.* Oxford University, 1938.

Lot, Ferdinand. *Étude sur le Lancelot en prose.* Champion, 1918.

Luttrell, Claude. *The Creation of the First Arthurian Romance.* Northwestern University, 1974.

Moorman, Charles. *The Book of Kyng Arthur.* University of Kentucky, 1965.

——, and Ruth Moorman. *An Arthurian Dictionary.* University of Mississippi, 1979.

Morris, John. *The Age of Arthur.* Scribner, 1973.

Morris, Rosemary. *The Character of King Arthur in Medieval Literature.* Brewer, 1982.

Owen, D. D. R., ed. *Arthurian Romance: Seven Essays.* Barnes and Noble, 1971.

Pickford, C. E., C. R. Barker, and R. W. Last. *The Arthurian Bibliography.* 3 vols. Brewer, 1981, 1983, 1985.

Reiss, Edmund, Lousie Horner Reiss, and Beverly Taylor. *Arthurian Legend and Literature: An Annotated Bibliography.* 2 vols. Garland, 1984 (Vol. 2 in preparation).

Schmolke-Hasselmann, Beate. *Der arthurische Versroman von Chrestien bis Froissart.* Niemeyer, 1980.

Tatlock, J. S. P. *The Legendary History of Britain.* University of California, 1950.

Treharne, R. F. *The Glastonbury Legends.* Cresset, 1967; rpt. Sphere, 1971.

Varty, Kenneth, ed. *An Arthurian Tapestry.* University of Glasgow, 1981.

Vinaver, Eugene. *The Rise of Romance.* Oxford University, 1971.

Weston, Jessie L. *From Ritual to Romance.* Cambridge University, 1920; rpt. Anchor, 1957.

Wilson, Anne. *Traditional Romance and Tale: How Stories Mean.* Brewer, 1976.

INDEX

addanc 49
Aeneid 5, 255
Agravain 248
Aguisel 16
Alier, Count 114–16
Anastew 262–63
Angharad Golden-Hand 45, 48
Anna (Morgawse) 15, 247–48
Argante (Morgan) 20, 28
Arthur: in Wace 6, 14–17; in
    Layamon 19–28; in
    Peredur 33–36, 39, 43–45,
    47–48, 54; in Chrétien 83,
    89–90, 105–10, 129–30, 140–
    46; in Béroul 152, 159–60,
    184, 188–89, 191–94; in *Prose*
    Merlin 245–52; in
    Suite 252–53, 258–59, 261–
    62, 266
Auctor (Hector) 250–53
Aurelius Ambrosius 6, 8–11. *See*
    also Pendragon
Avalon 15, 17, 20, 28

Bademagu 265
Badon 15
Ban, King 254
Bath 15
Bede, Venerable 19
Bedivere 21
Béroul 63, 151–97
Blaise 222–24, 228–29, 231, 235–
    36, 245, 249
Brangain (Brangane) 156–58, 174,
    202, 204–06
Breton lay 63, 199

Bron 234
Brutus 5, 19

Cador of Cornwall 16–17, 28
Cadwallader 19
Caen 21
Caerdin (Kaherdin) 204–06, 209–
    10
Cai. *See* Kay
Calogrenant 84–91
Camelford 27
Celtic myth 20, 63–65, 213
Childerich 24–25
Chrétien de Troyes: *Yvain* 81–149;
    29, 63, 81–83
Claudas of the Wasteland 254–55
Cligés 81–82
Constant, King 69
Constantine of Cornwall 17, 28
Cornwall, Duke of. *See* Gorlois

Denoalen 160–61, 163, 166, 183–
    84, 186, 189–90, 194–96
Diana 255–57
Dinabus 7
Dinas of Dinan 164, 177, 180–81,
    190
dragon 11–12, 116–17, 158, 177,
    231–32
dwarf of Tintagel. *See* Frocin

Edlym 52
Efrog 32
Eilhart von Oberge 152
Eleanor of Aquitaine 5, 19, 82

Erec and Enide 81–82
Excalibur 15, 251–52, 258–59, 266

Faunus 255–57
Felix 256–57
Frocin the Dwarf 153, 156, 158,
   159, 160, 162, 166

Ganelon, Baron 160–61, 163, 166,
   183, 186, 189, 190, 194–96
Gareth 248
Gawain: in Wace 16; in
   Layamon 22, 25; in
   Peredur 32, 43–45, 47, 54–
   56, 60; in Chrétien 83–84,
   105, 107, 110, 119, 121, 129–
   30, 140–46; in Béroul 184,
   186, 192; in *Prose Merlin* 248
Geoffrey of Monmouth 5–6, 19,
   213
Girflet 192
Gloucester, witches of 42, 61
Godoine 160–61, 163, 166, 183–
   84, 186, 189, 190, 194–97
Good Friday 57
Gorlois, Duke of Cornwall 12–14,
   236–45
Gottfried von Strassburg 203
Governal 153, 156, 162, 163, 165,
   166, 168, 174, 177, 181, 187,
   188, 191, 192, 195
Graelent 63–79
Grail, Holy 29, 213–14, 223, 234,
   266
Guillomer 10, 11
Guinevere: in Wace 16; in
   Layamon 22–27; in
   Peredur 34–35; in
   Chrétien 83–85, 89, 129,
   143
Gwalchmai. *See* Gawain
Gwenhwyfar. *See* Guinevere

Hangus. *See* Hengist
Harpin of the Mountain 121, 123–
   24
Hector. *See* Auctor
Helaine (wife of Ban) 254
Hengist (Hangus) 7, 224–26, 229
Henry II (England) 5, 19
Henry the Liberal (Champagne) 82
honeysuckle 201–02, 212
Howel 16; Howeldin 21;
   Howell 24; Hywel 54
Husdent 167–69, 179

Igerna (Ygerne) 6, 12–15, 236–48
incubus 7–8, 221
Isolde (of Ireland): in Béroul 151–
   97; in Marie 199–202; in
   Thomas 203–12
Isolde of the White Hands 204,
   208, 210
Ivain the leper 164–65

Joseph of Arimathea 213, 223–24,
   234
Judas 234

Kay: in Layamon 21; (Cai) in
   Peredur 34–36, 39, 43–45,
   47; in Chrétien 84–85, 89,
   90, 96, 105–06, 119, 121; in
   Béroul 184

Lady of the Lake. *See* Niviane
Lancelot 81–83, 129, 252, 254
Lanval 64–65, 199–200
Laudine 95–96, 98–111, 125–28,
   147–49; name given 105
Layamon 5–6, 19–28
lion, Yvain's 116–146
Lot of Lothian 15, 16, 247–48
Louis VII (France) 82
Lucius Hiberius (Rome) 17, 20–21
Lunete 93, 95–111, 118–20, 125–
   28, 131–32, 147–49; name
   given 107

Marie of Champagne 82
Marie of France 63–65, 199–202
Mark of Cornwall: in Béroul 151–
   97; in Marie 200–01
Meleagant 121–22, 129
Merlin: in Wace 6–14; in
   Layamon 22, 26, 28; in *Prose
   Merlin* 213–52; in
   Suite 252–66
Mordred: in Layamon 21–28; in
   Merlin 248, 252
Morgan: in Layamon 20, 28; in
   Merlin 248, 258, 262, 263,
   266
Morgawse. *See* Anna
Morholt 153, 161, 173
Morrois, Forest of 167–71, 173,
   175

Niviane 252–66

Ogrin the Hermit 166–67, 175, 177–80
Orri the Forester 180, 182, 185
Ovid 82
Owain. *See* Yvain

Parsifal. *See* Perceval
Paschent 11
Pendragon (Ambrosius Aurelius) 224–32; name given 229
Perceval 29, 81–82, 213
Peredur Son of Efrog 29–61
Perinis 180, 184–87
potion, love 166, 174
Pridwen 15
Prose Merlin 214–52
Pyramus, Bishop 16

Robert de Boron 213–14, 252
Roland 115
Ron (lance) 15
Round Table 6, 16, 185, 233–36

Salisbury, Battle of 230–33
Stonehenge 10, 11, 15
Suite du Merlin 252–66

Thomas of Britain (England) 63, 203–12

Tintagel Castle 13–14, 201, 239–45
Tristan: in Chrétien 82; in Béroul 151–97; in Marie 199–202; in Thomas 203–12
Troy 5

Ulfin 13–14; Urfin 225, 237–50
Urien 16
Uther Pendragon: in Wace 6–15; in Layamon 28; in *Merlin* 224–51

Vergil 255
Vortigern 6–7, 9; Vertiger 224–26

Wace 5–17, 19, 20, 213
Wagner, Richard 204
Walwain. *See* Gawain
Welsh myth 6, 29–31
Wenhaver. *See* Guinevere
Winchester 11–12, 20, 25–26
Wonders, Fortress of 57, 59, 61

York 16
Ygerne. *See* Igerna
Yvain: in *Peredur* 32–33, 35, 39, 48, 54, 186, 192; *Yvain* 81–149